I0112612

Python in Excel
Unlocking powerful data analysis and automation solutions

Liam Bastick
Kathryn Newitt

Python in Excel: Unlocking powerful data analysis and automation solutions
Published with the authorization of Microsoft Corporation by: Pearson Education, Inc.
Copyright © 2026 by Pearson Education, Inc.
Hoboken, New Jersey

ISBN-13: 978-0-13-543797-1
ISBN-10: 0-13-543797-0

Library of Congress Control Number: On file

1 2025

Trademarks

Warning and Disclaimer

Editor-in-Chief
Julie Phifer

Portfolio Manager
Loretta Yates

Acquisitions Editor
Shourav Bose

Development Editor
Kitty Wilson

Managing Editor
Sandra Schroeder

Senior Project Editor
Tracey Croom

Copy Editor
Dan Foster

Indexer
Valerie Haynes Perry

Proofreader
Kim Wimpsett

Technical Editor
Owen Auger

Cover Designer
Twist Creative, Seattle

Cover Illustration
stock.metket.com/stock.adobe.com

Compositor
Danielle Foster

Figures
01-01, 01-02, 03-01 /
Python Software Foundation

To my long-suffering wife, Nancy, and my little monster, Layla, thanks for the support while I pretended to work on this book. Here is yet another one that you will never read!

Since Layla was born, I have let my daughter add her sage words (literally, from cradle to tome) in every book: "Will the royalties be enough to buy me another guitar, Daddy?"

—LIAM

To my family, especially my daughters, for playing the "guess how many pages I wrote today?" game with such patience.

—KATHRYN

Contents at a Glance

Contents

Acknowledgments

I have always wanted to write "Thought 1 Not Applicable," and now I have. Thanks to my family (again) for supporting me while I buried my head in a keyboard, muttering something about pandas or koala bears.

Thanks, too, to all those who have taught me along the way. I have learned so much from my mistakes, but not half as much as from other practitioners. You know who you are. Thanks also to everyone who assisted in providing examples and technical input, believing in us to publish our book. And thanks to our editor, Kitty Wilson, who has finally gotten her way and made me put "gotten" twice in the same sentence. You have no idea how much that hurts.

But most of all, thanks to Kathryn Newitt. I may share authorship with Kathryn, but she drove it all the way. This is your book, Kathryn, not mine. Be proud of it.

—Liam

Since Liam came up with the concept for this book, it has steadily slithered toward existence. I am grateful to my colleagues at SumProduct who supported me as I cowrote the material and to the team at Pearson for making it possible. Thanks to Kitty for your patience while editing my contribution as a new author. I learned a lot from this process, and I hope we can work together again.

Python in Excel opens up the data analysis capabilities of Excel, and through this book, you'll acquire the tools to explore what you can do with it. You are not alone: Copilot is joining you for the ride, and the Python and Excel communities are there to support you. Please do get in touch with your creations and your discoveries. But no spam, please! (If you get that one, you are a true Python fan.)

—Kathryn

About the authors

Liam Bastick, FCA, FCMA, CGMA, MVP   Liam has over 40 years' experience in spreadsheets (more than Excel has). That's not bad, given he is only 21 (he just won't tell us the units). Little-known fact: The two authors were born on the same day and have antagonized each other ever since!

Liam has headed various modeling teams over the years, setting up the boutique consultancy SumProduct in late 2009. He has worked in various countries, with many internationally recognized clients, and written thousands of articles and more than a dozen books. One of them must be interesting.

He is a regular contributor to the American Institute of Certified Public Accountants (AICPA), Association of Chartered Certified Accountants (ACCA), Chartered Accountants in Australia and New Zealand (CAANZ), Certified Practising Accountants Australia (CPAA), the Chartered Institute of Management Accountants (CIMA), and the Institute of Chartered Accountants in England and Wales (ICAEW). He plans to collect the set and build a hotel.

Originally from the Channel Islands, Liam was educated in the UK before moving to sunnier climes in Australia. Although he is still a desperate Derby County supporter, the therapy is working well. Liam is still recognized by Crimewatch and by Microsoft as a Most Valuable Professional (MVP) in Excel (one of approximately 130 worldwide).

Further, he is a Fellow of the Institute of Chartered Accountants (ICAEW), a Fellow of the Institute of Chartered Management Accountants (CIMA), and a professional mathematician. Liam won the inaugural Lifetime Achievement Award for Financial Modelling (FMI) in 2021 and was one of three finalists for the Lifetime Achievement Award in Excel (GES) in 2023.

He tries hard not to be as boring as he sounds.

Kathryn Newitt With a BA in English Language and Literature and a BSc in Mathematics, writing a reference book for fellow nerds seems like a natural step.

Kathryn's first role in the workplace was marketing railway braking systems, and her career has stayed on track ever since.

Having spent over a quarter of a century working in various roles for a software house in Liverpool, Kathryn has traveled to Europe, Asia, and the United States while creating and maintaining software applications for communications, shipping, and warehousing clients.

During her time at SumProduct, she has used her programming and training experience to provide articles and training for many Microsoft Excel applications. She has edited many of her (unrelated) twin's books on Excel. She is excited to see collaboration with Excel in Python and is very happy to have been promoted to co-author for this book. She really needs to get out more!

Introduction

When businesses look for candidates with strong Excel skills, the aim is not to find the candidate who can name the most keyboard shortcuts or create complex formulas. It is also not to find an expert in Power Query who tries to use it for everything. Rather, the goal is to find the candidate who knows enough about all Excel features to choose and use the best tool for the job.

Turning data into information is crucial for businesses to make informed, wise decisions, and Excel includes excellent functionality for performing data analysis. Excel has been developed to make this process more efficient and productive, and new features are being added constantly. The challenge is that Excel users must stay up to date with all the new developments. This book focuses on one such recent development: Python in Excel.

This book aims to help you understand how to use Python in Excel, when you should use it, and how Python helps in performing data analysis. Using multiple Excel tools together—such as Python in Excel with Microsoft Copilot and Power Query—can provide powerful and efficient solutions, as you will see in this book.

Who this book is for

This book is written for business users of Excel. While it is not possible to know your exact requirements, we provide examples that allow you to explore Python in Excel using realistic data. We start with simple examples and build on them gradually. Eventually, the examples show how Python in Excel can join forces with Copilot and Power Query. The examples and tips provided in this book are intended to be transferable to your own data and your own analysis needs.

You may have some knowledge of Python or none whatsoever. There are many excellent Python handbooks; this is not one of them. However, by the time you finish this book, you will have practical knowledge of how to work with Python in Excel.

How this book is organized

This book covers how to use Python in Excel and how to use artificial intelligence (AI) effectively to assist with complex scenarios. Chapters 1 through 4 provide background information and introduce the basics of using Python in Excel. Chapters 5 through 7 describe how AI can help you quickly move on to complex data analysis. The epilogue provides a review of the book and a look to the future.

Chapter 1: Introduction to Python and Python in Excel

This book assumes you have no prior knowledge of Python. Chapter 1 gets you started by exploring what Python is and why it is now integrated into Excel. It provides a historical look at the partnership between Python and Excel and describes the qualities of Python that make it an ideal choice for expanding Excel functionality. It also explores the challenges that come with combining these two tools.

This chapter introduces how Excel can do more with Python integration and provides some simple examples that will be expanded in future chapters. To prepare you for the rest of the book, this chapter introduces Python concepts and vocabulary, as well as some key Python libraries that you need to be aware of from the start.

Chapter 2: Getting to know Python in Excel

This chapter explains the basics of using Excel as a frontend for Python, in preparation for the comprehensive examples to follow. It also explores the availability of Python in Excel and the differences between the paid and free versions. You will learn how to activate Python and get to know the interface through examples of Python functionality. You will also begin working with the downloadable resources that come with this book, including Excel workbooks that you can use to follow along with the examples and solution workbooks you can use for reference.

In this chapter, you will look at arrays, which are closely related to much of Excel, and pandas DataFrames, which are used to access Excel data entities. You will learn through examples which Excel syntax and functionalities are useful in interacting with DataFrames. You will also learn about the error codes you'll likely encounter, basic troubleshooting, and new keyboard shortcuts for efficiency.

Chapter 3: Using Python libraries

Python libraries are key to efficiently turning data into useful information. They enable access to functionality not easily achieved in Excel, as you will see in this chapter's examples.

All Python libraries, also known as *packages*, are accessible from the Python Package Index (PyPI). This chapter describes how to access the PyPI, which at the time of writing listed 673,608 Python libraries.

This chapter summarizes the properties of the libraries preloaded into Python in Excel and introduces the libraries that Microsoft recommends for use in Python in Excel. This chapter also explains the syntax you use with the preloaded libraries and provides examples that you can walk through to become familiar with using Python libraries. By the end of the chapter, you will have a solid base from which to explore some of the other libraries available.

Chapter 4: Using the Python Editor

Up to this point, the examples in the book use the Python in Excel formula bar. In this chapter, you will revisit some of those examples, now using the Python Editor, which provides a large editing space with color-coded text and formulas. It is useful for creating new Python code and reviewing and debugging existing code. In this chapter, you will encounter more involved examples that require more complex code.

Chapter 5: Introduction to AI and Copilot

This chapter is about the development of AI, focusing on ChatGPT and Copilot in particular. AI is an important part of this book because it can be used to create Python code in response to natural language prompts. Understanding how AI works is important to getting the best results. This chapter explores the possibilities and potential issues to equip you for creating Python in Excel using Copilot.

Chapter 6: Using Copilot with Python in Excel

Copilot makes Python in Excel accessible to users who would not consider themselves coders. Just as a macro recording can be used to learn about the syntax of Visual Basic for Applications (VBA), AI can be used to learn more about Python syntax. This chapter helps you understand how to use AI to write Python code and then adapt and refine it. You will also learn about Copilot advanced analysis, which obtains insights from Excel data using Python in a natural language exchange. You will see how you can use it to quickly create an informative dashboard. This chapter provides examples you can walk through to create effective solutions using Copilot and Python in Excel.

Chapter 7: Using Copilot and Power Query connectors with Python in Excel

This chapter covers the basics of Power Query, Excel's integrated extract, transform, and load (ETL) engine, and compares the processes of cleansing data with Power Query and with Python in Excel. The examples in this chapter show you how to use Power Query to connect to the external data provided in the downloads available with this book. The examples also show you how to use Python in Excel to perform data analysis. This chapter provides tips on which functionality to use, depending on the task and the data.

This chapter brings together everything covered in the book and provides some complex, realistic examples that will give you skills you can transfer to your workflows.

Epilogue

The Epilogue reflects on the journey taken throughout the book and the importance of staying up to date with new technologies.

About the companion content

A great way to become familiar with new technology is to use it. An even better way is to use it to solve problems. This book is intended to help you do that by providing examples you can work through and solutions to check your work. To support you with this, we have provided data and Excel files that you can download from *https://www.sumproduct .com/python-in-excel-book-resources*. These downloadable resources include the workbooks you need to work through all the examples in the book, as well as solutions to all the examples.

For each chapter, we have provided a starter file and a completed file:

- Each starter file has the words **Starter File** in the filename. Use this file to work through the examples presented in the chapter. As you progress through each chapter, you will be reminded of the location of the downloads and invited to open the appropriate starter file for that chapter.

- A file that includes the words **Completed File** in the filename contains completed examples for the chapter. You can view the completed files at any time, but we encourage you to attempt the examples yourself before checking the suggested solutions.

- The companion content for this book can also be downloaded from *MicrosoftPressStore.com/pythonexcel/downloads*.

System requirements

Before you begin working through the examples in this book, make sure your system meets the following requirements:

- **Operating system:** Windows 11, Windows 10, Windows 8.1, Windows Server 2019, or Windows Server 2016

- **Software:** Office 365

- **Python in Excel requirements:** Enterprise or Business license running the Current Channel on Windows, starting with Version 2408 (Build 17928.20114); Monthly Enterprise Channel on Windows, starting with Version 2408 (Build 17928.20216); or Excel on the web with an Enterprise or Business license

- **Copilot requirements:** Files in a OneDrive or SharePoint folder associated with a Copilot for Microsoft 365 license

Copilot Pro is available as a paid add-on for Microsoft 365 users or as part of Copilot for Microsoft 365 (Enterprise plan) for larger organizations.

Errata, updates, and book support

We've made every effort to ensure the accuracy of this book and its companion content. You can access updates to this book—in the form of a list of submitted errata and related corrections—at:

MicrosoftPressStore.com/pythonexcel/errata

If you discover an error not already listed, please submit it to us at the same page.

For additional book support and information, please visit:

MicrosoftPressStore.com/Support

Please note that product support for Microsoft software and hardware is not offered at this page. For help with Microsoft software or hardware, go to:

support.microsoft.com

## CHAPTER 1

Introduction to Python and Python in Excel

In this chapter, you will:

- Learn how and why Python was created
- Explore how Excel assists with data analysis
- Discover how Python came to be used for Excel data analysis

This book is designed to enable you to use Python in Excel to efficiently transform data into information that will help your business make wise decisions. To understand how Python in Excel can help with data interpretation, you first need to understand what Python is and what features make it so popular.

History and key features of Python

In the 1980s, Guido van Rossum created the language that would eventually be known as Python. It was a side project Guido took on when he realized that a new coding language could speed up the development of the Amoeba operating system.[1] His goal in creating the language was to make coding easy and accessible from the start. Guido named Python not for the snake but for the show *Monty Python's Flying Circus*, and he resisted the link to the snake for a long time. The initial Python logo, shown in Figure 1-1, was based on the name's text.

FIGURE 1-1 The first Python logo was snake-free.

---

[1] "Q&A with Guido van Rossum, inventor of Python," Microsoft, accessed March 24, 2025, *https://learn.microsoft.com/en-us/shows/reactor/qa-with-guido-van-rossum-inventor-of-python*.

It wasn't until 2006 that Tim Parkin designed the current logo, shown in Figure 1-2. Tim based the logo on Mayan representations of snakes rather than realistic pythons.[2]

FIGURE 1-2 Tim Parkin designed the snake logo in 2006.

A year into the development of Python, the team made the pivotal decision to make it an open-source language, which was a novel idea at the time. Python would be free for everyone to use and share. When it was released in 1991, Python was promoted to code-savvy users of Usenet—a network of discussion groups similar to today's online forums. Enthusiastic users around the world began using it for a variety of applications.

Python was designed to be easy to learn, with simple syntax. It is also object-oriented, focusing on data properties and manipulation rather than procedural code and lists of instructions.

Python embraced modular programming from its first release, and this methodology inspired the vast number of Python libraries available today. Alongside developments to the Python language by Guido and his team, other programmers wrote patches for functionality that they wanted to see included. The programming community was encouraged to develop and share Python, leading to the evolution of libraries to solve tasks in various disciplines across many platforms. As libraries made it easier to work, more people used Python, and more improvements were added to libraries.

Guido wanted to create a language that was not just aimed at experienced programmers. He and his team proposed "Computer Programming for Everybody" (CP4E) in 1999. The CP4E funding proposal expressed the intention to "come up with a programming language, a development environment, and teaching materials suitable to teach programming to children in junior and senior high school, as well as to adults with no previous computer experience."[3] Python was the obvious choice for an easy-to-learn, shared language as even at that early stage in its evolution, there was "enough (anecdotal) evidence that Python is easy to learn for people who are (nearly) computer-illiterate." The number of libraries and amount of information available for Python can be intimidating for Excel users with little coding experience, but Python is so easy to learn that even very inexperienced users can pick it up quickly.

While Python has been used for general-purpose programming for maintaining databases, for web development, and even for gaming, Guido did not initially envision its use in the development of machine learning, as he felt artificial intelligence (AI) had not lived up to the early promise of the 1960s and 1970s. However, since 2010, Python has been used extensively for machine learning and data analysis. Big data demands sophisticated tools for data analysis, and the cycle of writing and refining Python libraries in the community has created powerful and easily accessible code.

---

[2] "PSF Trademark Frequently Asked Questions (FAQ)," Python Software Foundation, accessed March 24, 2025, *https://www.python.org/psf/trademarks-faq/.*

[3] "Computer Programming for Everybody," Python.org, accessed March 24, 2025, *https://legacy.python.org/doc/essays/everybody/.*

Appreciating the key features of Python

Before moving on to consider Excel, let's look at some of the key features that make Python so popular:

- Python is a general-purpose programming language that can be used to do almost anything, and it is popular with seasoned programmers.

- Python is easy to learn. Python is used to teach children to code because it is simple to start with, and the code is easily readable since it uses recognizable words.

- Python is portable between platforms. Technically, this means that you can run Python code in different operating systems without needing to significantly rewrite sections of code. In practice, this means you can find the Python code that will perform the task you need in an open-source forum and use it in Python in Excel.

- Many open-source libraries contain code and modules that may be applied to various tasks.

- Python is an *interpreted language*, which means that each time a line of Python is created, it is translated into machine code for immediate execution. It is possible to test each line individually as written, rather than compiling a long program and then debugging by searching line by line for errors. You can quickly learn and apply new syntax, and you can use variables at runtime without predefining them.

- Because Python is open source and extremely popular, it is typically easy to find code to provide a starting point for a particular task.

Using Excel for data analysis

Excel for Windows appeared in 1987, several years before Python was first released. Excel began as a single-sheet system (only one worksheet per file) with integrated functions for mathematics and finance. It has since evolved into a multiple-sheet application that allows users to organize their data. Let's look at the features that make Excel so useful for data analysis.

Microsoft created the first Excel add-ins and then allowed the Excel community to create third-party add-ins for additional functionality. While Excel is not open source, and many add-ins are not free, the ability to create third-party add-ins enables collaboration between Microsoft and the Excel community, much like the Python environment fosters collaboration. Microsoft has created several Excel add-ins that enable efficient data analysis.

Transforming data into information often relies on visuals. Excel included basic charts from the beginning. PivotTables further enhanced dashboards beginning in 1994.

Visual Basic for Applications (VBA) allows users to automate tasks and interact with other Microsoft applications, such as Word and Access. In 2007, the Excel toolbar was upgraded to become the ribbon menu, and table functionality arrived, promoting consistent data in a columnar format.

In Excel 2010, Power Query transformed how data can be accessed and cleaned, further automating tedious jobs associated with data analysis. It allowed access to external data via connectors and enabled handling more data within an Excel workbook. In addition, Power Pivot complemented Power Query, enabling the transformation of data and linking of multiple tables in the Data Model. The Data Model has relationships and hierarchies; it stores a large amount of data and enables PivotTables and PivotCharts to be created from linked data.

Power Query and Power Pivot come with their own coding languages, M and DAX, respectively. Thanks to the Power Query user interface (UI), it is not necessary to learn M, although familiarity with the language is helpful to fully benefit from the application—particularly to ensure efficient load times. Similarly, knowledge of DAX makes it possible to create calculated columns and measures to assist with data analysis. If you find coding challenging, help is at hand in the form of AI.

AI has increasingly been incorporated into Excel:

- Recommended Charts is an AI feature that helps analysts tell compelling stories.

- Quick Analysis provides charts, formatting, and other useful visualizations.

- Analyze Data provides visualizations and can be prompted with natural language to perform specific analysis.

- Microsoft Copilot, which will be explored in detail later in the book, is designed to work with Microsoft products and is continually improving to help users get the most out of the data available. It can also be used to create M and DAX code. Figure 1-3 shows a sample Microsoft Copilot prompt, and Figure 1-4 shows a table you can create by pasting Copilot-generated M code into the Advanced Editor of a new blank query in Power Query. As you will see later in the book, Copilot will also be your ally in learning Python code.

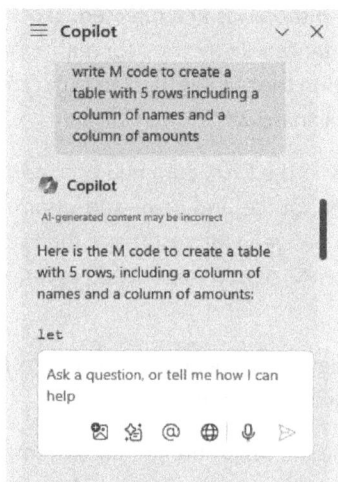

FIGURE 1-3 Copilot creates M code in response to a prompt.

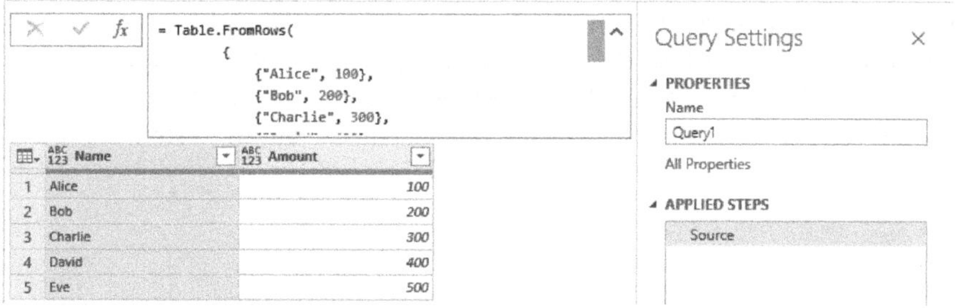

FIGURE 1-4 The table created by pasting the Copilot code into the Advanced Editor of a new blank query in Power Query

> **Tip** While Copilot can assist you with creating M and DAX code, it is advisable to learn the basics of these languages so you can spot errors and refine the code.

Integrating Python and Excel

Now that you have previewed the tools that make Excel useful for data analysis, let's look at how Python came to be integrated with Excel.

The journey to integrating Python into Excel began in 2015 with a request on what was then Microsoft UserVoice (see Figure 1-5), but it has since been migrated to Microsoft Feedback (see Figure 1-6).[4]

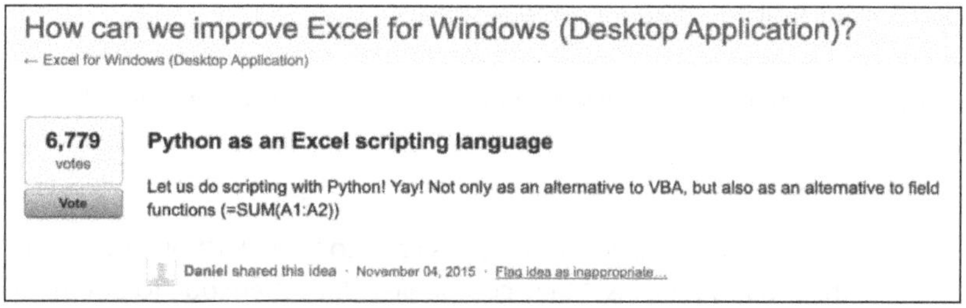

FIGURE 1-5 The request for Python scripting in Excel in Microsoft UserVoice in 2015

FIGURE 1-6 The request can now be seen in Microsoft Feedback.

---

[4] "Python as an Excel scripting language," Microsoft, accessed March 24, 2025, *https://feedbackportal.microsoft.com/feedback/idea/976c241d-74bd-ed11-83ff-000d3a1ab7d1.*

This integration became one of the most commonly requested features in the forums. Before the integration became official, developers took the opportunity to provide access to Python via third-party add-ins. Many of these add-ins are still available and can be accessed by clicking the Add-Ins button on the Developer tab in Excel. Figure 1-7 shows the results of a search for add-ins related to Python.

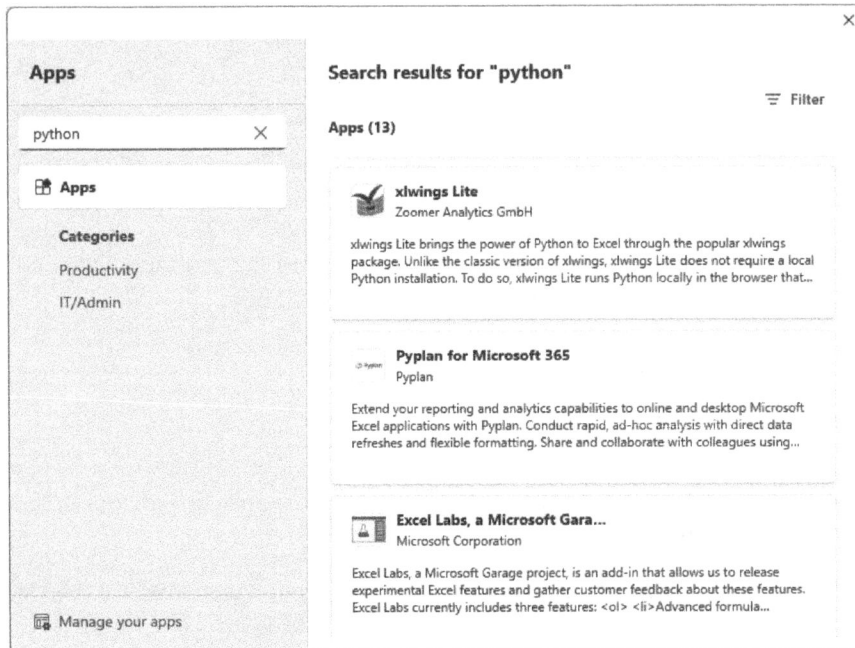

FIGURE 1-7 Third-party add-ins can be accessed from an Excel workbook.

As discussed earlier, Python is ideal for data analysis because much of the code needed to analyze data has already been written and is available in free libraries. Furthermore, Python's scalability means that large datasets can be easily analyzed.

If add-ins already allowed access to Python, why were users keen to bring Python into Excel? There are some drawbacks to using third-party add-ins. Many companies block them due to potential security risks: Third-party add-ins not only have access to company data but also have the potential to introduce viruses. Therefore, many companies view a fully integrated Python platform as the ideal way to extend their data analysis capabilities.

Python in Excel also appeals to organizations that may not have previously considered using Python with Excel. Analysts in these companies may be new to Python or may not have used Python in a business environment. Python in Excel makes it possible to combine Python and Excel analytics within the same workbook—with no setup required, as you will see in the next chapter.

Working with Python and Excel in the same environment does involve some challenges. As you will discover in Chapter 2, "Getting to know Python in Excel," although much of the Python code from other platforms is portable to Excel, there are differences and limitations.

Microsoft has been working with Anaconda, Inc., since 2017, when the companies partnered to embed the Anaconda platform into Azure Machine Learning, Visual Studio, and SQL Server. Anaconda was then the obvious platform choice for Python in Excel. Although not all Python libraries are available on the Anaconda platform, as you will see in Chapter 3, "Using Python libraries," there are many libraries to assist with data analysis.

Getting a taste of Copilot

To end this chapter, let's look at a task that is easy to carry out using Copilot with Python in Excel. We include this example to show the ease and logical order of the steps and provide a taste of what will follow later in the book.

To begin this example, open an empty worksheet and click **Analyze Data** on the **Home** tab (see Figure 1-8).

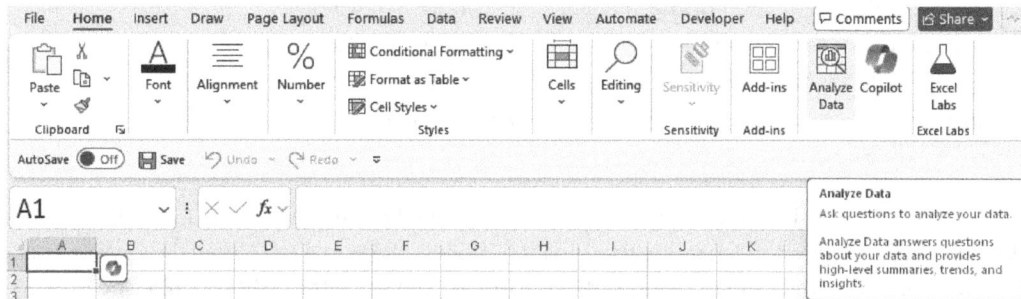

FIGURE 1-8 The Analyze Data functionality can be accessed from the Home tab in Excel.

The Analyze Data dialog appears. Because no data is available, the dialog suggests exploring the feature with sample data (see Figure 1-9).

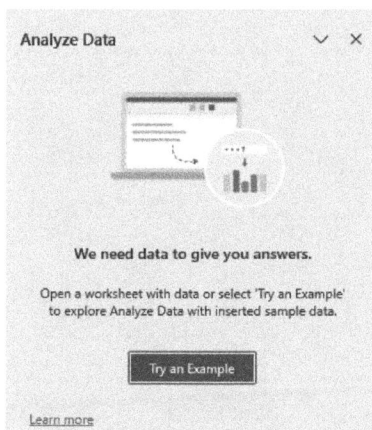

FIGURE 1-9 The Analyze Data dialog suggests using sample data if the current worksheet is empty.

Click **Try an Example** in the Analyze Data dialog, and Excel populates the current sheet with sample data generated by Microsoft (see Figure 1-10).

	A	B	C	D	E
1	Year	Category	Product	Sales	Rating
2	2017	Components	Chains	£20,000	75%
3	2015	Clothing	Socks	£ 3,700	22%
4	2017	Clothing	Bib-Shorts	£ 4,000	22%
5	2015	Clothing	Shorts	£13,300	56%
6	2017	Clothing	Tights	£36,000	100%
7	2015	Components	Handlebars	£ 2,300	35%
8	2016	Clothing	Socks	£ 2,300	28%
9	2016	Components	Brakes	£ 3,400	36%
10	2016	Bikes	Mountain Bikes	£ 6,300	40%
11	2017	Components	Brakes	£ 5,400	38%
12	2016	Accessories	Helmets	£17,000	90%

FIGURE 1-10 Sample data from the Microsoft training database is inserted into the worksheet.

Now, to go further than the Analyze Data function can take you, you can use Copilot. Choose App Skills from the dropdown menu under the Copilot button on the Home tab. When the Copilot App Skills pane appears, enter the prompt **using Python forecast the sales for 2018 to 2025** (see Figure 1-11).

Note You will learn all about using Copilot in later chapters.

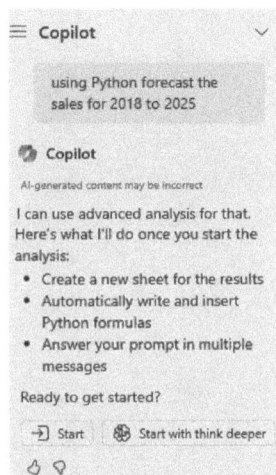

≡ Copilot ∨

using Python forecast the sales for 2018 to 2025

Copilot

AI-generated content may be incorrect

I can use advanced analysis for that. Here's what I'll do once you start the analysis:

- Create a new sheet for the results
- Automatically write and insert Python formulas
- Answer your prompt in multiple messages

Ready to get started?

→ Start ｜ ❀ Start with think deeper

FIGURE 1-11 Copilot responds to natural language prompts.

As you can see in Figure 1-12, in addition to generating forecasted results, Copilot suggests visualizations for the dashboard.

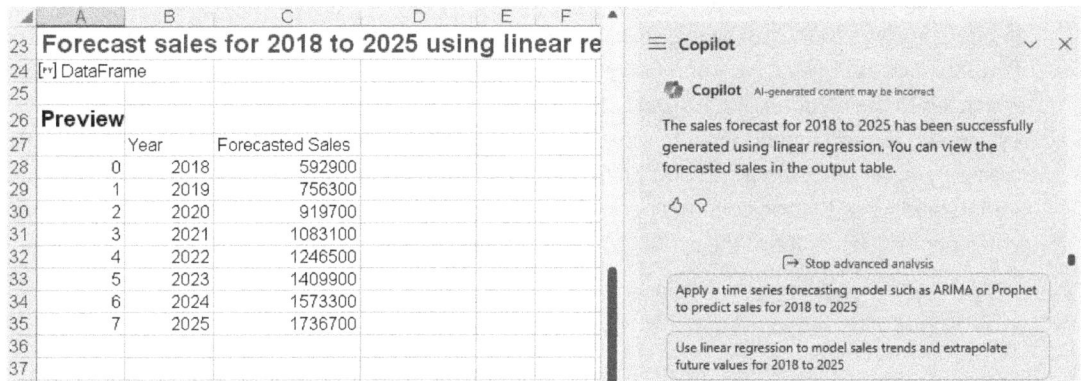

FIGURE 1-12 Copilot uses Python to create the answer and suggests next steps.

Figure 1-13 shows the Python Editor, where you can access the Python code that Copilot created to generate the results. To produce reliable results with Python in Excel, it is important to understand the code that is generated for you. You will begin to learn more about Python code in the next chapter.

> **Note** You will learn more about the Python Editor in later chapters.

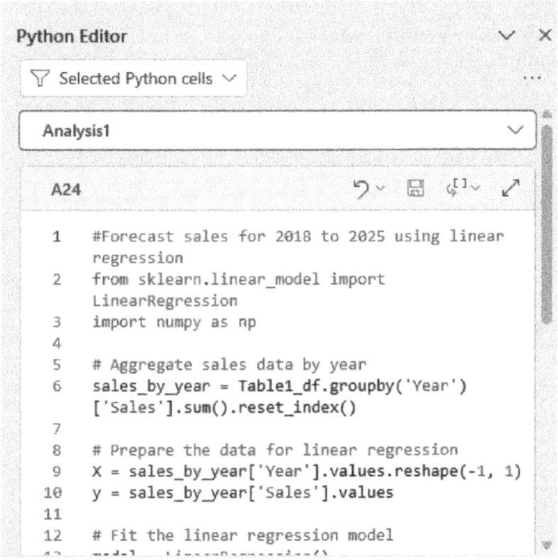

FIGURE 1-13 The Python code that Copilot created to forecast sales

This quick example has given you a taste of what you can do with Python in Excel and Copilot in just a few clicks.

Summary

In this chapter, you have learned about the history of Python and its popularity as a language for creating data analysis tools. You have also explored how Excel has evolved to support data analysis through features such as Power Query and Power Pivot. Data analysts wanted to combine Python and Excel, which led to the creation of third-party add-ins. Microsoft's official integration of Python in Excel has opened up Python functionality to more users. In addition, AI tools in Excel now make it possible to create Python code even if you don't have expert knowledge of Python. However, you must have some understanding of Python code to check and amend code created using AI tools. In the next chapter, you'll begin to learn about the syntax you'll encounter in Python in Excel.

## CHAPTER 2

Getting to know Python in Excel

In this chapter, you will:

- Learn how to access Python in Excel

- Start using Python in Excel

- Enter data using Python in Excel

- Preview the preinstalled Python libraries

- Define arrays with NumPy

- Learn about Python in Excel entities

- Recognize Python in Excel error codes

- Explore Python objects

Note To follow along with the examples in this chapter, you must download the resources that accompany this book. If you don't already have these resources, visit *https://www .sumproduct.com/python-in-excel-book-resources* and download the files to a folder associated with your Python in Excel license. For this chapter, you will begin by accessing the workbook **SP Python in Excel Example Starter File Chapter 2.xlsm**.

Accessing Python in Excel

At the time of writing, the standard version of Python in Excel is generally available to a variety of Microsoft 365 users:

- Users with Enterprise and Business licenses running the Current Channel (that is, the channel that receives the latest updates as they become available) on Windows with Version 2408 (Build 17928.20114) or later

- Users of the Monthly Enterprise Channel on Windows with Version 2408 (Build 17928.20216) or later

- Users of Excel on the web with Enterprise and Business licenses

Users of these licenses can access Python in Excel and do not need to perform any installations.

Python in Excel is also available as a preview for users with Family and Personal licenses in Excel on the web or running the Current Channel on Windows with Build 17628.20164.

Python in Excel is not currently available on the following editions:

- Excel for Mac
- Excel for iPad
- Excel for iPhone
- Excel for Android

> **Note** To see the latest availability of Python in Excel, visit *https://support.microsoft.com /en-us/office/python-in-excel-availability*.

If a user accessing a workbook containing Python formulas does not have access to Python in Excel, they can view the data but not recalculate it. You will learn more about this later in the chapter.

Using the standard version of Python in Excel

If you use the standard version of Python in Excel, you can complete all the Python in Excel examples throughout this book. You can also create Python formulas from an Excel workbook and access Python libraries compatible with the Anaconda platform. The calculations will be automatically performed in the cloud using enterprise-level security. The speed of the calculations will be standard, although you may have limited access to premium compute, a feature that enables faster computing speeds. We'll talk about this shortly.

Upgrading to the Python in Excel add-on license

If you have one of the Microsoft licenses listed earlier, you are eligible to purchase the Python in Excel add-on license, which is an upgrade to standard Python in Excel. You can do this through the Microsoft 365 admin center. At the time of writing, the cost is $24 per user per month. Compared to the standard version of Python in Excel, the Python in Excel add-on license allows you to perform calculations more quickly (via the premium compute feature) and gives you more control over how frequently the Python calculations are performed. You will find out more about this later in the chapter.

> **Note** For more information about licensing, see *https://support.microsoft.com/en-us/office /python-in-excel-add-on-licensing-faq-6d90fc0e-f080-4799-9d28-9754c77fb308*.

If you have recently upgraded to a Microsoft 365 license that includes Python in Excel or recently purchased the Python in Excel add-on, you may not see the Python in Excel features immediately. According to Microsoft, the features enabled by the license update may take time to update automatically, depending on your setup. If this happens and you need to access standard Python in Excel or premium add-on features, you can update your license manually. To do so, go to **File** > **Account**, and you will see the screen shown in Figure 2-1, where you can click **Update License**.

FIGURE 2-1 To access the option to manually update your license, go to the **File** tab and select **Account**.

Interpreting license messages in standard Python in Excel

As mentioned earlier, you have some limited access to faster computing speeds with the standard Python in Excel functionality. These pop-up messages let you know if you have this access and if you have reached your allotted monthly limit:

- **Python in Excel: You're using premium Python compute.** Your workbook is using Python in Excel, and you have access to faster formula calculation times with your Microsoft 365 subscription.

- **Python in Excel: You're close to using all of your monthly premium Python compute.** Your premium compute limit will soon be reached. After reaching the monthly premium compute limit, any Python code in your workbooks will be calculated using standard computing speeds for the rest of the month.

- **Limit Exceeded: You're using standard Python in Excel calculation speeds.** Any Python code in your workbooks will be calculated using standard computing speeds for the rest of the month.

Getting started with Python in Excel

Once you know that you have a license that provides access to Python in Excel, it is important to ensure that you are in a location associated with that license. If, for example, you try to use a personal OneDrive account when your license is associated with your company account, you'll need to switch to a local drive or folder associated with the company account. If you find that you do not have access to Python in Excel even though you have a license, check the file location. If you try to use Python in Excel in a location not connected to a valid license, you will encounter a #BLOCKED! error. You'll learn about the errors that can occur when using Python in Excel later in the chapter, in the section "Learning about Python in Excel error codes."

Once you have made sure that you are in an appropriate location to access Python in Excel, there are several ways to begin creating Python code:

- Click the **Insert Python** button on the **Formulas** tab.

- Enter Python directly into a cell in a sheet.

- Use the Python Editor, which you open from the **Formulas** tab.

The first method of using Python in Excel—clicking the Insert Python button—allows you to access the Python in Excel Help pane, which is useful when you're getting started. The other two methods of accessing Python in Excel do not offer the Python in Excel Help pane. You may want to use them once you are more familiar with using Python in Excel. We'll look at all three methods next.

> **Note** To follow along with the exercises in this section, go to the folder where you placed the resources for this chapter and open the workbook **SP Python in Excel Example Starter File Chapter 2.xlsm**. Then go to the **Python Syntax Examples** sheet.

Clicking the Insert Python button

To start using Python in Excel by clicking the Insert Python button, go to the **Formulas** tab in Excel, find the section labeled **Python**, and click the **Insert Python** option (see Figure 2-2). (You will use other options in the Python section of the Formulas tab later.)

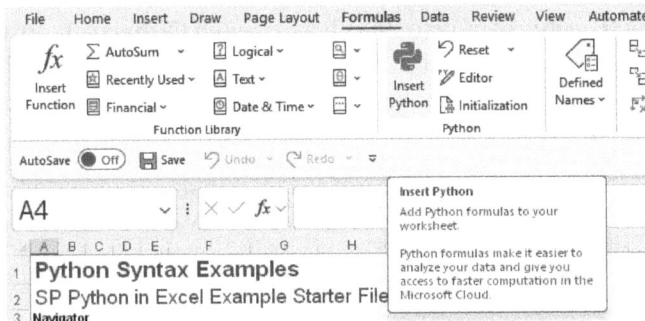

FIGURE 2-2 The Insert Python option is in the Python section of the Formulas tab.

When you click the **Insert Python** option, some changes occur:

- A green Python prompt appears in the formula bar, as shown in Figure 2-3, and a new symbol with square brackets appears next to the green checkmark, replacing the *fx* (insert function) symbol. (You will learn more about this new symbol later in this chapter.)

> **Note** When the formula bar shows the green PY prompt, the cell contains Python code, not Excel formulas.

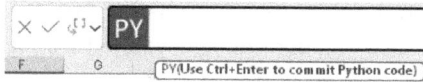

FIGURE 2-3 When you select the **Insert Python** button, the formula bar changes to show a green Python prompt.

- A hint is displayed, telling you to use Ctrl+Enter to commit the code. Whereas you can commit an Excel formula by pressing Enter, with a Python command, you need to press Ctrl+Enter to commit the code. In Python in Excel, clicking Enter takes you to the next line of Python code, which allows you to create multiple lines of Python code for a single cell. To signify that the Python code is complete, you must press Ctrl+Enter or click the green checkmark to the left of the Python prompt.

- A Python in Excel Help pane appears on the right side of the screen, offering help with Python in Excel. Because Python in Excel is a new development, Microsoft offers resources to help demystify the functionality (see Figure 2-4).

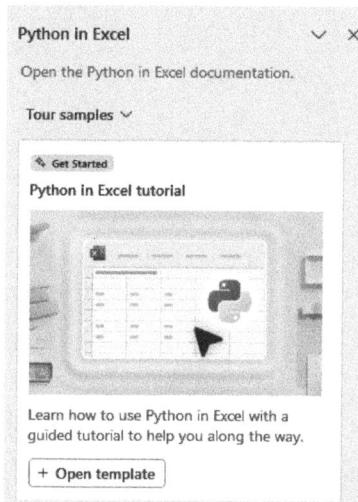

FIGURE 2-4 The Python in Excel Help pane offers resources to learn about this feature.

The Tour Samples dropdown filter allows you to choose which sections are displayed in the Python in Excel pane (see Figure 2-5). The default is to show all tour samples, but you can select the filter that best suits your needs.

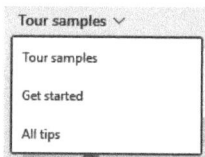

FIGURE 2-5 Select an option from the dropdown menu to choose which section to show.

From the Tour Samples dropdown filter, you can choose to view information, open a template to explore a topic, or open a feature. If you choose Tour Samples or All Tips, you will see everything you can explore. Figure 2-6 shows some of the samples you can explore.

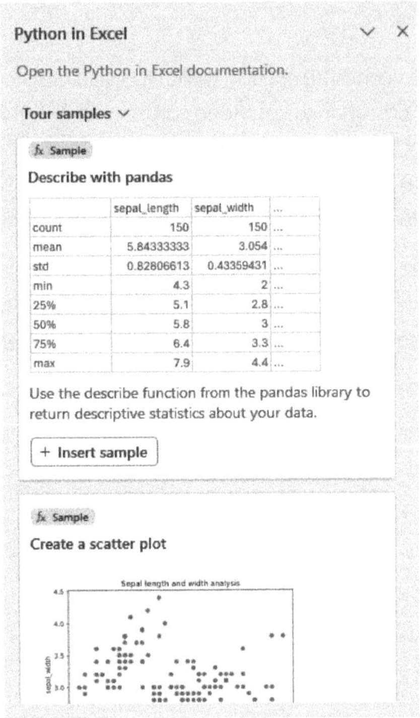

FIGURE 2-6 You can choose a sample to see what Python in Excel can do.

If you choose Get Started from the dropdown menu, you will see only the Get Started features.

Figure 2-7 shows one of the Get Started features, called Try Out the Python Editor. As its name indicates, it allows you to access the Python Editor.

Note The Try Out the Python Editor section is intended for users who are new to Python in Excel and may need more help finding the features available. This is not the method you will use to access the Python Editor when you work through the examples in this book.

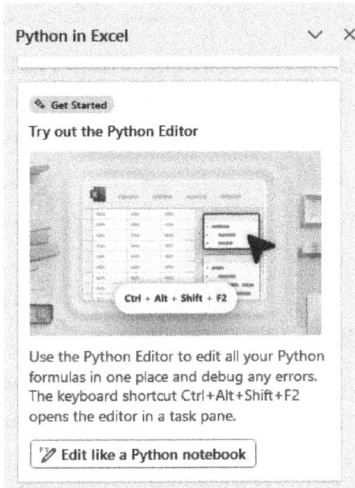

FIGURE 2-7 The Try Out the Python Editor section

> **Note** The sections shown in the Python in Excel Help pane will change as Python in Excel evolves. It's a good idea to check them out and become familiar with them as changes are made.

In some versions of Python in Excel, there is a Get More Premium Compute link at the bottom of the Python in Excel Help pane. You can click this link to sign up for the Python in Excel add-on (see Figure 2-8). If you do not see this link in your version, look for a diamond icon.

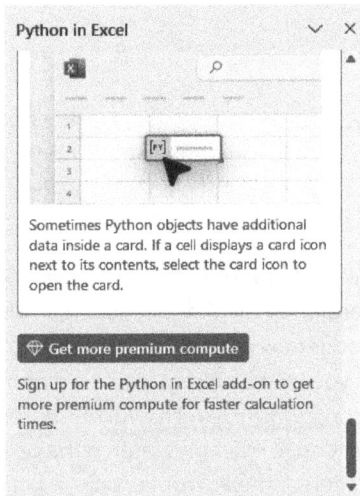

FIGURE 2-8 The option to sign up for the Python in Excel add-on is available from the Python in Excel pane.

Entering Python directly into a cell

The second method of accessing Python in Excel is to enter Python code directly into an Excel cell. To do this, you must enter the new Excel function PY(), which indicates that the cell will be used for Python code.

This is the syntax of the PY() function:

```
=PY(python_code, return_type)
```

where *python_code* is the Python code to be run, and *return_type* indicates whether the result is viewed as a Python object (*return_type* = 1) or as an Excel value (*return_type* = 0).

The PY() function is not a typical Excel function. It cannot be used with other Excel functions, and *python_code* and *return_type* must be static values. While it is possible to enter Python code using the previous syntax, you will enter **=PY** to change the prompt, enter Python code, and then choose the return type setting via the user interface. Using =PY rather than entering the full syntax of the Excel PY() function allows you to take full advantage of the Python environment for entering Python code.

Excel IntelliSense recognizes the PY() function as the function for creating Python formulas, as shown in Figure 2-9.

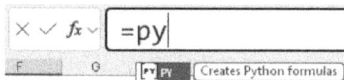

FIGURE 2-9 IntelliSense recognizes the function PY().

If you select the PY() function, the green Python prompt and the square bracket symbol shown in Figure 2-3 appear, but the Python in Excel pane does not.

Using the Python Editor

The two methods of accessing Python in Excel we've just discussed—clicking the Insert Python button and selecting the PY() function—enable you to type Python code in the formula bar. The third method of accessing Python in Excel, which we'll look at now, is to use the Python Editor. The Python Editor is a more recent development that gives you access to a Python notebook.

The Python Editor was developed while Python in Excel was available for preview. If you are looking online for information about Python in Excel, you may see mention of the Diagnostics pane. The Diagnostics pane no longer exists, and the functionality it provided is now part of the Python Editor. As the tooltip in Figure 2-10 indicates, the Python Editor provides you with an integrated development environment (IDE). It provides syntax help and error debugging and is particularly useful for more complex Python code. (You will use the Python Editor for comprehensive examples later in the book.) You access the Python Editor by clicking **Editor** in the **Python** section of the **Formulas** tab.

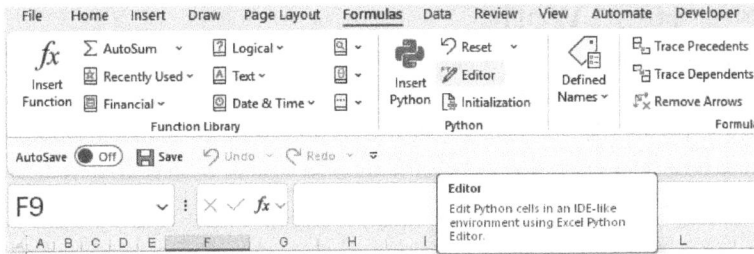

FIGURE 2-10 The Python Editor is accessed from the Formulas tab.

When you click the Editor option, the Python Editor appears on the right side of the screen (see Figure 2-11).

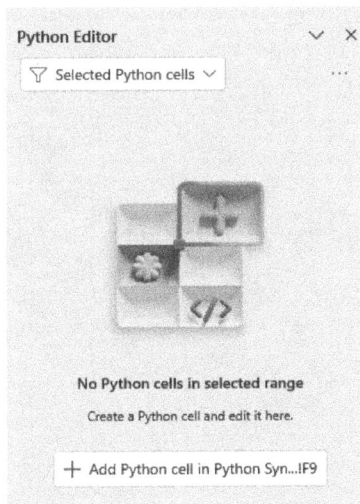

FIGURE 2-11 When you click Editor on the Formulas tab, the Python Editor appears on the right side of the screen.

Because you have not yet entered any Python code, you will not yet see any Python code in the Python Editor. There is an option at the bottom of the pane to start entering Python code in the currently selected cell. (You will become familiar with the features of the Python Editor in Chapter 4, "Using the Python Editor.")

Entering Python code in Excel

We will start with some basic examples where you will enter Python code from the formula bar. This section covers some of the Python syntax that allows you to access and manipulate Excel data by using Python in Excel. Later in this chapter, you will have the opportunity to explore more Python syntax to prepare for more involved examples later in the book.

Trying an example: "Hello World"

Let's start with a classic for learning a new programming language: "Hello World." If you are familiar with other Python interfaces, you may expect to use the `print` command for this. However, in Excel, the Python `print` command is not needed to get a value to appear in a cell. Let's look at what happens when the `print` command is entered.

For this example, indicate that cell F8 will contain Python code by entering the Excel function **PY()** in the formula bar or by selecting **Insert Python** on the **Formulas** tab. Once you see the green Python prompt, type the Python command **print("Hello World")**, as shown in Figure 2-12.

> **Note** Python is case sensitive. This means it treats uppercase and lowercase letters differently, and it is therefore important to pay attention to capitalization.

FIGURE 2-12 Entering Python code into a Python cell

Commit the code you typed by clicking the green checkmark or pressing **Ctrl+Enter**. The Python Editor appears, showing the results (see Figure 2-13).

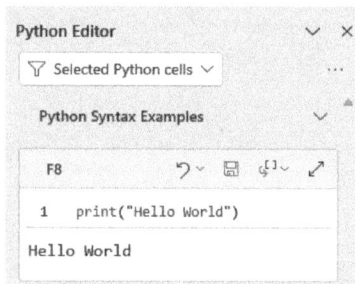

FIGURE 2-13 The Python Editor shows the Python code in cell F8.

While the phrase Hello World appears in the Python Editor, it does not appear in cell F8 on the Excel worksheet (see Figure 2-14).

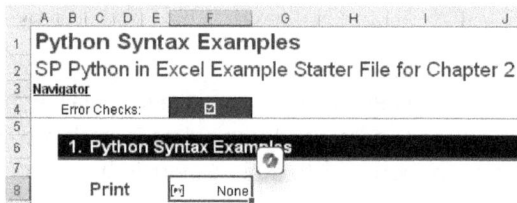

FIGURE 2-14 Hello World does not appear in cell F8.

In cell F8 of the Excel worksheet, you see the letters PY in square brackets ([PY]) and the word None. [PY] indicates that the Python object is shown. We noted earlier that there are two ways to show the results of Python code in a cell: either as a Python object or as an Excel value. Remember the new symbol that appears next to the formula bar? It is the Python Output option, and you can click it to toggle between the Python Object view and the Excel Value view (see Figure 2-15).

FIGURE 2-15 The Python Output option can be toggled to show the Python Object view or the Excel Value view.

Instead of clicking the symbol, you can use the keyboard shortcut **Ctrl+Alt+Shift+M** to toggle between these output options. If you toggle the Python Output option to Excel Value, you will still see None in the cell, as shown in Figure 2-16. With this output option chosen, the Python Editor shows the Python object first and then the Excel value 0 (None) (see Figure 2-17). What you now see in cell F8 is the equivalent of a null in Excel.

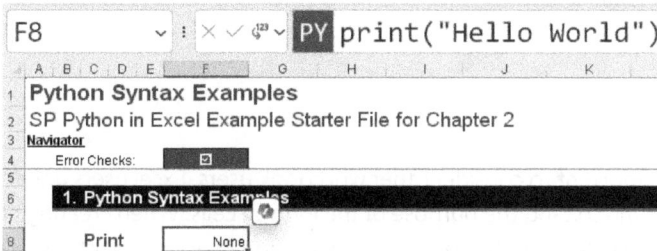

FIGURE 2-16 Selecting the Python Output option to show the Excel value causes None to appear in cell F8.

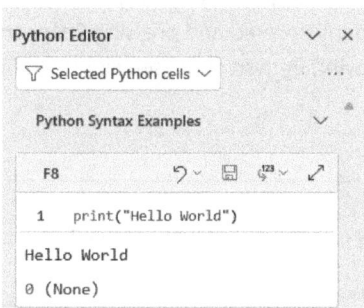

FIGURE 2-17 Selecting the Python Output option to show the Excel value causes Hello World and 0 (None) to appear in the box for cell F8 in the Python Editor.

To have the words He11o World appear in F8, you must omit the Python print command. Just enter **"He11o World"** in cell F8 and commit the Python code by clicking the green checkmark or pressing **Ctrl+Enter** (see Figure 2-18).

FIGURE 2-18 Enter **"He11o World"** with no print command in cell F8.

Cell F8 now shows the correct value (see Figure 2-19), and your first Python example is complete.

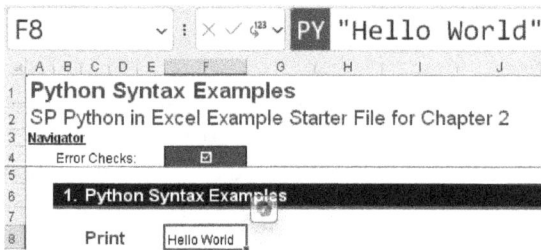

FIGURE 2-19 When you omit the print command, the correct value appears in cell F8.

Using comments

When creating Python code, it is important to consider other workbook users. Excel users unfamiliar with Python may find it difficult to understand the purpose of the Python cells. When creating code, it is helpful to enter comments to indicate what the code is doing. Python may be easier to read than many other programming languages, but it still helps the reader if you break up lines of code with an explanation of the purpose of each section. A comment line in Python begins with #.

To see how comments work, select cell F8 and prepare to enter a new line of Python code in the formula bar by going to the end of the "Hello World" code you already entered and pressing **Enter to start a new line of code**. Expand the formula bar and enter the following Python code (see Figure 2-20):

```
#This Python code displays 'Hello World'
```

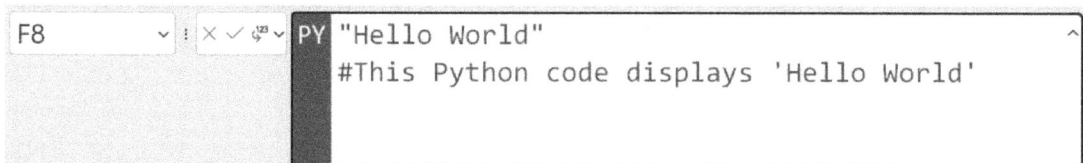

FIGURE 2-20 The comment line describes what the code does.

A comment line is used to improve the readability of the code and doesn't actually change the code or the output. So, when you commit the Python code you just typed, the output in cell F8 does not change.

Taking a first look at Python in Excel errors

You saw earlier that the Python `print` command is not needed to output text in Python in Excel. However, the Python interface does recognize `print` as a command, as shown in Figure 2-21.

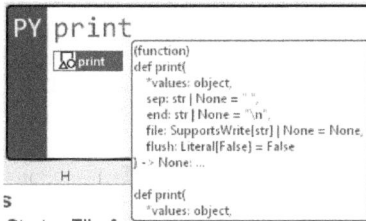

FIGURE 2-21 The Python interface recognizes the Python `print` command.

Some Python commands are not recognized in the Python in Excel frontend. An example is the `input` command. This command is used in other Python platforms to accept a user response. The following Python code on a platform that allows `input` prompts the user to enter a name and then outputs a response:

```python
print("Enter your name:")
x=input()
print("Hello, " + x)
```

You already know you need to omit the `print` command for Python in Excel. You will need to remove it from the previous code so that it looks like this:

```python
"Enter your name:"
x=input()
"Hello, " + x
```

Now you can indicate that cell F9 will be a Python cell and enter the modified Python code, as shown in Figure 2-22.

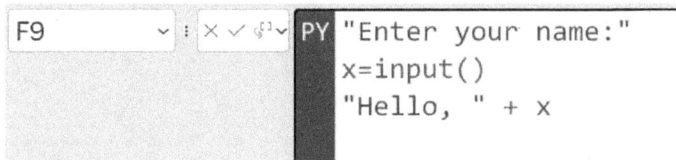

FIGURE 2-22 Trying to use the Python `input()` command.

Commit the Python code in cell F9 by clicking the green checkmark or pressing **Ctrl+Enter**. Figure 2-23 shows how the results appear in the worksheet.

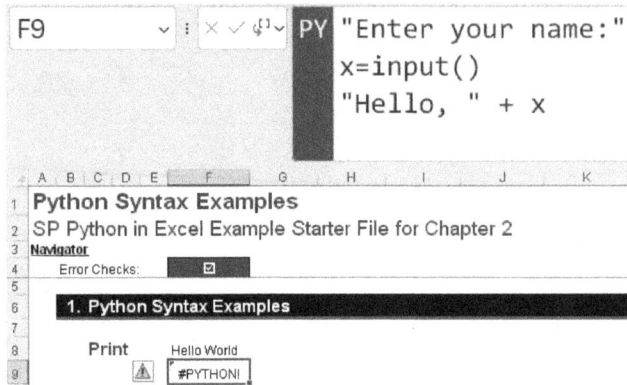

FIGURE 2-23 Using the Python command input causes a #PYTHON! error in cell F9.

You have already met the new Excel function PY(), and now you have caused the new Excel error #PYTHON!. Because it is an Excel error, you can view the issue by hovering over the warning symbol (see Figure 2-24).

FIGURE 2-24 Hover over the warning symbol to get more information about the error encountered.

The Python Editor also appears when an error occurs and shows the same error message (see Figure 2-25):

```
StdinNotImplementedError: raw_input was called, but this frontend does not support input requests.
```

FIGURE 2-25 The Python Editor shows the same error message.

While this is not a true Python error because `input` is recognized, it is a Python in Excel error. If you were to enter unrecognized Python syntax, you would trigger the same #PYTHON! error, but you would get a different message, as shown in Figure 2-26:

```
NameError: name 'InvalidSyntax' is not defined.
```

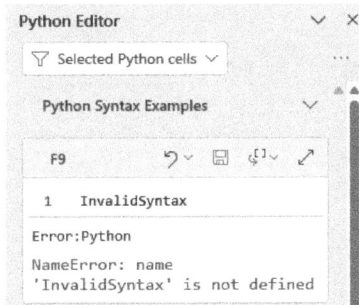

FIGURE 2-26 The Python Editor shows the error message that appears when unrecognized syntax is entered.

This is clearly a different message type. If you encounter this error message when entering Python code, you should check to make sure you have entered the commands correctly. (You will learn about the other error codes encountered when using Python in Excel and how to deal with them later in this chapter.)

Getting to know variables

It's time to move on to Python code that interacts with data. Python can handle a variety of data structures. For example, a *variable* is a name that you attach to an object so that you can give an indication of what it is and refer to it again. To keep your code easy to read, you can use variables to name your data structures.

Let's return to the "Hello World" example in cell F8 of the worksheet we've been working with in this chapter. Modify the Python code so it looks like this (see Figure 2-27):

message="Hello World"

FIGURE 2-27 The message variable names the object that outputs the words Hello World.

This does not impact the output in cell F8, as you can see in Figure 2-28.

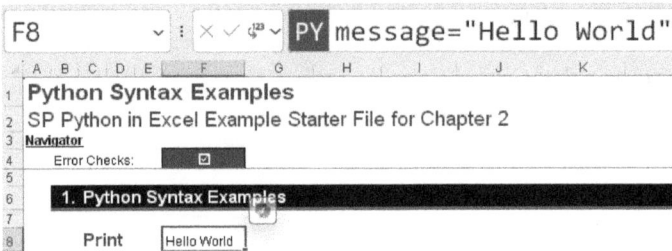

FIGURE 2-28 Using a variable to identify the code has no impact on the output in cell F8.

If you move to cell G8 and indicate that it will be a Python cell, you can refer to the variable `message` (see Figure 2-29).

> **Note** Remember that Python is case sensitive, so, for example, `message` and `Message` are not interpreted as the same variable.

FIGURE 2-29 The variable `message` is now recognized in Python cells.

IntelliSense recognizes the variable `message`. When you commit the Python code, cell G8 also contains the output `Hello World` (see Figure 2-30).

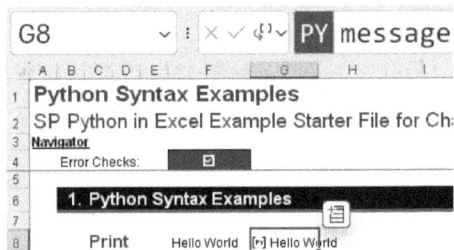

FIGURE 2-30 The variable links to the output `Hello World`.

You must follow these rules when choosing variable names:

- A variable name must begin with a letter or an underscore (_).

- A variable name can contain only letters, numbers, and underscores. It cannot include spaces.

- A variable cannot have the same name as a keyword. For example, assigning a value to True will result in an error.

- While you can use Python function names as variable names, doing so is not recommended since it can be confusing.

A variable takes the data type of the object it is attached to, and you can reassign a variable. If you reuse a variable for an object with a different data type, the variable's data type will change too.

Understanding calculation order

It is easy to see in a piece of Python code which definition of a variable comes first. But what is the order of the Python code when you use Python in Excel across multiple cells and sheets?

In the example you just completed, cell G8 is to the right of cell F8, and the variable defined in cell F8 is recognized in cell G8. Now, prepare cell E8 for Python code and enter the variable **message** in that cell. As you can see in Figure 2-31, the variable message is not recognized in cell E8.

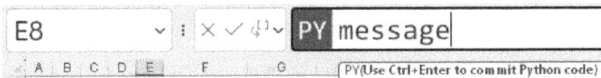

FIGURE 2-31 The variable message is not recognized in cell E8.

For Python in Excel, cell E8 comes before cell F8. So, in this case, trying to use the variable from F8 in E8 causes a Python error, as indicated by the following message (see Figure 2-32):

```
NameError: name 'message' is not defined.
```

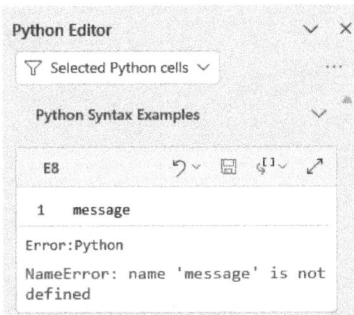

FIGURE 2-32 Trying to use the variable message in cell E8 causes an error.

The calculation order is from left to right and from top to bottom. This left-to-right order also applies to the sheets in the workbook. This means you must take care when moving sheets containing Python code.

Entering lists

Now that you have learned about the order of Python calculations and the importance of variable names, you can start entering data using Python in Excel. Let's begin with a familiar concept from Excel and Power Query: lists.

A list is simple and extremely useful. It can be thought of as a single column or row of data. It may contain data objects with different data structures. The Python syntax for creating a list uses square brackets ([]).

To try your hand at creating a list of numbers, enter the following Python code in cell E12 (see Figure 2-33):

```
numbers_list=[1,2,3,4,5]
```

FIGURE 2-33 Entering a list of numbers.

Using the Excel Value view, you see the list spilled from cell E12, as shown in Figure 2-34. (*Spilling* means that the formula is in cell E12, but the result spills into surrounding cells—in this case, E13:E16.)

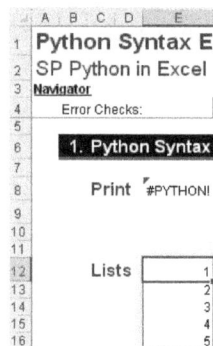

FIGURE 2-34 The Excel Value view shows the list spilled from E12.

You may be accustomed to creating lists in M code in Power Query. One difference in Python is the way that ranges generate lists. To use a range, you must use the Python nested function `list(range)`. For example, Figure 2-35 shows the use of the function `numbers_list=list(range(1,5))`.

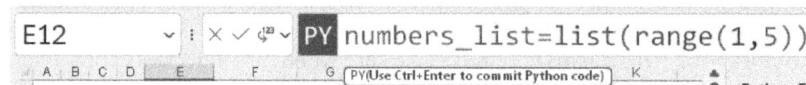

FIGURE 2-35 Using the Python command `list(range)` to create a list

If you use the method `numbers_list=list(range(1,5))`, the range that is generated extends to the number before the second parameter of the `range()` function (see Figure 2-36). That is, the list does not include the second parameter, which in this case is 5.

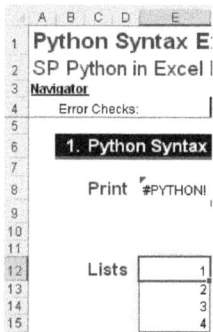

FIGURE 2-36 When you use `list(range)` to create a list, the list does not include the second parameter.

You have viewed the list as an Excel value. Now change the view to the Python Object view, as shown in Figure 2-37. (Note that in Figure 2-36, rows 8 and 9 are hidden so we can concentrate on cell E12.)

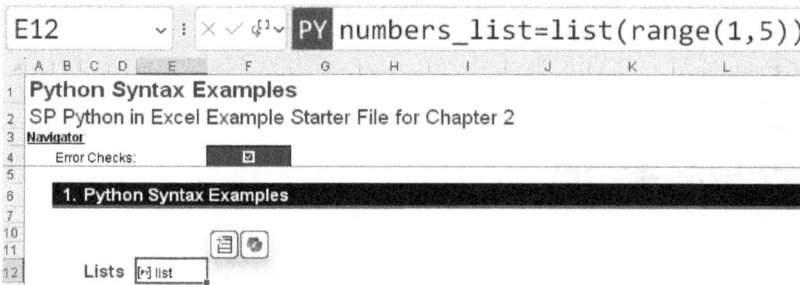

FIGURE 2-37 When you change the view to the Python Object view, you see `list` in cell E12.

An Insert Data icon appears next to the list (see Figure 2-38). You can click it to see more information.

FIGURE 2-38 The Insert Data icon is available for Python objects.

Click the **Insert Data** icon to open the menu shown in Figure 2-39.

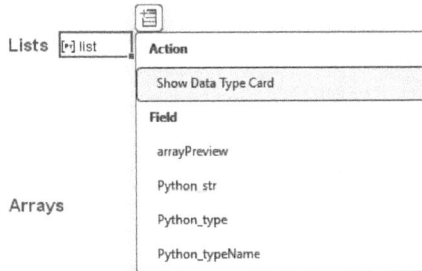

FIGURE 2-39 The Insert Data icon menu

You use the options under Field in this menu to enter data into the next available Excel cell. The following properties are used in Figure 2-40:

- `arrayPreview`, similar to the Excel Value view, is used in cell F12.

- `Python_str`, the list in Python syntax, is used in cell G12.

- `Python_type`, the Python object type, is used in cell H12.

- `Python_typeName`, the name of the Python object, is used in cell I12.

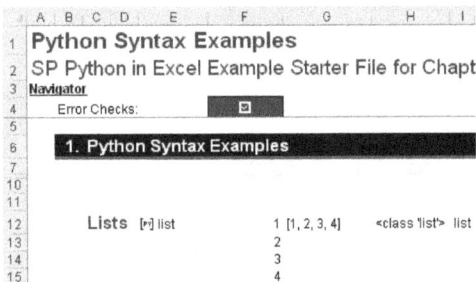

FIGURE 2-40 The Field property options from the Insert Data menu are shown in cells F12 to I12.

This information is displayed using new Excel functions for Python cells:

- `=E12.arrayPreview` in cell F12

- `=E12.Python_str` in cell G12

- `=E12.Python_type` in cell H12

- `=E12.Python_typeName` in cell I12

Ensure that you still have cell E12 selected, go back to the **Insert Data** menu, and choose **Show Data Type Card**. Figure 2-41 shows the data type card that appears. The data type card allows you to see the data in the Python object—in this case, the list object. In this example, data is in a 4x1 list, and you can see all the data without needing to extract it to a cell.

FIGURE 2-41 The Insert Data menu allows you to view the data type card.

Another way to access the data type card for cell E12 is to right-click this cell and select **Show Data Type Card** (see Figure 2-42).

FIGURE 2-42 The shortcut menu allows you to access the data type card.

Perhaps the easiest way to access the data type card is to click the Python object icon or, as you can see in Figure 2-43, use the keyboard shortcut **Ctrl+Shift+F5**.

FIGURE 2-43 Clicking the Python object icon also shows the data type card.

You can also view the Excel data in the Python Editor, as shown in Figure 2-44. (We will look at the Python Editor in more detail in Chapter 4.) This is the only place other than the formula bar where the variable name is shown.

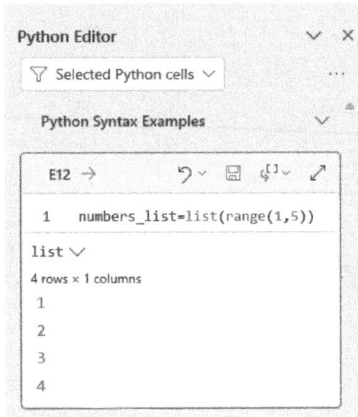

FIGURE 2-44 The Python Editor shows the Python syntax, the Python object, and the Excel value.

You can add data to the list by referencing the variable name. Enter the following Python code in cell J12:

```
numbers_list.append(5)
numbers_list
```

Because you are adding to an existing variable, you do not need to enter a new variable, but you do need to add a line of Python to output the existing variable. Figure 2-45 shows the results in the Excel Value view: The value 5 is added to the end of numbers_list.

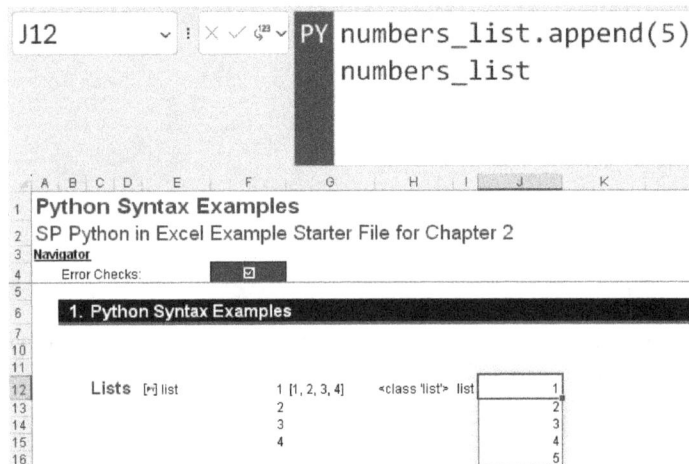

FIGURE 2-45 Appending values to an existing list by using the variable name

It is possible to create a nested list. Our next example shows the difference between a nested list and an array. Enter the following Python code into cell K12:

```
number_nested_list = [[1,2],[3,4],[5,6]]
```

Figure 2-46 shows the results in the Excel Value view.

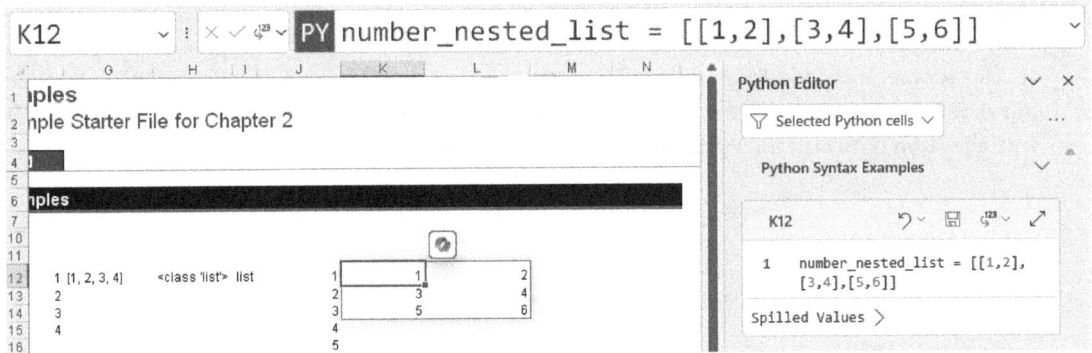

FIGURE 2-46 Entering a nested list

The numbers 1 to 6 are now displayed in pairs on three rows. Although the nested list looks like an array, it has the properties of a list. To see what we mean, in cell M12, use the following Python code to add `number_nested_list` to itself:

```
number_nested_list+number_nested_list
```

Figure 2-47 shows the results. More values are added to the list, and there are now six rows; the values in the list are not added together. Arrays can handle arithmetic operations, whereas lists (even nested lists) cannot. Mathematically, arrays are related to matrices.

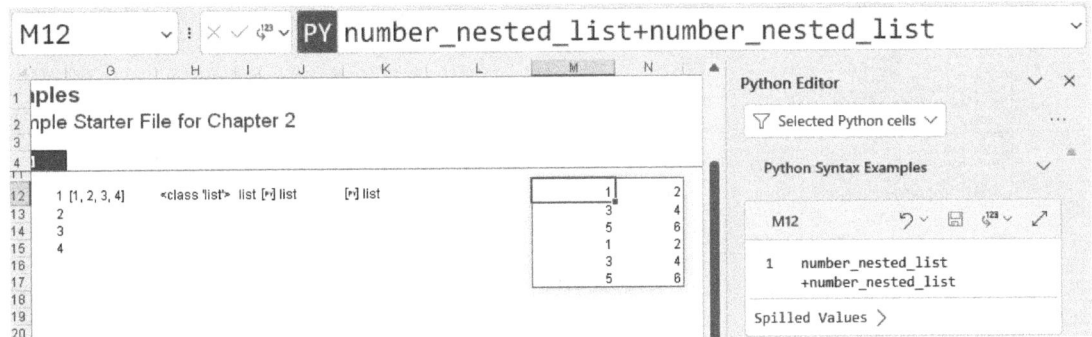

FIGURE 2-47 Nested lists do not behave like arrays.

The Python library NumPy allows you to define arrays and use them in complex mathematical and statistical operations. We'll look at it and other preloaded Python libraries next.

A quick preview of the preloaded Python libraries

Before we look specifically at the NumPy library, we need to briefly discuss the basics of the Python libraries you will likely encounter. A *Python library* is a collection of code modules, functions, and other Python objects that can be reused. The Python standard library is written in C and is always distributed with Python. You will find out much more about Python libraries in the next chapter. For now, let's concentrate on the libraries needed to read Excel data with Python.

The libraries preloaded in Python in Excel have been chosen because of their suitability for working with Excel data. To open the Initialization pane, where you can see the preloaded libraries, click the **Initialization** button in the **Python** section of the **Formulas** tab (see Figure 2-48).

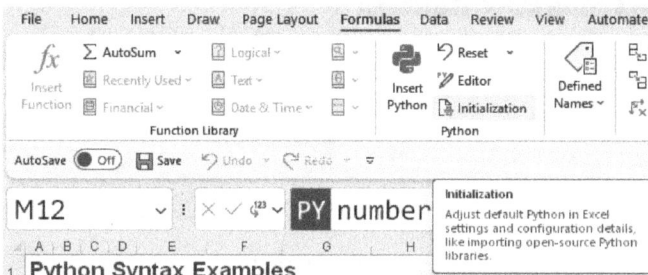

FIGURE 2-48 The Initialization button in the Python section of the **Formulas** tab opens the Initialization pane.

The tooltip shown in Figure 2-48 suggests that you can change the default settings. At the time of writing, these details are for information only.

The Initialization pane shows the loaded libraries (see Figure 2-49).

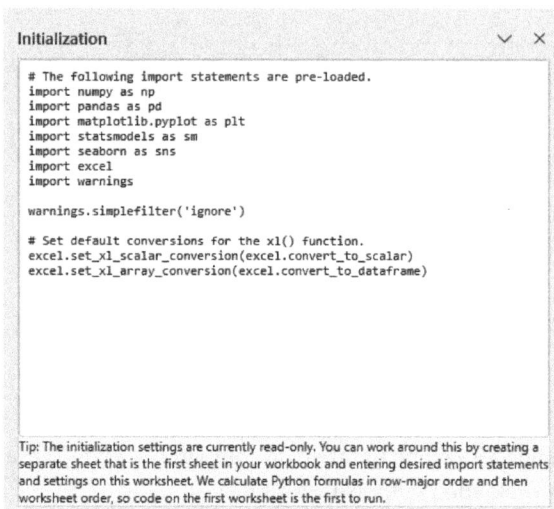

FIGURE 2-49 The Initialization pane shows the initialization settings in a read-only environment.

You can see in the Initialization pane that the Python syntax to load a library is `import` *library _full_name* `as` *library_alias*. You can also see that these libraries are currently preloaded:

- **NumPy:** This library allows you to perform mathematical and logical operations, working with arrays rather than the more cumbersome Python lists you have already seen in action.

- **pandas:** This library, which is built on the NumPy library, is designed for data manipulation and data analysis. The pandas DataFrame is similar to data in an Excel worksheet and is key to reading Excel data as a Python object. A DataFrame contains two-dimensional data and data labels.

- **Matplotlib:** This library allows you to quickly create plots. You will use it in some of the examples later in this book.

- **statsmodels:** As its name implies, this library is for creating and analyzing statistical models.

- **seaborn:** This library has functions that use matplotlib.pyplot to provide access to more complex and varied visualizations.

The remaining libraries and settings allow Python in Excel to function and interact with the user interface. You will learn more about the functionality available with each library and try out some examples in the next chapter. The library we are concerned with here is NumPy.

Defining arrays with the NumPy library

As stated, the preloaded Python library NumPy allows you to define arrays. We'll now look at the arrays available in NumPy. In the following examples, you will enter some simple arrays and see how they interact. While arrays are often used for mathematical operations, for the first example, you will enter numbers and characters. The syntax is similar to the syntax for a nested list, but it is enclosed in the `np.array` function, where `np` is the short name, or alias, for the NumPy library.

For this example, you will enter the longest line of Python you have entered so far:

```
array1 = np.array([["Red","Orange","Yellow","Green","Blue","Indigo","Violet"],[1,2,3,4,5,6,7]])
```

How do you enter such a long line of code? You can do so in two ways: Either ensure that you do not press the Enter key between the sections of this code or break up the way the line is displayed. Let's look at how to do this.

Adding line breaks in Python

Python has been designed to be easy to use and often offers multiple ways to accomplish the same task. For example, it gives you two ways to split a line:

- You can explicitly define where you want the line to be split.

- You can use implicit splits when Python expects the line to continue.

Figure 2-50 shows the `array1` code mentioned earlier typed or copied into cell E21 as one long line.

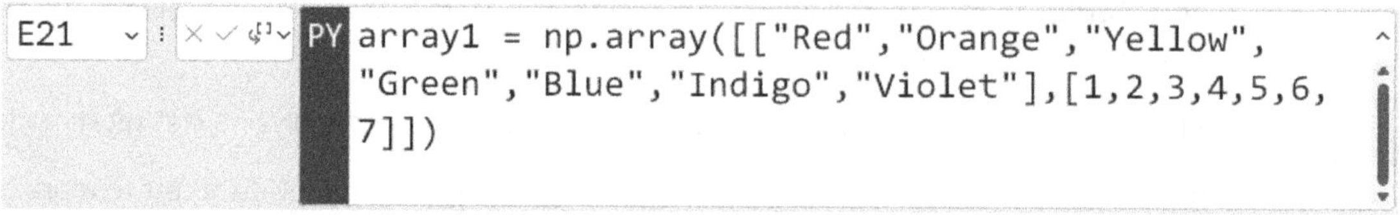

```
E21        PY array1 = np.array([["Red","Orange","Yellow",
                "Green","Blue","Indigo","Violet"],[1,2,3,4,5,6,
                7]])
```

FIGURE 2-50 The code for `array1` is entered as a single line of code.

The appearance of the code will vary depending on your display settings. A single line of Python code may be displayed over several lines in the Excel formula bar. The Python Editor shows the Python line numbers so you can see the Python code in each line (see Figure 2-51).

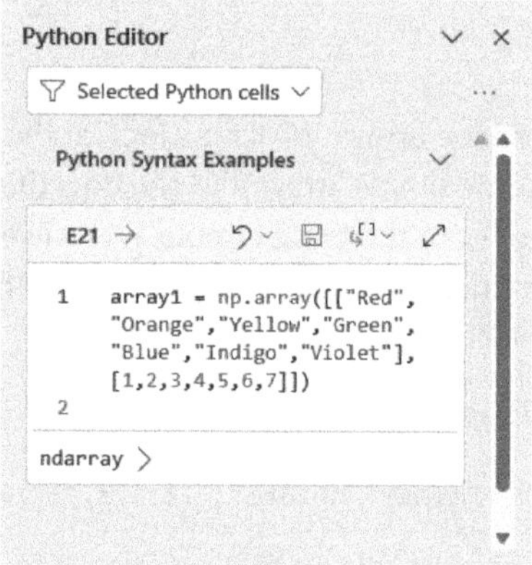

Python Editor

Selected Python cells

Python Syntax Examples

E21 →

```
1   array1 = np.array([["Red",
        "Orange","Yellow","Green",
        "Blue","Indigo","Violet"],
        [1,2,3,4,5,6,7]])
2
```

ndarray >

FIGURE 2-51 The code for `array1` is all on line 1 of the Python code, even though it took up three lines in the formula bar.

To control where the code is broken over the lines and improve readability, you can use a backslash (\). The following example deliberately uses excessive breaks to show how you can use them:

```
array1 = np.array([ \
          [ "Red","Orange",   \
           "Yellow","Green",        \
           "Blue","Indigo",         \
           "Violet"                 \
                              ], \
          [1,2,3,4,5,6,7]])
```

Figure 2-52 shows how this code looks in the formula bar, which has been extended in this case to show all the code.

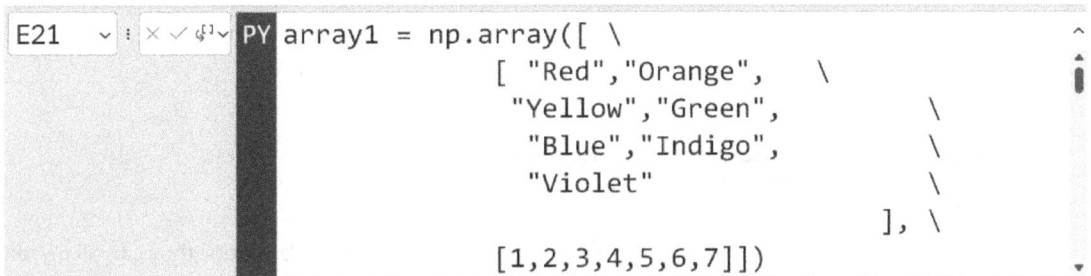

FIGURE 2-52 Backslashes can be used to change how code is displayed.

In the Python Editor, the code is now on different line numbers (see Figure 2-53).

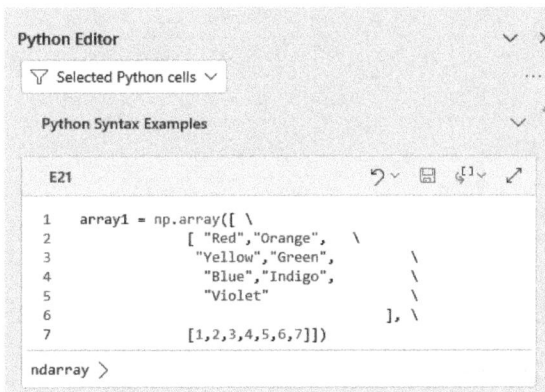

FIGURE 2-53 A backslash moves the following code to the next line but keeps the integrity of the code by indicating that it will continue.

You can also break the code into lines at logical points due to the way Python is programmed. For example, if you remove the backslash after the first square bracket, as shown in Figure 2-54, the code still evaluates successfully.

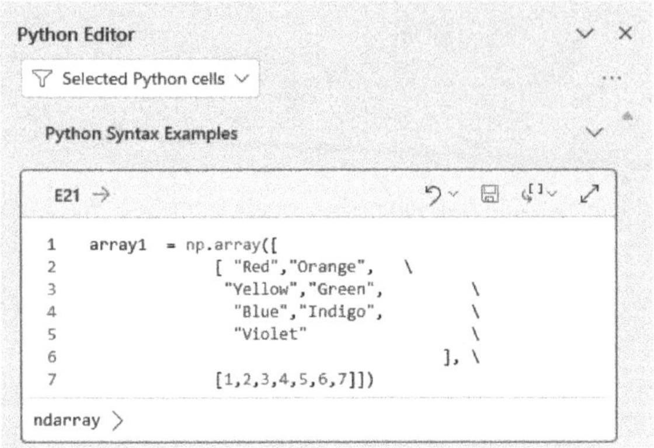

Python Editor   ∨ ✕
⊽ Selected Python cells ∨   ···
Python Syntax Examples   ∨

E21 →   ↻∨ ▦ ⟲¹∨ ↗

```
1    array1 = np.array([
2              [ "Red","Orange",    \
3                "Yellow","Green",        \
4                "Blue","Indigo",         \
5                "Violet"                 \
6                                  ], \
7              [1,2,3,4,5,6,7]])
```

ndarray ⟩

FIGURE 2-54 The opening square bracket on line 1 tells Python the code will continue on the next line.

In fact, because all the continuation lines in this case occur within brackets, they can all be removed (see Figure 2-55). The same is true with parentheses and curly braces. The code is much easier to read when it is split this way.

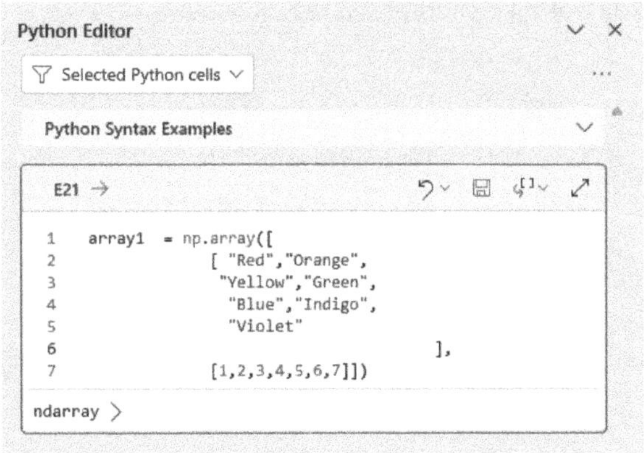

Python Editor   ∨ ✕
⊽ Selected Python cells ∨   ···
Python Syntax Examples   ∨

E21 →   ↻∨ ▦ ⟲¹∨ ↗

```
1    array1 = np.array([
2              [ "Red","Orange",
3                "Yellow","Green",
4                "Blue","Indigo",
5                "Violet"
6                                  ],
7              [1,2,3,4,5,6,7]])
```

ndarray ⟩

FIGURE 2-55 Python allows code to be split inside all types of brackets for readability.

Tip If you break up your code for readability, use the implicit breaks within the brackets. If you encounter syntax errors after you break up a line, you can resort to the backslash approach.

Indentation is an important concept in Python code. The indentation in this example allows for readability in this single Python command to create an array. This example follows an important Python rule that says the first line cannot be indented. To see what happens if the first line is indented, look at Figure 2-56, which shows the Python Editor with the Python code in cell E21 indented on the first line. This produces an error and the following error message:

```
IntentationError: unexpected Indent (4036100023.py,line 1)
```

The error message indicates that there is an unexpected indent. You can easily rectify this problem by removing the space before the first line of code.

You will learn more about the indentation of multiple Python commands and its impact when we look at more complex Python code later in the chapter.

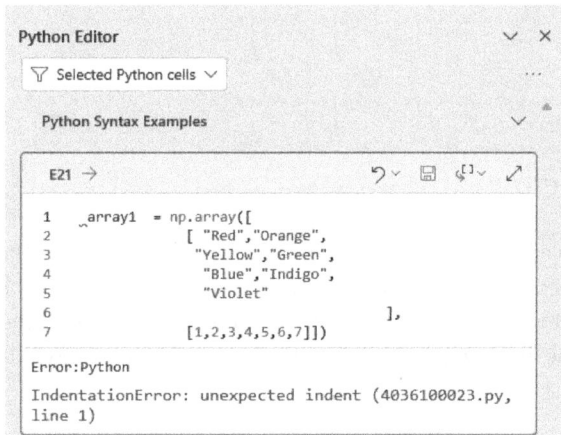

FIGURE 2-56 You are never allowed to indent the first line of Python code.

Viewing properties of arrays

Now that you have created your first array and arranged the Python code, you can investigate your creation. Use the Excel Value view to look at the data in cell E21 (see Figure 2-57).

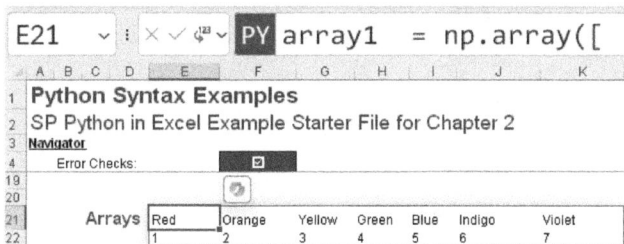

FIGURE 2-57 Viewing the array by using the Excel Value view causes the array values to spill.

The `np.array` function has created an array with the values in the first list in a row above the values in the second list. When you use the Python Object view, you can access the data type card to see the properties of the Python object (see Figure 2-58).

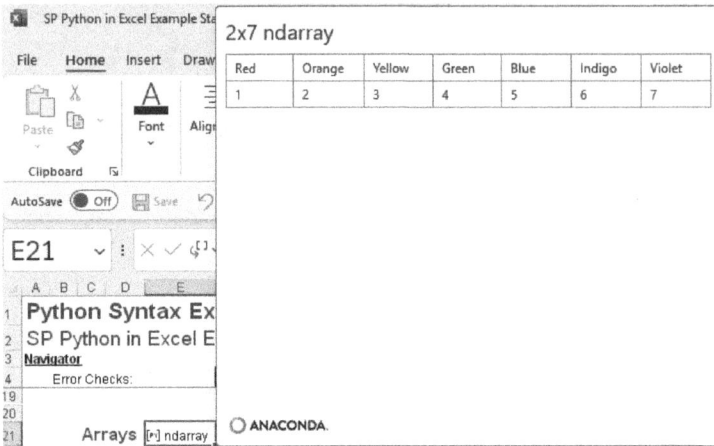

FIGURE 2-58 Viewing the data type card for an ndarray

Note that the Python object in this example is called an ndarray. An *ndarray* is an N-dimensional array, a multidimensional array that typically contains items of the same size and type. We will look at operations with numeric ndarrays soon, but it is useful to first work with different data types to see how the lists are arranged. To see them side by side in columns, you can enter a new ndarray `array2` that consists of lists of pairs in cell E25 (see Figure 2-59):

```
array2  = np.array([
            ["Red",1],
            ["Orange",2],
            ["Yellow",3],
            ["Green",4],
            ["Blue",5],
            ["Indigo",6],
            ["Violet",7]])
```

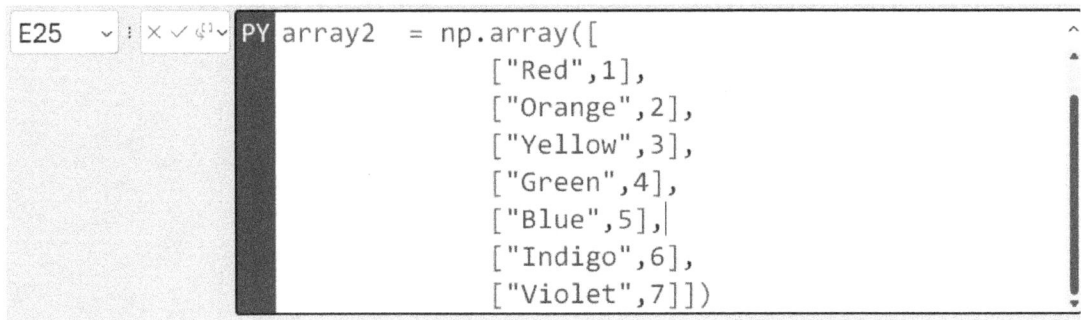

FIGURE 2-59 Creating an ndarray using data pairs in each list

You can view cell E25 by using the Excel Value view to see the values of `array2` in columns (see Figure 2-60).

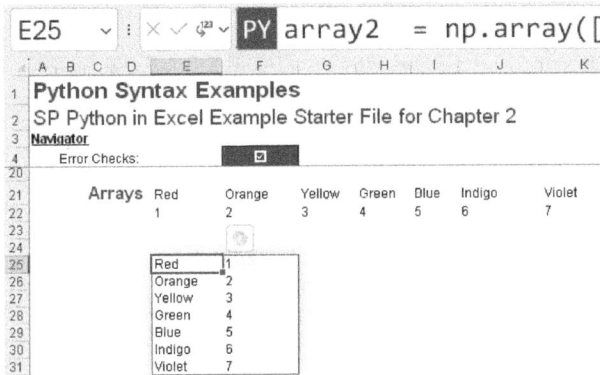

FIGURE 2-60 An ndarray using pairs of data in each list results in columns of data.

You can view the data type card for the corresponding object to see that the data is now stored in a 7x2 ndarray (see Figure 2-61).

FIGURE 2-61 An ndarray using data pairs in each list results in a 7x2 ndarray.

Trying out array examples

Now that you know how to organize data into ndarrays, you can try creating some numeric ndarrays and performing some simple operations.

In cell E33, enter the following Python code to create a simple ndarray in a columnar format:

```
num_array1 = np.array([1,2,3,4,5])
```

The resulting ndarray is the column vector shown in Figure 2-62.

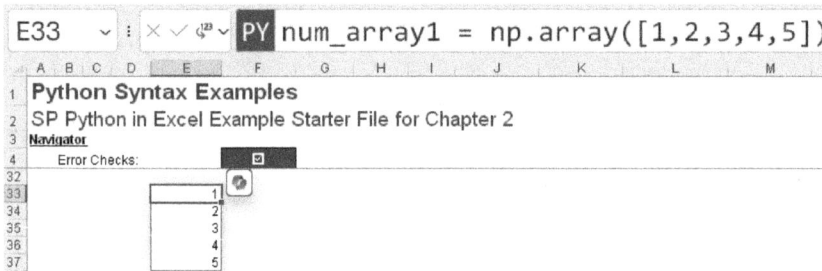

FIGURE 2-62 A numeric ndarray in columnar format

Next, create another numeric ndarray in a row by entering the following code in cell G33:

```
num_array2 = np.array([[1,2,3,4,5]])
```

Figure 2-63 shows the row vector that results.

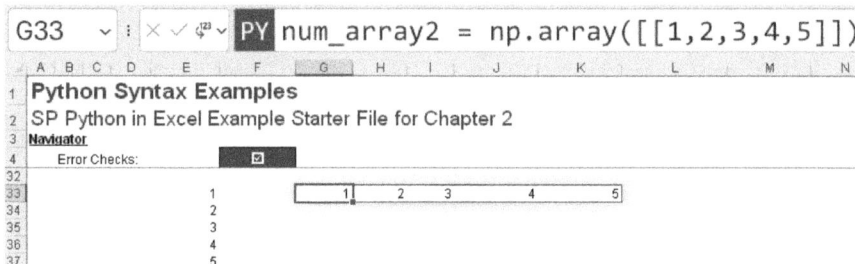

FIGURE 2-63 A numeric ndarray in row format

Now let's use another NumPy function, `np.dot()`, to multiply the vectors. Vectors must be multiplied in the correct order. Let's start by attempting the wrong order to see the error message produced. Checking the error messages in these simple examples will make it easier to spot what is going on in more complicated code.

Enter the following Python code in cell E39:

```
array_dot_result = np.dot(num_array1,num_array2)
```

As you can see in Figure 2-64, the Python Editor shows the following error message:

```
ValueError: shapes (5,) and (1,5) not aligned: 5 (dim 0) != 1(dim 0)
```

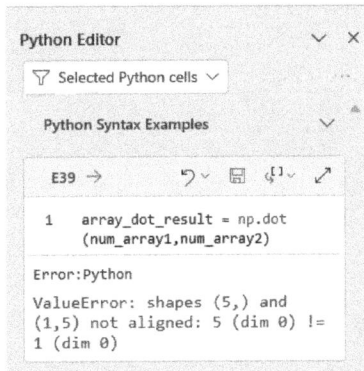

FIGURE 2-64 Arrays must be aligned before they can be multiplied.

The shape of the 5x1 vector is a (5,) shape because Python sees it as a one-dimensional array. If you needed to multiply the arrays, you would need to reshape the arrays by using further NumPy functionality. The point of this example, though, is not to solve the error but to recognize it.

You can multiply these arrays if you change the order of the vectors and enter the following code:

```
array_dot_result = np.dot(num_array2,num_array1)
```

Figure 2-65 shows the results.

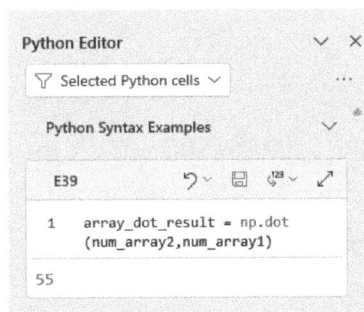

FIGURE 2-65 Aligned arrays can be multiplied.

Now that the corresponding shapes (1,5) and (5,) are aligned, the calculation result is 55 (=(1x1)+ (2x2)+(3x3)+(4x4)+(5x5)). The data type card for the result shows a 1x1 ndarray (see Figure 2-66).

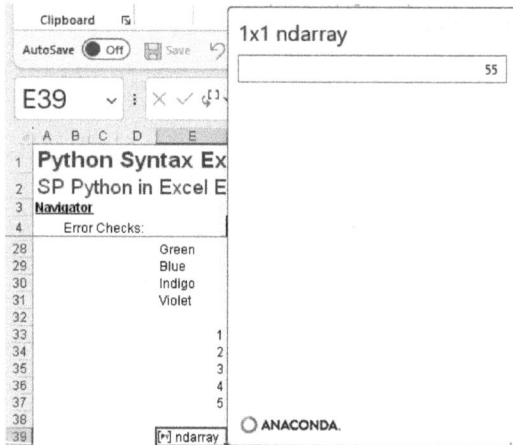

FIGURE 2-66 The result is a 1x1 ndarray.

As long as you follow alignment rules, you can multiply any arrays. For example, you can create a 3x3 ndarray in cell E41 by entering this code:

```
num_array3 = np.array([[1,2,3],[4,5,6],[7,8,9]])
```

Figure 2-67 shows the results.

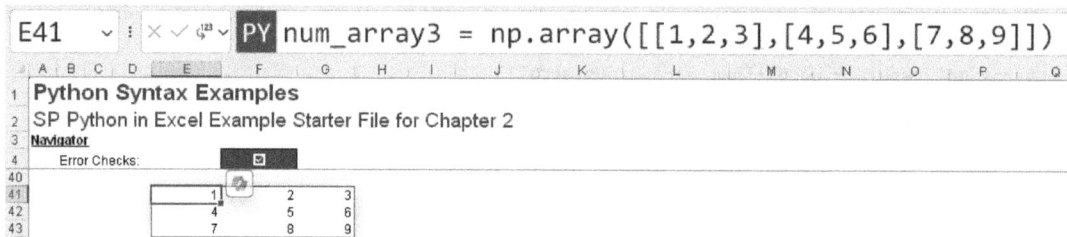

FIGURE 2-67 Creating a 3x3 ndarray

You can create a 3x1 ndarray in cell I41 by entering the following code:

```
num_array4 = np.array([1,2,3])
```

Figure 2-68 shows the results.

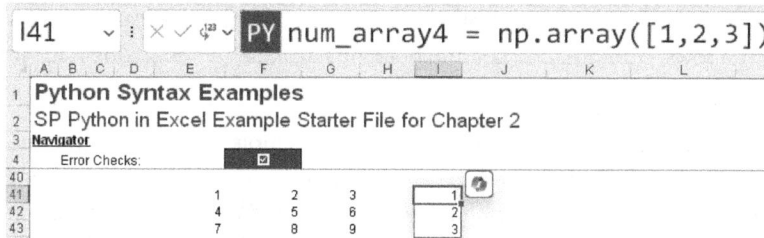

FIGURE 2-68 Creating a 3x1 ndarray

You can now use `np.dot()` to multiply the arrays in cell K41:

```
array_dot_result2 = np.dot(num_array3,num_array4)
```

Figure 2-69 shows the results—another 3x1 array:

```
14 =(1x1)+(2x2)+(3x3)
32 =(1x4)+(2x5)+(3x6)
50 =(1x7)+(2x8)+(3x9)
```

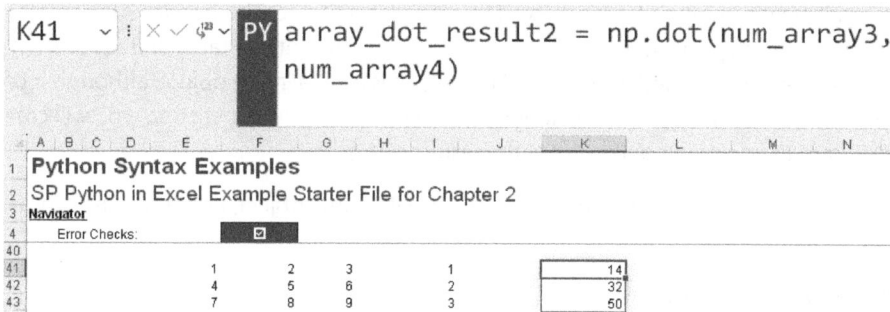

FIGURE 2-69 Using `np.dot()` to multiply the arrays

The examples you have worked through in this section are simple, but they are scalable. You can use NumPy library functions to manipulate massive arrays of data. You will see more NumPy examples in Chapter 3, "Using Python libraries."

Accessing Excel entities

In this chapter, you have created Python objects by entering data directly into Python cells. Let's move on to manipulating the other data in an Excel workbook. You may recall that pandas is one of the preloaded Python libraries. The purpose of the pandas library is to share code that assists with manipulating and analyzing data. In particular, the pandas DataFrame is vital to Python in Excel; it enables you to work with tabular data. The rows, columns, and column headings of DataFrames are ideal for storing and analyzing Excel data.

pandas attempts to infer the data type of data, which works well in simple cases, as you will see. In this section, you will see how to examine DataFrames by using the data type card and the Python Editor to become familiar with the properties associated with Excel entities stored in Python objects. In this section, you will also encounter the one-dimensional form of a DataFrame, known as a series.

Extracting Excel data with the Python x1() function

To extract Excel data into a pandas DataFrame, you use a specific Python function, x1(), which is unique to Python in Excel. It has the following syntax:

```
x1("source", headers = True/False)
```

In this syntax, *source* is the Excel object, which can be identified by a cell reference or an Excel identifier. The *headers* option is a Boolean.

You may be familiar with creating tables in Excel by using Insert Table. The *headers* parameter is similar to the choice of specifying whether column headings are present in a table. If *headers* is True, the first row of Excel data will be used as headers. The output is a DataFrame object, although it could be a series or a scalar (that is, a single value), depending on the source. In this section, you will create examples for different Excel objects and explore the results.

It is good practice to specify a variable to assign to the DataFrame object, and this is the syntax you will use to do so:

```
x=x1("source", headers = True/False)
```

where *x* is the variable you are using to identify a Python object.

> **Note** For the Excel entities in this section, you will use the workbook SP Python in Excel Example.xlsm, which contains some sample data from the Microsoft AdventureWorks dataset.

Working with cells

The smallest Excel entity is a single cell. In this section, we'll look at how to extract the data from an Excel cell into a Python object. Figure 2-70 shows the Range Data sheet with a dataset that has not been converted to a table.

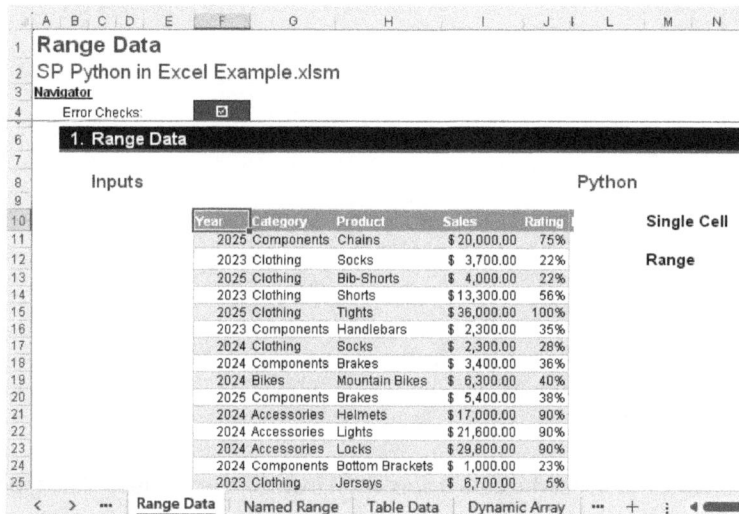

FIGURE 2-70 The data in the Range Data sheet has not been converted into a table.

Enter the following Python code in cell O10 to select the data in cell F11:

```
df_single_cell = xl("F11")
```

Figure 2-71 shows this Python code in the formula bar and the results in the worksheet.

> **Note** You do not need to enter the syntax after the equal sign (=). Instead, you can select the cell, and Python in Excel will generate the syntax for you.

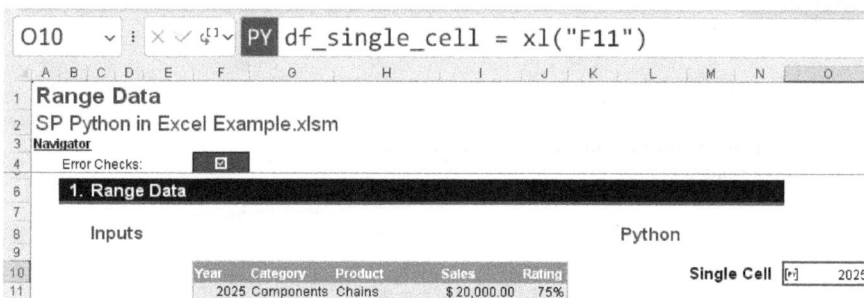

FIGURE 2-71 The Python object when Python reads a single Excel cell shows the value of that cell.

The data type card indicates that because you have extracted a single numeric value, it has been recognized as an integer (see Figure 2-72).

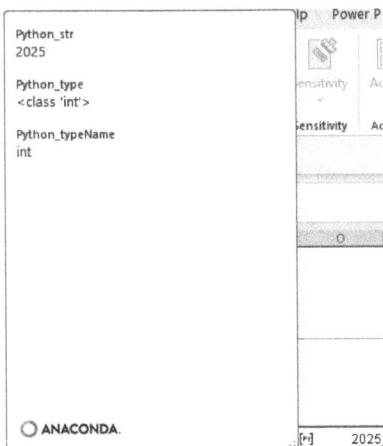

FIGURE 2-72 The Python object when Python reads a single numeric cell with no decimal point is an integer.

If you change the Python syntax to select the data from cell J11 instead, the resulting data type card will be for a float. The Excel formatting is ignored, and the data value is extracted as 0.75 rather than 75% (see Figure 2-73).

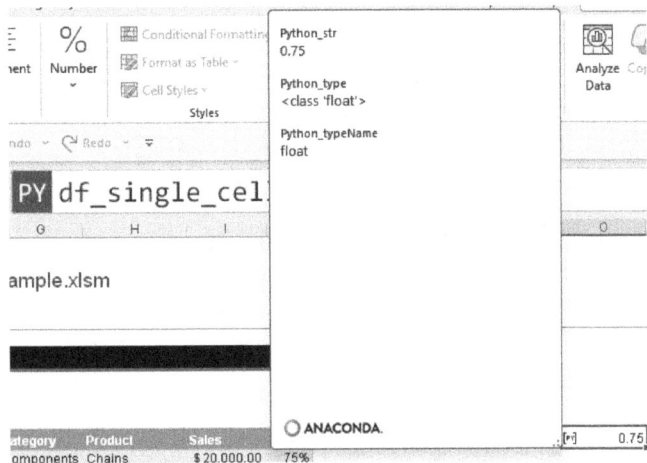

FIGURE 2-73 The Python object when Python reads a single numeric cell with a decimal point is a float.

The Python object for a single cell corresponds to the data found in the cell. A text cell is read as a Python string. For example, if you amend the Python code in O10 to extract the data from H11, the string will have the value Chains (see Figure 2-74).

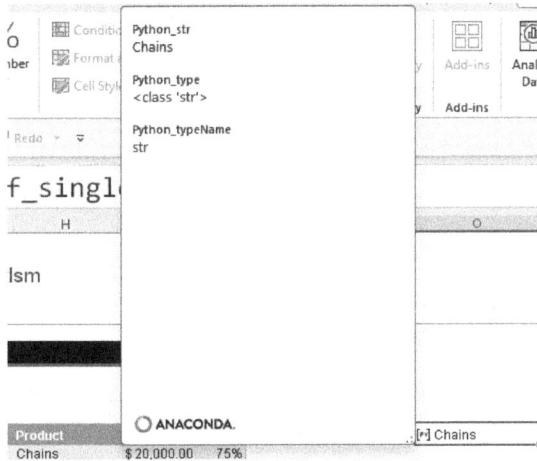

FIGURE 2-74 The Python object when Python reads a single text cell is a string.

Finally, let's see how Python recognizes dates for the single-cell example. Add the heading **Dates** to cell K10 and enter the date **01 January 2025** in cell K11. Then change the Python code in cell O10 to extract data from cell K11. Figure 2-75 shows the results.

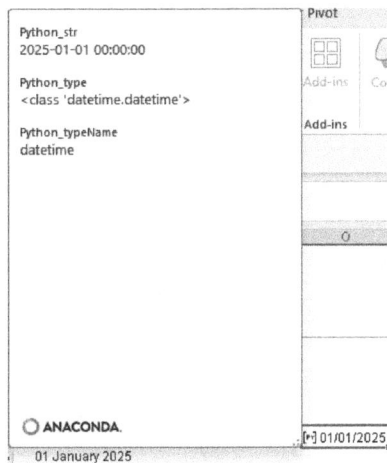

FIGURE 2-75 The Python object when Python reads a single cell containing a date is a datetime object.

The examples for single-cell values have demonstrated how Python interprets data types from data values. The way that dates can be detected is a useful feature of Python in Excel. You will learn more about the `datetime` object later in this chapter. Next, we will look at examples where multiple cells are extracted.

Using contiguous ranges

A *contiguous range* is a range of cells directly next to each other. Using the data on the Range Data sheet as a reference, F11:J12 would be contiguous, but F11:J11, H12 would not.

Enter the following Python code into cell O12 to extract data from the range F10:J18:

```
df_contig_range = xl("F10:J18",headers = True)
```

Figure 2-76 shows the Python code and the result.

> **Note** Just as you can select a single cell instead of typing code after the equal sign, you can select the range instead of typing the code after the equal sign.

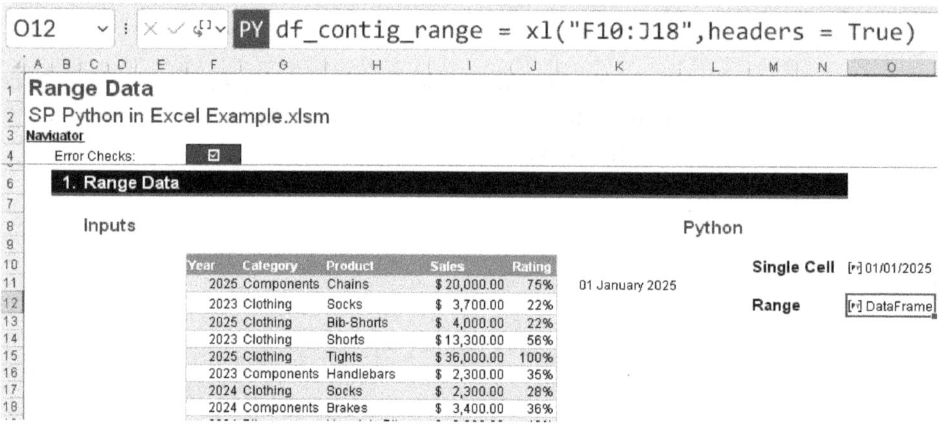

FIGURE 2-76 The Python object when Python reads a contiguous range is a DataFrame.

Notice that when you select the range, the second parameter, `headers=True`, is included in the generated syntax. The data type card in Figure 2-77 shows an 8x5 DataFrame with the headers from the data. The row number is also included in the card, but not in the five columns of the 8x5 DataFrame. The card has been expanded by dragging the bottom-right corner.

8x5 DataFrame

	Year	Category	Product	Sales	Rating
0	2025	Components	Chains	20000	0.75
1	2023	Clothing	Socks	3700	0.22
2	2025	Clothing	Bib-Shorts	4000	0.22
3	2023	Clothing	Shorts	13300	0.56
4	2025	Clothing	Tights	36000	1
5	2023	Components	Handlebars	2300	0.35
6	2024	Clothing	Socks	2300	0.28
7	2024	Components	Brakes	3400	0.36

○ ANACONDA.

FIGURE 2-77 The data type card for the contiguous range F10:J18 shows an 8x5 DataFrame.

The data types have been determined in much the same way as they were in the single-cell example. Year and Sales are right-justified numeric columns, Category and Product are left-justified text, and the decimal point in the Rating column has been preserved, indicating that it is a float.

The Excel value of cell O12 spills from cell O12 (see Figure 2-78).

Year	Category	Product	Sales	Rating
2025	Components	Chains	$ 20,000.00	75%
2023	Clothing	Socks	$ 3,700.00	22%
2025	Clothing	Bib-Shorts	$ 4,000.00	22%
2023	Clothing	Shorts	$ 13,300.00	56%
2025	Clothing	Tights	$ 36,000.00	100%
2023	Components	Handlebars	$ 2,300.00	35%
2024	Clothing	Socks	$ 2,300.00	28%
2024	Components	Brakes	$ 3,400.00	36%
2024	Bikes	Mountain Bikes	$ 6,300.00	40%
2025	Components	Brakes	$ 5,400.00	38%

Single Cell [▸] 01/01/2025

01 January 2025

Range

Year	Category	Product	Sales	Rating
2025	Components	Chains	20000	0.75
2023	Clothing	Socks	3700	0.22
2025	Clothing	Bib-Shorts	4000	0.22
2023	Clothing	Shorts	13300	0.56
2025	Clothing	Tights	36000	1
2023	Components	Handlebars	2300	0.35
2024	Clothing	Socks	2300	0.28
2024	Components	Brakes	3400	0.36

FIGURE 2-78 The Excel value of the 8x5 DataFrame spills from cell O12.

Amend the Python code in cell O12 so that the second parameter, headers=True, is not entered:

```
df_contig_range = xl("F10:J18")
```

In the Excel Value view, the results look the same (see Figure 2-79).

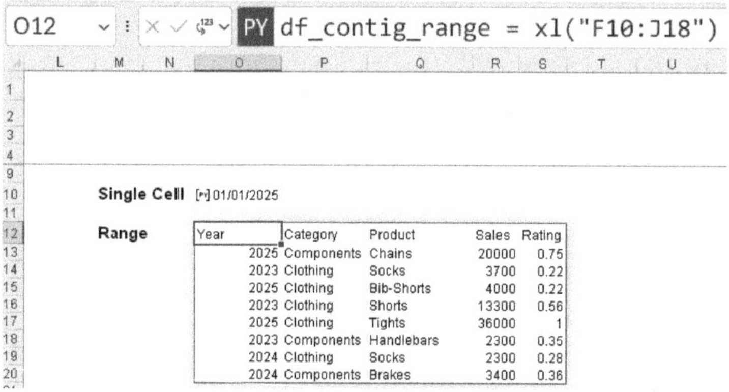

FIGURE 2-79 The Excel value spilling from cell O12 remains the same when the headers parameter is not defined.

Change to the Python Object view. The data type card shows the header detail in the first row, and the DataFrame is now 9x5 (see Figure 2-80).

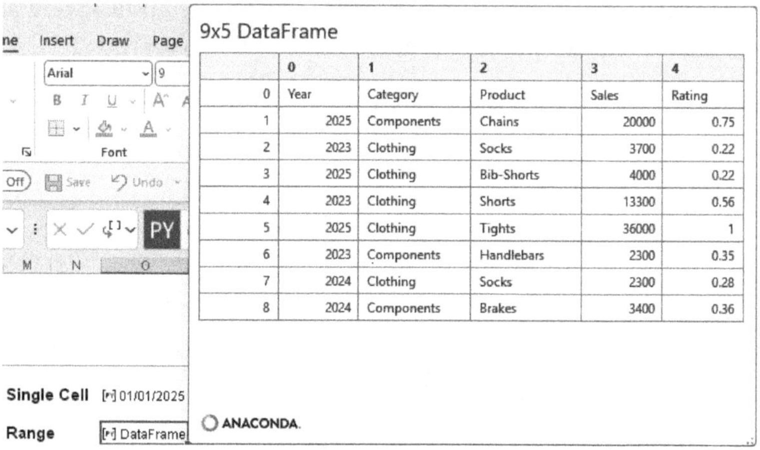

FIGURE 2-80 The data type card for cell O12 shows a 9x5 DataFrame where the first row contains the header values.

You can conclude that if you define the value of the headers parameter as True, the first row of data will be treated as headers in the DataFrame.

Now, amend the Python code in cell O12 to remove everything to the right of the equal sign and then select another contiguous range by selecting the data F11:J18 from the sheet (rather than by typing in the range). Figure 2-81 shows the selection and the Python code that is generated.

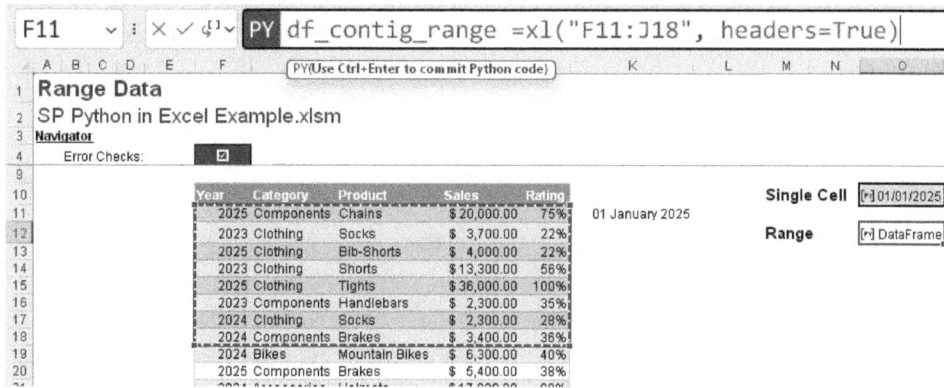

| F11 | | | × ✓ ⫶ | PY | df_contig_range =xl("F11:J18", headers=True) |

	A	B	C	D	E	F		K	L	M	N	O
1	Range Data						PY (Use Ctrl+Enter to commit Python code)					
2	SP Python in Excel Example.xlsm											
3	Navigator											
4		Error Checks:			☑							
9												
10			Year	Category	Product	Sales	Rating		Single Cell		[*] 01/01/2025	
11			2025	Components	Chains	$ 20,000.00	75%	01 January 2025				
12			2023	Clothing	Socks	$ 3,700.00	22%		Range		[*] DataFrame	
13			2025	Clothing	Bib-Shorts	$ 4,000.00	22%					
14			2023	Clothing	Shorts	$ 13,300.00	56%					
15			2025	Clothing	Tights	$ 36,000.00	100%					
16			2023	Components	Handlebars	$ 2,300.00	35%					
17			2024	Clothing	Socks	$ 2,300.00	28%					
18			2024	Components	Brakes	$ 3,400.00	36%					
19			2024	Bikes	Mountain Bikes	$ 6,300.00	40%					
20			2025	Components	Brakes	$ 5,400.00	38%					

FIGURE 2-81 The data selected contains no header values, but headers=True is generated in the Python code.

This example shows that the default behavior when you select Excel data to be extracted to a DataFrame is that the headers parameter value defaults to True. Therefore, the DataFrame containing the extracted data has the dimensions 7x5, with the first line of data in the headings (see Figure 2-82). This is something to watch out for when selecting data to be extracted to Python objects.

7x5 DataFrame

	2025	Components	Chains	20000	0.75
0	2023	Clothing	Socks	3700	0.22
1	2025	Clothing	Bib-Shorts	4000	0.22
2	2023	Clothing	Shorts	13300	0.56
3	2025	Clothing	Tights	36000	1
4	2023	Components	Handlebars	2300	0.35
5	2024	Clothing	Socks	2300	0.28
6	2024	Components	Brakes	3400	0.36

○ ANACONDA.

FIGURE 2-82 The data selected contains no header values, but because headers=True, the first line of data is in the headings.

Now remove the second parameter so the formula looks like this:

```
df_contig_range = xl("F11:J18")
```

The data type card now shows an 8x5 DataFrame, and the header information contains numbers for the columns (see Figure 2-83). By default, if the headers parameter is not specified, the value of this parameter is False.

8x5 DataFrame

	0	1	2	3	4
0	2025	Components	Chains	20000	0.75
1	2023	Clothing	Socks	3700	0.22
2	2025	Clothing	Bib-Shorts	4000	0.22
3	2023	Clothing	Shorts	13300	0.56
4	2025	Clothing	Tights	36000	1
5	2023	Components	Handlebars	2300	0.35
6	2024	Clothing	Socks	2300	0.28
7	2024	Components	Brakes	3400	0.36

ANACONDA.

FIGURE 2-83 The data selected contains no header values, and the headers parameter is not defined, so the first line of data is in the first DataFrame row.

These examples help you understand the default behavior when extracting Excel data into DataFrames. By default, if you select the data rather than enter it as a formula, the first line of the data appears in the headings. If you enter the data as a formula without specifying the headers parameter, all the data appears in the DataFrame rows. It's important to look out for the headers parameter as your Python code gets more complex.

Referencing DataFrames

In the example we've been working with, the variable df_contig_range allows you to use the DataFrame in other Python code. You can enter the following code in cell O21 to access the data that has been extracted to the Python object identified by df_contig_range:

```
df_point_at_contig_range = df_contig_range
```

Figure 2-84 shows the result, using the Excel Value view for cells O12 and O21.

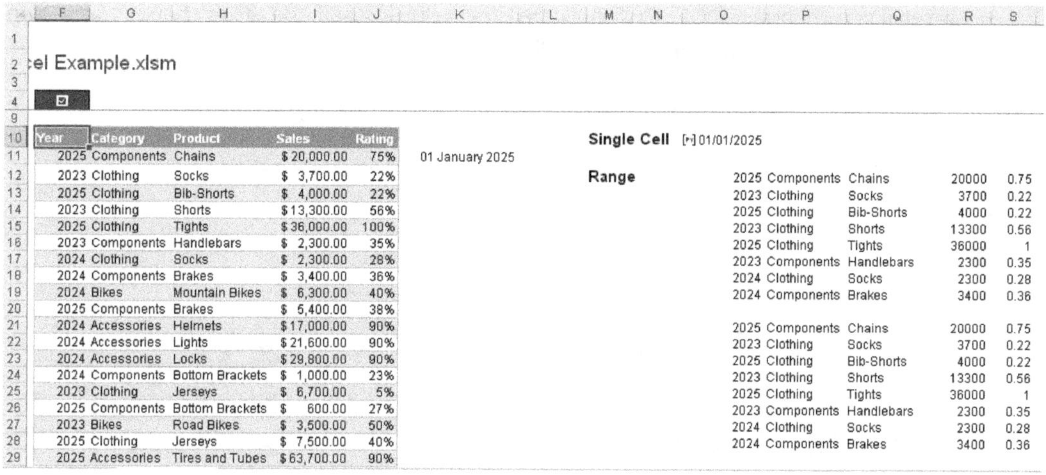

FIGURE 2-84 Cell O21 accesses the variable `df_contig_range`, which is defined in cell O12.

In Python in Excel, it is also possible to point to the data in other cells, including cells containing Python objects. You must be careful with this method, though. The results can vary depending on how the original Python cell is displayed. To see an example of why it is important to take care when referencing Python objects using the Excel cell reference, enter the following Python code, where the original Python object is in cell O12, and you are referencing that object in cell O21:

```
df_point_at_contig_range = xl("O12")
```

Figure 2-85 shows the results: The original Python object is displayed in cell O12, and the Excel value is displayed in cell O21.

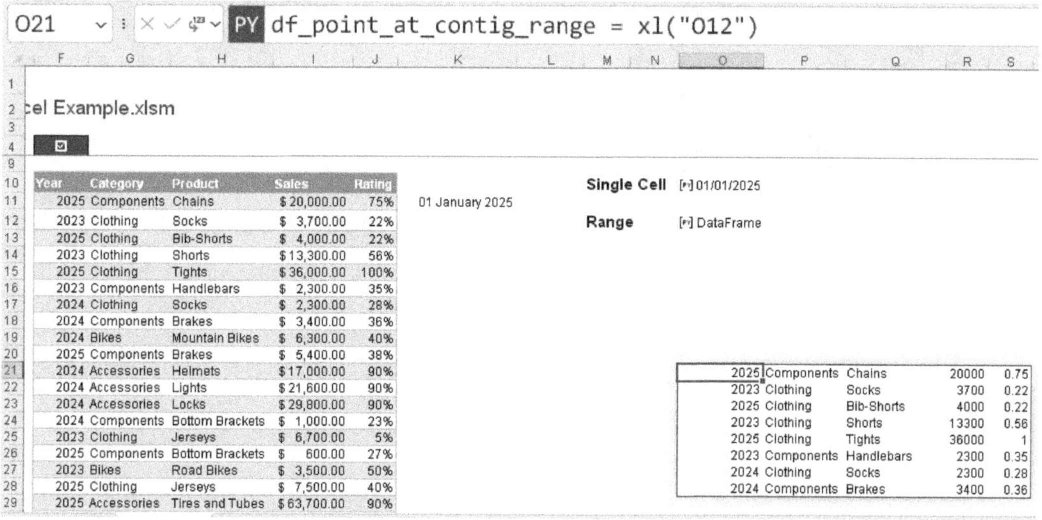

FIGURE 2-85 Cell O21 displays the spilled range, which is the same as the Excel value of the Python object in cell O12.

However, if you change cell O12 to display the Excel value instead, the result changes, as shown in Figure 2-86. Now only one value appears in cell O21.

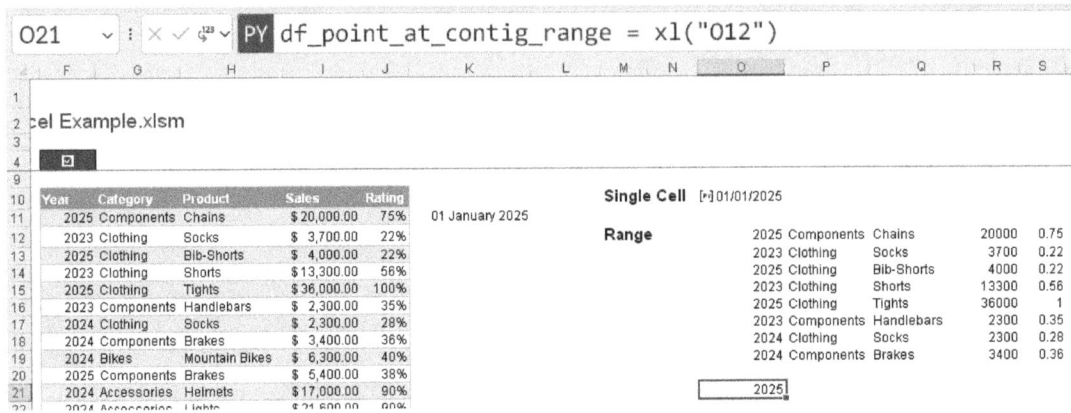

FIGURE 2-86 Cell O21 selects only the first value of the spilled range when extracting data from O12.

With dynamic arrays, you can add a pound sign (#) after the cell reference to select all the spilled data (see Figure 2-87). (You will learn more about the properties of dynamic arrays later in this chapter.)

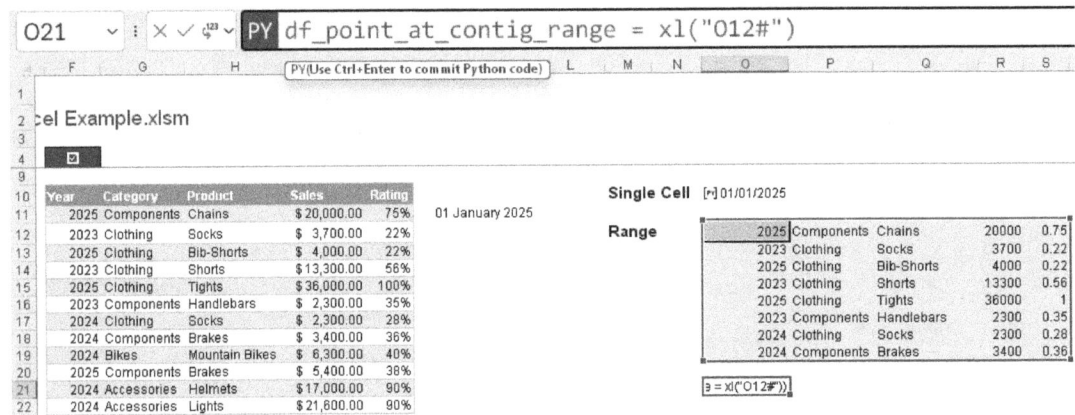

FIGURE 2-87 Using O12# to select the spilled array

If you use cell references to identify Python cells, you must ensure you always add the pound sign after the cell reference in case the Excel value of a Python cell is displayed as a dynamic array. This works with any cell value other than null, including a Python object (see Figure 2-88).

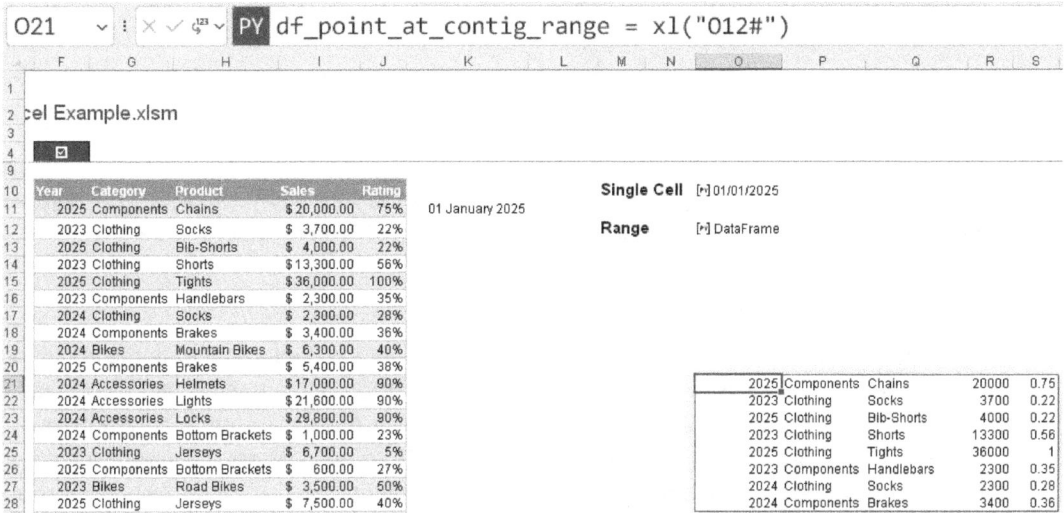

FIGURE 2-88 Using O12# also works with a Python object

The other consideration when using Excel cells as references for Python objects is that Excel referencing is relative. If you copy cell O21 to cell U21 and give the Python object a new variable name, the Excel cell referencing moves, too, as shown in Figure 2-89.

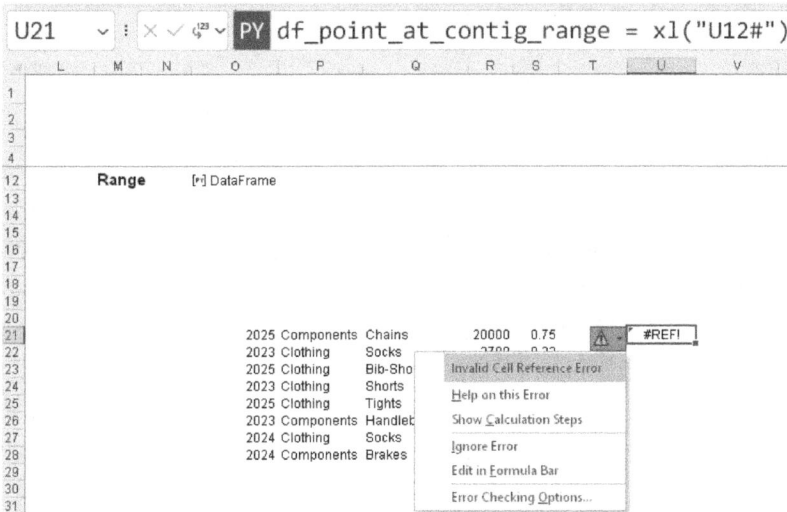

FIGURE 2-89 Copying a Python cell that uses an unanchored cell reference to identify another Python object can cause errors.

Because the Excel cell reference is not anchored, it now points at cell U12 instead of O12. U12 is empty, so it is an invalid target for the dynamic array reference. If you amend the formula in cell U21 to remove the pound sign, the result would be None, which is the equivalent of a null value in Excel. The #REF! error results from the dynamic array referencing an empty cell.

Another problem, the #SPILL! error, crops up when you reference the cell that contains the Python object rather than using the variable name. (We will look at this error in detail later in this chapter.) If the target cell is displayed in Excel Value view and has a #SPILL! error, the Python cell that references that cell also triggers a #SPILL! error.

To summarize, when creating and referencing DataFrames, you should assign and use variable names unless you have an unusual task that requires relative referencing of Excel data.

Carrying out Python calculations

You already know that Python code can refer to data that has occurred above or to the left (or on a previous sheet). This impacts the way that calculations in Python cells are refreshed. The default behavior for Python cells that use Excel data is that Python formulas recalculate automatically in row-major order when a value used in a Python formula is changed. This means across row 1 from column A to column XFD and then row 2 and so on, from the first worksheet to the last. If this behavior becomes a problem, it may be possible to control the way the Python cells are recalculated from the Calculation Options settings in the Formulas tab (see Figure 2-90).

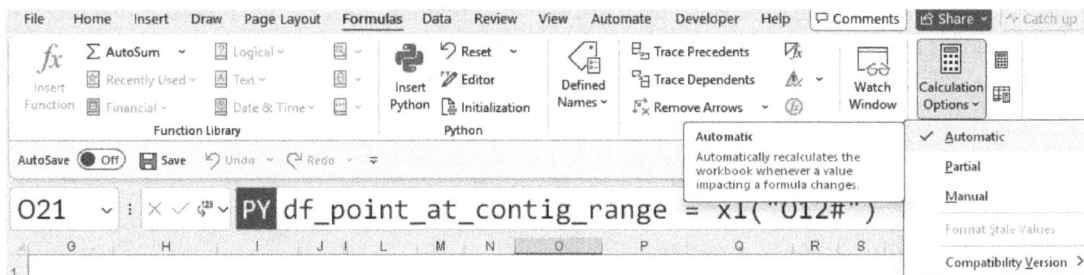

FIGURE 2-90 The default calculation option is Automatic.

The default option for Calculation Options is Automatic, which means Python cells that use Excel data and Excel formulas will be recalculated if a value that the formula refers to changes. You can change the Calculation Options to Partial or Manual.

Selecting the partial calculation option The Partial calculation option changes how formulas are calculated for Excel entities (excluding Data Tables and automatic PivotTables) (see Figure 2-91). At the time of writing, this impacts Python objects that use Excel data if you have the Python in Excel add-on. If you do not have the add-on, you will be prevented from manually recalculating cells if you select **Partial** or **Manual**. (You will learn more about this later in the chapter.)

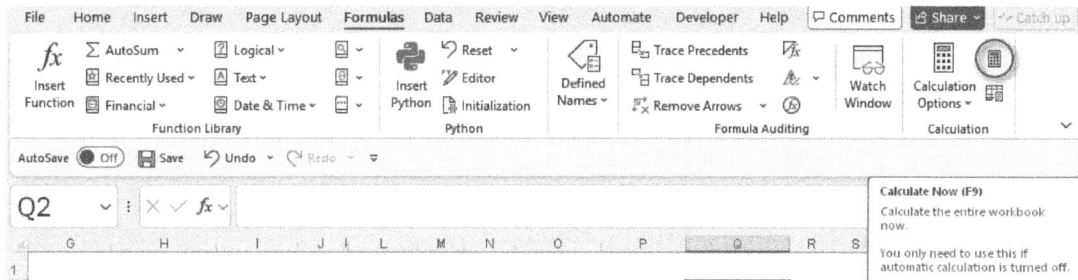

FIGURE 2-91 The Partial calculation option excludes some Excel entities.

If you have the Python in Excel add-on and Partial is selected, there are four ways to manually recalculate the Python cells that use Excel data:

- Click **Calculate Now** on the **Formulas** tab (or press **F9**).

- Click **Calculate Sheet** on the **Formulas** tab (or press **Shift+F9**).

- Update the Python formula in the cell.

- Click the **Reset** option in the **Python** section of the **Formulas** tab.

Figure 2-92 shows the Calculate Now option.

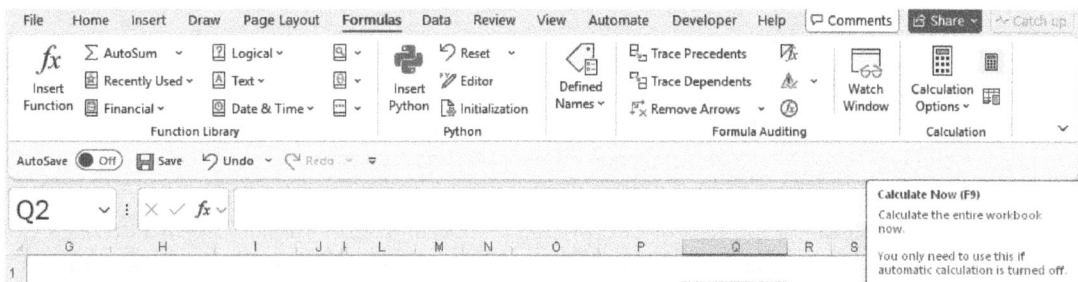

FIGURE 2-92 The Calculate Now option recalculates the entire workbook, including Python cells that use Excel.

You may have noticed that in this section, we have referred to Python cells that use Excel data. This is because the Calculate Now and Calculate Sheet options do not recalculate Python cells that do not reference Excel data. Before we look at the options to refresh Python calculations in the Python section of the Formulas tab, let's look at what happens to Python cells that do not reference Excel data.

In cell O30, enter the following Python code:

```
import random
No_Excel = random.randint(1,10)
```

This Python code loads the Python library `random` and then generates a random number from 1 to 10. Figure 2-93 shows one result, which will probably not be the same as yours.

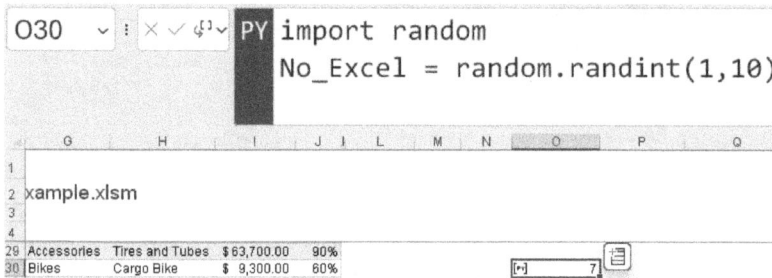

FIGURE 2-93 Using Python to generate a random number

Now select cell **F9** and notice what happens to the value in cell O30: It stays the same.

In the **Python** section of the **Formulas** tab, click **Reset** (see Figure 2-94).

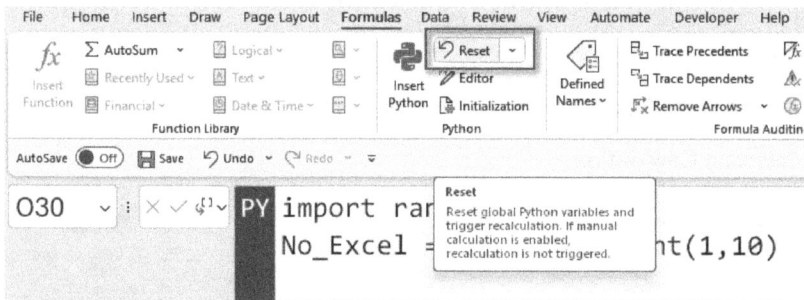

FIGURE 2-94 The Reset functionality in the Python section of the Formulas tab resets global Python variables and triggers calculation if the calculation type is Automatic.

Note that the Reset dropdown list has two items: Reset and Reset Runtime (see Figure 2-95). Reset is the default, and Reset Runtime is similar, except that it does not reset the global Python variables.

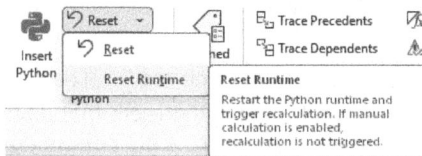

FIGURE 2-95 Reset Runtime triggers the recalculation of Python cells.

When you click Reset or Reset Runtime, the value in cell O30 is recalculated (see Figure 2-96).

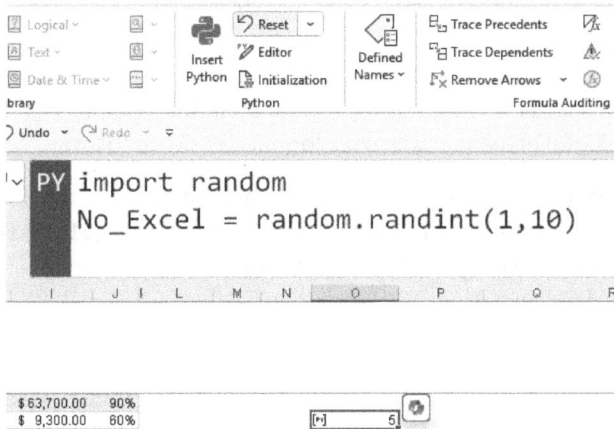

```
PY import random
   No_Excel = random.randint(1,10)
```

FIGURE 2-96 Select **Reset** to recalculate cell O30 and generate a different random number.

In summary, you can use the Reset options in the Python section of the Formulas tab to recalculate all Python cells. The Calculate Now and Calculate Sheet options only recalculate Python cells that use Excel data in the workbook or sheet, respectively. The Partial calculation setting works with Python cells only if you have the Python in Excel add-on. The same is true for the Manual calculation setting.

Calculating manually The Manual calculation option in the Calculation Options dropdown menu applies to all formulas in the workbook. If this option is selected, Excel formulas can be recalculated by using Calculate Now or Calculate Sheet. Python formulas that use Excel references are also recalculated. Python cells not using Excel data must be recalculated by using the Reset options in the Python section of the Formulas tab. If you set the Calculation option to Manual when the Python in Excel add-on is not installed, you get errors when updating the Python cells. (You'll learn more about this later in the chapter.)

In this section, you have created Python cells that extract Excel data from contiguous ranges into DataFrames. You have also seen how to reference other DataFrames and how to recalculate Python cells. This experience will be helpful as you move on to extracting data from other Excel entities, beginning with named ranges.

Identifying cells with named ranges

Much like the variables you use to reference Python objects, a *named range* is a name that can be used in Excel formulas to identify a cell or a group of cells.

Rules related to creating a name for a cell or a range of cells apply when naming tables too:

- Names are not case sensitive.

- A name must begin with a letter, an underscore (_), or a backslash (\).

- A name cannot be longer than 255 characters.

- A name cannot contain spaces, and most punctuation is not allowed.

- r and c are not valid names because they are reserved for row and column.

- A name cannot be the same as a default cell name.

The default name for a cell is the column letter followed by the row number (for example, A1). A named range allows you to enter a meaningful name that will make formulas easier to follow.

In the same Excel workbook you have been using (SP Python in Excel Example.xlsm), open the sheet **Named Range**. Select the data in cells F10:I15. In the name box, enter the name **NamedRange1** (see Figure 2-97). You must press Enter after typing the named range in the Name Box to assign it to the cells.

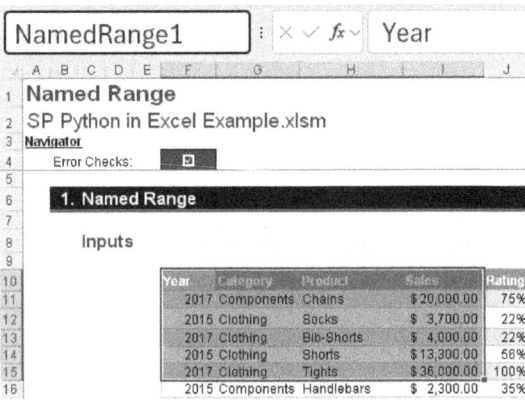

FIGURE 2-97 Defining a named range

You can also define a named range in the Name Manager on the Formulas tab (see Figure 2-98). The Name Manager also shows any Excel table names, which you will use in the next section.

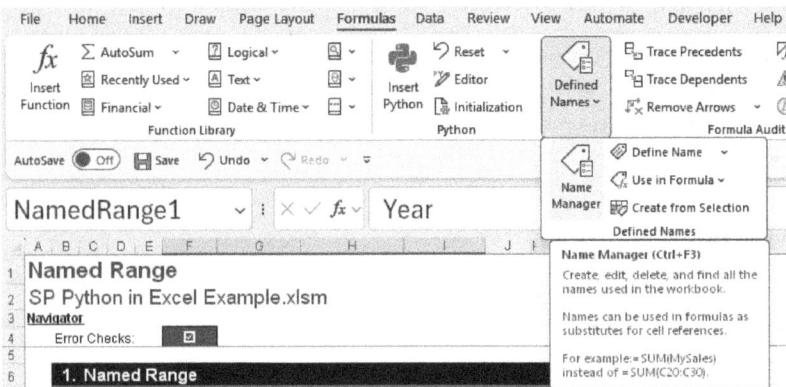

FIGURE 2-98 Named ranges can be created, amended, and deleted in the Name Manager.

Open the Name Manager, and the names in the workbook are shown, including NamedRange1 (see Figure 2-99).

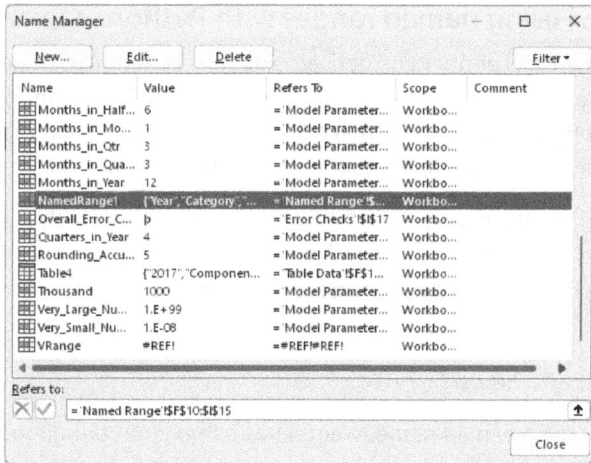

FIGURE 2-99 The named range NamedRange1 appears in the Name Manager.

> **Note** Deleting a worksheet causes the cells referenced by a name to be deleted, but it does not delete the name itself. For example, VRange still exists as a name in Figure 2-99 even though the associated reference has been removed (as the #REF! error indicates). To delete a name, you must delete it in the Name Manager.

Python in Excel recognizes named ranges. To see how it works, enter the following Python code in cell O10:

```
df_named_range=xl("NamedRange1", headers=True)
```

The headers parameter behaves in the same way it does for cell ranges. Figure 2-100 shows the results of entering the code: The original data is shown on the sheet, and the data in the named range NamedRange1 spills from cell O10.

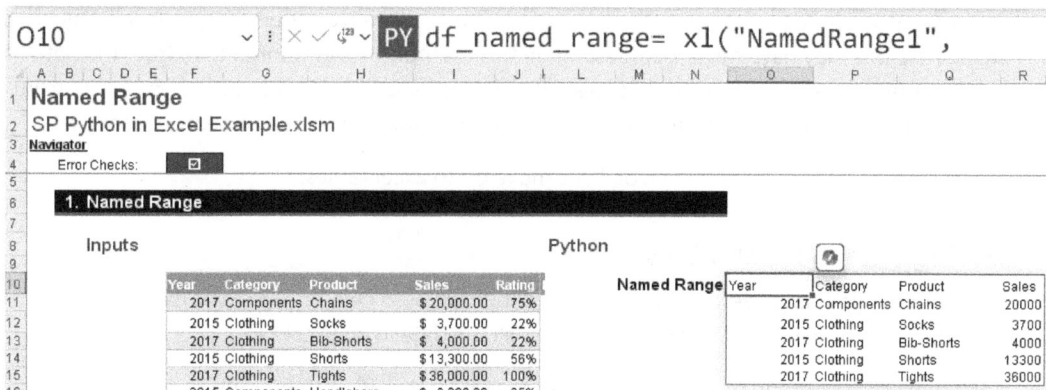

FIGURE 2-100 NamedRange1 is extracted to a DataFrame, and the Excel value is displayed.

Understanding the limitations of using named ranges with Python in Excel

The Python function xl() allows only one Excel entity to be defined. You may be tempted to get around this by including more than one range in a named range (that is, by creating a noncontiguous range where multiple sets of data are not right next to each other). Don't do it. The next example demonstrates what happens if you try to extract a noncontiguous named range into a DataFrame.

In this example, you will attempt to extract the headings and some data that is not directly under the headings, which would create a subset of the data and retain the headings. Select cells F10:J10 and F12:J14 to create a named range and give it the name **NamedRangeNonContig**. Enter the following Python code in cell O17:

```
df_named_range_nc=xl("NamedRangeNonContig", headers=True)
```

Figure 2-101 shows the results of trying to use a named range to enter more than one contiguous range: Cell O17 contains the error code #BUSY!, and an error message is displayed.

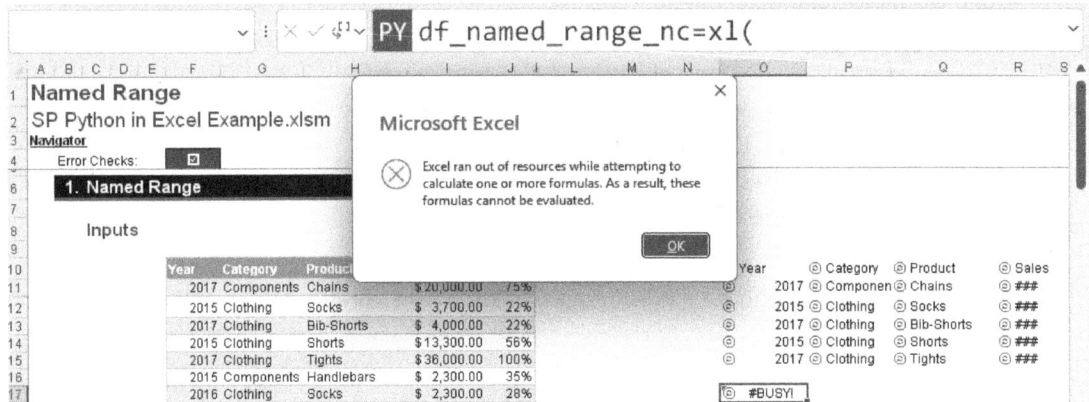

FIGURE 2-101 Trying to extract a named range that references more than one contiguous range prompts an error.

The error message is "Excel ran out of resources while attempting to calculate one or more formulas. As a result, these formulas cannot be evaluated." Do not try to extract data by using a named range that references more than one contiguous range. The results have varied as Python in Excel has been developed, but they have never been useful! In this example, if you wanted to extract the data from the noncontiguous range, you could extract the data in cells F10:J14 and then remove data from the DataFrame. (You will learn how to transform the data in DataFrames in the next chapter.)

Delete cell O17 to remove the error. Let's move on to Excel tables.

Storing data in Excel tables

The examples you have seen so far with Excel data have used cell references or named ranges to access the data. In Python in Excel, you can also select all the data in an Excel table.

One major advantage of using Excel tables to store data rather than using ranges is that they are dynamic—so if you add or remove rows or columns, the table will reference the current data.

Open the sheet **Table Data** in the current workbook. The data is currently in a range that extends from F10 to J85. Enter the following Excel formula in cell L10:

```
=MAX(F11:F85)
```

This formula simply finds the maximum Year column value, which is 2025 (see Figure 2-102).

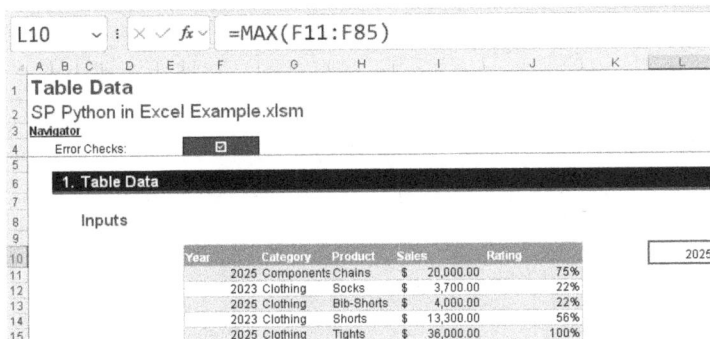

FIGURE 2-102 Determining the latest year in the data

Now add a row to the bottom of the data, using the following values:

- Year=2026

- Category=Tools

- Product=Spanner

- Sales=1000

- Rate=50%

The value in cell L10 is still 2025, and you may get a warning notice that the formula omits adjacent cells, as shown in Figure 2-103.

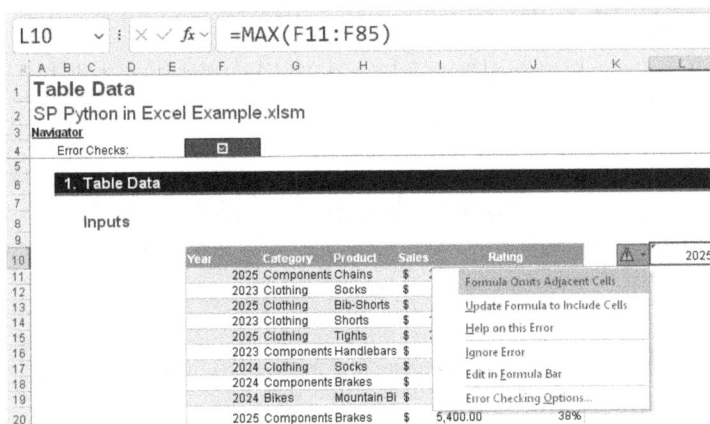

FIGURE 2-103 The extra row is not included in the MAX calculation, and a warning appears.

Now, you will create a table for the original data. Delete the bottom row and the contents of cell L10. Click anywhere in the data and press **Ctrl+A** to select the whole range. On the **Insert** tab, choose **Insert Table** (see Figure 2-104).

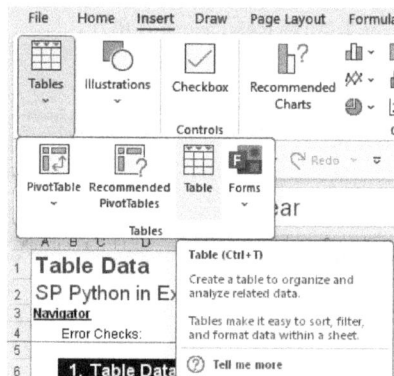

FIGURE 2-104 The Insert Table option allows you to organize and analyze related data.

The tooltip tells you that creating a table is useful for organizing and analyzing related data, and a table makes it easier to sort, filter, and format data. Because you will analyze data in this example, tables will be particularly useful.

When you select the Table option, you are prompted to confirm the range and whether headers exist in the data, as shown in Figure 2-105.

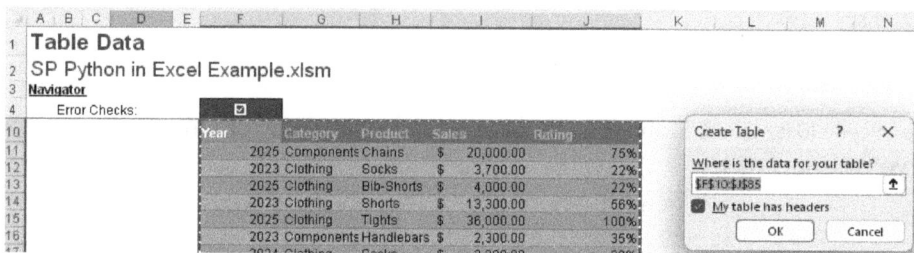

FIGURE 2-105 The Create Table dialog allows you to change the range and confirm the existence of headers.

Accept the defaults and click **OK**. The format of the data changes, and the contextual tab Table Design appears (see Figure 2-106). Your table may have different colors if your default table format is different from ours. (If you are reading a printed copy of the book, you will see only black-and-white text and figures.)

Note The Table Design tab appears only if you have selected a cell in the table.

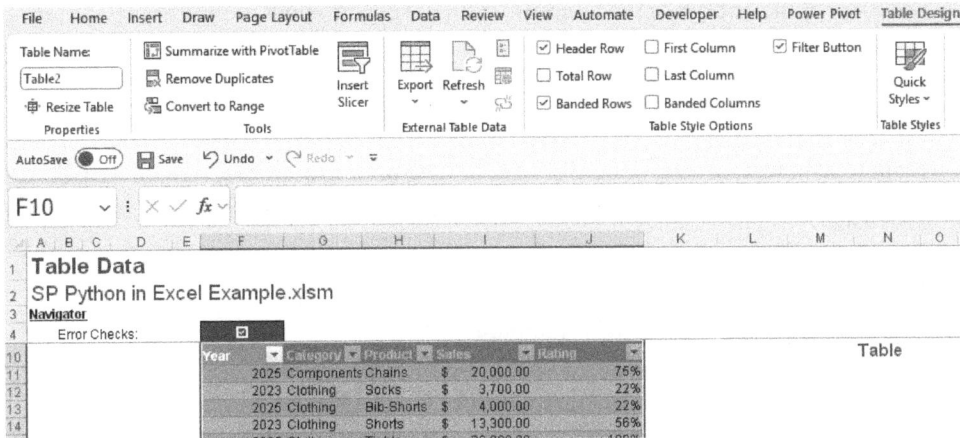

FIGURE 2-106 The Table Design tab is available when a table is inserted.

A filter button is added to each column by default. You can toggle this option by using the Filter Button checkbox in the Table Style Options section of the Table Design tab. There is a Table Name box, where the table in this example is currently named Table2. Your table name may include a different number if you have already tried creating tables in your workbook. No matter what your table is currently named, rename it **TblExcelData** so that the name is more helpful. Make sure you enter the name by pressing **Enter** after typing it in.

> **Note** The rules for table names are the same as those for names of named ranges discussed in the previous section.

Now you can find the latest year again. When you enter the MAX formula in cell L10 again, select all the data in the Year column (including the column heading), and the formula bar shows the table syntax for the column:

```
=MAX(TblExcelData[[#All],[Year]])
```

As shown in Figure 2-107, the result in cell L10 is 2025.

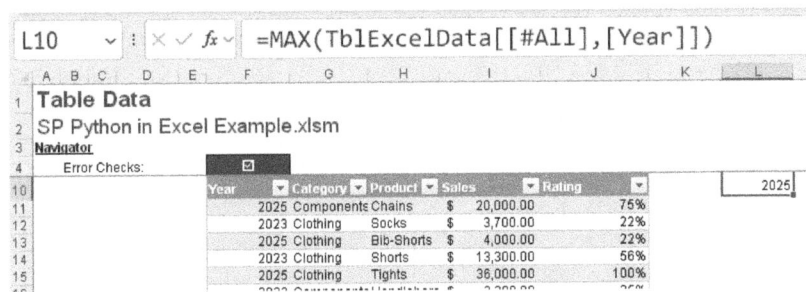

FIGURE 2-107 Selecting the whole column causes table references to be inserted into the formula.

Now add a row at the bottom of the table, using the following values:

- Year=2026

- Category=Tools

- Product=Spanner

- Sales=1000

- Rate=50%

The result is updated to 2026, as shown in Figure 2-108.

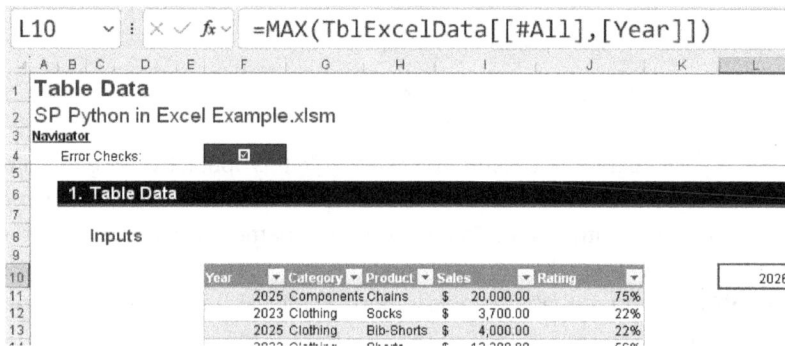

FIGURE 2-108 Adding rows to a table dynamically changes the result of the formula.

This is a simple example, but it demonstrates a powerful property of tables: The syntax for a table will also be used by Python. In this example, the data in the Year column is referenced by TblExcelData[[#All],[[Year]], which begins with the table name and then has square brackets ([]) to indicate that column data is being referenced. [#All] means that headers and data are included, and [Year] is the column you are interested in for this example.

You can also use these table references:

- [#Data] is the data in the table, excluding the headings.

- [#Headers] is just the headings.

- [#Totals] selects the total row if Total Row is toggled on in the Table Design tab; otherwise, it returns null.

Referencing Excel tables

Let's move on to creating a Python cell to read the data. Continuing with the same worksheet you've been using, in cell O10, enter the following Python code:

```python
df_table=xl("TblExcelData[#All]", headers=True)
```

Figure 2-109 shows the Excel value of cell O10.

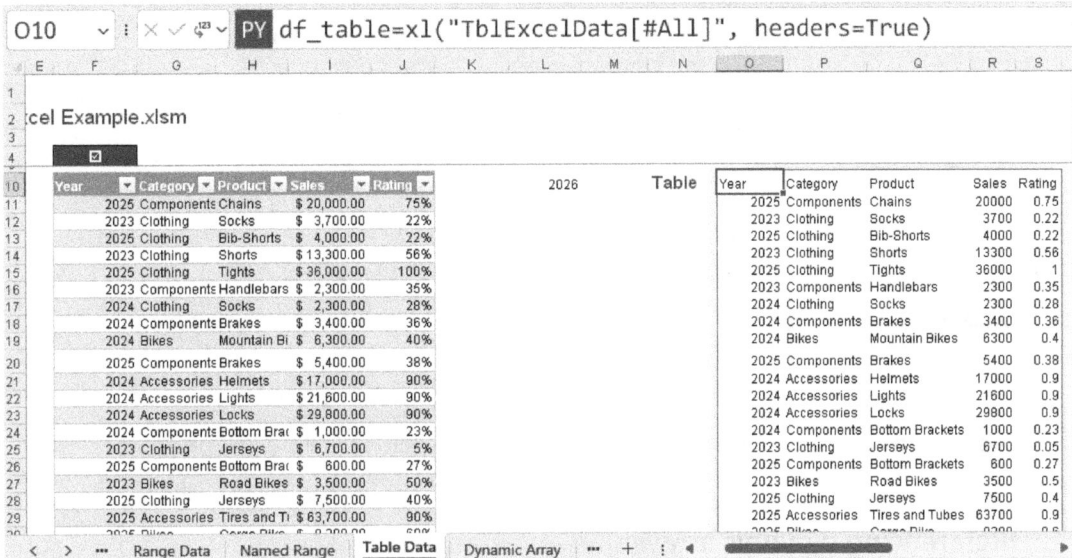

FIGURE 2-109 Using Python to extract an Excel table into a DataFrame

Change the view to Python Object view for cell O10 and look at the data type card (see Figure 2-110).

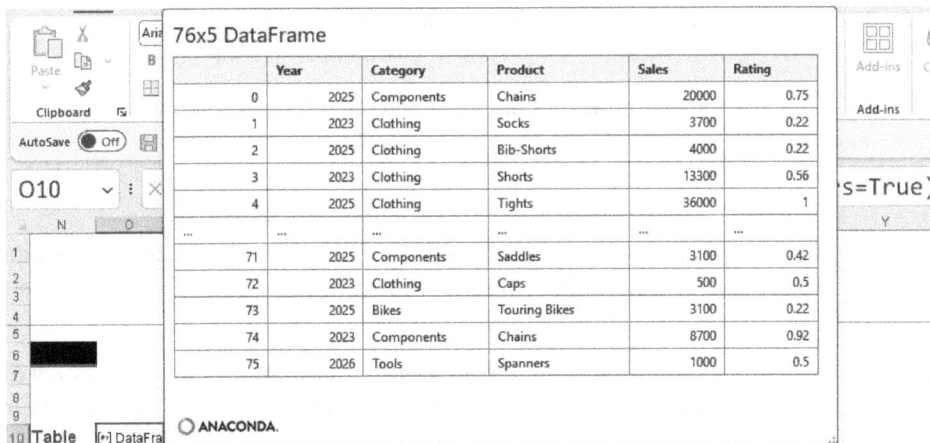

FIGURE 2-110 The Python object for an Excel table with 5 columns and 76 rows is a 76x5 DataFrame.

When dealing with very large datasets, you cannot view all the rows on the data type card. The alternatives are to view the Excel value or to use the Python Editor. (You will review the examples from this chapter using the Python Editor in Chapter 4.)

To complete this section on Excel tables, remove the final row you added at the bottom of the table and then check the data type card to see the results (see Figure 2-111).

75x5 DataFrame

	Year	Category	Product	Sales	Rating
0	2025	Components	Chains	20000	0.75
1	2023	Clothing	Socks	3700	0.22
2	2025	Clothing	Bib-Shorts	4000	0.22
3	2023	Clothing	Shorts	13300	0.56
4	2025	Clothing	Tights	36000	1
...	...	...	...	...	...
70	2024	Clothing	Tights	22100	0.99
71	2025	Components	Saddles	3100	0.42
72	2023	Clothing	Caps	500	0.5
73	2025	Bikes	Touring Bikes	3100	0.22
74	2023	Components	Chains	8700	0.92

FIGURE 2-111 Remove the final row to update the Python code automatically.

Referencing dynamic arrays

The Excel Value view for a DataFrame is a dynamic array, so it is no surprise that Python in Excel can extract dynamic arrays. A *dynamic array* function returns a result that can be more than one value. The result can spill to the right and below the cell that contains the function. If the result of the Python code in a Python cell in Excel is more than one value, then the Excel value is displayed as a dynamic array. (You encountered this concept in the "Referencing DataFrames" section earlier in this chapter.) You can use Python in Excel to reference dynamic arrays created by other Excel functions.

Let's start by entering a dynamic array formula. Open the sheet **Dynamic Array** and then use the Excel function RANDARRAY() in cell F10:

`=RANDARRAY(5,6,10,300,TRUE)`

This function generates an array with five rows and six columns. The minimum value is 10, and the maximum is 300. The final parameter indicates that the array should contain integers (whole numbers).

> **Note** Even when you use the same parameters shown in this example, your results will differ from the results shown here. Your array will have five rows and six columns, but each number in the array will be a randomly generated number between 10 and 300.

In cell P10, enter the following Python code:

```
df_dynamic_array= xl("F10#")
```

When you view the Excel value of P10, you should find that the array spilling from P10 has the same values as the array spilling from F10 (see Figure 2-112).

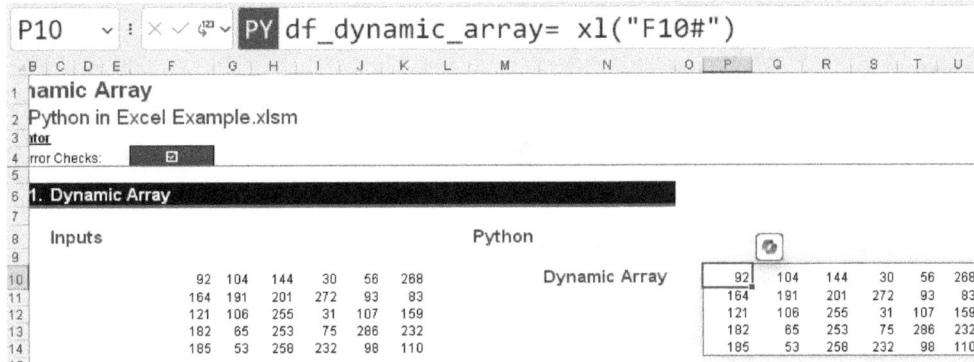

FIGURE 2-112 The Python cell displays the same dynamic array values as the referenced dynamic array.

Accessing data in Power Query queries

The data for the examples in this chapter has been in an Excel workbook. To work with external data, Python in Excel can access data in Power Query queries. This section is particularly important because Python in Excel needs to use the Power Query data connectors to access external data. In case you are unfamiliar with Power Query, we will walk you through how to extract the data we will use for the example.

Power Query is also known as Get & Transform. You can find it in the Data tab, in the section Get & Transform Data (see Figure 2-113). Power Query is an integrated extract, transform, and load (ETL) engine that allows you to access data from a wide range of sources.

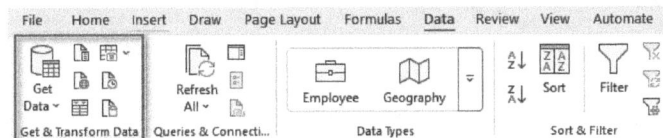

FIGURE 2-113 The Get & Transform Data section of the Data tab

In this example, you will use the Power Query connectors to extract data from external sources for use in Python in Excel. You do not need to load the data into the Excel workbook to do this. The Get Data dropdown menu shows the available source groups. In Figure 2-114, the From File dropdown menu has been opened to show the sources for that group.

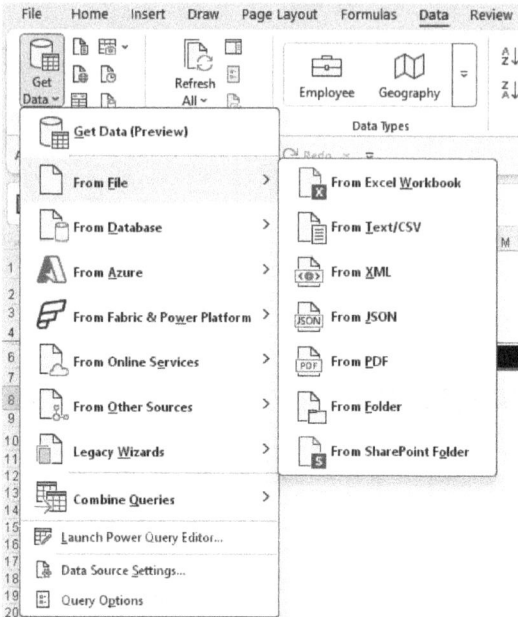

FIGURE 2-114 The Get Data dropdown menu in the Get & Transform Data section on the Data tab

At the time of writing, a new alternative to the Get Data dropdown menu was in preview: the Get Data (Power Query) dialog (see Figure 2-115). This new dialog allows you to view all the connectors in one place rather than opening multiple dropdown menus.

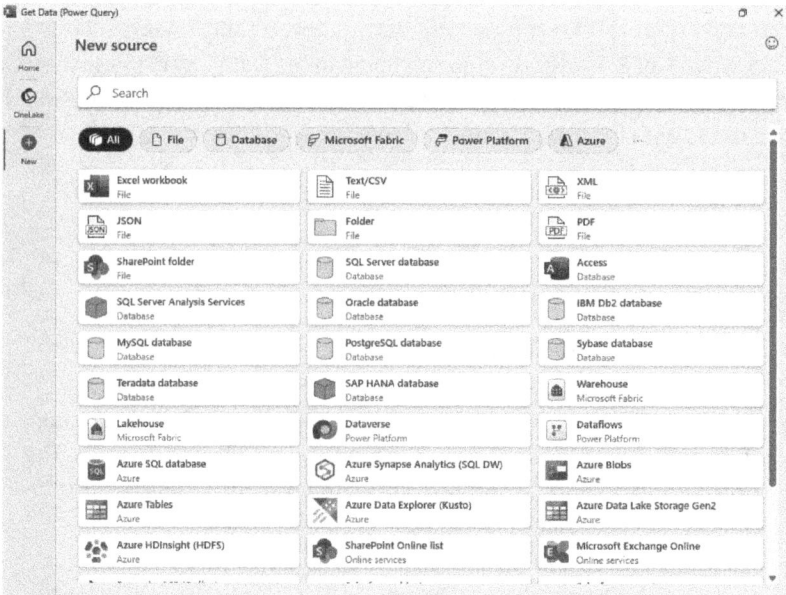

FIGURE 2-115 The Get Data (Power Query) dialog shows all the sources that can be accessed.

One of the workbooks you downloaded as part of the downloadable resources for this book is the Financial Sample.xlsx Excel workbook. This is a sample data workbook available from Microsoft that you can also access at *https://learn.microsoft.com/en-us/power-bi/create-reports/sample-financial-download*. If you haven't already downloaded it, do so now and note its location. You will browse to this location for the next example.

In the **Get & Transform Data** section on the **Data** tab, use the **Get Data** dropdown menu to access the **From File** group and then select the **From Excel Workbook** option (see Figure 2-116).

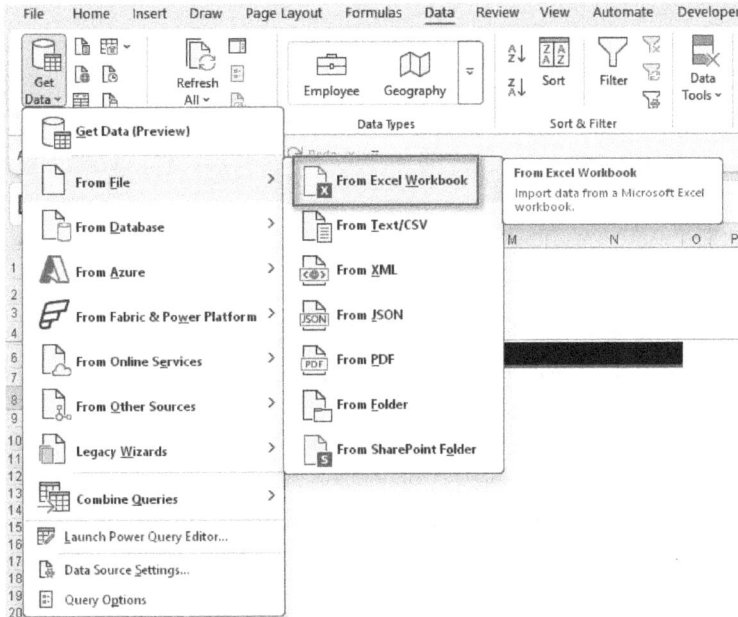

FIGURE 2-116 The From Excel Workbook connector is in the From File group.

When prompted to browse to the workbook's location, select the workbook in the browser and choose Import. The Navigator dialog will appear (see Figure 2-117).

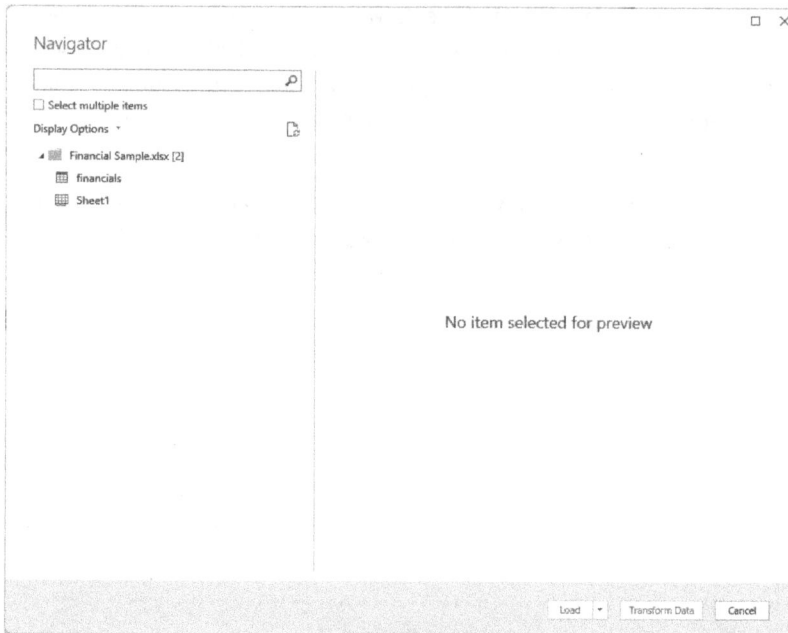

FIGURE 2-117 The Navigator dialog for an Excel workbook

When you extract data by using Power Query, the Navigator dialog varies depending on the type of data you are accessing. In a workbook, you can access sheets and tables from the Navigator dialog. Select the table **financials** to preview the data, as shown in Figure 2-118.

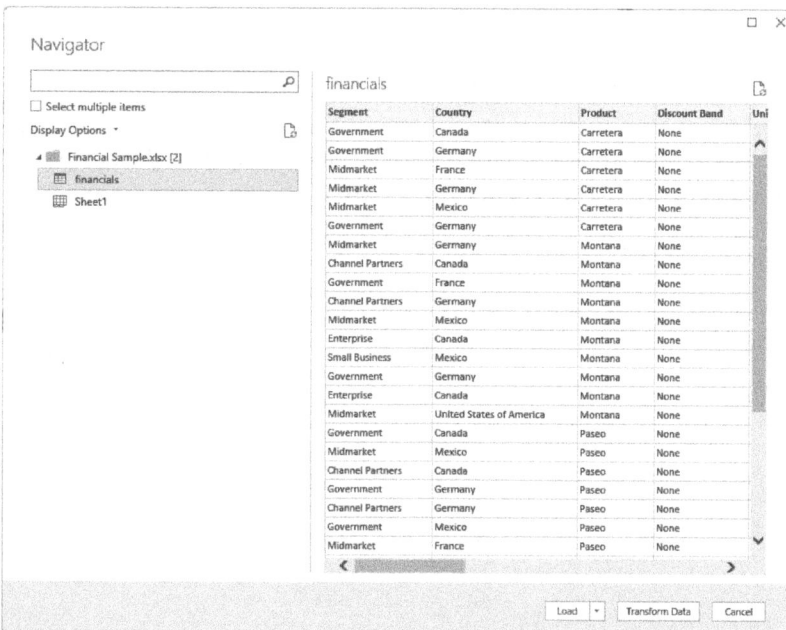

FIGURE 2-118 A preview of the data in the financials table

Once you have selected the table, you can see a preview of the data, and you can choose to transform the data. Do not choose to load it, or you will write all the data into the workbook in a new sheet called financials. (If you do this accidentally, delete the financials sheet.)

Click the **Transform Data** button to display the Power Query Editor (see Figure 2-119).

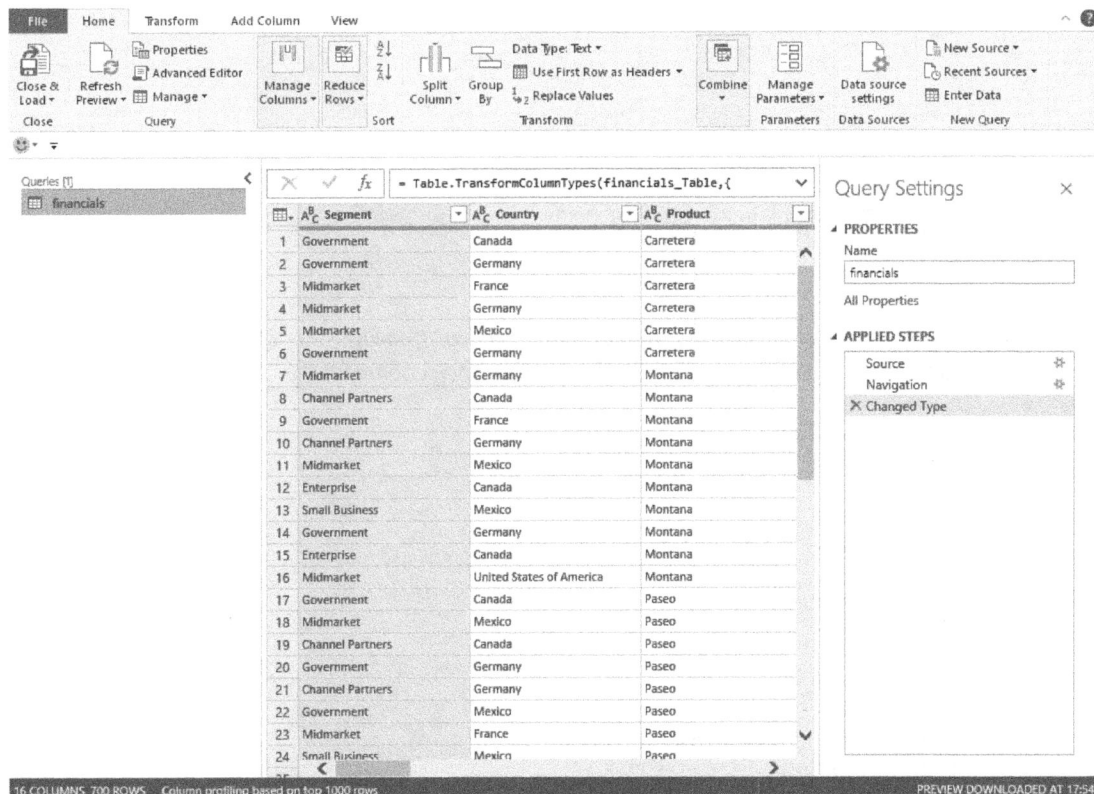

FIGURE 2-119 The Power Query Editor

A snapshot has been taken of the financials table in the Financial Sample workbook. The menu options can be used to transform the data. Every transformation creates a new step, and all steps are recorded in the Applied Steps section. Some steps can be performed automatically, which is why there are three steps shown. Every query has a Source step: For this example, the Source step identifies the workbook. The Navigation step selects the table. The Changed Type step detects the data type of each column based on algorithms performed on a sample of the data.

For this example, you will not perform further transformations. Instead, you will load the data into a Power Query query not loaded to the workbook. To do this, select the **Close & Load** dropdown menu on the **Home** tab and select **Close & Load To** (see Figure 2-120).

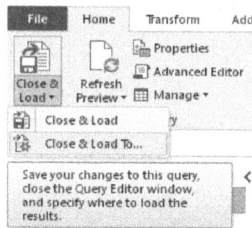

FIGURE 2-120 On the **Close & Load** dropdown menu, choose the **Close & Load To** option to specify where to load the results.

The Import Data dialog appears, with defaults selected (see Figure 2-121). It allows you to control the output so the data can be accessed from the query without being written to a new worksheet.

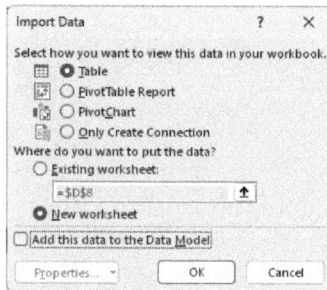

FIGURE 2-121 The Import Data dialog allows you to specify how the data is stored in the workbook.

Note The defaults shown in Figure 2-121 are used for new queries if you select the Close & Load option shown in Figure 2-120. If you choose the Close & Load option after entering a new query, Python in Excel bypasses the Import dialog and assumes that the defaults should be used.

In the Import Data dialog, select **Only Create Connection**. Leave the option **Add This Data to the Data Model** unchecked because Python in Excel cannot access data in the Data Model. Click **OK**, and the Queries & Connections pane opens (see Figure 2-122).

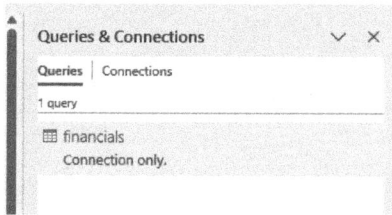

FIGURE 2-122 The financials query appears in the Queries & Connections pane as a connection-only query.

Now that you have created a connection to the external data, you can use a Python cell to access the data. Open the sheet called **Power Query**. In cell F10, enter the following Python code:

```
df_power_query = xl("financials")
```

Figure 2-123 shows the results in the Excel Value view.

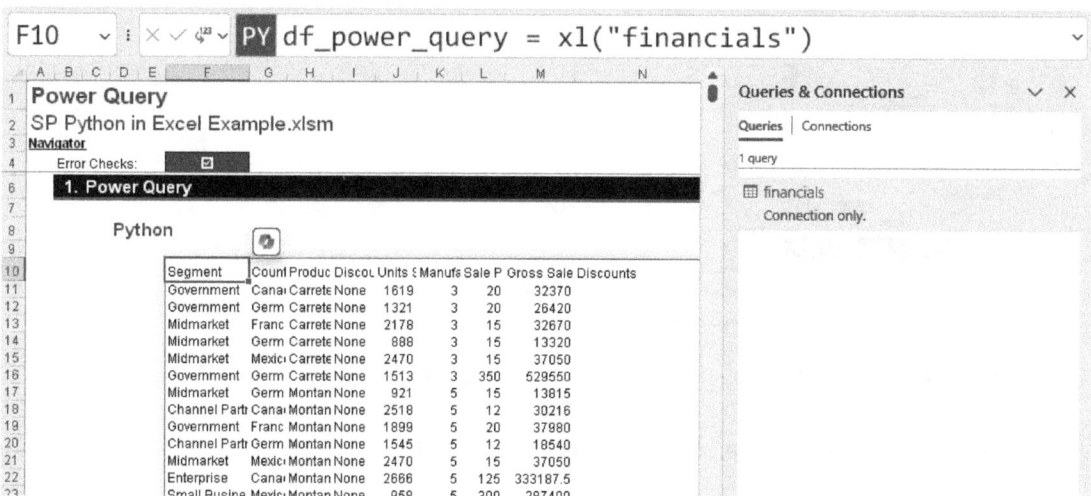

FIGURE 2-123 The financials query has been extracted to a DataFrame, and the Excel Value view displays the data from the external workbook.

The query is a snapshot of the table in the external workbook. If you hover over the financials query in the Queries & Connections pane, you can then click the **Refresh** icon to refresh the query (see Figure 2-124). If the calculation mode is automatic, Excel automatically refreshes the Python cell.

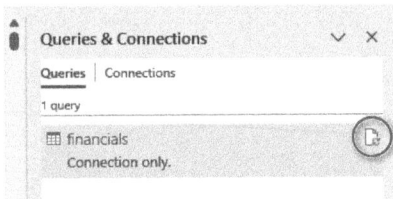

FIGURE 2-124 Clicking the icon refreshes the query.

To complete this example, change cell F10 to the Python Object view and look at the data type card (see Figure 2-125).

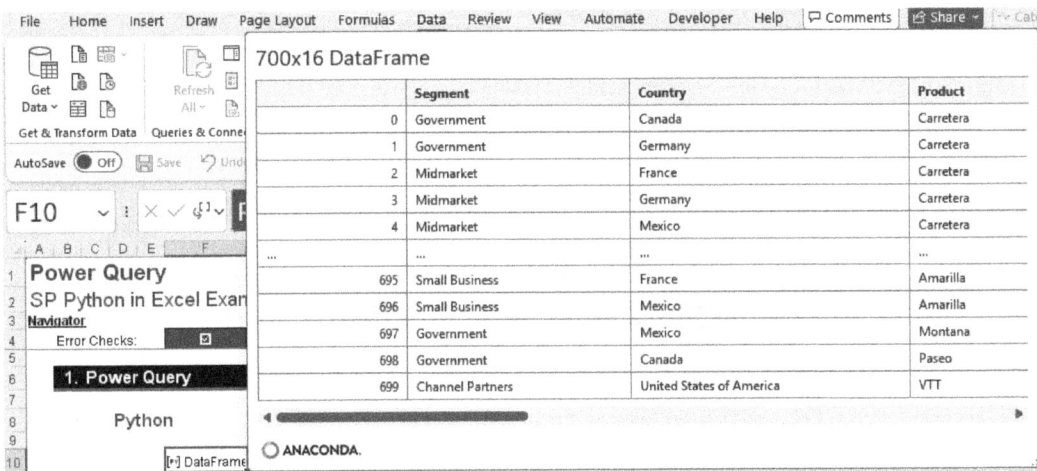

FIGURE 2-125 The DataFrame for the Power Query query is a 700x16 DataFrame.

You have now seen all the Excel entities that Python in Excel references.

> **Note** Python in Excel cannot reference some parts of Excel. You cannot use a Python cell to reference the following Excel entities:
>
> - **Formulas:** You cannot use Excel formulas in Python code.
> - **Charts:** Python code cannot reference charts. If you try to reference a cell with a sparkline, the result is None.
> - **PivotTables and PivotCharts:** Using x1() to access a PivotTable or PivotChart name fails with a #PYTHON! error because these names are not recognized by Python in Excel.
> - **Macros and VBA code:** You cannot reference macros or VBA code in a Python formula.

Referencing elements of DataFrames

Now, let's look at how to reference parts of the DataFrames you have created. As you discovered earlier, you can reference other Python DataFrames by using either the variable name associated with a DataFrame name or the cell location. The best practice is to use the variable name to avoid errors with unanchored cell referencing and to make formulas easier to understand.

It is also possible to reference part of a DataFrame. To see how this works, on the sheet Table Data, enter the following Python code in cell V10:

```
df_table_column = df_table['Category']
```

This code selects the column Category from the DataFrame df_table. Figure 2-126 shows the Excel Value view for cell V10.

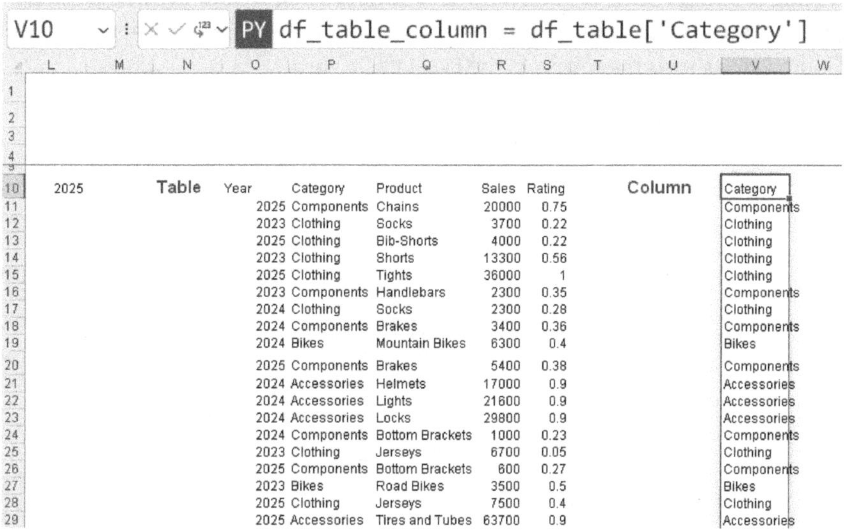

FIGURE 2-126 You can reference a column on an existing DataFrame.

Change cell V10 to the Python Object view and look at the data type card (see Figure 2-127).

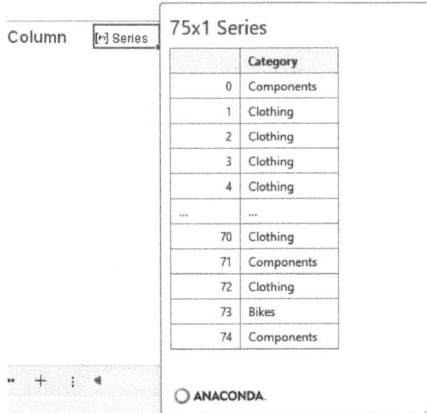

FIGURE 2-127 The DataFrame for a single column is a series.

> **Note** A DataFrame that contains one column is referred to as a *series*.

Before you can reference rows, you must identify the row(s) you want to extract. One way to do this is to specify the column values. In cell Y10, enter the following Python code to extract all the rows from 2025:

```
df_table_row=df_table.loc[(df_table["Year"]==2025)]
```

In this code, you locate the data where the column Year of df_table has the numeric value 2025. The double equal sign (==) is the Python code required to indicate that the column value should equal the value specified. Figure 2-128 shows the results in the Excel Value view.

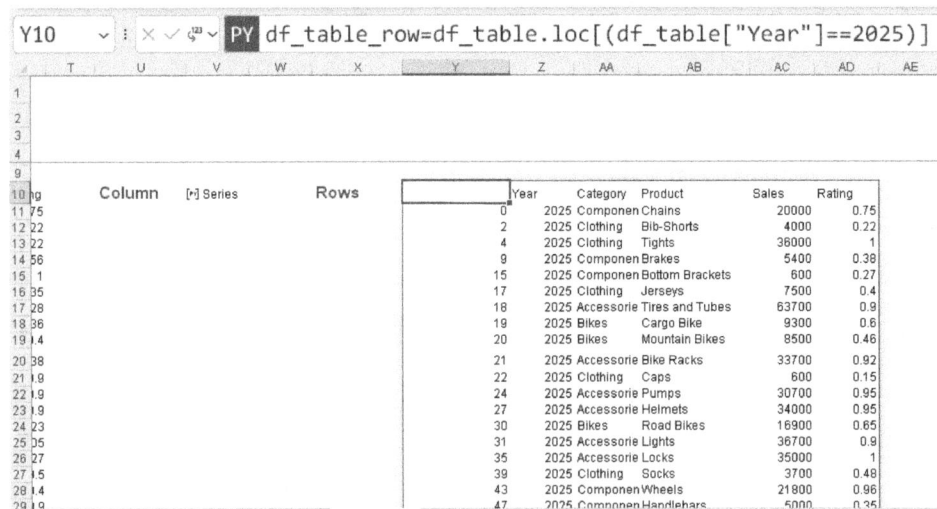

FIGURE 2-128 Extracting rows from a DataFrame based on column values

Note that the row number column, also known as the index column, is also shown for the Excel Value view for this DataFrame. The Excel Value view does not usually show this. We will look more closely at the use of this index in a moment, but first let's expand this example to show rows for 2025 where the category is Components. Change the Python code in cell Y10 to the following:

```
df_table_row=df_table.loc[(df_table["Year"]==2025)&(df_table["Category"]=="Components")]
```

Figure 2-129 shows the results.

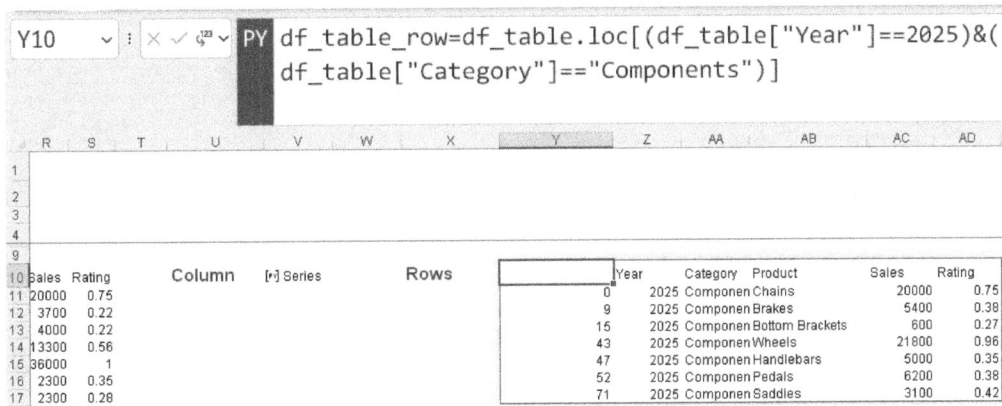

FIGURE 2-129 Extracting rows from a DataFrame based on multiple column values

Change the view to Python Object view and look at the data type card for cell Y10 (see Figure 2-130). This DataFrame is a reduced version of the DataFrame df_table, and the row numbers shown here are the row numbers from df_table.

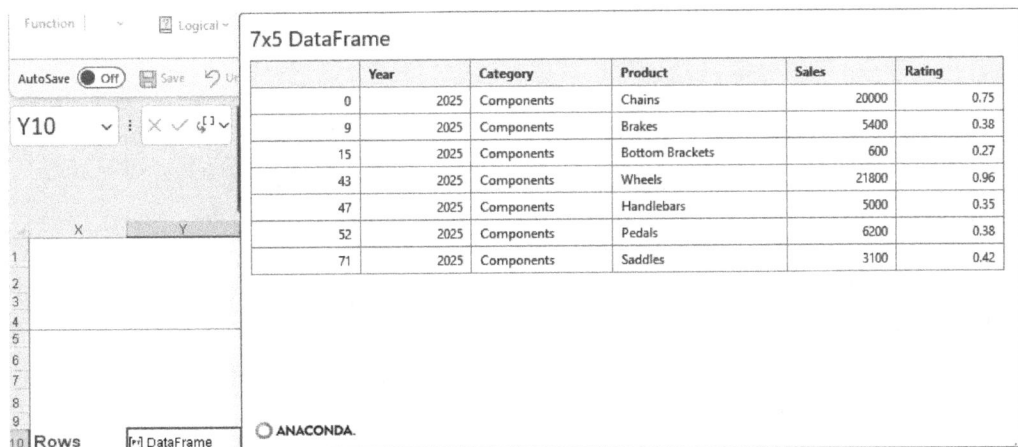

FIGURE 2-130 The DataFrame for the selected rows

You can also reference a row in a DataFrame by using the row number column that appears on the data type card. To see this in action, in cell Y20, enter the following Python code:

```
df_table_row_index = df_table.iloc[0]
```

This extracts the first row of the DataFrame df_table, as shown in Figure 2-131.

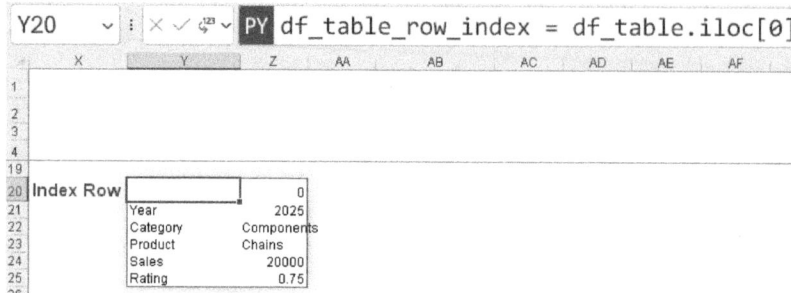

FIGURE 2-131 Using the row index to extract a row returns the results in a series displayed in columns in the Excel Value view.

Change to the Python Object view for cell Y20 and look at the data type card (see Figure 2-132).

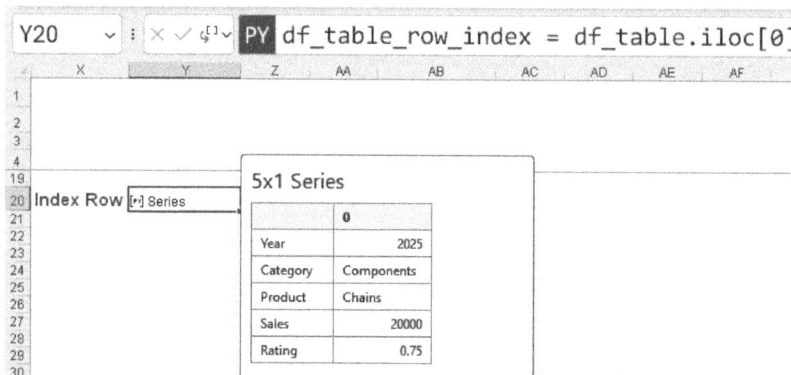

FIGURE 2-132 Using the row index to extract a row returns the results as a 5x1 series, not a 1x5 series.

It is important to understand that extracting the row in this way will return a column of data with the headings as row identifiers; it will not return a row of data.

The final example in this section uses the iloc() function to identify a cell. Enter the following Python code in cell AC20:

```
df_table_cell_index = df_table.iloc[0,2]
```

This code finds the value in the first row and the third column, as shown in Figure 2-133. (We will consider the iloc() function in more detail when discussing the pandas library in the next chapter.)

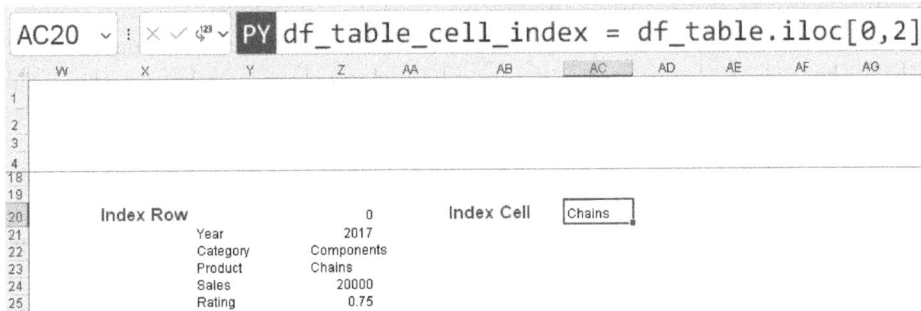

FIGURE 2-133 Using the row index and the column index to extract a value

Change cell AC20 to the Python Object view and look at the data type card (see Figure 2-134).

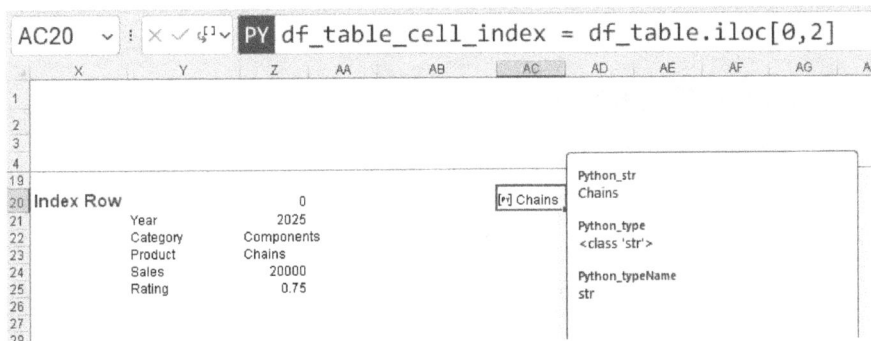

FIGURE 2-134 Using the row index and the column index results in a Python string.

If you expected the result to be a Python string, then you are getting the hang of this!

Solving an Excel entities challenge

In this section, you'll have a chance to use some of the code from the Excel entity examples along with some new Python code to solve a challenge. In the same workbook you have been using (SP Python in Excel Example.xlsm), open the **Challenge** sheet (see Figure 2-135).

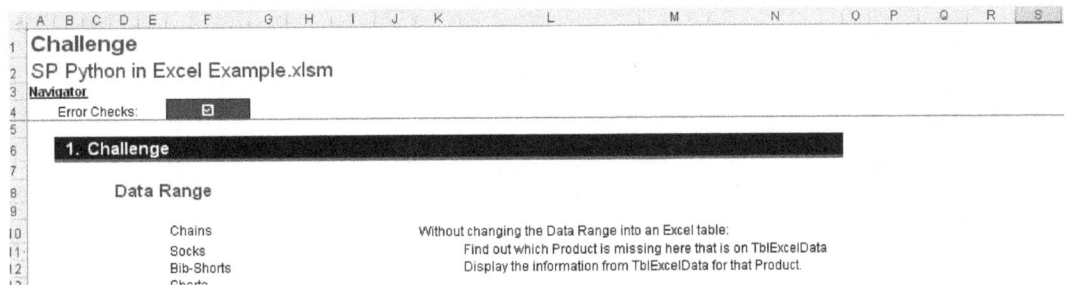

FIGURE 2-135 The Challenge sheet

If you use Power Query regularly, you know that when you extract data from the current workbook, it is converted into a table. This can be a problem for users who prefer to keep their data as a range. Python comes to the rescue for these users: It can extract the data into a DataFrame without impacting the data format. To see how this works, start by creating a DataFrame for the data range in cell M14:

```
df_data_range=xl("F10:F33")
```

Leave cell M14 as a Python object and look at the data type card (see Figure 2-136).

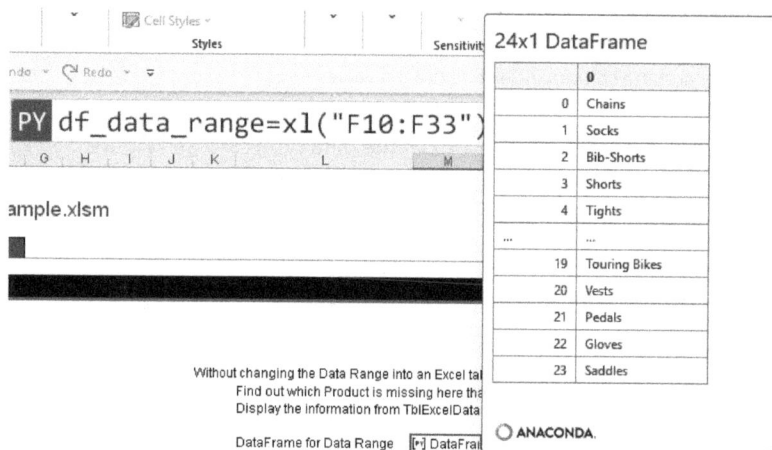

	24x1 DataFrame	
		0
0	Chains	
1	Socks	
2	Bib-Shorts	
3	Shorts	
4	Tights	
...	...	
19	Touring Bikes	
20	Vests	
21	Pedals	
22	Gloves	
23	Saddles	

Without changing the Data Range into an Excel tab
Find out which Product is missing here tha
Display the information from TblExcelData

DataFrame for Data Range   [▾] DataFra

FIGURE 2-136 Start by creating a 24x1 DataFrame for the data range.

Note While we will step through each stage in this example, it is possible to solve this challenge by using several lines of Python code. You will see how to do this when you explore the Python Editor in Chapter 4.

You have already given the DataFrame for TblExcelData the name df_table. Now, you will join the DataFrames to see what values are not in both of them. This process is called *merging*. The type of merge, or join, you need to perform here is called a *left anti join* (see Figure 2-137).

LEFT ANTI JOIN

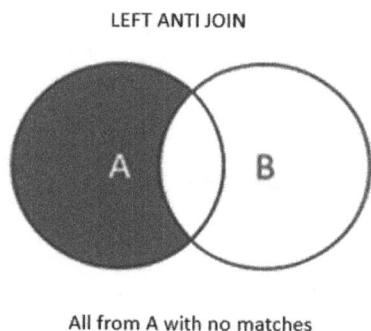

All from A with no matches

FIGURE 2-137 A left anti join takes everything in DataFrame A that does not exist in DataFrame B.

You need to take two steps in Python. First, you create an outer join, which is everything in each of the DataFrames, and then you exclude the data in the second DataFrame. To do this, in cell M15, enter the following Python code:

```
df_outer=pd.merge(df_table,df_data_range,how='outer',left_on='Product',right_on=0,indicator=True)
```

Let's break this up. You are using the pandas `merge` functionality to join DataFrame df_table (the left DataFrame) to DataFrame df_data_range (the right DataFrame). You have defined the join type (`how`) to be an outer join. You need to specify what columns to use to join the DataFrames. In df_table, the column is called Product, and in the data type card for df_data_range, the column header is the number 0. Finally, because `indicator` is `True`, a column is created to provide information about the merge. (You will need this for the next step.) The result, as shown in Figure 2-138, is a DataFrame.

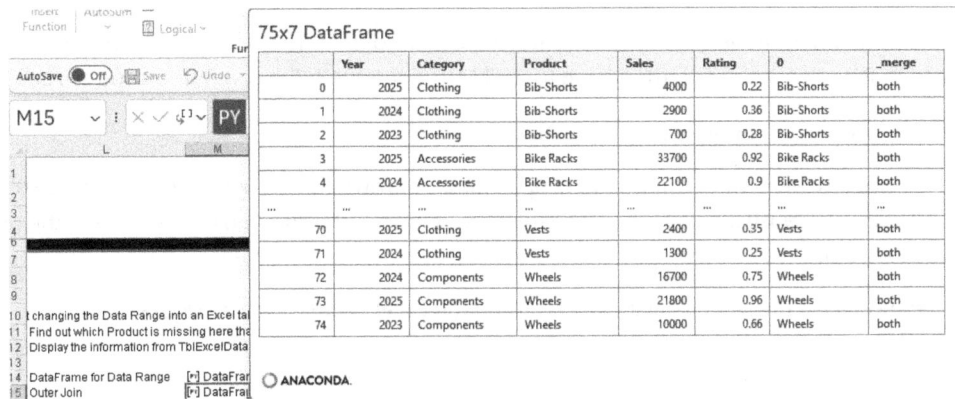

FIGURE 2-138 The outer join produces a 75x7 DataFrame.

Next, you keep the rows where the `_merge` column has the value `left_only`. This means the product is in df_table but not in df_data_range. In cell M16, enter the following Python code:

```
df_anti_join = df_outer[df_outer['_merge']=='left_only'].drop(columns=['_merge'])
```

Figure 2-139 shows the results.

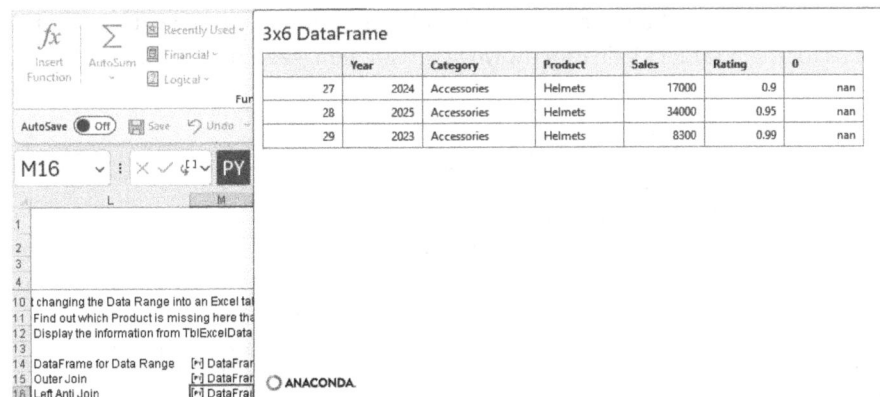

FIGURE 2-139 The result when selecting the rows where the merge is `left_only` is a 3x6 DataFrame.

The final column contains the value nan (which sometimes appears as NaN and stands for "not a number") because the data is missing or undefined. It cannot be displayed in the Excel Value view (see Figure 2-140).

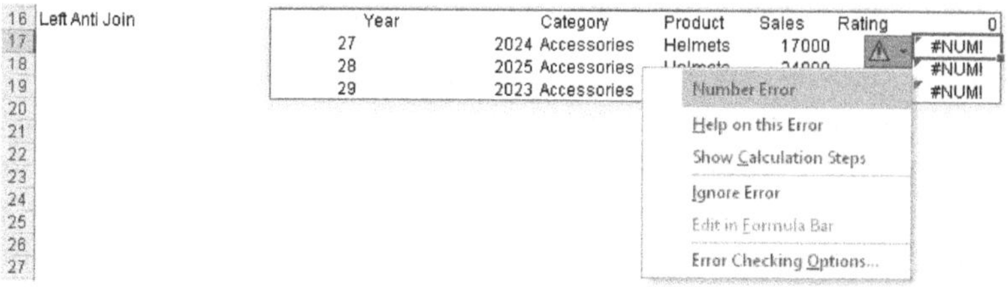

FIGURE 2-140 The NaN values cannot be viewed in the Excel Value view.

To complete this example, you need to remove the final column. To do so, you can use the `drop` command that was part of the Python code for cell M16. Enter the following Python code in cell M18:

```
dp_solution= df_anti_join.drop(0,axis='columns')
```

`axis` is required to tell Python whether to drop columns or rows. For this example, you could substitute 1 for `'columns'` because it means the same thing to Python, but using `'columns'` makes the purpose of the code clearer.

You can now view the results of cell M17 by using the Excel Value view (see Figure 2-141).

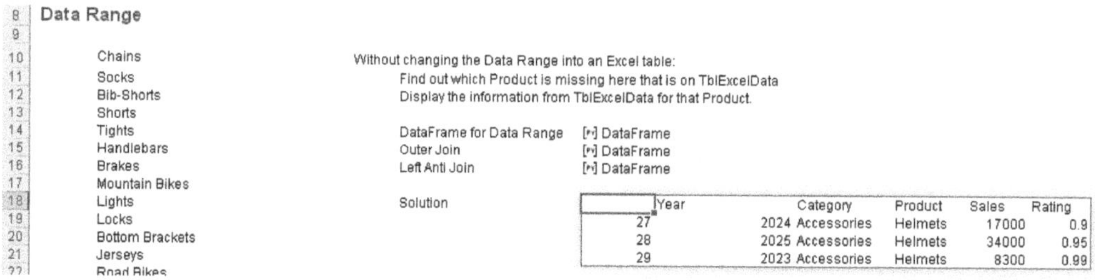

FIGURE 2-141 The Excel Value view for the solution displays three rows.

The solution is dynamic. To test this, delete the value Chains from cell F10. The Python results update, and the rows for the product Chains are shown in the solution (see Figure 2-142).

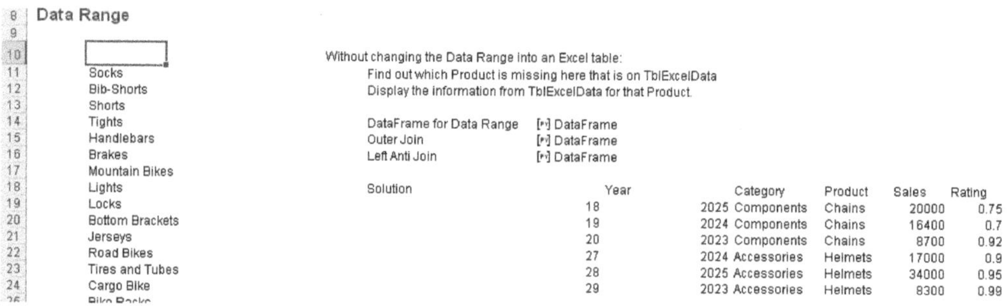

FIGURE 2-142 Deleting the product Chains from the list causes the results to update.

This example demonstrates how you can use Python to solve a practical problem. You may have encountered some errors while experimenting with the Python code you entered. In the next section, you'll learn about possible errors and how to deal with them.

Learning about Python in Excel error codes

New functionality brings new errors. This section describes when and why each Python error occurs and how to avoid errors. You met the #PYTHON! error earlier, so let's start there. Open the Excel workbook SP Python in Excel Example Starter File Chapter 2.xlsm and select the sheet called **Python Syntax Examples**.

#PYTHON!

Essentially, the #PYTHON! error occurs when the Python code cannot be compiled. You encountered this error when you used the input Python function (see Figure 2-143).

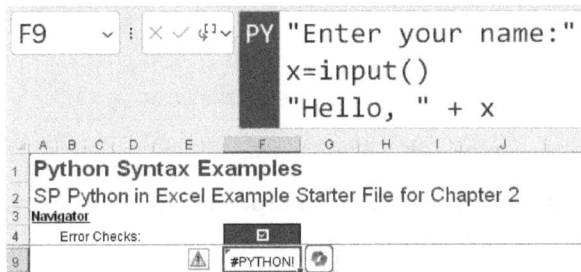

FIGURE 2-143 Using the input function results in an error.

When the #PYTHON! error occurs, you can click the warning triangle to learn more about the cause (see Figure 2-144).

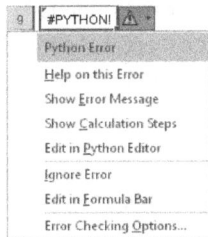

FIGURE 2-144 You can click the warning triangle to open the Python Error menu, which has options for handling an error.

Let's explore the list of options in the Python Error menu, beginning with Help on This Error.

Help on This Error

The Help on This Error option opens a Help pane on the right side of the screen (see Figure 2-145).

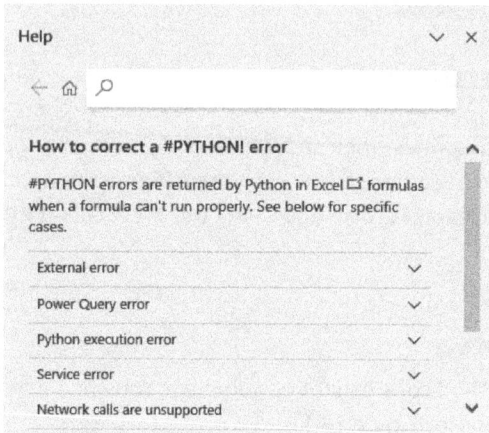

FIGURE 2-145 The Help pane for dealing with a #PYTHON! error

The Help pane options give further information about possible causes of the error:

- **External Error:** An error occurred in an external calculation service.

- **Power Query Error (although it really should be Python Interpreter Error):** The Python interpreter returned an error when running the Python code.

- **Python Execution Error:** Python in Excel was unable to execute the Python code. You can check the Python formula for errors and try again.

- **Service Error:** Something went wrong with the service. You can try again.

- **Network Calls Are Unsupported:** Python in Excel supports importing data from an Excel worksheet or a Power Query data source. To protect your security, common external data functions in Python, such as pandas.read_csv and pandas.read_excel, are not compatible with Python in Excel. To import external data, use the Get & Transform feature in Excel to access Power Query.

> **Note** At the time of writing, the second section is titled Power Query Error. This does not match the description, which is for a Python interpreter error.

Show Error Message

The Show Error Message option displays more information about the specific error in an error dialog box, as shown in Figure 2-146.

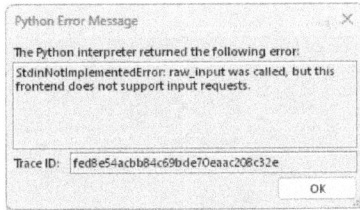

FIGURE 2-146 The Python Error Message dialog gives more information about the cause of a #PYTHON! error.

The message is the same as the one you saw when hovering over the warning triangle when you first entered the Python code in cell F9. You also saw it in the Python Editor. The trace ID can be used to find more information about errors that are difficult to diagnose. It may be recognized by Excel support or in Excel forums. In this case, it is clear from the message that the input request is not supported in Python in Excel.

Show Calculation Steps

The Show Calculation Steps option is designed to help you find the issue in a complex formula. Clicking it opens the Evaluate Formula dialog (see Figure 2-147).

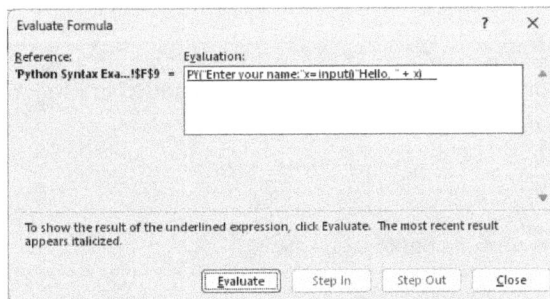

FIGURE 2-147 The Evaluate Formula dialog helps you to locate the line of Python code that triggers the error.

The Evaluate Formula dialog is not particularly useful in this example because there is only one line of Python code. For longer sections of code, though, the Evaluate Formula dialog could help you locate the line of code that triggers the error. If you click Evaluate for the current line of code, the result is #PYTHON!.

Edit in Python Editor

As its name suggests, the Edit in Python Editor option opens the Python Editor, showing information on the currently selected cell (see Figure 2-148).

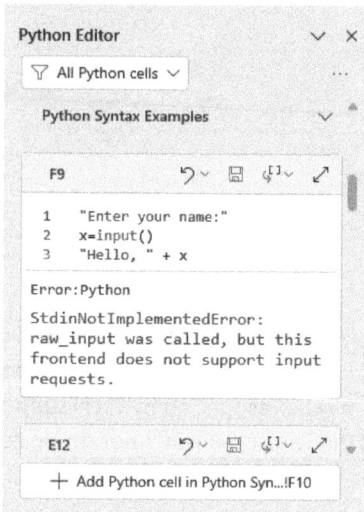

FIGURE 2-148 The Edit in Python Editor option in the Python Error menu opens the Python Editor.

We will explore error troubleshooting in the Python Editor in Chapter 4.

Ignore Error

The Ignore Error option changes the setting for the cell so that the error is not flagged in Excel. You can select it to remove the icons indicating an error.

Edit in Formula Bar

The Edit in Formula Bar option takes you to the formula bar for the cell.

Error Checking Options

The Error Checking Options item takes you to the Excel Options dialog with the Formulas tab open (see Figure 2-149).

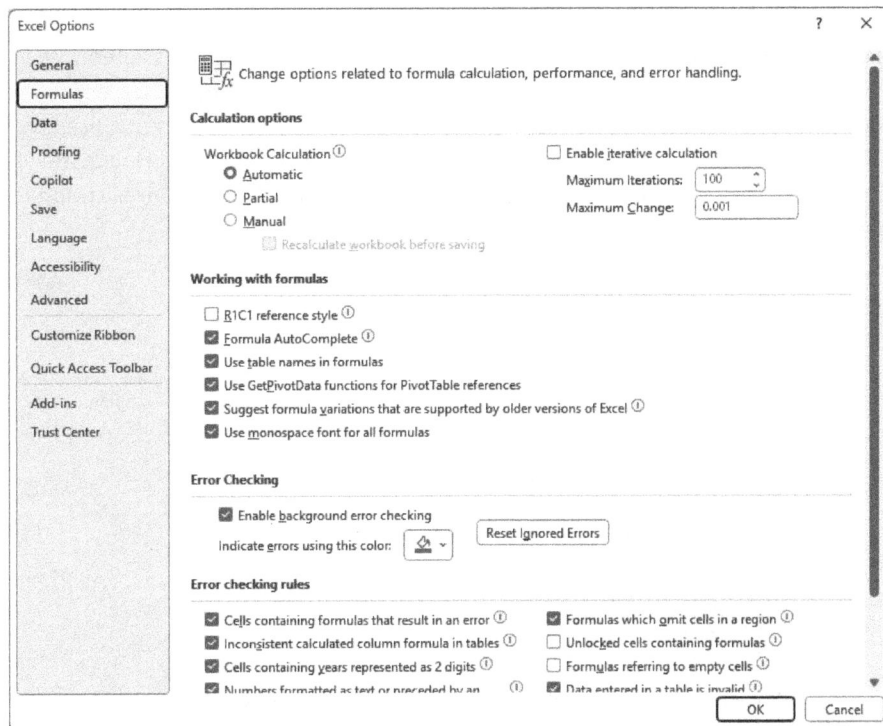

FIGURE 2-149 The Error Checking Options item in the Python Error menu opens the Excel Options dialog.

The Excel Options dialog includes some useful options for working with Python in Excel. The Calculation Options section of the Formulas tab allows you to view and change the workbook calculation settings. You can run Python in Partial or Manual mode with the Python add-on. (See the section "Upgrading to the Python in Excel add-on license," earlier in this chapter, for more details.) Reset Ignored Errors is a good option if you chose Ignore Error and have changed your mind. (You will learn about more items in the Excel Options dialog as they become pertinent to our discussion.)

> **Note** As you have seen, the #PYTHON! error means the Python code cannot be evaluated. The error message provided should give you a clue about where to look. If the error message is unfamiliar, you can often find help online. One of the significant advantages of using Python is that the Python community is encouraged to share code and solutions to problems.

#BLOCKED!

#BLOCKED! errors are not unique to Python in Excel. This type of error can be returned when a required resource can't be accessed. For example, you may encounter it when using the IMAGE function to insert images into cells from a source location.

Earlier in this chapter, we noted that if you are using a Python in Excel license associated with your company account, you cannot use your personal OneDrive account to work with Python in Excel; instead, you need to work on a local drive or in a folder that is associated with the company account. If you try to use Python in Excel in a location not connected to a valid license, you will encounter a #BLOCKED! error. The example in Figure 2-150 shows an attempt to edit a Python formula using a location not associated with a Python license.

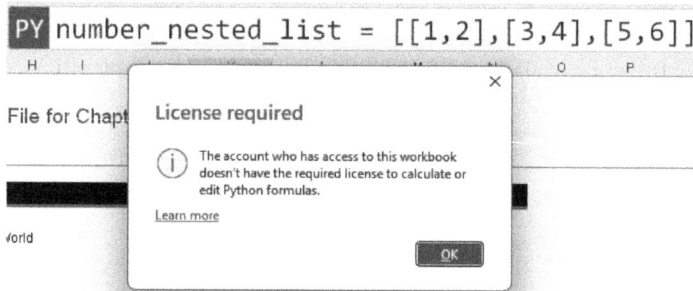

FIGURE 2-150 Trying to edit a Python cell when the workbook is not in a location associated with a valid Python in Excel license

Accessing the Excel Value view for this cell causes the #BLOCKED! error to be issued (see Figure 2-151).

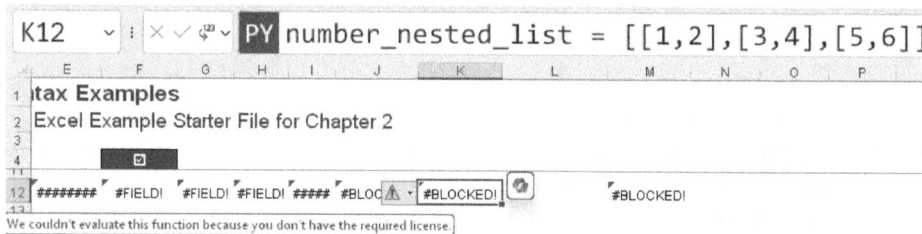

FIGURE 2-151 Evaluating a Python cell causes a #BLOCKED! error and a message that the license is not associated with the file location.

Note that some of the cells show #FIELD! instead of #BLOCKED!. These cells contain the Python attributes accessed from the Insert Data menu of the associated Python cell (see Figure 2-152).

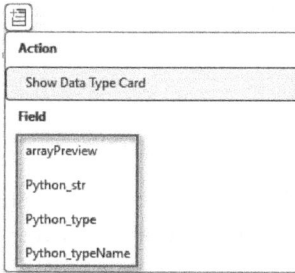

FIGURE 2-152 Cells containing the field values associated with a Python cell cannot be recalculated without a valid Python license.

> **Note** You may also see #UNKNOWN! in Python cells if a valid Python in Excel license is not associated with the workbook location.

There are other possible causes of the #BLOCKED! error when using Python in Excel. The following sections cover some alternative error messages you might see.

Allow Connection Experience

Python in Excel, like many other features, uses cloud-based services. Some companies have security concerns about using cloud-based services. If yours does, you can turn off connected experiences by going to **File** > **Account** > **Manage Settings** and making the appropriate changes in the Privacy Settings dialog that appears (see Figure 2-153).

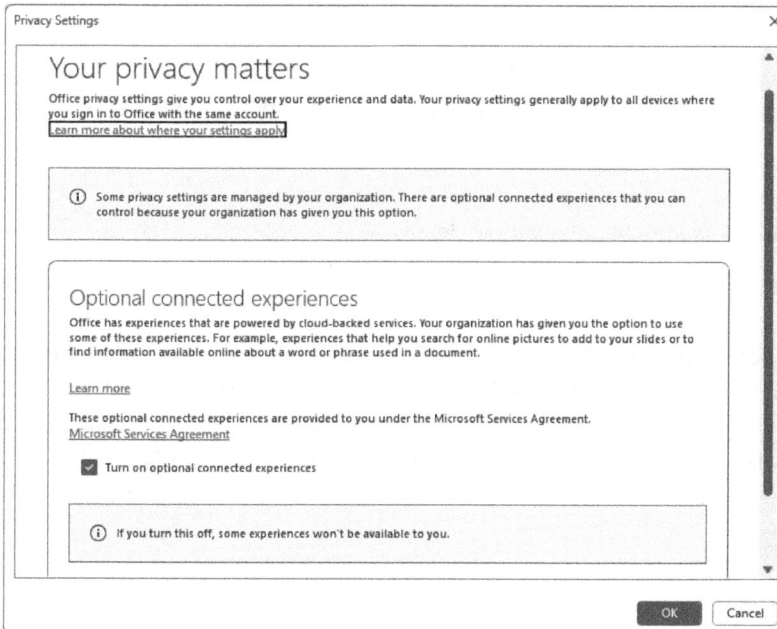

FIGURE 2-153 The Privacy Settings dialog allows you to turn off optional connected experiences.

You can click the **Learn More** link to find out how the Turn on Optional Connected Experiences setting affects your Microsoft Office applications. You cannot calculate Python cells if you switch off this setting.

Compute Resource Error

The Compute Resource Error message is also connected with the use of the Microsoft Cloud. It indicates that a compute resource was recycled and the attempt to automatically retry failed. Microsoft advises that if you get this error message, you should reset the Python runtime. As discussed earlier in the chapter, the reset options are in the Python group on the Formulas tab. You can reset the Python runtime by selecting **Reset Runtime** in the **Python** group on the **Formulas** tab or by using the keyboard shortcut **Ctrl+Alt+Shift+F9**.

Resetting the Python runtime is often the solution for errors encountered using Python in Excel, since it is the equivalent of "turning it off and back on again." You may also find that closing and re-opening the Excel workbook helps.

Connection Limit Exceeded

The Connection Limit Exceeded message indicates that you have multiple Excel workbooks open that contain Python cells. The solution is to close some of those workbooks.

Daily Quota Exceeded

While there are not currently any published limits associated with using Python in Excel, the Daily Quota Exceeded message indicates that the daily or monthly quota has been exceeded. Check the latest licensing information.

Limit Exceeded

The Limit Exceeded message could indicate that the connection limit or the quota has been exceeded.

Login Failure

If you get the Login Failure message, check your login details.

Not Supported

As noted in the Introduction to this book, Python in Excel is available on several platforms and versions. Using a platform or version where Python in Excel is not available to open an Excel workbook containing Python cells would trigger the Not Supported error message. You might also see one of the alternative messages: Unmet Requirements, Unsupported Environment, or Wrong Account Type.

Python Functions Disabled

If you are in a location with a valid license and you get the Python Functions Disabled error message, contact your administrator.

> **Note** If you encounter the #BLOCKED! error and you have not run Python in Excel before, check the reasons listed earlier. If you have been running Python in Excel successfully and then get a #BLOCKED! error, you should check the status of your Python license. If the license is valid, check to ensure the Excel file's location is associated with that license.

#BUSY!

The #BUSY! error does not necessarily indicate a problem. It may appear when Python in Excel recalculates a Python cell (see Figure 2-154).

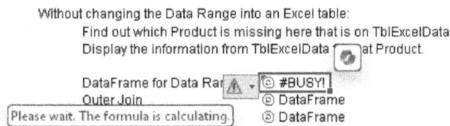

FIGURE 2-154 The #BUSY! message may appear when a formula is calculating.

The #BUSY! error means that Python calculations are running in the Microsoft Cloud. If this error remains on the screen for more than a minute, you can reset the Python runtime. As a reminder, you can reset the Python runtime by selecting **Reset Runtime** in the **Python** group on the **Formulas** tab or by using the keyboard shortcut **Ctrl+Alt+Shift+F9**.

#CALC!

At the time of writing, Microsoft documentation says that Python in Excel cannot handle volatile functions and gives the Excel function RAND() as an example. RAND() returns a random decimal value from 0 to (but not including) 1 and recalculates every time the worksheet is recalculated. We tested this on the Power Query sheet in the current workbook. You can try it too: Enter the Excel formula =**RAND()** in cell M10 and then drag it down to cell M19. You now have a range M10:M19 of randomly generated numbers. Now enter the following Python code in cell P10:

```
df_rand = xl("M10:M19")
```

Figure 2-155 shows our results, with the Excel value in cell P10. (Remember that because the function returns random numbers, your results will differ from ours.)

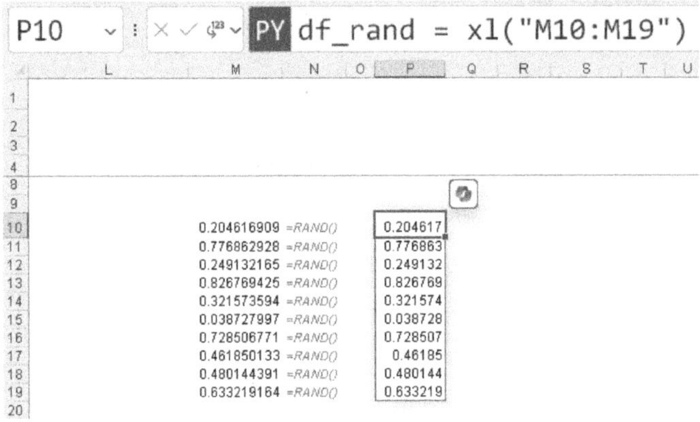

FIGURE 2-155 Python in Excel coping with volatile functions

At the time of writing, Python in Excel does not appear to get a #CALC! error when referencing volatile functions.

> **Tip** If you choose to replicate this example, delete the contents of cells M10:M19 and P10 afterward to avoid wasting resources by continually recalculating them.

There are limits to the amount of data that can be calculated. If you are working with a dataset that contains more than 100 MB of data, you may encounter the #CALC! error. When that happens, it is a good idea to reduce the size of the dataset. How you would reduce the dataset size depends on how the dataset is created. For example, if dataset A is created by combining two smaller datasets, B and C, and then the #CALC! error occurs when performing transformations that would reduce the data in dataset A, you should consider whether the data in datasets B and C could be reduced before combining them to make dataset A.

#CONNECT!

The #CONNECT! error indicates an issue with communications with the cloud. In Python in Excel, several error messages may be connected to this error. Let's look at each of them.

Service Not Available

If a value cannot be retrieved from the service, you may get the Service Not Available message. It means the service has probably timed out. The recommended solution is to reset the Python runtime. As a reminder, you can reset the Python runtime by selecting **Reset Runtime** in the **Python** group in the **Formulas** tab or by using the keyboard shortcut **Ctrl+Alt+Shift+F9**.

Resource Not Available

The Resource Not Available message also indicates that the value cannot be retrieved, but in this case it is because the compute resource of the service is not available. If this is the first Python value you have tried to refresh in this session, check the license and location. If the license and location are fine or if the error occurs mid-session, then follow the familiar advice to reset the Python runtime: Select **Reset Runtime** in the **Python** group in the **Formulas** tab or use the keyboard shortcut **Ctrl+Alt+Shift+F9**.

Unable to Upload

The Unable to Upload message usually indicates a temporary issue with the data upload. Try again. If the issue persists, you can (as you may have guessed by now) reset the Python runtime: Select **Reset Runtime** in the **Python** group in the **Formulas** tab or use the keyboard shortcut **Ctrl+Alt+Shift+F9**.

> **Note** As you have seen, connection errors can usually be fixed by trying again or resetting the Python runtime. As mentioned for other error types, if resetting does not fix the problem, you can try closing and reopening the Excel workbook.

#SPILL!

If you use dynamic arrays, you will know how to deal with the #SPILL! error. When the formula in a Python cell returns a result, it can be displayed as a Python object or an Excel value. When you display a Python cell as an Excel value and the result is more than one value, it will spill from the Python cell. Any formula that could return multiple values can be called a *dynamic array formula*. Python formulas expressed as Excel values usually fall into this category.

Let's return to our earlier example in workbook SP Python in Excel Example.xlsm and locate df_contig_range on the Range Data sheet. When the spill area is empty, the Excel Value view is displayed, as shown in Figure 2-156.

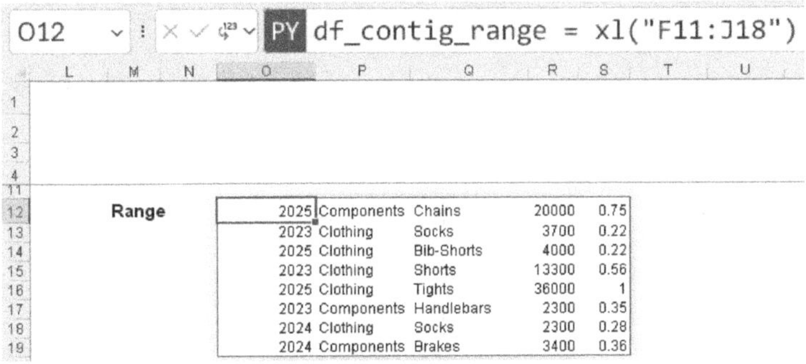

FIGURE 2-156 The Excel value spills from cell O12.

In this example, the border around the range O12:S19 indicates the spill area. If we enter a value into cell Q16 or any other cells in the spill area, we get the #SPILL! error, as shown in Figure 2-157.

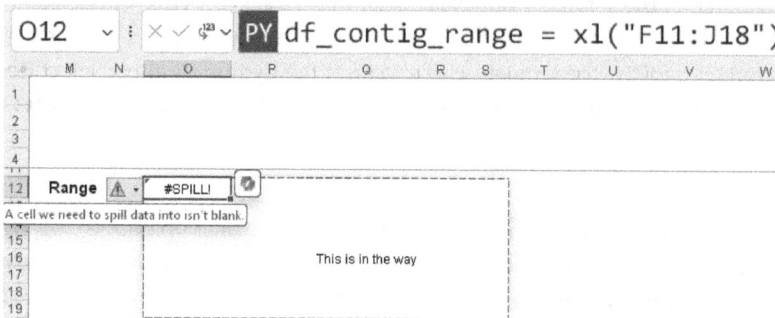

FIGURE 2-157 The Excel value cannot spill if a cell in the spill range already contains data.

You may recall that when we created the Python formula in cell O21, we used the cell reference df_contig_range rather than a variable:

```
df_point_at_contig_range = xl("O12")
```

Therefore, cell O21 also contains a spill error (see Figure 2-158).

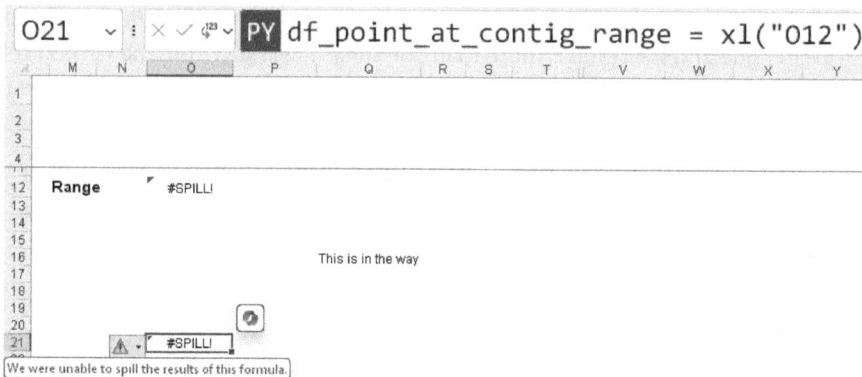

FIGURE 2-158 Referencing a cell with a #SPILL! error triggers another #SPILL! error.

Because the cell is being used, the error is referenced. Note that the error message is slightly different since there is nothing in the spill area for cell O21. Even if we change the view for cell O21 to the Python Object view, the error persists (see Figure 2-159).

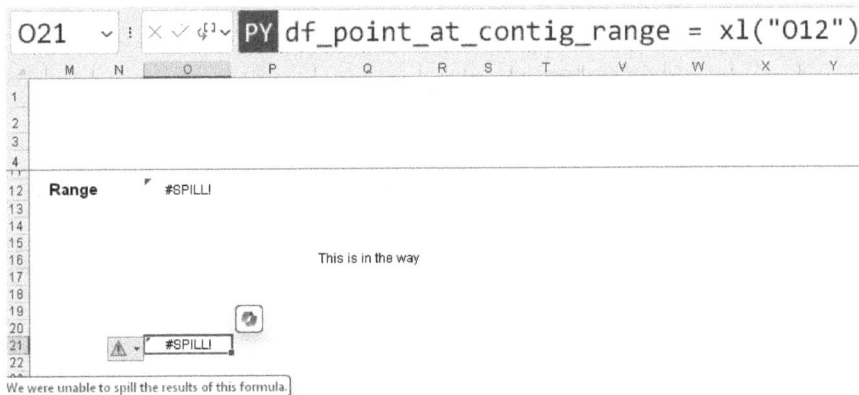

FIGURE 2-159 Referencing a cell with a #SPILL! error triggers another #SPILL! error even if the cell is shown in Python Object view.

This is another reason to use a variable and not the cell. If you change cell O21 to use the variable `df_contig_range`, the error is not triggered (see Figure 2-160).

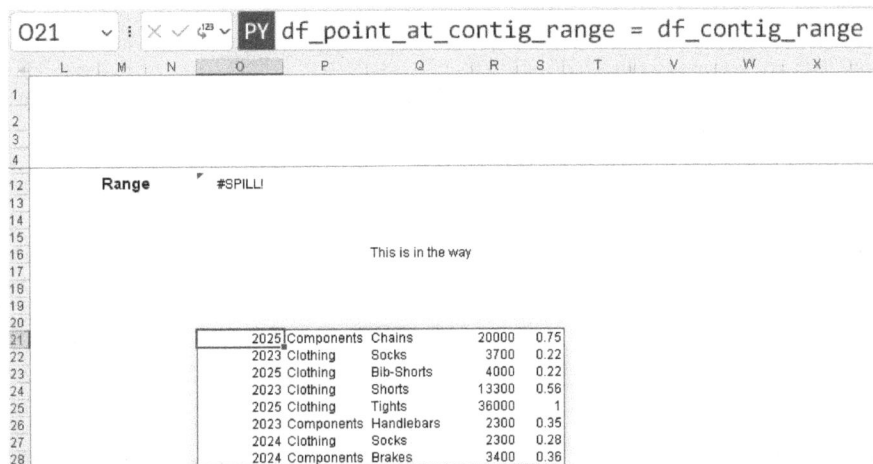

FIGURE 2-160 Referencing the variable, not the cell that has a #SPILL! error, does not trigger the same error, and the Excel value may be spilled.

So, as you have seen, one way to avoid #SPILL! errors when using Python in Excel is to use variable references rather than cell references. In our example, the offending cell in the spill range for O12 is easy to spot (refer to Figure 2-160). For more complex examples, you can use the error menu to find the problem (see Figure 2-161).

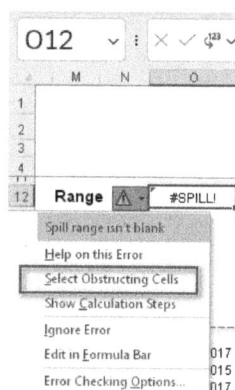

FIGURE 2-161 Clicking the warning arrow next to the #SPILL! error brings up a menu where you can choose the Select Obstructing Cells option.

If you choose Select Obstructing Cells, the offending cell is highlighted, and you are taken to that cell. If more obstructing cells exist, they are all highlighted, and you are taken to the first cell (see Figure 2-162).

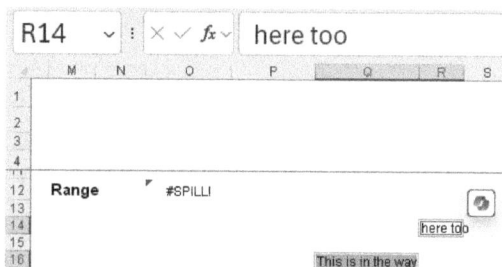

FIGURE 2-162 If you choose Select Obstructing Cells, you are taken to the first obstruction.

Once the obstruction is removed, the formula can spill in the Excel Value view. If you are only using the Excel Value view to see the contents easily, you can avoid #SPILL! errors by using the Python Object view and checking the Excel values in the Python Editor instead. This is a good choice for busy worksheets and when dealing with large datasets that could exceed the size of the worksheet.

#TIMEOUT!

The #TIMEOUT! error is often triggered when a Python formula takes longer to calculate than the maximum allotted time. There are two messages that may accompany this error: Formula Timed Out or Python Formula Timed Out. Let's look at them.

Formula Timed Out

If you get the Formula Timed Out message, try the calculation again. If the problem persists, you know the drill: Reset the Python runtime. As a reminder, you can reset the Python runtime by selecting **Reset Runtime** in the **Python** group in the **Formulas** tab or by using the keyboard shortcut **Ctrl+Alt+Shift+F9**.

Python Formula Timed Out

Again, the first course of action for the Python Formula Timed Out message is to try the calculation again. If the problem persists, reset the Python runtime: Select **Reset Runtime** in the **Python** group in the **Formulas** tab or use the keyboard shortcut **Ctrl+Alt+Shift+F9**.

If this message appears frequently, go to **File** > **Options** to open the Excel Options dialog. Then, on the **Advanced** tab, make the selections shown in Figure 2-163 under **When Calculating This Workbook**.

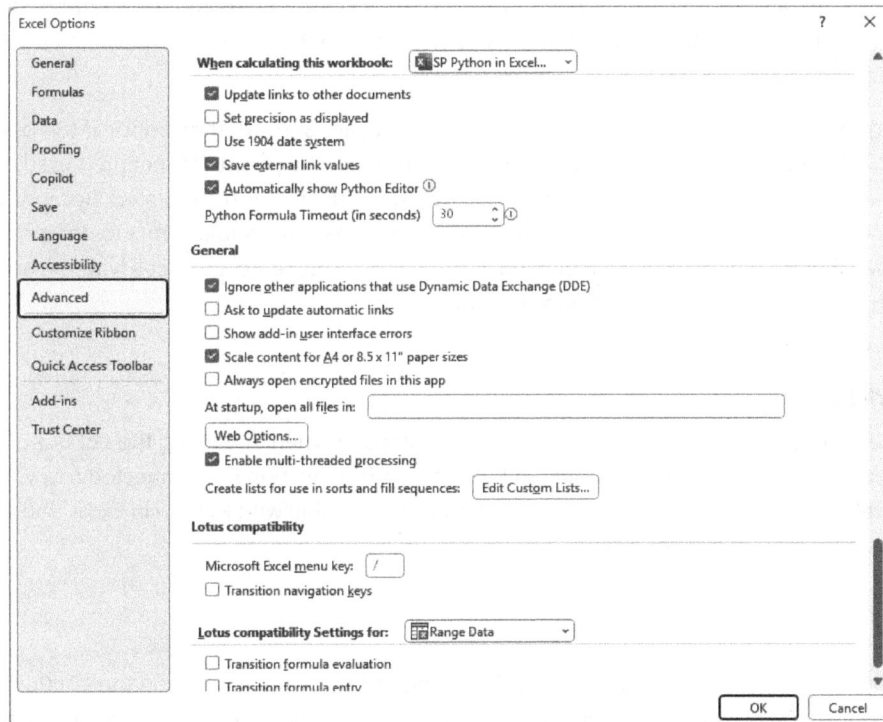

FIGURE 2-163 The Python Formula Timeout value can be changed in the Excel Options dialog.

By clicking the information icon next to the Python Formula Timeout option, you can get more information about what happens if you change the value, but you won't get information about what the values can be (see Figure 2-164).

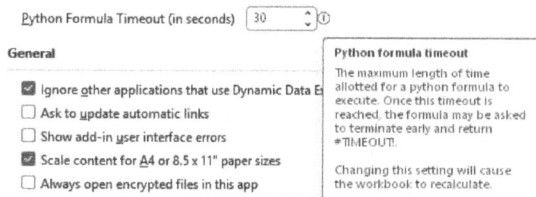

FIGURE 2-164 Changing the Python Formula Timeout value causes the workbook to recalculate.

The Python Formula Timeout setting applies to the workbook selected and cannot be set to less than 30 seconds or more than 7,999 seconds (2 hours and 13 minutes). You should not increase the timeout limit unless you get timeout errors regularly. If you have to set a long timeout limit for multiple workbooks with standard Python in Excel, you might consider getting the Python in Excel add-on for faster computing times.

If you are experiencing #TIMEOUT! errors, your first step should be to reset the Python runtime. Also consider closing and reopening the workbook. If multiple workbooks containing Python calculations are open, you can try closing some of them. You can increase the Python Formula Timeout setting in the Excel Options dialog if issues persist.

Note in Figure 2-163 that there is another option: Automatically Show Python Editor. If this option is selected, the Python Editor will open if an error is triggered or if the print() function is used. It will also open when the cell that contains the error or the print() function is recalculated. Because you are working with examples in this chapter that are sometimes meant to trigger errors to demonstrate a point, you will find that the pane keeps opening. If this annoys you, remove the cell with the error or change the Automatically Show Python Editor setting.

#UNKNOWN!

We briefly mentioned the #UNKNOWN! error earlier in this chapter when discussing the #BLOCKED! error. If you open an Excel workbook containing Python cells in a location not connected to a valid Python in Excel license or use a version of Excel that is not compatible with Python in Excel, you could see the #UNKNOWN! error in a Python cell.

#FIELD!

We also briefly mentioned the #FIELD! error earlier in this chapter when discussing the #BLOCKED! error. If you open an Excel workbook containing Python cells in a location that is not connected to a valid Python in Excel license or use a version of Excel that is not compatible with Python in Excel, you could see this error in a cell that is extracting Python properties from a Python cell. Figure 2-165 shows an associated error message, which indicates that the field that would have been extracted from the Python cell cannot be found.

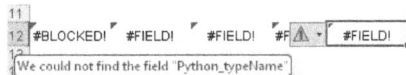

FIGURE 2-165 If a workbook containing Python data extracted to Excel cells from a Python cell is recalculated and Python in Excel is not available, a `#FIELD!` error is triggered.

Leveling up with Python objects

Now that we have covered a lot of building blocks, you are ready to be introduced to more Python concepts that will help you transform and analyze data in Excel and build effective dashboards. As promised earlier, this last section covers several key Python concepts. The concepts you have already encountered are summarized in this section, and new concepts are explored with Excel data.

You are familiar with displaying a Python cell as a Python object or an Excel value. Virtually everything in Python is considered to be an object. This section focuses on objects that are useful when working with Python in Excel. You can read this section all at once and follow along with the examples or dip into the section when you meet a particular object in the wild. The examples for this section are on a new sheet called More Python Syntax in the workbook SP Python in Excel Example.xlsm.

> **Note** Remember that this is not a Python manual. We have chosen examples and information that will help you begin your Python in Excel journey.

Revisiting variables

You already understand how important it is to use variable names to identify Python objects. And you have already learned the rules for variable names:

- A variable name must begin with a letter or an underscore (_).

- A variable name can contain only letters, numbers, and underscores. It cannot include spaces.

- A variable cannot have the same name as a keyword. For example, assigning a value to `True` will result in an error.

- While you can use Python function names as variable names, doing so is not recommended since it can be confusing.

Remember that variable names are case sensitive, so `df_frame` and `Df_frame` are different variables. You may change the assignment of any variable by using a new statement. This is something to watch out for in Python in Excel.

Tip Use an Excel cell reference only if it is required in your solution.

Let's look at an example. Open the worksheet **More Python Syntax** in the workbook SP Python in Excel Example.xlsm. In cell F10, enter the following Python code:

```
df_variable_name = xl("'Range Data'!F10:J15", headers=True)
```

Figure 2-166 shows the results.

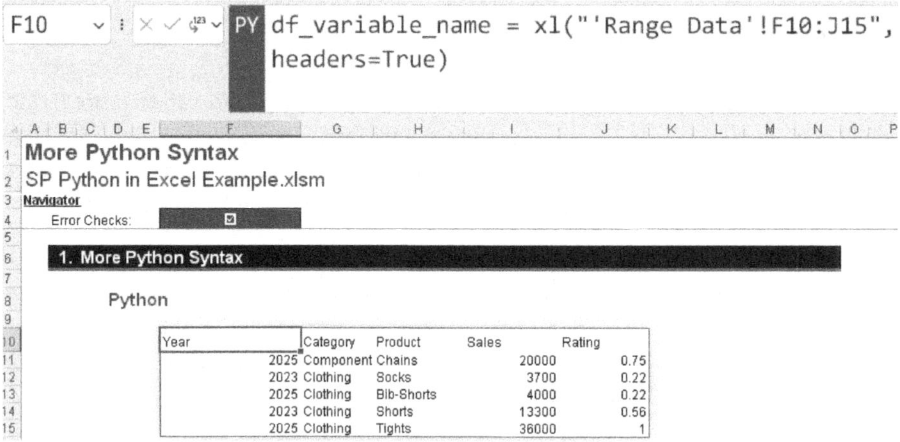

FIGURE 2-166 Using the variable `df_variable_name` to point to an Excel range.

Next, enter the following Python code, which references `df_variable_name`, in cell R10:

```
df_variable_name_ref=df_variable_name
```

Figure 2-167 shows the results.

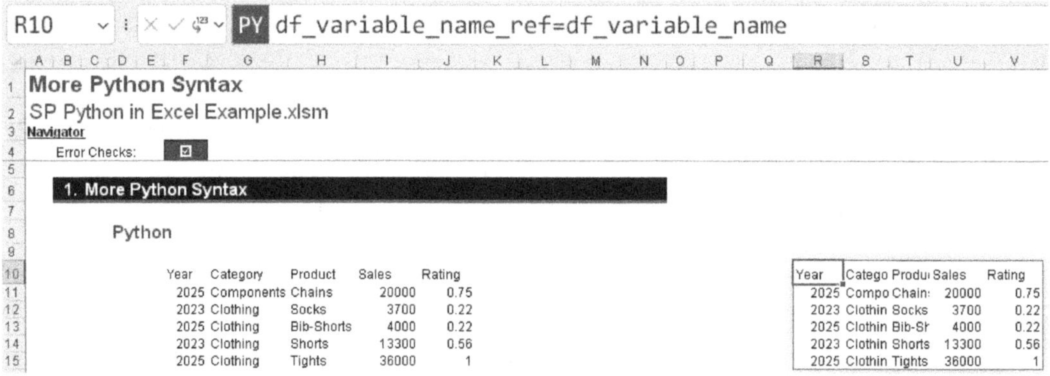

FIGURE 2-167 Creating another Python cell that points to `df_variable_name` produces a copy of those results.

Now you will use the variable `df_variable_name` in cell L10. This time, enter the following Python code to reference a single cell:

```
df_variable_name=xl("'Range Data'!G11")
```

Figure 2-168 shows the impact on cell R10.

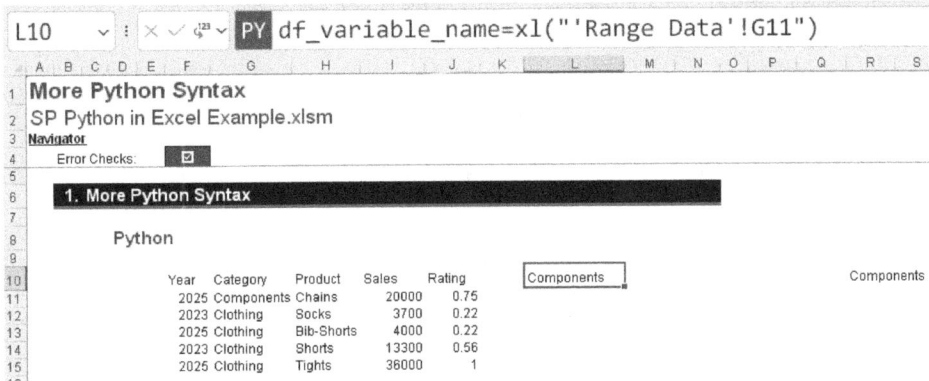

FIGURE 2-168 Reassigning the variable name to a single cell changes the Python cell that references the variable.

So, you can use the same variable name again without encountering errors, and you can also assign it to a different Python object. This is known as *dynamic typing*. It is a flexible feature but can be problematic. If you accidentally use the same variable name for a different object, you will reassign its target, and you will get no warnings. As you saw in this example, reassigning a variable name to a different object is not an obstacle. The variable `d_variable_name` went from referencing a DataFrame to referencing a string, as shown in Figure 2-169.

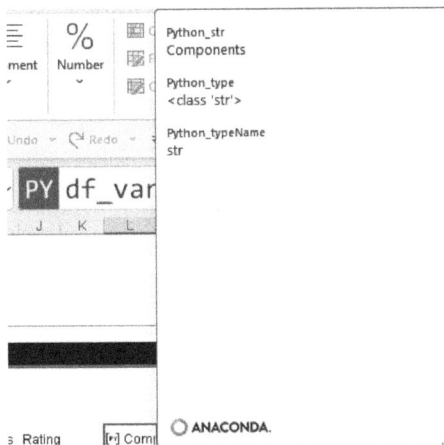

FIGURE 2-169 Reassigning the variable name to a single cell changes the Python object to a string.

Storing data in strings

Now let's look at the properties of a Python string. You have been using Python strings throughout this chapter. In F18, enter the following Python code:

```
message="Hello World"
```

Figure 2-170 shows the data type card for the resulting Python object.

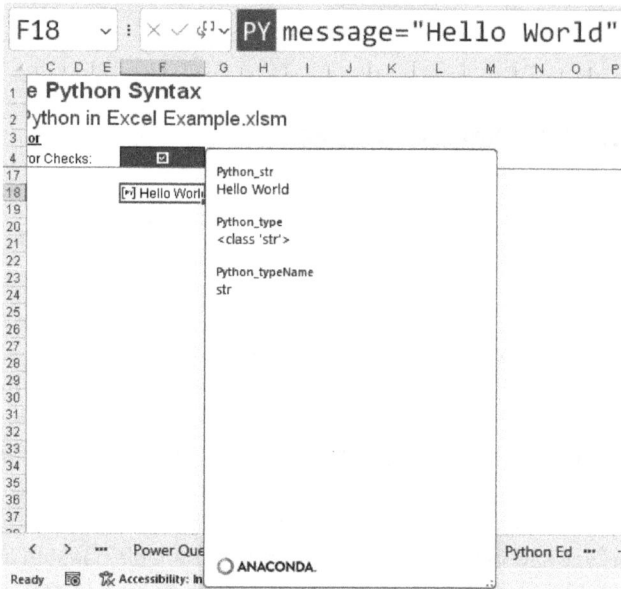

FIGURE 2-170 The Python code df_message = "Hello World" results in a Python string.

A string is textual data, and using strings in Python is easier than in many other languages (including VBA). In this example, you can see that you use double quotes (") to start and end a string. You can also use single quotes ('), but you must be consistent with your choice: If you start a string with a single quote, you must end it with a single quote.

You can concatenate strings by using the plus (+) symbol. To see this in action, enter the following Python code in cell F19.

```
message_plus="Hello "+'World'
```

Figure 2-171 shows the results.

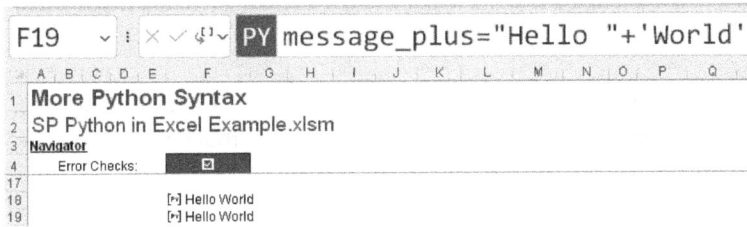

FIGURE 2-171 It is easy to concatenate Python strings.

Note that this example uses double and single quotes. If you use single quotes, then double quotes can be part of the text and vice versa. To see how this works, enter the following Python code in cell F20:

```
message_plus_quotes="Hello "+'"World"'
```

As Figure 2-172 shows, the result has double quotes around `World`.

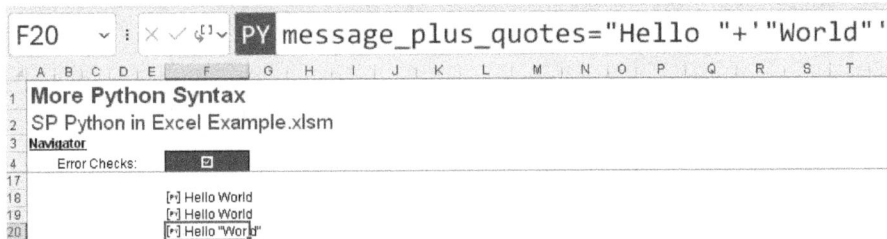

FIGURE 2-172 You can mix quote types to include quotes in a string.

Before we move on to using strings with Excel data, enter the following Python code in cell F21 to see how easy it is to repeat a string:

```
message_repeated_plus_quotes="Hello "*3+'"World"'
```

Figure 2-173 shows the results.

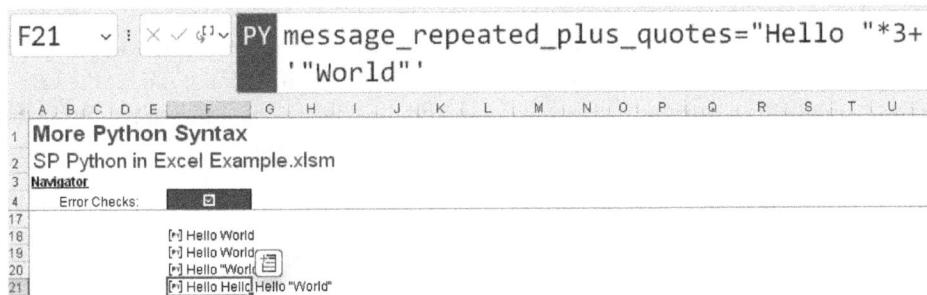

FIGURE 2-173 You can use * and an integer to repeat a string in the result.

A common use for strings is to describe the results of a calculation. To see how this works, enter the following Python code in cell F22:

```
df_Sales = sum(xl("TblExcelData[[#Data],[Sales]]")[0])
```

This code extracts the data from the Sales column of the Excel table TblExcelData, puts it into a DataFrame, and then sums column 0 of the DataFrame, which is the column that contains the sales data. Figure 2-174 shows the results.

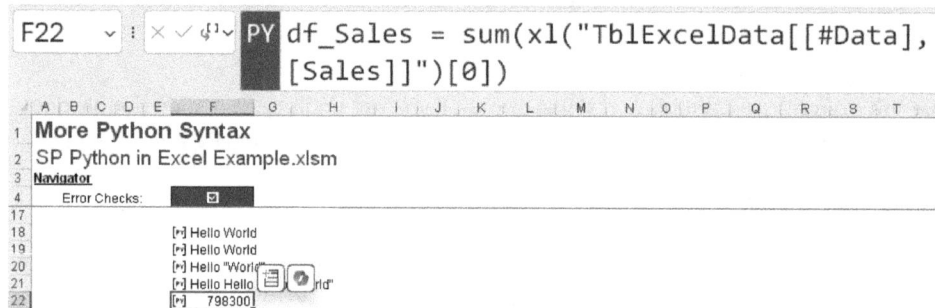

FIGURE 2-174 An example of summing a column from a DataFrame

To make the results easier to understand, enter the following Python code in cell H22:

```
df_Sales_desc = f"The total sales is {df_Sales}"
```

Figure 2-175 shows the results.

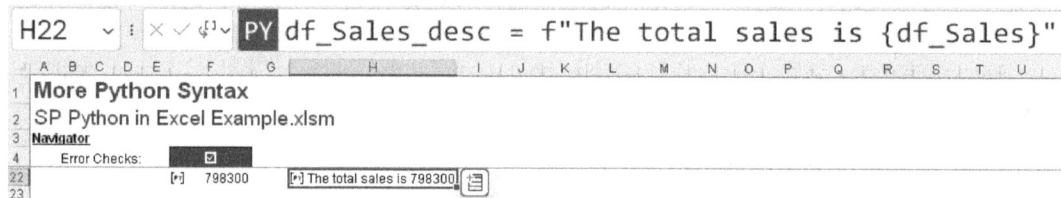

FIGURE 2-175 An example of using an fstring to combine variables with text

This example shows the use of an *fstring*, a formatted string used to include variables in text. The variable is indicated by using curly braces ({}). You do not need to specify a data type for the variable df_Sales. Because it is a number, though, you can add the comma separator so it is displayed as 798,300. To see this in action, amend the code in cell H22 so it looks like this:

```
df_Sales_desc = f"The total sales is {df_Sales:,}"
```

Figure 2-176 shows the results.

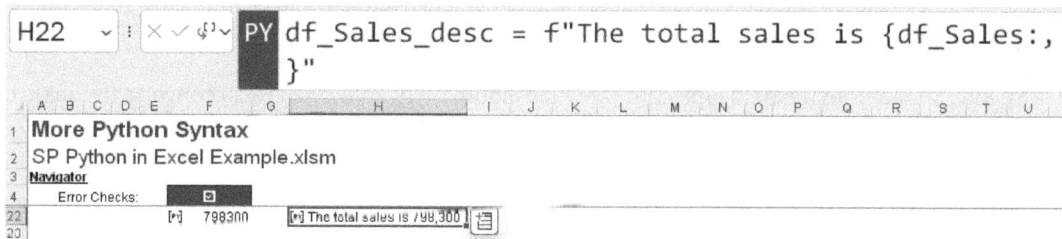

FIGURE 2-176 If the variable is numeric, you can add the comma separator.

Storing numbers with number types

We have been looking at displaying numeric values in strings, so let's move on to how numbers can be stored. To see how the DataFrame df_Sales is stored, you can use the data type card for that object. Using Python code, you can also use the type() function. To see how it works, enter the following Python code in cell J22:

```
type (df_Sales)
```

If you view the Excel value, you see that the class is int, for an integer (see Figure 2-177).

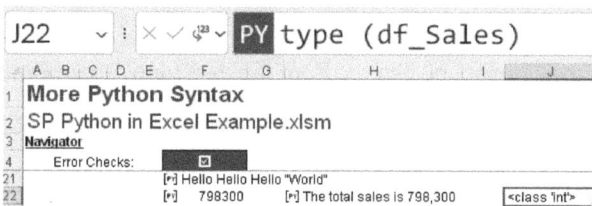

FIGURE 2-177 The type() function reveals how a number is stored.

The other number type you will work with in examples in this book is a float. To get an idea of how it works, enter the decimal number **56.78** in cell F23 and enter the following Python code in cell J23:

```
type(xl("F23"))
```

Figure 2-178 shows the results.

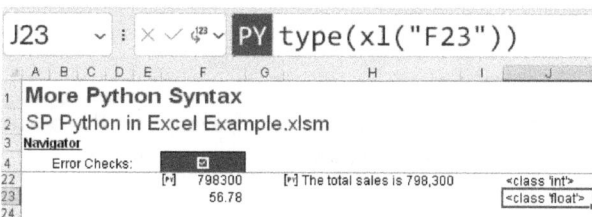

FIGURE 2-178 The type() function reveals how a decimal number is stored.

You may sometimes need to convert an integer to a float or vice versa. There are functions you can use to do this. To see how it works, enter the following Python code in cell H23:

```
int(xl("F23"))
```

As you can see from the data type card shown in Figure 2-179, Python in Excel converts the value into an integer.

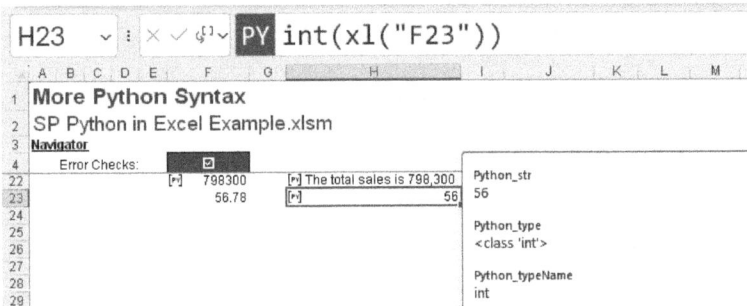

FIGURE 2-179 The `int()` function converts a float into an integer by removing the value after the decimal point.

To convert an integer to a float, you use the `float()` function. To see it in action, enter the following Python code in cell H24:

```
float(xl("H23"))
```

The result may look misleading in the Excel cell, but as you can see from the data type card in Figure 2-180, Python in Excel has converted 56 into a float.

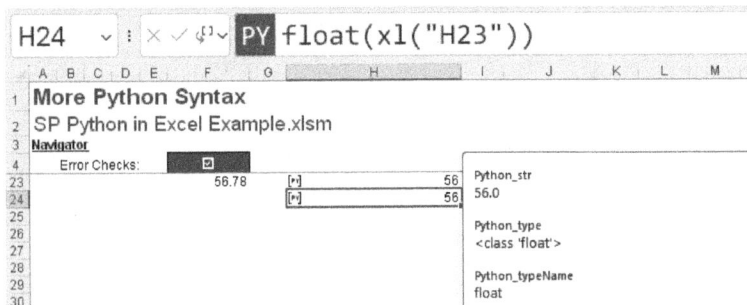

FIGURE 2-180 The `float()` function converts an integer into a float by adding a decimal point.

Note The mathematical operators in Python are the same as in Excel, except for the power operator. If you want to calculate 2 to the third power, the Python expression is 2**3.

Simplifying with decimal numbers

The float and integer types will be sufficient for the examples in this book. However, there are a few more types that may help you with calculation problems. For example, the decimal type can be useful if you get inaccurate results using floats. In such a situation, you need to convert the float to a string and then convert the string to a decimal. To do this, you need the decimal library. To try it, enter the following Python code in cell H25:

```
import decimal
decimal.Decimal(str(xl("F23")))
```

The function `str()` converts a number to a string, and then the function `Decimal()` converts the string into a decimal. Figure 2-181 shows the results.

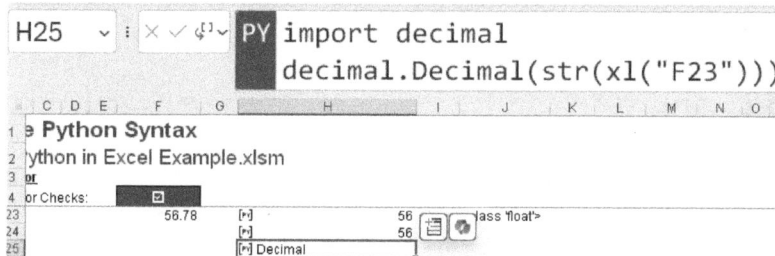

FIGURE 2-181 You can import the decimal library to convert floats to decimals.

The decimal type cannot be expressed as an Excel value. Figure 2-182 shows the data type card for cell H25.

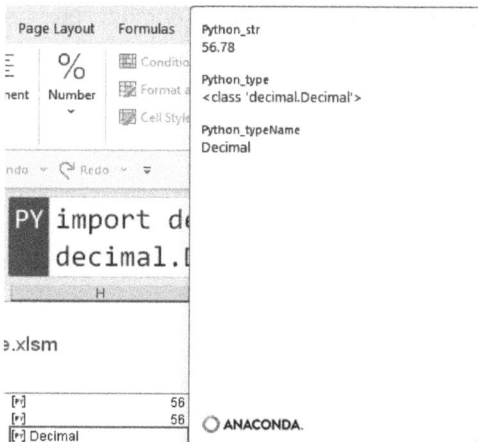

FIGURE 2-182 The data type card shows the decimal value and the class `decimal.Decimal`.

Because decimals cannot be viewed as Excel values, this conversion would only be needed to correct rare float calculation issues.

Creating and using complex numbers

Some mathematical calculations use complex numbers. A complex number is expressed as a real part and an imaginary part. The unit of imaginary numbers is the square root of -1, known as i. The expression for a complex number is a + bi, where a is the real part and b is the imaginary part. This is the Python function to create a complex number:

```
complex(real, imaginary)
```

The parameters *real* and *imaginary* default to zero if they are not specified.

To see a complex Python type, enter the following Python code in cell H27:

```
complex(3,2)
```

Figure 2-183 shows the results.

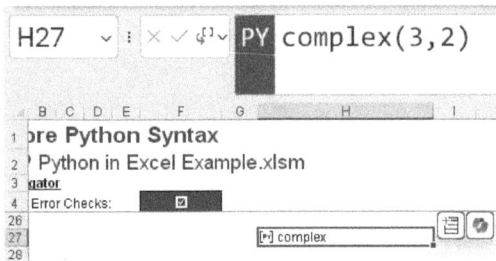

FIGURE 2-183 A complex number can be created by using the complex() function.

As shown in Figure 2-184, the data type card for cell H27 shows the complex number you created.

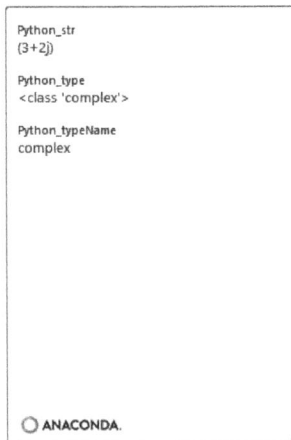

FIGURE 2-184 The complex number is expressed as (3+2j).

As expected, a complex number cannot be viewed as an Excel value.

> **Note** The use of j instead of i for the complex number unit in Python comes from the engineering convention of using j. This has the advantage of being easier to distinguish from numbers. There are debates about using j instead of i in Python forums, but it will not change.

Using Booleans for **True/False** values

Now that you have learned about numeric objects, let's move on to Booleans, which are used for True/False values. You used True and False earlier, with the Python function xl():

```
xl("source", headers = True/False)
```

> **Note** The Boolean types True and False are capitalized. Remember that Python is case sensitive.

Interpreting the Boolean type can be useful for testing whether data exists in an object. These are the Boolean operators:

- and (or False and True)

- or (or False or True)

- not (or not True)

- ==

- !=

- <

- >

Every object has a Boolean property, and most objects evaluate to True. Some evaluate to False, 0, and other empty values, such as an empty string. You came across the Python object None when you used the print() command, as this command is not used in the Excel frontend. None is a Python constant that represents the absence of a value, and it evaluates to False.

To check whether an object is `True` or `False`, you can use the `bool()` function. To see how this works, enter the following code in cell H28:

bool(xl("H27"))

Figure 2-185 shows the result.

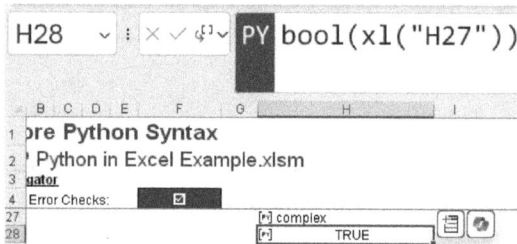

FIGURE 2-185 The Boolean type of the complex Python object is `True`.

Figure 2-186 shows the data type card for the cell H28.

Python_str
True

Python_type
<class 'bool'>

Python_typeName
bool

○ ANACONDA.

FIGURE 2-186 The Boolean value is `True`, and the class and type of the result are both `bool`.

Extracting partial strings with indexing

Now we're ready to look at how to extract partial strings. To do this, you need to understand more about Python indexing.

Python uses *zero-based indexing*, which means that you start counting at 0. We already looked at indexing in DataFrames, but it can also be used in many other Python objects. The simplest example is using indexing in a string. To use Python to get parts of a string in Excel, enter the following string as an Excel formula in cell F30:

```
"Sales for Department Admin in June 2024"
```

Then extract this data into a DataFrame in cell F31:

```
df_string_for_index = xl("F30")
```

Each character (including spaces) in this string can be accessed with an index. Python counts from 0 at either end. To extract a character using indexing, you use square brackets ([]) around the index of the character. To see how it works, enter the following Python code in cell H31:

```
df_string_for_index[10]
```

The result is D. The same result can be achieved by counting from the other end. To see this in action, enter the following code in cell H31:

```
df_string_for_index[-29]
```

It is more useful to extract words from a string, which is called *slicing*. Slicing has something in common with creating a list from a range, which we looked at earlier when learning Python syntax, in this example:

```
numbers_list=list(range(1,5))
```

You saw earlier that, with this method, the range goes up to the number just before the second number of the range. Slicing works the same way: The start interval is included, but the stop is not. To extract the word Department from `df_string_for_index`, replace the Python code in cell H31 with the following code:

```
df_string_for_index[10:20]
```

The second number is the index of the character after the last letter, not the length of the string to be extracted. You can also start from the other end, as you did for the single character. To try it, enter this code:

```
df_string_for_index[-29:-19]
```

You can also add a third parameter: `step`. The `step` parameter can be useful for other Python objects, such as lists. Here, it would take every third character from the beginning to the end:

```
df_string_for_index[0::3]
```

The result is Sef ptnAiiJe0. Collecting every third character is not likely to be useful, but how about every third item in an Excel data range? To see if that's useful, enter the following range of data in cells F33:F45:

```
Company: A
Sales: 1000
Region: 1
Company: B
Sales: 200
Region: 2
Company: C
Sales: 4000
Region: 3
Company: D
Sales: 1500
Region: 4
```

Then enter the following Python code in cell H33:

```
xl("F33:F44")[0::3]
```

Figure 2-187 shows the results.

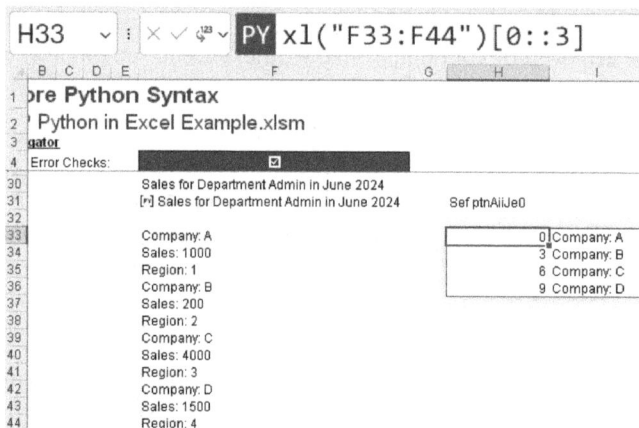

FIGURE 2-187 You can slice the data range to extract the company data.

The four company names are stored in a DataFrame with their row numbers. Note that this is not the same as selecting a row number. To prove this, you can replace the Python code in cell H33 with the following:

```
xl("F33:F44")[-12::3]
```

This gives the same result but does so by using reverse indexing.

Storing and using dates

As an Excel user, you are probably familiar with how Excel stores dates. A date is a serial number, counting from January 1, 1900. You can change this in the Excel Options dialog, but for the purposes of this book, you will use the standard setting. When you enter a date into a cell, Excel formats the date for you to look like a date, but it stores the value as a float. If you also specify the time, you can specify it to the nearest millisecond.

There is no option to enter a time zone. The default format for a date is based on the Windows Language & Region settings on your computer (see Figure 2-188). You can also change the cell format to show a different date format, but the stored float remains the same.

FIGURE 2-188 Excel bases its date formatting on the user's Language & Region settings.

In Python, dates and datetimes are stored in `datetime` objects. Before we explore how to create a `datetime` object, you need to see how easy it is to convert an Excel datetime to a Python object in Python in Excel. Enter the date **23 January 2025** in cell H46. The example in Figure 2-189 shows the UK region, with the cell formatted to show the month name to avoid any confusion.

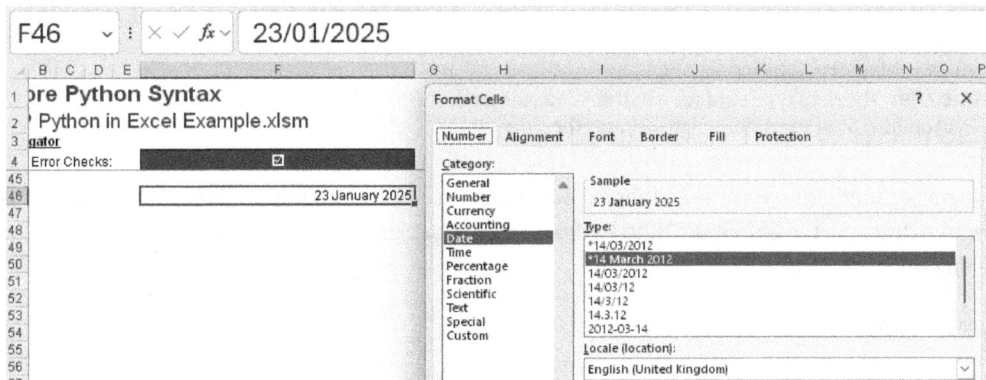

FIGURE 2-189 Cell formatting can be applied to change the way the date is displayed.

> **Note** You can display the date any way you like because the formatting does not change the way it is stored.

To see date formatting in action, enter the following Python code in cell H46:

```
df_date = xl("F46")
```

The Python object is displayed in an Excel cell and uses the default date formatting. Figure 2-190 shows the results for this example, although your results will show your default date formatting.

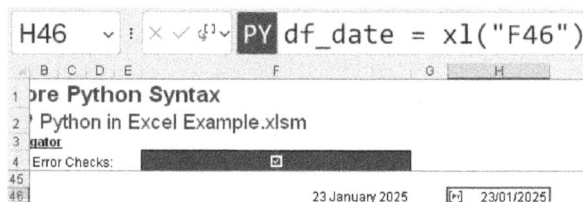

FIGURE 2-190 When a Python date is displayed as a Python object, the Excel default date format is used.

The data type card for cell H46 reveals the Python type and class (see Figure 2-191).

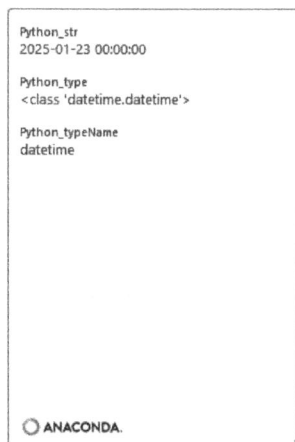

FIGURE 2-191 The data type card for a Python date shows the Python format of the date, which includes the time.

In this example, you have seen that extracting an Excel date into Python is easy. Now, let's look at how to extract part of a date by using Python. Enter the following Python code in cell H47 to extract the day from `df_date`:

```
df_day=df_date.day
```

Enter the following Python code in cell H48 to extract the month from `df_date`:

```
df_month=df_date.month
```

Enter the following Python code in cell H49 to extract the year from `df_date`:

```
df_year=df_date.year
```

The result for each example is an integer, as shown in Figure 2-192.

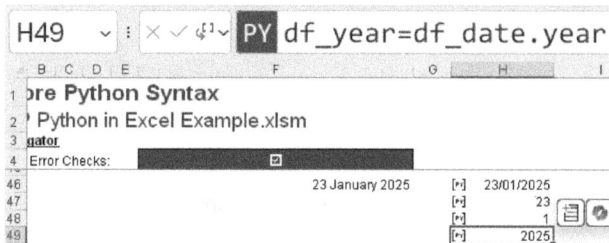

FIGURE 2-192 Extracting the day, the month number, and the year from a `datetime` object.

To extract the month name, you must use a different function to convert the datetime to a string first. To do so, enter the following Python code in cell H50:

```
df_month_name=df_date.strftime("%B")
```

Figure 2-193 shows the result.

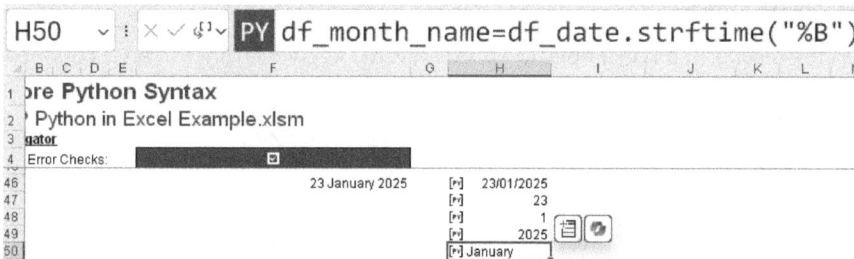

FIGURE 2-193 You can extract the month name by using the `strftime()` function.

You can use `strftime()` (which stands for "string from time") to reformat how the date is displayed. To see how it works, enter the following Python code in cell H51:

```
df_reformat = df_date.strftime("%A  %d - %m - %Y")
```

This example demonstrates the main symbols for extracting date components. The other common components from the time segment are %H for hours and %M for minutes. As you can see, the case is important here too. Figure 2-194 shows the result of using df_reformat.

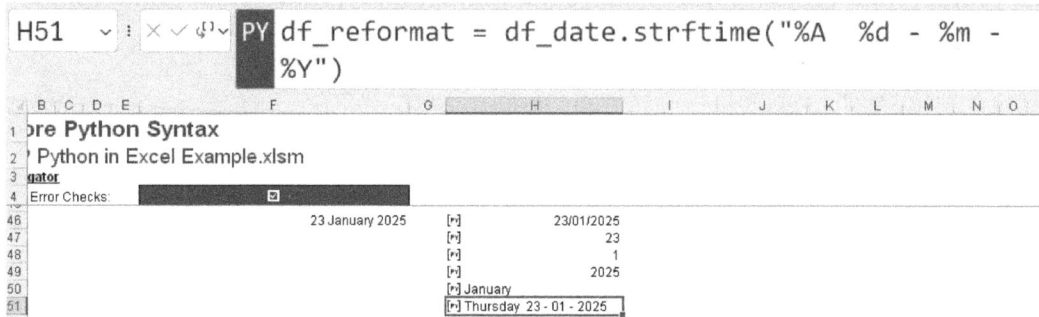

FIGURE 2-194 You can also use the strftime() function to control how the date is displayed.

Creating and using dictionaries

A Python dictionary is similar to a list in that it is a collection of Python objects. However, each object has a key. To create a simple dictionary that links products to account codes, enter the following Python code in cell F53:

```
dict_Products = {"Chains":14827,
                 "Socks":14786,
                 "Shorts":14928,
                 "Tights":14848}
```

Figure 2-195 shows the results. In this example, the product is the key, which links to an account code.

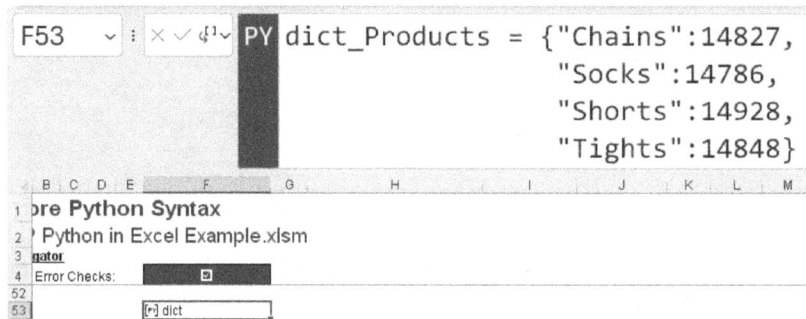

FIGURE 2-195 Creating a Python dictionary

Figure 2-196 shows the data type card for cell F53.

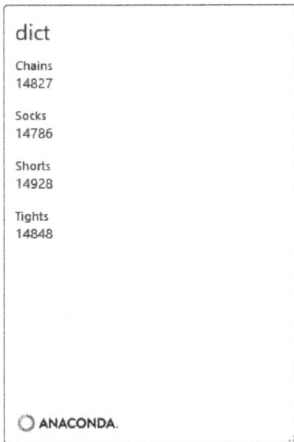

FIGURE 2-196 The data type card for a Python dictionary

This data type card contains different information from the cards you have seen so far. There is no Python class. The type `dict` is the title, and each pair is shown with the value underneath the key. The Excel value view for a `dict` object also shows a dictionary icon next to the word `dict`. You can click the dictionary icon, which looks like a stack of two sheets, to view a similar card, as shown in Figure 2-197.

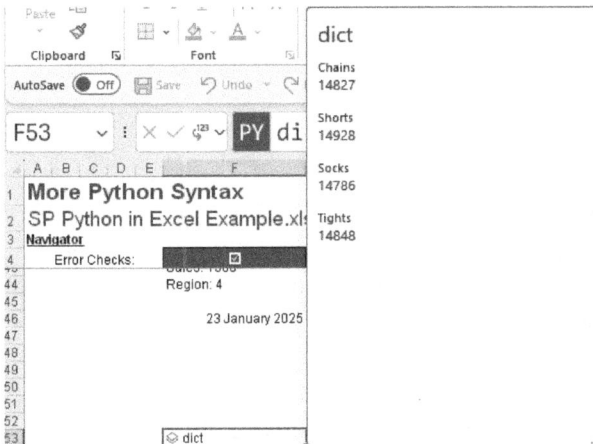

FIGURE 2-197 The data type card for a Python dictionary can be accessed from the dict icon when in the Excel value view.

You can change or add a pair to a dictionary by using similar syntax. To see this in our dictionary example, enter the following Python code in cell F54:

```
dict_Products = dict_Products | {"Bells":14852}
```

The new value will be assigned to the key `"Bells"`. If the key exists, it will be assigned the new value. If the key does not exist, a new pair will be added. Remember that Python is case sensitive, so it is important to take care when updating a key.

Check the results in cell F54 and then enter similar Python code with a new value for "Bells" in cell F55:

```
dict_Products = dict_Products | {"Bells":17852}
```

You can extract a value from the dictionary by using get(). Enter the following Python code in cell F56 to get the account code for the "Bells" key:

```
dict_Products.get("Bells")
```

You should see the value you gave to the key "Bells". You can also include an error trap if the key doesn't exist. To do this, enter the following Python code in cell F57:

```
dict_Products.get("jackets","N/A")
```

Python in Excel returns the value "N/A" because "jackets" is not in the dictionary.

Figure 2-198 shows the results for this section.

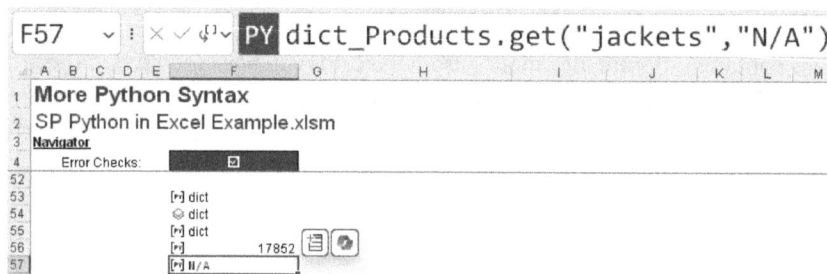

FIGURE 2-198 An error trap can be specified if the key is not found.

Accident-proofing with tuples

If you want to create a list that cannot be changed, you need a Python object called a *tuple*, which is similar to a list. You can use tuples to avoid accidentally changing data. To create a tuple of the department regions, for example, enter the following Python code in cell F59:

```
tp_regions="NORTH","SOUTH","EAST","WEST"
```

The Excel Value view for this tuple looks like a list, as you can see in Figure 2-199.

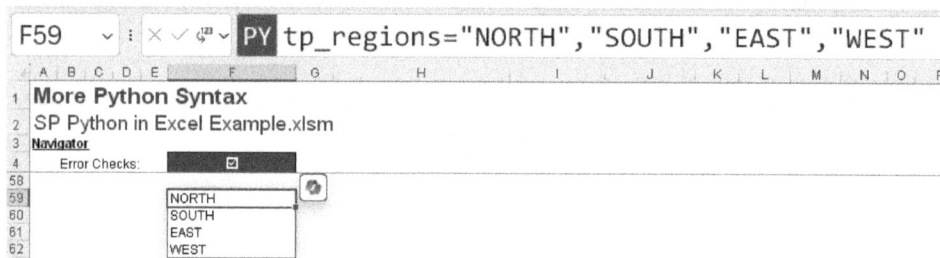

FIGURE 2-199 The Excel Value view of a tuple looks like a list.

To see what happens if you try to change one of the elements of the tuple, enter the following Python code in cell H59:

```
tp_regions[0]="North"
```

In this case, you are attempting to change the first item in the tuple `tp_regions` from "NORTH" to "North". Figure 2-200 shows the results.

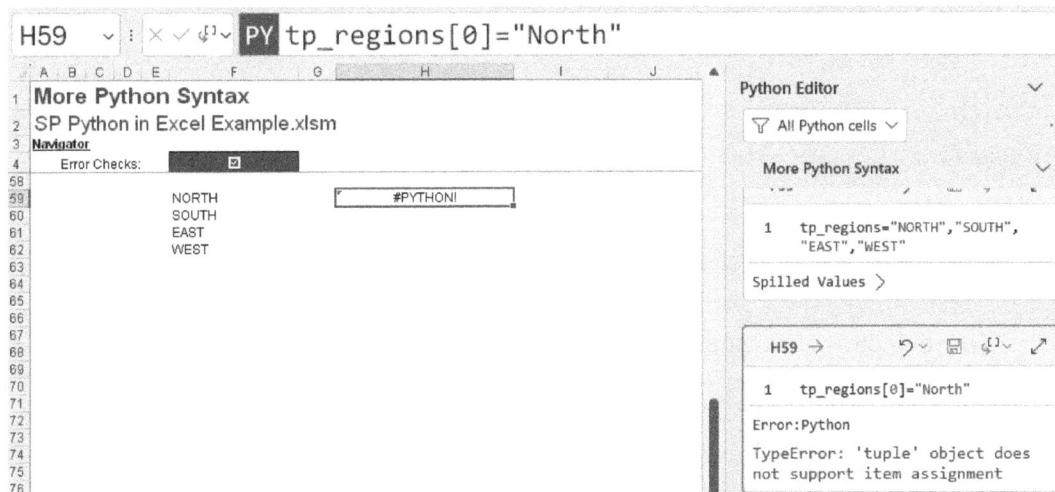

FIGURE 2-200 Trying to change the value of an item in a tuple is not allowed.

As you've seen, you are only prevented from changing values in an existing tuple. However, you can use the same variable `tp_regions` to point to a new tuple.

> **Note** Don't be concerned if working with tuples is difficult to understand; it is an advanced concept in programming. It is used in some Python code generated by Copilot later in the book, where we will look at how to access the data contained in a tuple.

Finding unique list values with sets

A *set* is a list that cannot contain duplicate elements. A practical use of a set is to find the unique values in a list. To see how it works, enter the following Python code in cell F64:

```
set_Products=set(df_contig_range[2])
```

Figure 2-201 shows the results, using the Excel Value view.

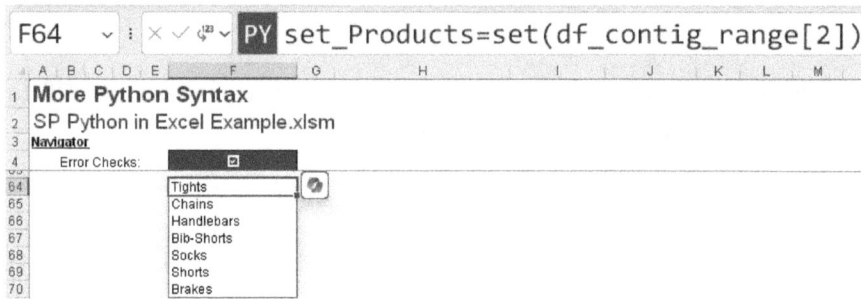

```
F64        PY set_Products=set(df_contig_range[2])
```

A B C D E	F	G	H	I	J	K	L	M
1 **More Python Syntax**								
2 SP Python in Excel Example.xlsm								
3 **Navigator**								
4 Error Checks:	☑							
64	Tights	○						
65	Chains							
66	Handlebars							
67	Bib-Shorts							
68	Socks							
69	Shorts							
70	Brakes							

FIGURE 2-201 A set can be used to find unique values in a list or column.

> **Note** You must select a column of a DataFrame and not a whole DataFrame.

To create another set in cell H64, enter the following Python code in that cell:

```
set_challenge_Products=set(df_data_range[0])
```

Part of the challenge earlier in this chapter was to find the products in `df_contig_range` that are not in `df_data_range`. One way to find the products would be to create sets and use `difference()`. To do this, enter the following code in cell J64:

```
set_ProductsMatch = set_Products.difference(set_challenge_Products)
```

Figure 2-202 shows the results.

> **Note** You can enter the sets in either order to get the same result.

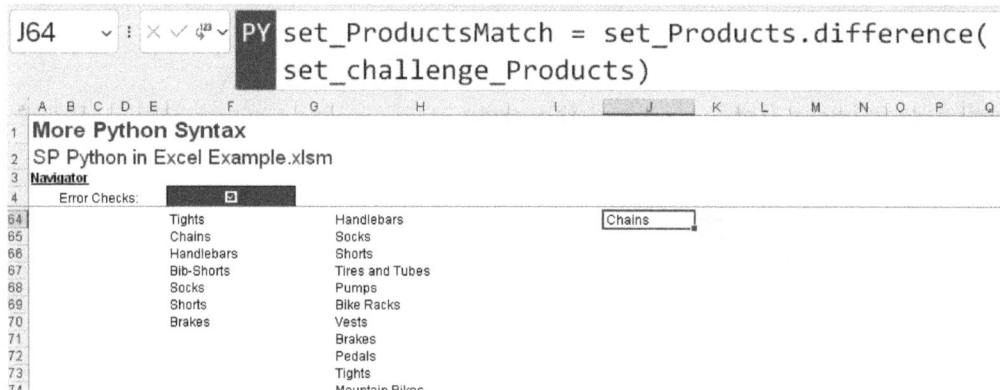

```
J64        PY set_ProductsMatch = set_Products.difference(
                  set_challenge_Products)
```

A B C D E	F	G	H	I	J	K	L	M	N	O	P	Q
1 **More Python Syntax**												
2 SP Python in Excel Example.xlsm												
3 **Navigator**												
4 Error Checks:	☑											
64		Tights		Handlebars		Chains						
65		Chains		Socks								
66		Handlebars		Shorts								
67		Bib-Shorts		Tires and Tubes								
68		Socks		Pumps								
69		Shorts		Bike Racks								
70		Brakes		Vests								
71				Brakes								
72				Pedals								
73				Tights								
74				Mountain Bikes								

FIGURE 2-202 You can use the `difference()` function to find the missing values from one set.

There are two other common set operators:

- **Union:** Finds the elements that exist in either set.

- **Intersection:** Finds the elements that exist in both sets.

You can also perform operations with more than two sets. For example, if you have three sets—A, B, and C—you can use the following code to find elements in A that are not in B or C:

```
set_differences = A.difference(B,C)
```

In this section, you have just glimpsed what is possible with sets. Set theory is used extensively in mathematics and data analytics.

Using conditional expressions

Conditional expressions allow you to follow a path according to the answers to questions. In Python, the keywords for conditional expressions are if, elif, and else.

For example, to set a rate according to a value, you could enter this Python code:

```
value = 44
if value <=10:
    rate = 50
elif value <=30:
    rate = 40
elif value <=50:
    rate = 20
else:
    rate = 10
rate
```

When this Python code is executed in a Python cell, the result is 20.

> **Note** The indentation in the code shown here is required. The Python interpreter will let you know if you get it wrong!

If you wanted to run this code with different values, you would use a loop.

Counting with loops

To explore loops, let's start with another simple example. Start with the set set_Products that you created earlier. You can count the entities in the set by using the following Python code:

```
count=0
for product in set_Products:
    count=count+1
count
```

When this Python code is executed, the result in a Python cell is 7.

You could stop counting when `count` is 3. There are two ways to do this. The first method is to use `break` to get out of the loop:

```
count=0
for product in set_Products:
    if count==3:
      break
    else:
        count=count+1
count
```

The second method is to use `continue` to keep going through the loop but skip the `count+1`:

```
count=0
for product in set_Products:
    if count==3:
        continue
    else:
        count=count+1
count
```

Finally, here is a simple example of a `while` loop that also returns the value 3:

```
count=0
while count<=2:
    count=count+1
count
```

The Python syntax in this section should be enough to get you started, but there is one more area to cover before we finish the chapter: You need to know how to write your own Python functions.

Creating your own Python functions

You have been using preloaded Python functions for the examples so far. You can also create your own functions.

A Python *function* is a block of code that is assigned a function name. The rules for naming functions are the same as those for naming variables. As with variables, assigning a new function to a name means that the name no longer refers to the previous function. Once a function has been created, you can call it with the Python code in any Python cell by using the function name. Remember the Python calculation order: Cells to the left of and above the cell defining the function occur before the function is defined, so they will not recognize it.

You will find functions useful when repeating the same code lines. When maintaining your Python code, calling a function is more efficient than making changes each time those lines occur. It also saves time and space when creating new code that can use the function. To create a function, you begin with the keyword `def`. For example, enter this Python code in cell F91:

```
def fn_hello():
    return "Hello, I am a function"
fn_hello()
```

Figure 2-203 shows the results.

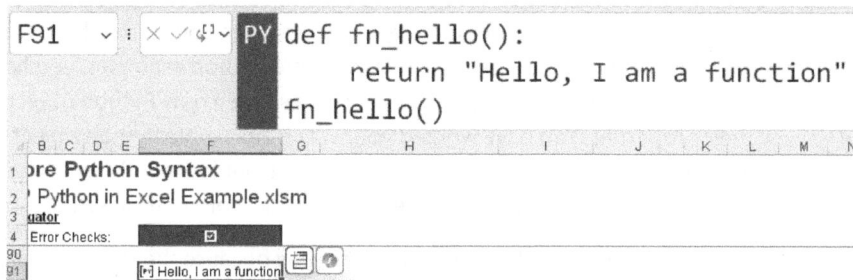

FIGURE 2-203 Creating a basic function

This simple example shows you the basic syntax required to write your own function. You must use parentheses after the function name when defining it and calling it, even if there are no parameters. You must use a colon (:) after the def statement, and you must indent the return statement. As always with Python, everything is case sensitive.

Consider this example with parameters and conditions:

```
def fn_UKtoUS(uk_word):
    if uk_word.lower() =="colour":
        return "color"
    elif uk_word.lower() =="analyse":
        return "analyze"
    else:
        return "No, I'm not changing it"
fn_UKtoUS("Colour")
```

In this example, we use lower() to lower the case of uk_word. The result of running the function with the argument set to "Colour" is "color". The argument uk_word is required. To enter an optional argument, you must specify the default value, as in the following code:

```
def fn_UKtoUS(uk_word,skip_colour=True):
    if uk_word.lower() =="colour" and not skip_colour:
        return "color"
    elif uk_word.lower() =="analyse":
        return "analyze"
    else:
        return "No, I'm not changing it"
fn_UKtoUS("Colour")
```

Because we have not specified a value for skip_colour, the value is True. The function would return "No, I'm not changing it". In Python code, it is not necessary to declare arguments in the same order as the function definition. We can put them in any order, specifying them by name, as shown here:

```
fn_UKtoUS( skip_colour=False,uk_word="Colour")
```

This would return the value "color".

Summary

You have learned a lot and worked through a lot of examples in this chapter. You started by learning where Python in Excel is available and how to access it. Through simple Python examples, you have explored how the Excel frontend differs from other platforms. You have seen how Python objects are created and how to view their properties. You have worked your way from simple Python objects to arrays, and you have extracted Excel entities. You have learned how to troubleshoot the errors encountered when using Python in Excel. Finally, you have become familiar with more Python syntax.

We decided to divide the introduction to Python objects in this way because the star of the show is the way that Python interacts with Excel data. You have learned enough about Python objects and constructs to move on to more complex Python code, and you are ready for the examples in the rest of the book. Even if you plan to use AI to write Python code, you must understand what is being created so that you can troubleshoot and adapt the code produced to tell the story of the data.

In the next chapter, you will learn about some Python libraries that the Python community has created to help you perform advanced data analysis by using tried and tested modules of Python code.

## CHAPTER 3

Using Python libraries

In this chapter, you will:

- Get an overview of Python libraries

- Explore the libraries preloaded with Python in Excel

- Learn about libraries Microsoft recommends using with Python in Excel

Note To follow along with the examples in this chapter, you must download the resources that accompany this book. If you don't already have these resources, visit *https://www .sumproduct.com/python-in-excel-book-resources* and download the files to a folder associated with your Python in Excel license. For this chapter, you will begin by accessing the workbook **SP Python in Excel Example Starter File Chapter 3.xlsm**.

What is a Python library?

We previously defined a Python library as a collection of code modules, functions, and other Python objects that can be reused. The Python standard library is included on all platforms that use Python. Python is an open-source language, and the programming community has been encouraged to develop and share code. As a result, myriad libraries are now available to solve tasks in various disciplines across many different platforms.

Some Python libraries are so popular and vital to organizations that the nonprofit organization NumFOCUS was created to sponsor select Python libraries. The goal was to provide a more formal structure to support and organize the community. NumFOCUS has since expanded to encompass many open-source projects. The organization "envisions an inclusive scientific and research community that utilizes actively supported open-source software to make impactful discoveries for a better world." NumFOCUS is sponsored by large corporations as well as member donations. To find out more, see *https://www.numfocus.org*.

The Python libraries supported in Python for Excel include pandas, NumPy, and Matplotlib. You have already discovered that pandas is vital to Python in Excel, and you will learn about NumPy and Matplotlib (including the pyplot module), as well as some other preloaded libraries, in this chapter.

A variety of terms are used when referring to collections of Python code, which can get confusing:

- A *project* refers to a collection of files and information, often under different releases. As features are requested and provided, multiple releases are created.

- A *release* is a version of a project created when the project is modified and shared with the community. A release contains one or more files.

- A *file*, also known as a package or a library, is what you can search for and download for use with Python in Excel.

You can see how many Python projects, releases, and files are currently available by visiting *https://pypi.org*. At the time of writing, there are 673,608 Python projects available on PyPI (see Figure 3-1).

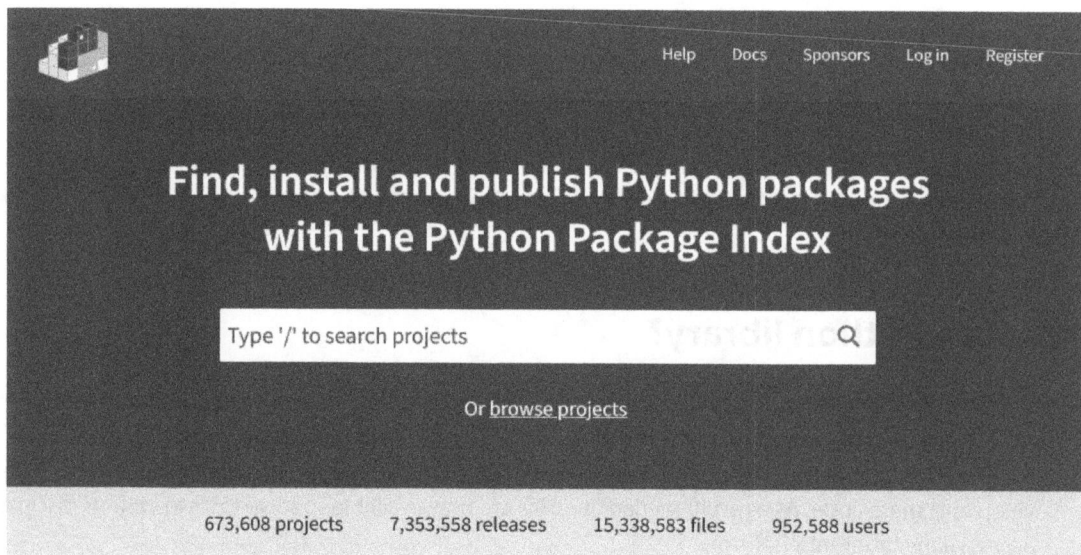

Help   Docs   Sponsors   Log in   Register

Find, install and publish Python packages
with the Python Package Index

Type '/' to search projects   🔍

Or browse projects

673,608 projects   7,353,558 releases   15,338,583 files   952,588 users

FIGURE 3-1 The number of available Python projects, releases, and files can be viewed on the PyPI website.

Because Python in Excel uses the Anaconda platform, the libraries you can import into Python in Excel are those supported by Anaconda. Anaconda enables you to access more than 400 packages for use in Excel.[1] Rather than try to cover all the available libraries in this chapter, we focus on preloaded libraries and libraries that Microsoft recommends for their suitability to support Python in Excel. As with many of the features of Python in Excel, the list of recommended libraries may have been extended since we wrote this chapter. Figure 3-2 shows the beginning of the list as of this writing.

As you saw in Chapter 2, "Getting to know Python in Excel," to load a library in Python in Excel, you use the syntax `import library_full_name as library_alias`. However, the recommended libraries do not all use this standard `import` statement, as you will see at the end of this chapter, where you can also find a list of all the recommended libraries.

List of recommended libraries

The following table shows a subset of the open-source libraries provided by Anaconda that you can use with Python in Excel. The libraries Matplotlib, NumPy, seaborn, statsmodels, and pandas are imported by default. The additional libraries listed in the table are not automatically imported, but you can choose to import them if desired.

Important: To protect your data security, these libraries will not have the ability to make network requests or access your files and data on your local machine. To learn more, see Data Security and Python in Excel.

Note: Python in Excel supports English, Chinese (Simplified), French, German, Japanese, and Spanish fonts.

Library	Description
Astropy	A Python library for astronomy. License: BSD-3-Clause.
beautifulsoup4	A Python library designed for screen-scraping. License: MIT.
Faker	Generates fake data. License: MIT.
imbalanced-learn	Helps tackle classification issues by offering re-sampling techniques. Relies on scikit-learn. License: MIT.
IPython	A library for interactive computing. License: BSD-3-Clause.
Matplotlib	Creates publication-quality charts and figures in Python. License: PSF.

FIGURE 3-2 Microsoft recommends a subset of Anaconda-supported libraries for Python in Excel.

---

[1] "What Are Python Packages in Excel?" Anaconda blog, accessed June 10, 2025, *https://www.anaconda.com/blog /what-are-python-packages-in-excel*.

Working with the preloaded libraries in Python in Excel

The pandas library is necessary for working with Excel data, and the other libraries that are preloaded in Python in Excel were chosen because of their suitability for working with Excel data. You may recall that you can see the libraries already loaded by clicking the **Initialization** button in the **Python** section on the **Formulas** tab to open the Initialization pane (see Figure 3-3).

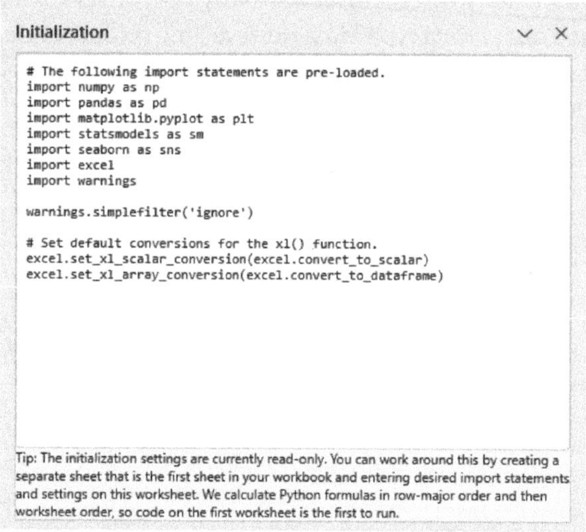

Initialization ⌄ ✕

```
# The following import statements are pre-loaded.
import numpy as np
import pandas as pd
import matplotlib.pyplot as plt
import statsmodels as sm
import seaborn as sns
import excel
import warnings

warnings.simplefilter('ignore')

# Set default conversions for the xl() function.
excel.set_xl_scalar_conversion(excel.convert_to_scalar)
excel.set_xl_array_conversion(excel.convert_to_dataframe)
```

Tip: The initialization settings are currently read-only. You can work around this by creating a separate sheet that is the first sheet in your workbook and entering desired import statements and settings on this worksheet. We calculate Python formulas in row-major order and then worksheet order, so code on the first worksheet is the first to run.

FIGURE 3-3 The Initialization pane shows the preloaded Python libraries.

These Python libraries are currently preloaded:

- **NumPy:** This library allows you to perform mathematical and logical operations, working with arrays rather than the more cumbersome Python lists you have already seen in action.

- **pandas:** This library, which is built on the NumPy library, is designed for data manipulation and analysis. The pandas DataFrame is similar to data in an Excel worksheet and is key in reading Excel data as a Python object. A DataFrame contains two-dimensional data and data labels.

- **Matplotlib:** This library makes it possible to quickly create plots. The pyplot module is preloaded in Python in Excel. matplotlib.pyplot is an application programming interface (API) that allows you to use the Python code in the Matplotlib library to quickly create plots, as you will see in several examples in this chapter.

- **statsmodels:** As its name implies, this library assists with the creation and analysis of statistical models.

- **seaborn:** This library has functions that use matplotlib.pyplot to provide access to more complex and varied visualizations.

In Chapter 2, you already saw some examples of using pandas and NumPy. Next, we'll look closely at each of the preinstalled libraries, beginning with pandas.

pandas

You used pandas extensively when you looked at how to extract Excel entities into Python objects in Chapter 2. According to Anaconda, the purpose of pandas is to enable data analysis in Python. Because pandas is also the main tool for reading data from Excel, it is the star of Python in Excel. pandas is especially useful for transforming large raw datasets into useful information, and in this section, we'll look at how to use pandas for cleaning and preparing data:

- *Cleaning data* means improving data quality by removing or correcting data that contains errors or that is inconsistent or irrelevant to the task; it can also involve filling in missing values.

- *Preparing data* involves transforming it into a format that readies it for analysis. It can include merging (which we looked at in the challenge example in Chapter 2) and removing duplicates. Transformations such as pivoting and unpivoting data may also be required to prepare data.

To try cleaning data, open the **SP Python in Excel Example Starter File Chapter 3.xlsm** workbook and go to the **Pandas Clean and Transform** sheet. You should see a dataset that is missing some data, as shown in Figure 3-4.

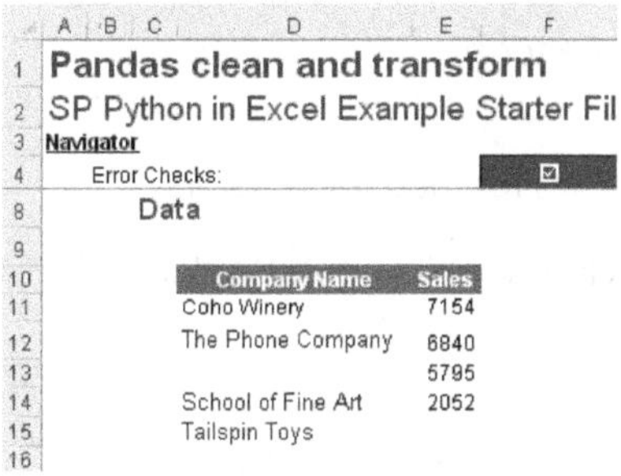

FIGURE 3-4 A dataset that is missing some values

Your task is to remove the rows that are missing data. To do this, enter the following two lines of Python code in cell G10:

```
df_raw_data=xl("D10:E15", headers=True)
df_company_data=df_raw_data.dropna()
```

The first line is familiar: You use it to extract the Excel data range into a DataFrame. The second line includes the function dropna(), which has the following syntax:

```
DataFrame.dropna(*, axis=0, how=<no_default>, thresh=<no_default>, subset=None, inplace=False,
ignore_index=False)
```

As you can see in the syntax, several parameters can be passed to this function:

- ***:** This parameter indicates that a tuple may be passed to the function.

- **axis:** This parameter indicates whether rows (0 or 'index') or columns (1 or 'columns') that contain missing values are removed. The default is 0.

- **how:** This parameter indicates whether a row or column is removed from the DataFrame when you have at least one NA (empty) value (`any`) or all NA values (`all`). The default is `all`.

- **thresh (integer):** This parameter allows you to optionally specify the number of non-NA values for the row or column to be valid. This parameter cannot be combined with how.

- **subset:** You can optionally specify labels along the other axis (rows/columns) to consider. For example, if you are dropping rows, this would be a list of columns to include.

- **inplace (bool):** This parameter indicates whether to modify the DataFrame rather than create a new one. The default is `False`.

> **Note** Many Python functions have been designed and revised to be flexible so that they can be used in various applications. This means there is often a long list of parameters that can be used in different ways, depending on the context in which the function is used. For the functions defined in this chapter, we have provided more parameters than you will need for the exercises in this book. We want to give you an idea of how the functions can be used and provide information that will benefit you as you become a more advanced Python user. As a Python beginner, you may not yet understand all the terms.

In the Python code used in cell G10, you use the default values for these parameters.

The Python code in this example removes any row that includes a missing (NA) value and creates a new DataFrame (see Figure 3-5).

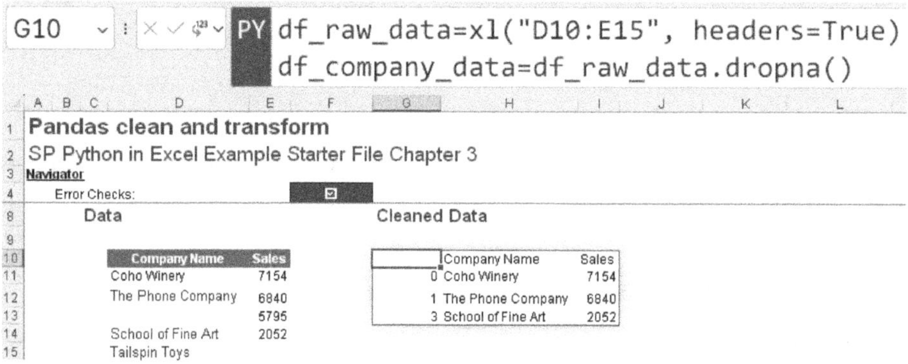

FIGURE 3-5 The function dropna() can be used to remove rows or columns with a specified number of missing values.

In this case, we deliberately left the Python row index in the DataFrame to show which rows are selected. If you want to display the data without the index, though, you can add a `reset_index()` function to the `dropna()` function:

```
df_raw_data=xl("D10:E15", headers=True)
df_company_data=df_raw_data.dropna().reset_index(drop=True)
```

An alternative is to specify values to use if data is missing. To see how it works, enter the following Python code in cell K10:

```
df_company_filled_data=df_raw_data.fillna("Data Missing")
```

This time, you are using `fillna()`, which has the following syntax:

```
DataFrame.fillna(value=None, *, method=None, axis=None, inplace=False, limit=None)
```

These are the parameters you can specify with `fillna()`:

- **value:** This parameter, which may be a scalar, a dict, a series, or a DataFrame (but not a list), is the value to use to fill holes (in this example, `value` is `"Data Missing"`). For a more complex dataset, you might use a dict, a series, or a DataFrame of values and specify which value to use for each index (for a series) or column (for a DataFrame). Values not in the dict, series, or DataFrame would not be filled.

- **method:** This parameter can be set to `'bfill'`, `'ffill'`, or None. This is the equivalent of filling down or filling up. In a reindexed series, `'ffill'` (which stands for *forward fill*) indicates to propagate the last valid observation forward to the next valid observation, and `'bfill'` (which stands for *backward fill*) indicates to use the next valid observation to fill the gap.

- **axis:** This parameter, which specifies the axis along which to fill missing values, can be set to 0 or `'index'` or 1 or `'columns'` for a DataFrame. For a series, this parameter is unused. `axis` defaults to 0.

- **inplace (bool):** This parameter indicates whether to modify the DataFrame rather than create a new one. The default is `False`. Note that if it is set to `True`, this will modify any other views on this object (such as a no-copy slice for a column in a DataFrame).

- **Limit:** If `method` is specified for this parameter, this is the maximum number of consecutive NaN (not a number) values to forward fill or backward fill. In other words, if there is a gap with more than this number of consecutive NaNs, it will be only partially filled. If `method` is not specified, this is the maximum number of entries along the entire axis where NaNs will be filled. This parameter must be greater than 0 if it is not set to None. The default is None.

As you can see in Figure 3-6, the code you have entered specifies a value to use in place of the blanks.

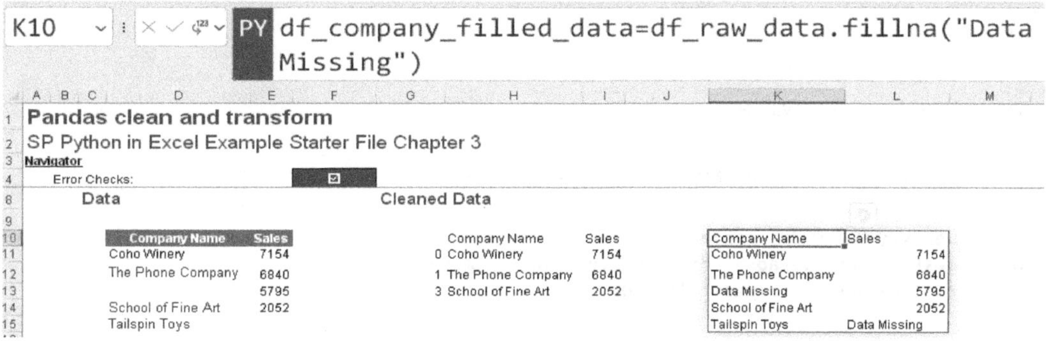

FIGURE 3-6 The function `fillna()` can be used to replace missing values with specified replacements.

You could fill down the data instead. To do this, change the Python code in cell K10 to the following:

```
df_company_filled_data=df_raw_data.fillna(method="ffill")
```

This code specifies the method parameter instead of specifying the value. Figure 3-7 shows the results you get when you enter this code.

> **Note** In Excel, you can skip parameters by using commas—for example, **=PIVOTBY(tbl [Item],tbl[Year],tbl[Rating],AVERAGE,,,-2)**. This is not the case in Python. In Python, if you want to skip parameters, you must name the ones you are specifying. If you enter commas instead, you will trigger a Python error.

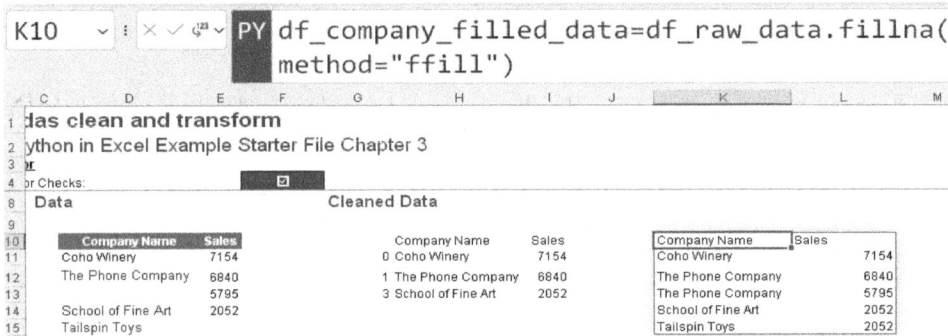

FIGURE 3-7 The function `fillna()` can also be used to replace missing values by filling down.

You can also use pandas to create additional columns to shape data. To see how this works, let's calculate the moving average for the values shown in Figure 3-8.

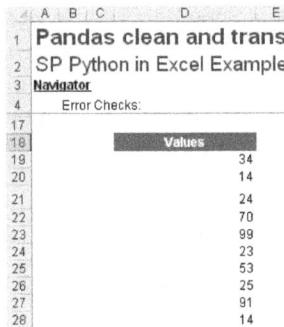

FIGURE 3-8 A column of values

Enter the following lines of Python code in cell G18:

```
df_values=xl("D18:D28", headers=True)
df_values["Moving Average"]=df_values.rolling(3).mean()
df_no_null_values=df_values.fillna(0)
```

Some of this code will be familiar from the examples you have already encountered. The first line is extracting the Excel data into a DataFrame called df_values. The second line is not creating a new DataFrame; rather, it is adding a new column, "Moving Average," to df_values. This line includes the functions rolling() and mean(), which we'll take a moment to look at.

This is the syntax for rolling():

```
DataFrame.rolling(window, min_periods=None, center=False, win_
type=None, on=None, closed=None, step=None, method='single')
```

You can use these parameters to influence the way the rolling() function performs:

- **window:** This parameter can be set to integer, timedelta, str, offset, or BaseIndexer. You can apply this function over a moving window (in this example, a window of three values) or a fixed period. The interpretation of this parameter depends on the data type. If it is an integer, it is the fixed number of observations used for each window. Negative integers are not allowed. If the column type is datetime and the parameter type is timedelta, str, or offset, it is the time period of each window. Each window is a variable size, based on the observations included in the time period. The BaseIndexer subclass is another parameter type that you might want to look into when you are more experienced at using the rolling() function.

- **min_periods:** This parameter is the minimum number of observations in a window required to have a value; if the number of observations is smaller, the result is np.nan (that is, empty). For a window specified by an offset, min_periods defaults to 1. For a window specified by an integer, as in this example, min_periods defaults to the window size. (The final line of code in this example replaces the empty values, allowing the DataFrame to be displayed using the Excel Value view.)

- **center (bool):** If this parameter is False, the window labels are set as the right edge of the window index. If it is True, it is the center of the window index. The default is False.

- **win_type:** This string parameter allows you to create a weighted moving average. The default is None, which means all points are evenly weighted. If it is not null, the string value must be a valid scipy.signal.windows() function. Some SciPy window types require additional parameters to be passed in the aggregation function. The additional parameters must match the keywords specified in the SciPy window type method signature.

- **on:** For a DataFrame, this parameter would be a string containing a column label or an index level on which to calculate the rolling window, rather than the DataFrame's index. Because you are creating a new column in this example, the on parameter is not specified.

- **closed:** This parameter is a string that can be set to None, 'right', 'left', 'both', or 'either'. 'right' means that the first point in the window is excluded from calculations, and 'left' means that the last point in the window is excluded from calculations. 'both' is essentially the same as None, meaning that all points are included. 'either' means that the first and last points in the window are excluded from calculations. The default is None.

- **step:** This parameter can be specified if `window` is an integer. The function evaluates the `window` value at every step result and is equivalent to slicing as `[::step]`. Using a `step` value other than None or 1 will produce a result that has a different shape than the input.

- **method:** This parameter can be set to `'single'` (the default) or `'table'`. If it is `'single'`, the rolling operation is performed for a single column. If it is `'table'`, the rolling operation is performed over the entire object.

This is the syntax for the `mean()` function:

```
DataFrame.mean(axis=0, skipna=True, numeric_only=False, **kwargs)
```

These are the possible parameters:

- **axis:** This parameter denotes the axis the function is applied on; for rows, it is set to 0, and for columns, it is set to 1. For a series, this parameter is unused and defaults to 0. For a DataFrame, you can specify `axis=None` to apply the aggregation across both axes.

- **skipna (bool):** If this parameter is set to True (the default), then NA/null values will be excluded from the result (as they are in this example).

- **numeric_only (bool):** If this parameter is set to True, then only `float`, `int`, and `boolean` columns will be included. This parameter is not used for a series. The default is `False`.

- ****kwargs:** This parameter specifies additional keyword arguments to be passed to the function. The data type is `dict`.

Based on what you have learned about the functions in this example, you can see that you are creating a rolling window of three values and taking the average of those values. Because there are not three values in the window for the first two rows, the returned value for the moving average would be empty. The final line of code replaces each empty value with 0. Figure 3-9 shows the results.

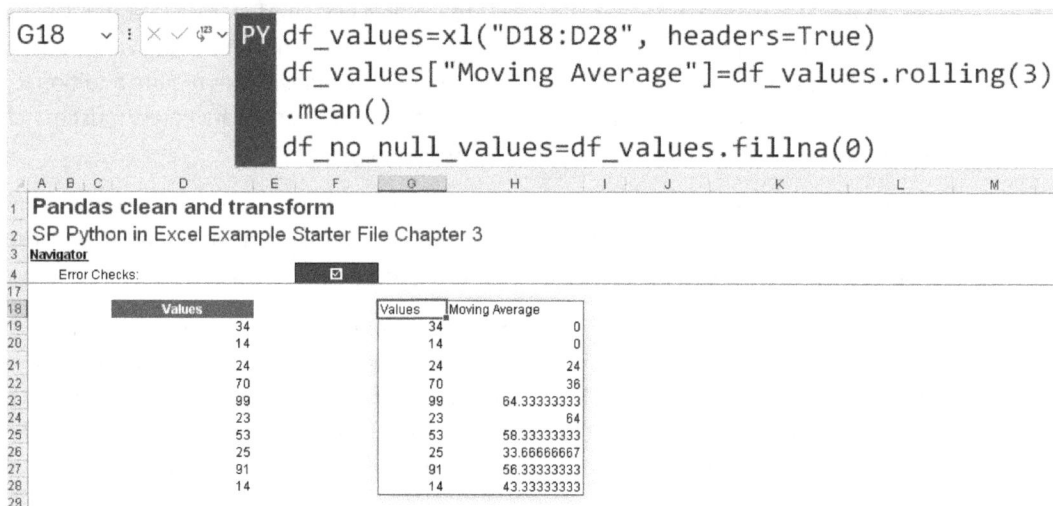

G18			PY	`df_values=xl("D18:D28", headers=True)`

```
df_values["Moving Average"]=df_values.rolling(3)
.mean()
df_no_null_values=df_values.fillna(0)
```

	A	B	C	D	E	F	G	H	I	J	K	L	M
1	**Pandas clean and transform**												
2	SP Python in Excel Example Starter File Chapter 3												
3	Navigator												
4	Error Checks:				☑								
17													
18		**Values**					Values	Moving Average					
19				34			34	0					
20				14			14	0					
21				24			24	24					
22				70			70	36					
23				99			99	64.33333333					
24				23			23	64					
25				53			53	58.33333333					
26				25			25	33.66666667					
27				91			91	56.33333333					
28				14			14	43.33333333					
29													

FIGURE 3-9 Using pandas to add a moving average column

Instead of calculating values only if there are three values available to average, you can calculate a running average by changing the `min_period` setting in `running()`. To do this, change the Python code in cell K18 to the following:

```
df_values=xl("D18:D28", headers=True)
df_values["Moving Average"]=df_values.rolling(3,min_periods=1).mean()
df_values
```

Now, you are working out the running average with a window of three values (or the available window). Figure 3-10 shows the results.

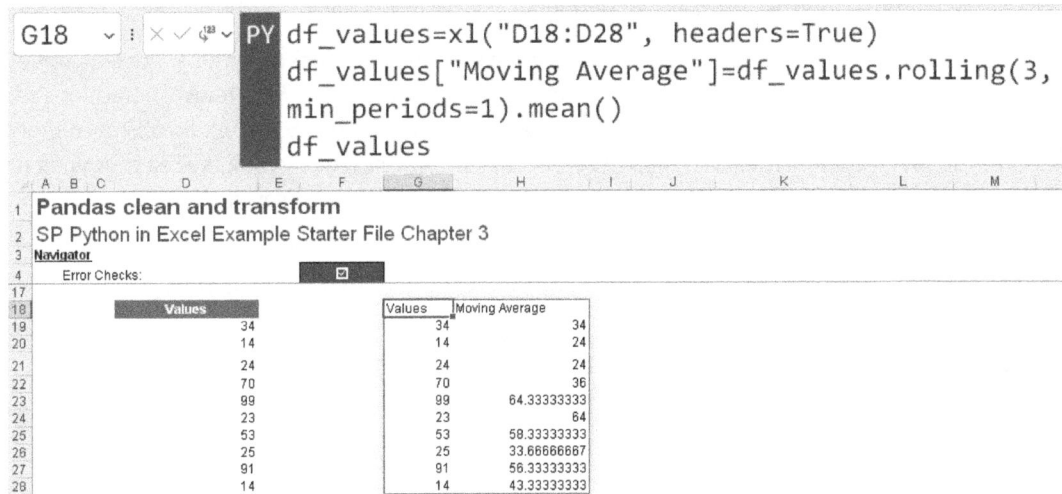

FIGURE 3-10 Using pandas to add a moving average column with a flexible window

Understanding how you can change the way a function works by using parameters will help you manipulate Python code generated by AI to get the results you need.

pandas is a versatile library that can support many of your data analysis needs. Everything we have covered with pandas is scalable; pandas can handle DataFrames with several million rows.

No matter the size of the DataFrame, another pandas function, `describe()`, can tell you more about it. To see how this works, enter the following Python code in cell J18:

```
df_desc_values=df_values.describe()
```

This function creates a new DataFrame with statistics to tell you more about the central tendency, dispersion, and shape of a dataset's distribution, excluding empty values. The type of data provided depends on the nature of the data in the DataFrame. You can also specify these parameters:

- **percentiles:** You can use this parameter to specify numbers in a list-like format to determine which percentiles to include. The default is [.25, .5, .75], which returns the 25th, 50th, and 75th percentiles.

- **include:** You can use this parameter to specify the data types you want to include. (This parameter will not affect the current example because there is only one data type.) Possible values are `'all'`, dtypes (that is, Python data types) in a list-like format, and None. None is the default. This parameter is ignored for a series. To limit the result to numeric types, set `include` to the `numpy.number` data type. To instead limit the result to object columns, set `include` to the `numpy.object` data type. You can also use strings by using `select_dtypes()`; for example, `df.describe(include=['O'])`, where `'O'` represents an object, will include strings. To select pandas categorical columns, use `'category'`. This parameter allows you to determine what Python objects to include in the `describe()` output. For example, categorical columns are used in statistics to represent gender or observation time.

- **exclude:** You can use this parameter to specify what data types to exclude. Possible values are dtypes in a list-like format and None. None is the default. This parameter is ignored for a series. To exclude numeric types, submit the data type `numpy.number`. To exclude object columns, submit the data type `numpy.object`. You can also use strings by using `select_dtypes` (for example, `df.describe(exclude=['O'])`). To exclude pandas categorical columns, use `'category'`.

Figure 3-11 shows the results when you use the default values for the parameters.

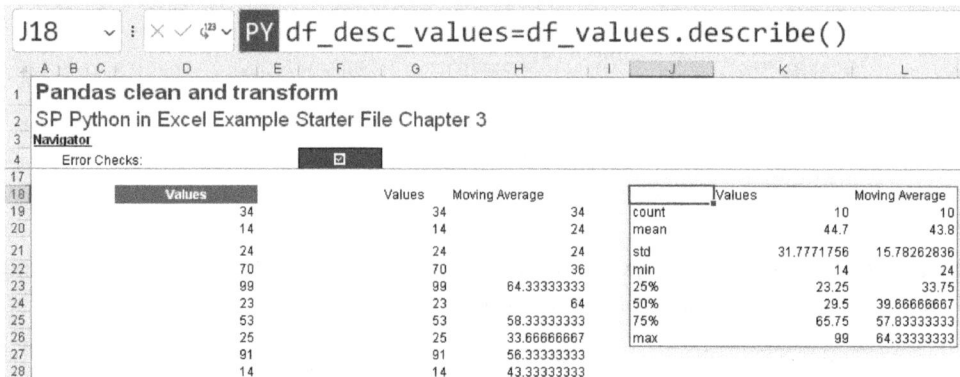

FIGURE 3-11 Using pandas to describe a DataFrame

You can change the data returned by entering a parameter. To see how this works, change the Python code in cell J18 to the following:

```
df_desc_values=df_values.describe(percentiles=[.10,.25,.40,.60,.80])
```

Here, you are specifying the percentiles to include. Figure 3-12 shows the results.

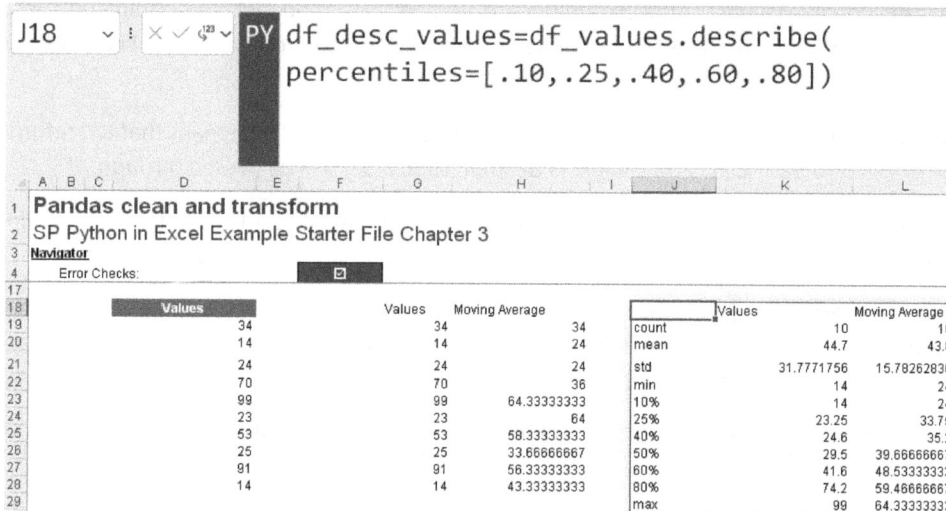

FIGURE 3-12 Specifying the `percentiles` parameter when using pandas to describe a DataFrame

Note that 50% is included in the results even though it is not specified in the code as a value for `percentiles`.

NumPy

Now let's look at the library that pandas was built on: NumPy. NumPy stands for Numerical Python, and it allows you to work with arrays, which are an important tool in mathematics. It also includes functions that work in linear algebra and matrices. Like pandas, both scikit-learn (aka sklearn) and SciPy (which we cover later in this chapter) were built on NumPy.

We used the NumPy library earlier, when we looked at examples of Python syntax to create and manipulate arrays and used the `np.array()` function to create arrays (where `np` is the alias for NumPy). The `np.array()` function has the following syntax:

```
numpy.array(object, dtype=None, *, copy=True, order='K', subok=False, ndmin=0, like=None)
```

This function accepts the following parameters:

- **object:** This parameter is defined as an array-like object. It can be an array, any object that exposes the array interface, an object whose `array` method returns an array, or any (nested) sequence. If `object` is set to a scalar, a 0-dimensional array that contains `object` is returned.

- **dtype:** This parameter is the desired data type for the array. If you do not specify a value for `dtype`, NumPy will try to use a default value for this parameter (by applying promotion rules when necessary).

- **copy (bool):** This parameter defaults to `True`, which means the array data is copied. If it is set to `None`, a copy will be made only if the array returns a copy. If this parameter is set to `False`, Python raises a `ValueError` if a copy cannot be avoided.

- **order:** Possible values for this parameter are `'K'`, `'A'`, `'C'`, and `'F'`. This parameter specifies the memory layout of the array. Its impact depends on whether copy is set to `True` or `False`. The default is `'K'`, which does not impact the order.

- **subok (bool):** The default value for this parameter is `False`, which means that the returned array will be a base-class array. If it is `True`, then subclasses will be passed through.

- **ndmin:** This parameter defaults to 0. It can also be set to an integer to specify the minimum number of dimensions in the returned array.

- **like:** This array-like parameter defaults to None. It allows the creation of arrays that are not NumPy arrays. However, we will only create NumPy arrays in the examples in this book.

> **Note** To find out more about these parameters, check out the *www.numpy.org* documentation.

Using NumPy to reshape ndarrays

In Chapter 2, you created ndarrays by passing in numeric values. Let's re-create one of the examples from that chapter, using NumPy. Open the **NumPy Arrays** sheet. In cell D10, enter the following Python code to create a simple ndarray in a columnar format:

```
num_array1 = np.array([1,2,3,4,5])
```

The resulting ndarray is a column vector.

Next, create another numeric ndarray in a row that spills from cell D17:

```
num_array2 = np.array([[1,2,3,4,5]])
```

Figure 3-13 shows the resulting row vector, along with the column vector in cell D10.

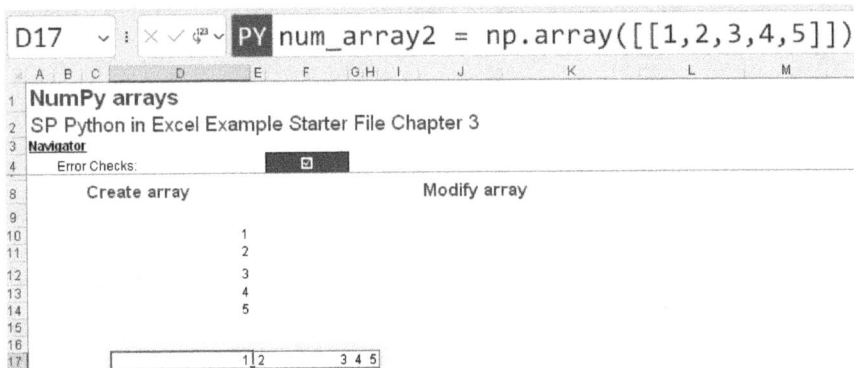

FIGURE 3-13 A numeric ndarray in row format and an ndarray that was already created in a column

Now let's use another NumPy function, `np.dot()`, to multiply the vectors. The vectors must be multiplied in the correct order. Let's start by attempting the wrong order to see the error message produced. Enter the following Python code in cell J17:

```
array_dot_result = np.dot(num_array1,num_array2)
```

You may recall that the default shape for a single-column array is one-dimensional, which caused issues. As you can see in Figure 3-14, because the arrays are not the same shape, you get the following error:

```
ValueError: shapes (5.) and (1,5) not aligned: 5 (dim 0) !- 1(dim 0)
```

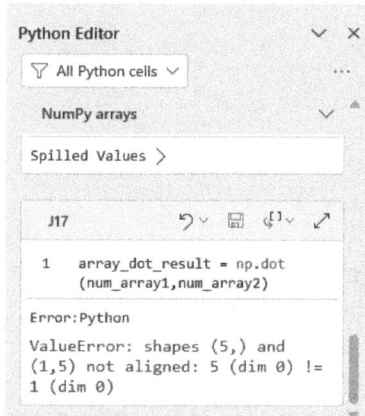

FIGURE 3-14 Arrays must be aligned to be multiplied.

As mentioned in Chapter 2, if you need to multiply the arrays in this order, you must reshape them. You can do the reshaping by using further NumPy functionality. Let's look at how to do that.

You can start by using the `shape` parameter with `np.array()` to manipulate the array `num_array1`. Enter the following Python code in cell J10:

```
num_array1.shape = (5,1)
num_array1
```

As soon as you commit this code, you see that the `#PYTHON!` error in cell J17 is fixed. Figure 3-15 shows all the ndarrays using the Excel Value view.

> **Note** The second line is included in this example to display `num_array1`; without it, you would see the Python object `None` in cell J10 because there would be no output.

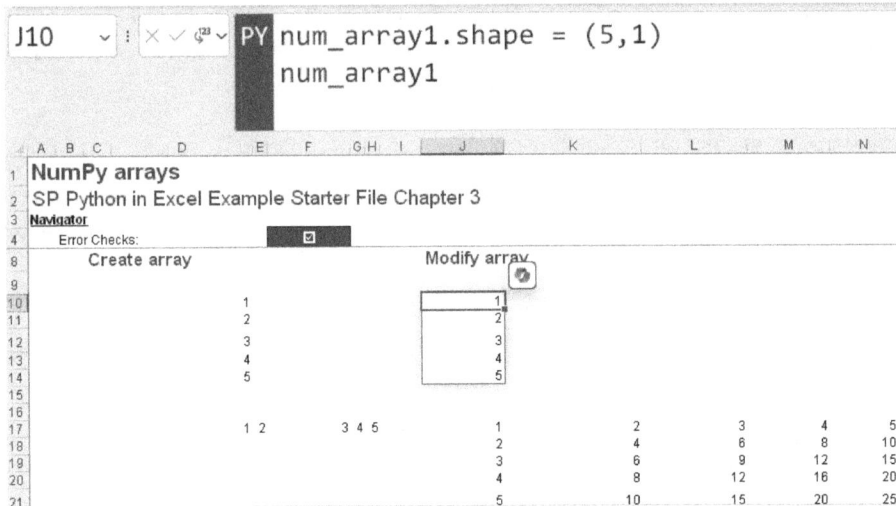

FIGURE 3-15 Using the shape() function to solve the multiplication issue

If you go back to the parameters for `np.array()`, you might think that changing the Python code in cell D10 to the following code would eliminate the need for the `shape()` function in cell J10:

```
num_array1 = np.array([1,2,3,4,5],ndmin=2)
```

However, as you can see in Figure 3-16 (where we have removed the code from cell J10 so you can see the result), this creates a horizontal array.

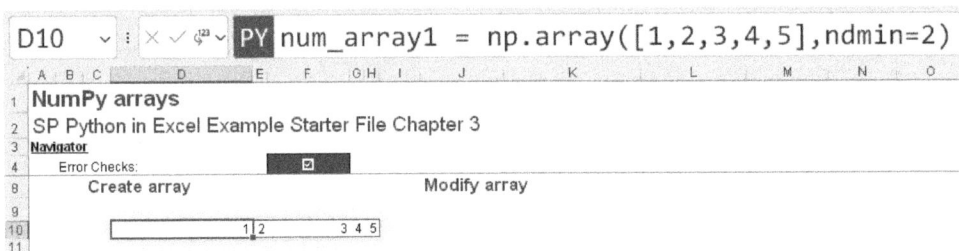

FIGURE 3-16 Using the ndmin parameter changes the direction of the ndarray.

The function algorithms have determined that this array is best represented as a horizontal array. But there are a few ways you can change the alignment. The first is to use another NumPy function, `transpose()`. To see how this works, add another line of code to cell D10:

```
num_array1 = np.array([1,2,3,4,5],ndmin=2)
num_array1 = num_array1.transpose()
```

This transposes the array, and then the multiplication works, as shown in Figure 3-17.

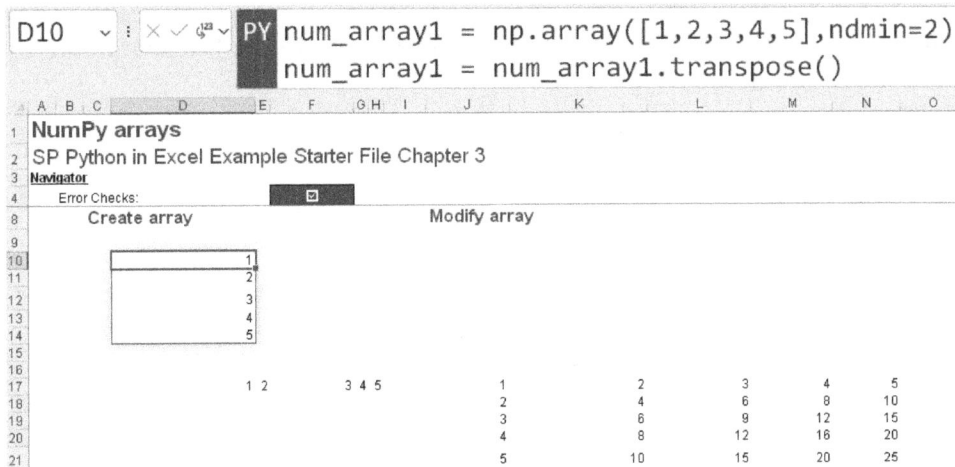

```
D10          PY  num_array1 = np.array([1,2,3,4,5],ndmin=2)
                 num_array1 = num_array1.transpose()
```

	A	B	C	D	E	F	G	H	I	J	K	L	M	N	O
1	**NumPy arrays**														
2	SP Python in Excel Example Starter File Chapter 3														
3	Navigator														
4	Error Checks:														
8	Create array						Modify array								
9															
10				1											
11				2											
12				3											
13				4											
14				5											
15															
16															
17		1 2		3 4 5				1		2	3	4	5		
18								2		4	6	8	10		
19								3		6	9	12	15		
20								4		8	12	16	20		
21								5		10	15	20	25		

FIGURE 3-17 You can use the `transpose()` function to transpose the axes of an ndarray.

Another way to reshape an array is to use the `reshape()` function. To see it in action, change the code in cell D10 to the following Python code:

```
num_array1 = np.array([1,2,3,4,5],ndmin=2)
num_array1 = np.reshape(num_array1,(5,1))
```

Many of the examples in this book rely on NumPy. As you will see, the NumPy library really shines when used with functions from the other libraries.

Now that we have looked at some ways to clean and manipulate Excel data, let's look at the pre-loaded libraries in Python in Excel that enable you to produce visualizations quickly and easily, starting with Matplotlib, which includes the preloaded module matplotlib.pyplot.

Matplotlib

As the name suggests, Matplotlib is a plotting library. It provides the plotting basis for other libraries, such as SciPy, and is used extensively in the mathematical and scientific communities. Visualizations are important tools in telling the story of data, and Matplotlib is also useful when carrying out data analysis. It allows you to create line, scatter, bar, pie, and contour charts, as well as histograms.

> **Note** At the time of writing, animations do not work in Python in Excel. Although you can use the Python code from the matplotlib.animation library module to animate visuals, the animation does not occur in Excel.

To try examples using Matplotlib, you will use a new worksheet in the same workbook you've been using, SP Python in Excel Example Starter File Chapter 3.xlsm. Open the worksheet **Matplotlib**, which contains a data range, as shown in Figure 3-18.

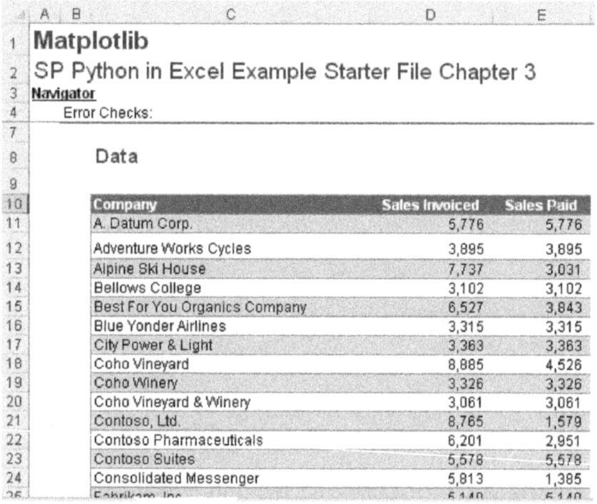
Matplotlib
SP Python in Excel Example Starter File Chapter 3
Navigator
Error Checks:
Data

Company	Sales Invoiced	Sales Paid
A. Datum Corp.	5,776	5,776
Adventure Works Cycles	3,895	3,895
Alpine Ski House	7,737	3,031
Bellows College	3,102	3,102
Best For You Organics Company	6,527	3,843
Blue Yonder Airlines	3,315	3,315
City Power & Light	3,363	3,363
Coho Vineyard	8,885	4,526
Coho Winery	3,326	3,326
Coho Vineyard & Winery	3,061	3,061
Contoso, Ltd.	8,765	1,579
Contoso Pharmaceuticals	6,201	2,951
Contoso Suites	5,578	5,578
Consolidated Messenger	5,813	1,385

FIGURE 3-18 Sample data on the Matplotlib sheet

Bar chart example

Let's start with a simple bar chart since this chart type is familiar and easy to understand. One of the strengths of Matplotlib is that it enables you to customize plots easily. You may recall that when Matplotlib is preloaded to Python in Excel, it is actually the matplotlib.pyplot module that is referenced and imported using the alias `plt`. The matplotlib.pyplot module is the plotting interface and, therefore, the only part of the Matplotlib library you need for these Matplotlib examples. Since these are the first examples where we will produce Python images, we will also explore the Python in Excel functionality available when displaying and identifying the properties of images.

The function we will use for the first example is `plt.bar()`, which has the following syntax:

```
matplotlib.pyplot.bar(x, height, width=0.8, bottom=None, *, align='center', data=None)
```

> **Note** The syntax that can be used with this function is extensive, and we have chosen not to show some of the advanced options. When you become more experienced with Python plotting or if AI uses a parameter in a way you are unfamiliar with, you can consult the *www.matplotlib.org* site for more information.

These are the parameters in this syntax:

- **x:** This parameter, which may be a float or an array-like object, is used to provide the x coordinates of the bars.

- **height:** This parameter, which may be a float or an array-like object, is used to provide the heights of the bars.

- **width:** This parameter, which may be a float or an array-like object, is used to provide the widths of the bars. The default setting is 0.8, with inches as the units because that was the printing industry standard when Matplotlib was being developed.

- **bottom:** This parameter, which may be a float or an array-like object, is used to provide the y coordinates of the bottoms of the bars. The default value is 0.

- **align:** This parameter determines the alignment of the bars relative to the x coordinates. Possible values are 'center' and 'edge', and the default is 'center'. Depending on the value, either the base of the bar is centered on the x position or the left edge of each bar is aligned with the x position. To align right, you must enter a negative width.

These are some of the other parameters you could use to customize a plot:

- **color:** This parameter can be set to a single color or a list of colors for the bar faces. There is no point in specifying both color and facecolor because facecolor will override color.

- **facecolor:** This parameter can be set to a single color or a list of colors for the bar faces.

- **edgecolor:** This parameter can be set to a single color or a list of colors for the bar edges.

- **linewidth:** This parameter, which may be a float or an array-like object, determines the width of the bar edges. If the parameter is set to 0, edges are not drawn.

- **tick_label:** This parameter is a string that can be used for the tick labels, if required.

- **label:** Usually, this parameter is a string that specifies a single label. However, it can be a list if each bar is to be labeled.

In this example, let's start with the defaults and then add some parameters to refine the chart. Enter the following Python code in cell J10:

```
df_range=xl("C10:E13", headers=True)
plt.bar(df_range['Company'],df_range['Sales Paid'])
```

This creates a Python object called an image. Figure 3-19 shows the data type card for the Python object in cell J10.

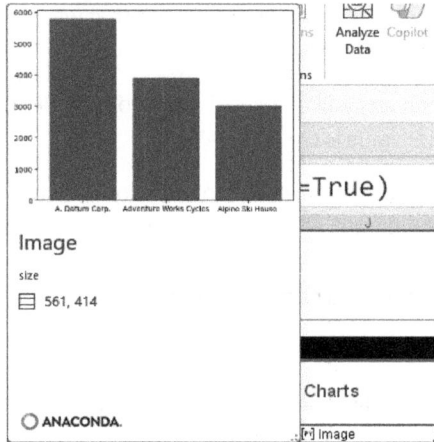

FIGURE 3-19 Viewing the data type card for a Python image

If you change the view for cell J10 to Excel Value, you see the bar plot—but in only one cell (see Figure 3-20).

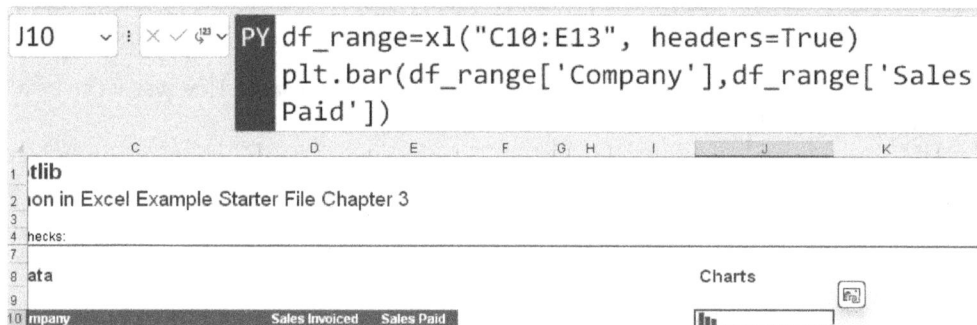

FIGURE 3-20 If you view the Python image as an Excel Value, Python in Excel creates a chart in a single cell.

One solution would be to merge cells to enlarge the image. However, there is another way to view the bar plot, and it can be accessed from several different paths. One way is to remain in the Excel Value view and right-click the image. The context menu shown in Figure 3-21 appears.

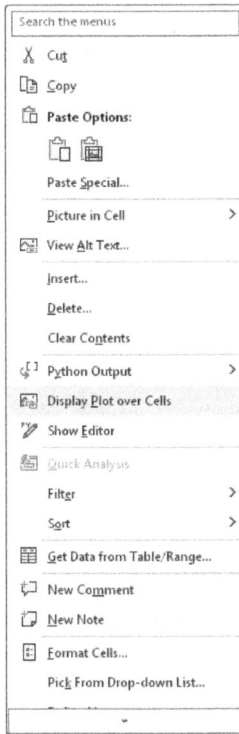

FIGURE 3-21 Right-clicking the image while in the Excel Value view reveals the option Display Plot over Cells.

Select the option **Display Plot over Cells** to create a floating image object that you can select, drag into a new position in the worksheet, and resize by dragging the nodes (see Figure 3-22).

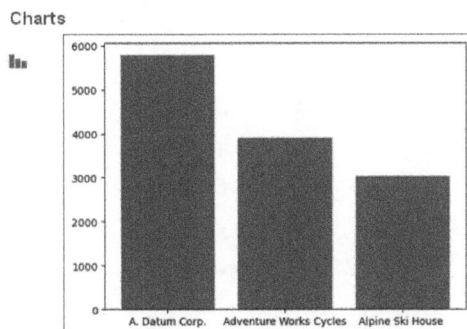

FIGURE 3-22 The Display Plot over Cells option provides a picture of a bar chart that can be dragged and resized.

Another way to access this floating image is to remain in the Excel Value view, right-click the image, and select the **Picture in Cell** option from the context menu. Then select **Create Reference** from this expanded menu (see Figure 3-23).

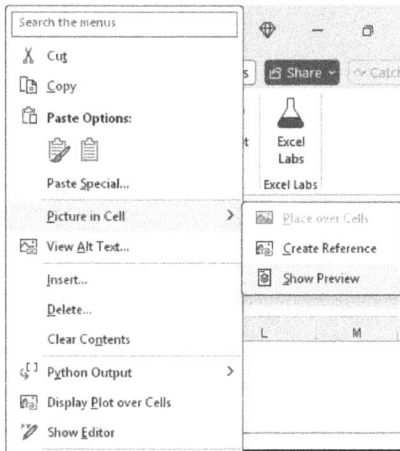

FIGURE 3-23 Right-clicking the image while in the Excel Value view and selecting **Picture in Cell** > **Create Reference** is another way to access the floating image.

Rather than inserting a floating image in the workbook, you can use the Show Preview option to view what the chart would look like (see Figure 3-24). You can enlarge this preview of the image by clicking and dragging the bottom-right corner.

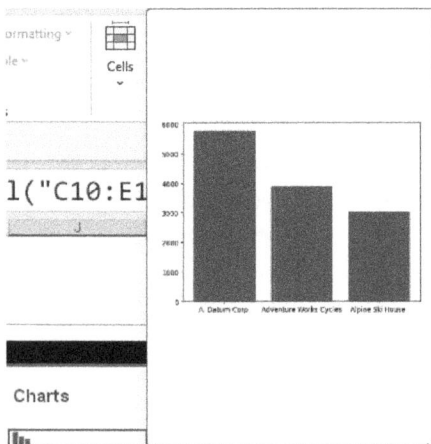

FIGURE 3-24 Show Preview allows you to view what the bar chart looks like without importing it into the worksheet.

Perhaps the easiest way to insert the floating image in the workbook is to click the icon next to the cell containing the Python image displayed as an Excel value (see Figure 3-25).

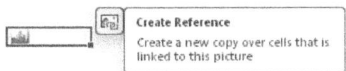

Create Reference
Create a new copy over cells that is linked to this picture

FIGURE 3-25 The Create Reference icon appears near the cell that contains the Python image.

Now that you know how to view the chart in the workbook, you can add some parameters to the `bar()` function to customize the bar chart. Change the Python code in cell J10 to the following:

```
df_range=xl("C10:E13", headers=True)
plt.bar(df_range['Company'],df_range['Sales Paid'],color="red",tick_label =["1","2","3"])
```

This code changes the bar chart so it has red bars with new labels across the bottom (see Figure 3-26).

> **Note** If you're reading the print version of this book, you won't see colors in our figures, but if you are following along with the examples on your computer, you will see the colors mentioned here. As a bonus, working through all the examples will help you learn this material more quickly.

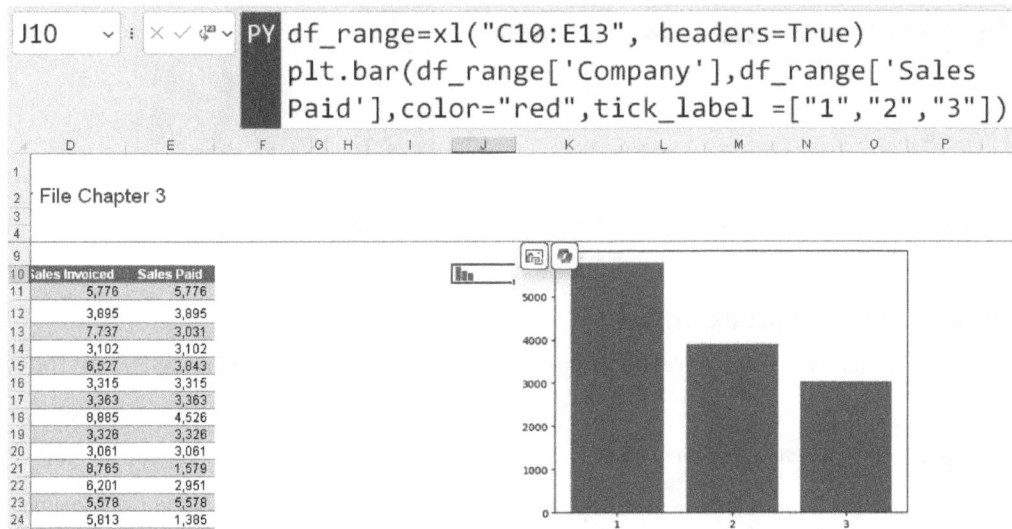

FIGURE 3-26 You can add parameters to change the format of the bar chart.

You could add other labels. Because adding labels is common to many types of plots—and not just bar plots—the functionality is separate from the `bar()` function. To see this in action, add some more lines to the Python code in cell J10:

```
df_range=xl("C10:E13", headers=True)
plt.bar(df_range['Company'],df_range['Sales Paid'],color="red",tick_label =["1","2","3"])
plt.xlabel('Company')
plt.ylabel('Sales Paid')
plt.title('My Python Bar Plot ')
```

By adding these lines, you have specified labels for the x axis and the y axis, and you have given the chart a title. Figure 3-27 shows the results.

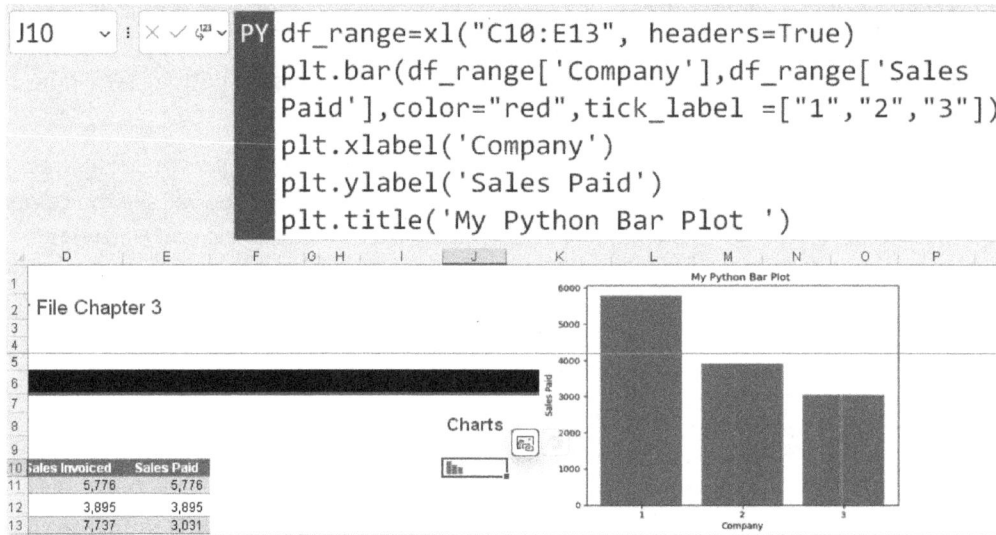

FIGURE 3-27 You can use other Matplotlib functions to create labels and titles for many chart types.

Box and whisker plot example

Now, let's look at an example of creating a box and whisker plot. Enter the following Python code in cell J23:

```
plt.boxplot(xl("D10:E50", headers=True))
```

You can display the floating image for this plot by clicking the icon next to the cell in the Excel Value view (see Figure 3-28).

```
PY  plt.boxplot(xl("D10:E50", headers=True))
```

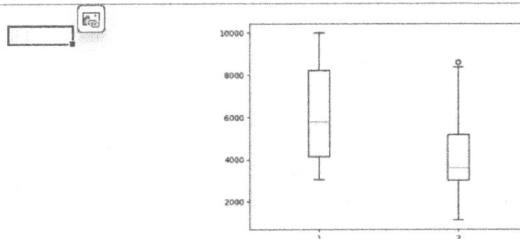

FIGURE 3-28 You can also use Matplotlib to create a box and whisker plot.

We won't review all the parameters for each chart, but let's look at some of them for this example. Change the Python code in cell J23 to the following:

plt.boxplot(xl("D10:E50", headers=True),vert=False,patch_artist=True)

This changes the plot's orientation and adds more color, as shown in Figure 3-29.

```
PY  plt.boxplot(xl("D10:E50", headers=True),
    vert=False,patch_artist=True)
```

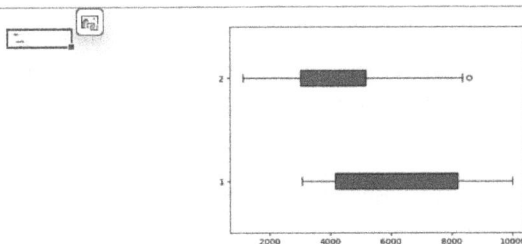

FIGURE 3-29 You can use parameters to change the presentation of a box and whisker plot.

Violin chart example

You may be thinking that you can create bar charts and box and whisker plots in Excel, so why do you need Python in Excel? To see how Python in Excel can take you beyond what Excel offers, let's create a violin chart. A violin chart is based on a box and whisker plot but shows peaks in the data and can be used to visualize the distribution of numeric data.

Enter the following Python code in cell J36:

```
plt.violinplot(xl("D10:E50", headers=True),vert=False)
```

The `vert` parameter you used when manipulating the box and whisker chart can also be used here. Figure 3-30 shows the results in the cell and the floating image.

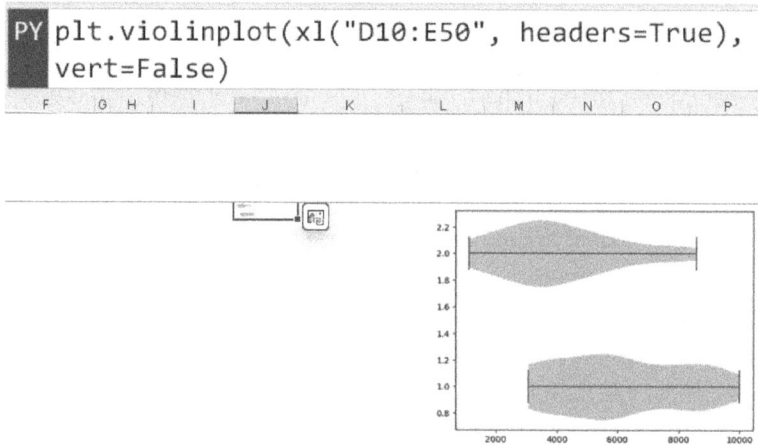

FIGURE 3-30 You can use Matplotlib to easily create a violin chart.

When creating a violin chart, there is no parameter to use different colors, but you can change the colors after the chart has been created. To see how this works, change the Python code in cell J36 to the following:

```
violin_plot=plt.violinplot(xl("D10:E50", headers=True),vert=False)
for pc in violin_plot['bodies']:
    pc.set_facecolor('red')
    pc.set_edgecolor('black')
```

Figure 3-31 shows the results.

```
violin_plot=plt.violinplot(xl("D10:E50",
headers=True),vert=False)
for pc in violin_plot['bodies']:
    pc.set_facecolor('red')
    pc.set_edgecolor('black')
```

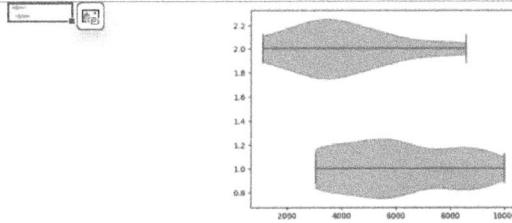

FIGURE 3-31 Changing the colors on a violin chart

> **Note** For more information on customizing violin charts, see the documentation and examples at *www.matplotlib.org*.

You have learned the basics of creating Python plots and manipulating them in Python in Excel. As mentioned earlier, Matplotlib contains functions used by other, more specialized plotting libraries. In particular, the seaborn library builds on the matplotlib.pyplot module to give you access to more complex and varied visualizations.

seaborn

seaborn, which is based on Matplotlib, enables you to create visualizations of statistical data. It integrates well with pandas data structures, making it ideal for Python in Excel, which is why it is preloaded in Python in Excel.

To try examples using seaborn, you will use a new worksheet in the same workbook you've been using, SP Python in Excel Example Starter File Chapter 3.xlsm. Use the worksheet **Seaborn** for these examples.

> **Note** Because the Seaborn worksheet comes after the Matplotlib sheet in the workbook, you can use the DataFrames defined on the Matplotlib sheet when working with seaborn.

We introduced Matplotlib with a bar chart, so let's also start our look at seaborn with a bar chart. Enter the following Python code in cell C10:

```
sns.barplot(df_range,x="Company", y="Sales Invoiced")
```

In the Excel Value view, click the **Create Reference** icon to create a floating image (see Figure 3-32).

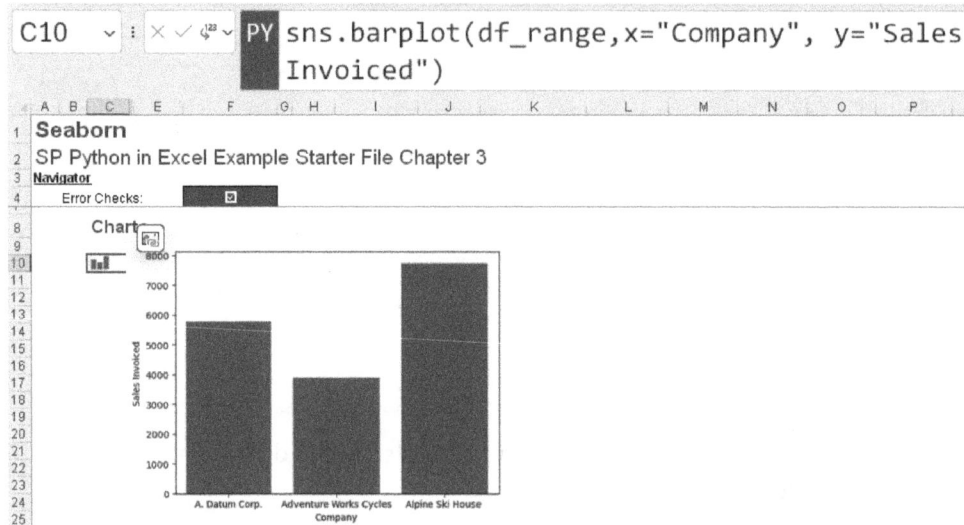

FIGURE 3-32 Using the Python seaborn library to create a bar chart

The main difference between the seaborn bar chart you just created and the Matplotlib bar chart you created in the previous section is that the x and y axes now have labels. The syntax is also different because with seaborn, you must specify the x and y axes rather than just entering the column names.

This is the complete syntax for `sns.barplot()`:

```
seaborn.barplot(data=None, *, x=None, y=None, hue=None, order=None, hue_order=None,
estimator='mean', errorbar=('ci', 95), n_boot=1000, seed=None, units=None, weights=None,
orient=None, color=None, palette=None, saturation=0.75, fill=True, hue_norm=None, width=0.8,
dodge='auto', gap=0, log_scale=None, native_scale=False, formatter=None, legend='auto',
capsize=0, err_kws=None, ci=<deprecated>, errcolor=<deprecated>, errwidth=<deprecated>,
ax=None, **kwargs)
```

Don't let the number of parameters scare you. You won't usually need them all, but they're available to give you many options when you want to customize a plot. Let's look at a selection of the parameters you're most likely to use:

- **data:** This parameter specifies the data source, which may be a DataFrame, series, dict, array, or list of arrays. If you do not specify x and y (see the next parameters), the data is interpreted as wide form—like an Excel PivotTable—which is suitable for simple datasets. For example, for time-series data, there would be a column for each month and a row for each year, and each value would appear in the appropriate position in the grid. Otherwise, the data is expected to be long form, as in this example. In long form, the time-series data would be arranged in columns for year, month, and value. If you chose not to specify x and y in this example, there would be two bars for the numeric data and lines to show the distribution.

■ **x, y, and hue:** These parameters are the inputs for plotting long-form data and come from the data. In this example, x is Company, and y is Sales Invoiced. hue indicates how the color should be applied. If you added hue="Company" to your example, the bars would be different colors.

■ **order and hue_order:** These parameters are lists of strings that determine the order in which to plot the categorical levels; if these parameters are not set, the levels are inferred from the data objects.

■ **estimator:** This parameter can be a string or a callable function that maps a vector to a scalar. It is a statistical function for estimating within each categorical bin.

■ **errorbar:** barplot() places error bars on the chart by default. The errorbar parameter is used when creating an error bar, and it can be set to a string or a (*string, number*) tuple, or it can be set to callable (which includes functions) or None. It represents the errorbar method. As a string, it can be 'ci', 'pi', 'se', or 'sd'. These values represent the statistical approaches' confidence interval, percentile interval, standard error, and standard deviation, respectively. If errorbar is set to a tuple, it has a method name and a level parameter. If it is set to a function, it maps from a vector to a (*min, max*) interval. If it is set to None, the error bar is hidden.

■ **n_boot:** This parameter specifies the number of bootstrap samples used to compute confidence intervals. Bootstrapping is useful with atypical data or small datasets.

■ **seed:** This parameter is an integer that may be created by numpy.random.Generator or numpy.random.RandomState. It is the seed or random number generator for reproducible bootstrapping.

■ **units:** This parameter, which is used by the errorbar() function, identifies the sampling units.

■ **weights:** This parameter computes weighted statistics. Its use may limit other statistical options.

■ **orient:** This parameter specifies the plot's orientation (vertical or horizontal). Values may be 'v' | 'h' or 'x' | 'y'. The values are usually inferred based on the type of the input variables, but you can set this parameter intentionally to resolve ambiguity when both x and y are numeric or when plotting wide-form data.

■ **color:** This parameter, which can be set to any Matplotlib color, specifies a single color to use for the elements in the plot.

■ **palette:** This parameter can be a palette name, a list, or a dict. It indicates the colors to use for the different levels of the hue variable. It should be something that can be interpreted by color_palette() or a dictionary that maps hue levels to Matplotlib colors.

■ **saturation:** This float indicates the proportion of the original saturation to use for fill colors. Large patches often look better with desaturated colors, but you should set this parameter to 1 if you want the colors to perfectly match the input values.

- **fill:** This parameter is a Boolean. If it is set to `True`, a solid patch will be used. If it is set to `False`, the line art will have no fill.

- **hue_norm:** This parameter can be a tuple or a `matplotlib.colors.Normalize` object. The setting indicates the normalization in data units for the colormap applied to the hue variable when it is numeric. It has no effect if hue is categorical.

- **width:** This parameter is a float that indicates the width allotted to each element on the orient axis (the axis at the base of the bars). When `native_scale=True`, the width is relative to the minimum distance between two values in the native scale.

- **dodge:** This parameter can be set to `'auto'` or a Boolean. When hue mapping is used, dodge indicates whether elements should be narrowed and shifted along the orient axis (the axis at the base of the bars) to eliminate overlap.

- **gap:** This parameter is a float that indicates the amount of shrinkage that will occur on the orient axis (the axis at the base of the bars) to add a gap between dodged elements.

- **log_scale:** This parameter may be a Boolean, a number, or a pair of Booleans or numbers. If you are working with a large range of values in the dataset, you may find that the smaller values are hard to distinguish on a standard linear scale. You can use this parameter to apply a logarithmic scale to the axes. When this parameter is set to `None` or `False`, seaborn defers to the existing axis scale.

- **native_scale:** By default, the `barplot()` function assumes that one of the axes is categorical. In this example, there is a bar for each company. If you use numeric or datetime data for the categorical grouping but need to preserve the underlying data properties, you can use `native_scale`. This parameter is a Boolean. When set to `True`, numeric or datetime values on the categorical axis will maintain their original scaling rather than being converted to fixed indices on the axis. For example, if the value is 2.4 and the index on the axis is 2, the data will not be changed to convert the value to 2 if `native_scale` is `True`.

- **formatter:** This parameter is a callable function for converting categorical data into strings. It affects both grouping and tick labels.

- **legend:** This parameter indicates how to draw the legend, and it can be set to `'auto'`, `'brief'`, `'full'`, or `False`. If `'brief'`, numeric hue and size variables will be represented with a sample of evenly spaced values. If it is set to `'full'`, every group will get an entry in the legend. If it is set to `'auto'`, you must choose between brief or full representation, based on the number of levels. If it is set to `False`, no legend data is added, and no legend is drawn.

- **capsize:** This parameter is a float that indicates the width of the caps on error bars (that is, the lines perpendicular to the ends of the error bars), relative to bar spacing.

To try some of these parameters, change the Python code in cell C10 to the following:

```
sns.barplot(df_range,x="Company", y="Sales Invoiced", hue="Company",legend="full",fill=False)
```

This changes the plot to use different colors for the companies and show a full legend. Setting `fill` to `False` causes only the outlines of the bars to appear (see Figure 3-33).

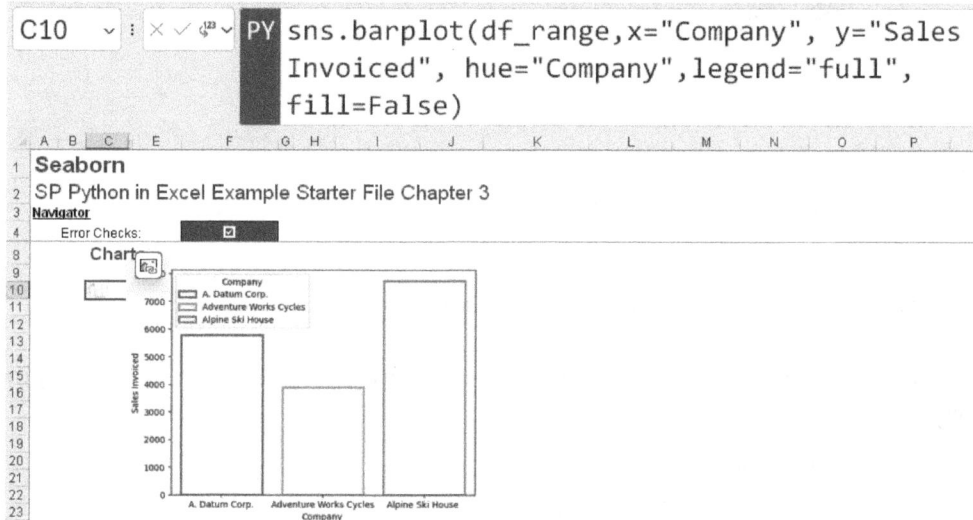

FIGURE 3-33 Adjusting the parameters in the seaborn bar chart can have a visual impact.

You can also use some of the Matplotlib functions to add details to the plot, such as a title. To do so, add a second line to the Python code in cell C10:

```
sns.barplot(df_range,x="Company", y="Sales Invoiced", hue="Company",legend="full",fill=False)
plt.title("Seaborn and Matplotlib Together")
```

You may recall using the `plt.title()` function in the Matplotlib examples. You can also use it to add a title to plots created using other libraries, as shown in Figure 3-34.

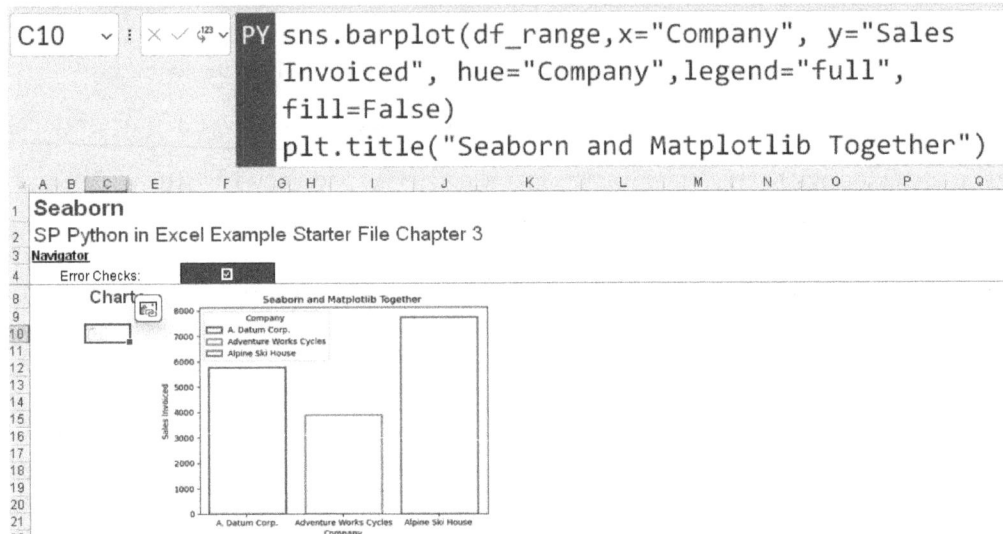

FIGURE 3-34 You can use Matplotlib functions to manipulate a chart created in seaborn.

You can create many more types of plots with seaborn, in a variety of categories, including the following:

- Relational charts, such as scatter plots

- Distribution charts, such as histograms

- Categorical charts, such as the bar chart you just created

- Regression charts, such as linear regression charts

- Multi-plot grids, such as for small multiples

We will explore more charts as we encounter them in examples throughout this book.

statsmodels

The statsmodels library is preloaded into Python in Excel to enable you to access statistical computations and models. It complements SciPy, which is one of the libraries recommended by Microsoft for use with Python in Excel. You'll learn about Microsoft-recommended libraries in the next section, but first, let's look at what statsmodels can do.

The statsmodels library includes the following functionality:

- It provides extensive support for regression analysis, including ordinary least squares (OLS), weighted least squares (WLS), and generalized least squares (GLS).

- It provides autoregressive (AR) models, moving average (MA) models, autoregressive integrated moving average (ARIMA) models, and other models that allow you to study temporal data.

- Its hypothesis-testing tools include t-tests, chi-square tests, and goodness-of-fit tests.

- It accommodates non-normal distributions of data.

- It allows you to use error estimation techniques.

- It gives you access to residual plots and influence diagnostics for regression models.

You are unlikely to use statsmodels alone. You may also need to perform another import to get the API module, which provides classes and functions for creating various statistical models. The command to import the API module is `import statsmodels.api`.

Let's look at an example that involves generating data and performing an OLS regression. (This example is based on an example available in the statsmodels documentation pages, at *https://www.statsmodels.org/stable/index.html*.)

To try examples using statsmodels, you will use a new worksheet in the same workbook you've been using, SP Python in Excel Example Starter File Chapter 3.xlsm. Use the worksheet **Statsmodels** for this example. Enter the following Python code in cell C10 on the Statsmodels worksheet:

```
import statsmodels.api as sm
ncount = 100
X = np.random.random((ncount, 2))
X = sm.tools.tools.add_constant(X)
beta = [1, .1, .5]
e = np.random.random(ncount)
y = np.dot(X, beta) + e
result=sm.OLS(y, X).fit()
```

Figure 3-35 shows the results. The code creates a new Python object that cannot be displayed as an Excel value.

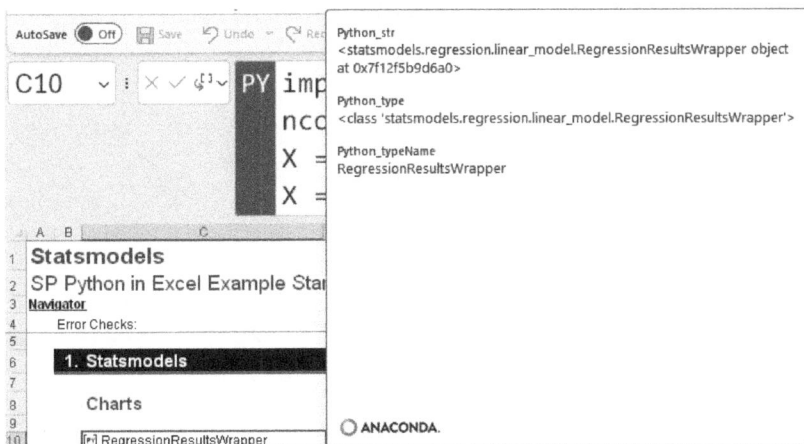

FIGURE 3-35 The results from the OLS regression are stored in a Python object of type RegressionResultsWrapper.

To display the results, you must concatenate the results into an ndarray, so add another line of Python code to cell C10:

```
import statsmodels.api as sm
ncount = 100
X = np.random.random((ncount, 2))
X = sm.tools.tools.add_constant(X)
beta = [1, .1, .5]
e = np.random.random(ncount)
y = np.dot(X, beta) + e
result=sm.OLS(y, X).fit()
df_result = np.concatenate((result.params, result.tvalues))
```

Now you should have an ndarray, for which you can display the Excel value (see Figure 3-36).

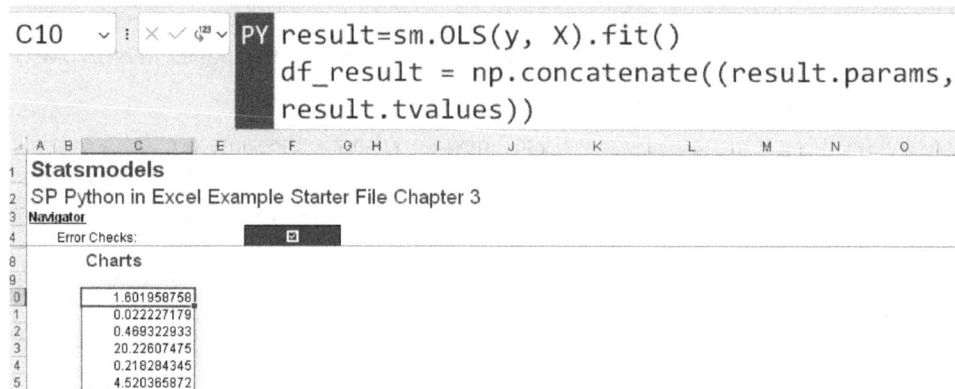

FIGURE 3-36 The results from the OLS regression can be extracted to an ndarray.

> **Note** If you are not familiar with OLS regression, you may not be following the statistical calculations shown here. Don't worry: The point of this example is to demonstrate how the libraries work together to produce results you can export to Excel.

Microsoft-recommended Python libraries

This section summarizes all the libraries that Microsoft recommends for Python in Excel at the time of writing (see Table 3-1). This list will grow as the Excel community adopts Python in Excel.

> **Note** Most libraries can be imported using the standard Python `import` statement, which has the following syntax:
>
> ```
> import library_full_name as library_alias
> ```
>
> There are exceptions, however. For example, to import the beautifulsoup4 library, you enter the following Python code:
>
> ```
> from bs4 import beautifulsoup
> ```
>
> If the standard `import` statement does not import a library, check out the documentation for that library to find the recommended `import` statement.

TABLE 3-1 Microsoft-recommended libraries[2]

Library	Description	Functionality
Astropy	The Astropy package provides functionality and common tools for performing astronomy and astrophysics with Python. Astropy allows you to analyze and visualize astronomical data. To use Astropy, you need some knowledge of astronomy.	■ Flexible coordinate systems ■ Time handling ■ Data manipulation ■ Support for physical units and quantities ■ Spectral analysis ■ Visualization and integration with Matplotlib to produce high-quality plots, including sky maps and spectral graphs ■ Astrometric calculations
beautifulSoup4	Not all websites provide links to download useful information. This library helps in scraping webpages. You can use it to remove HTML markup and efficiently save data from the web.	■ Efficient parsing and support for HTML and XML ■ Flexible searching and use of attributes, CSS selectors, tags, and regular expressions ■ Easy navigation throughout the parse tree (parent, sibling, descendant) ■ Content manipulation, such as modification of various elements ■ Encoding support
Faker	This library can be useful for testing code, since it can produce lots of realistic fake data, such as names, addresses, phone numbers, and dates. Faker can waste processing time if it regenerates every time you update a Python cell. You can avoid this by specifying `Faker.seed`.	■ Customization to meet particular data requirements ■ Diverse array of data types ■ Reproducibility, so that if you use the same random generator seed, you will receive the same results ■ Support for multiple locales, languages, and regions ■ Privacy protection, since real data is replaced with fake data for testing and development

continues

---

[2] "Open-Source Libraries and Python in Excel," Microsoft, accessed June 24, 2025, *https://support.microsoft.com/en-gb /office/open-source-libraries-and-python-in-excel-c817c897-41db-40a1-b9f3-d5ffe6d1bf3e#:~:text=How%20to%20import %20libraries,assigns%20it%20the%20alias%20np.*

Library	Description	Functionality
imbalanced-learn	This library uses scikit-learn, and like scikit-learn, it is used for machine learning. Its purpose is to ensure that datasets that are highly skewed toward some classes are rebalanced, ensuring more even sampling. It could be used, for example, in fraud detection datasets, where suspicious transactions might represent only a small fraction of the total data.	■ Resampling techniques ■ Class-balancing algorithms ■ Integration with scikit-learn's pipelines, which allows you to resample into machine learning workflows
IPython	IPython (short for "Interactive Python") is a system for interactively running Python. Although it is not listed as one of the preloaded libraries for Python in Excel, it is already an integral part of the way Python in Excel works.	■ Ability to show the results of Python code in a cell without using the Python `print()` function ■ Ability to view charts without the `plt.show()` function
Matplotlib	matplotlib.pyplot, as you have already seen, is preloaded into Python in Excel and is the main plotting tool. Many other packages are based on Matplotlib, such as seaborn. Keep in mind that animation is not currently supported in Python in Excel.	■ High-quality plots ■ Customization of most elements ■ Integration with other Python libraries, such as NumPy and pandas
mlxtend	The name mlxtend comes from "machine learning extensions," and this library is intended to provide useful tools for data science.	■ Data preprocessing ■ Visualizations (with Matplotlib) ■ Model evaluation ■ Ensemble methods ■ Feature selection algorithms ■ Association rule mining (to identify patterns in large datasets)
NetworkX	NetworkX allows you to create and manipulate complex networks. It supports various graphs and charts, including undirected graphs, directed graphs, and multigraphs. Graphs in this context represent multiple nodes/vertices and connections/edges.	■ Graph creation, using either automatic or manual methods ■ Graph manipulation ■ Algorithms for shortest-path computation, centrality measures, connectivity testing, and community detection ■ Integration with Matplotlib and other visualization libraries ■ Ability to store data in graphs using Python dictionaries (as discussed in Chapter 2) ■ Integration with pandas and NumPy
NLTK	NLTK stands for "Natural Language Toolkit," and this library is used for natural language processing. At the time of writing, the following corpora are preloaded for use with Python in Excel: brown, punkt, stopwords, treebank, vader, and wordnet2022.	■ Tokenization (splitting up text, such as into words or sentences) ■ Text classification (for example, spam) ■ Part-of-speech tagging ■ Identification of proper nouns ■ Parsing ■ Stemming ■ Availability of a corpus or canon of texts ■ Wordnet interface that makes it possible to perform semantic analysis with synonyms, antonyms, and hypernyms
NumPy	NumPy, as you already know, is useful for performing mathematical and logical operations and is preloaded into Python in Excel.	■ ndarrays that are optimized for performance and manipulation ■ Broadcasting, which allows operations to be performed on arrays of differing dimensions that don't have to be resized first ■ Integration with SciPy and scikit-learn

continues

Library	Description	Functionality
pandas	As you have seen, pandas is key to Python in Excel, reading Excel data in DataFrames.	■ Operation with series (one-dimensional data) and DataFrames (two-dimensional data, similar to tables) ■ Data manipulation tools for slicing, indexing, merging, reshaping, and aggregating data ■ Data cleaning functions for handling missing values, filtering, and transforming data ■ Advanced functionality for working with time-based data ■ Integration with Matplotlib and NumPy
Pillow	Pillow supports image formats such as JPEG and PNG and makes it possible to open, read, edit, manipulate, and save images.	■ Image opening and saving in formats such as JPEG, PNG, GIF, BMP, TIFF, and WebP ■ Image transformations, such as cropping, resizing, rotating, and flipping images ■ Image enhancement, such as filters and functions for altering brightness, contrast, sharpness, and color balance ■ Drawing tools ■ Image analysis ■ Images with transparency layers
plotnine	plotnine is a data visualization and plotting library for describing and building graphs with layered visuals.	■ Graphics framework grammar that makes it possible to build plots in a systematic way, defining aesthetics, geometries, scales, and themes ■ Flexibility to create scatter plots, line charts, bar graphs, histograms, and more by constructing layers sequentially ■ Integration with pandas DataFrames (and, therefore, Excel data) ■ Customization of labels, themes, and annotations ■ Faceting, which makes it possible to create subplots for data grouped by categories
Prince	Prince builds on functionality in the pandas, Matplotlib, and scikit-learn libraries and is designed for multivariate exploratory data analysis. Some of the methods included for summarizing tabular data include principal component analysis (PCA), correspondence analysis (CA), multiple correspondence analysis (MCA), and discriminant correspondence analysis (DCA), which are extremely useful for analyzing complex datasets, detecting patterns, and simplifying data in preparation for predictive modeling.	■ PCA to reduce the dimensionality of numeric datasets while preserving variability ■ MCA for categorical data, which allows datasets to be simplified using multiple variables ■ CA for summarizing relationships between rows and columns of categorical datasets in contingency tables ■ DCA, which is a combination of CA and discriminant analysis for classifying observations
PyTables	PyTables is designed to help you browse, process, and search large amounts of data. Memory is optimized using efficient compression and disk resources.	■ Hierarchical structure ■ Support for large datasets ■ Optimization for speed, especially for reading and writing operations ■ Efficient querying of datasets, using index-based search mechanisms ■ Use of multiple compression algorithms to reduce storage space while maintaining data integrity ■ Integration with NumPy, enabling processing of ndarrays and advanced numeric computations ■ Customization of data models

continues

Library	Description	Functionality
PyWavelets	Wavelets are mathematical basis functions localized in time and frequency. They can be used to analyze data that is not stationary, where the patterns are not consistent over time. PyWavelets allows you to perform wavelet analysis, which in turn allows you to analyze signals and images. Wavelet transforms enable you to decompose or reconstruct signals of interest. PyWavelets can be used in financial analysis, where understanding frequency composition and time localization is important.	■ Support for multiple wavelet families ■ Hierarchical signal analysis ■ Analysis of signals for continuous frequency bands ■ Image processing tasks, including denoising and compression ■ Integration with NumPy
qrcode	qrcode generates quick response (QR) code images.	■ Customized QR code generation ■ Support for error correction, allowing QR codes to be read if damaged or obscured
scikit-learn	scikit-learn (commonly known as sklearn) is designed to facilitate machine learning. It provides solutions for classification, regression, clustering, dimensionality reduction, model selection, and preprocessing. It is a specialized tool that uses modules from NumPy, SciPy, and Matplotlib. You can use it to create machine learning algorithms and solve data analysis tasks.	■ Identification of categories within datasets (such as for spam detection) ■ Prediction of values within a continuous range (for example, house price predictions) ■ Grouping of similar data points (clustering) ■ Transformation of data into information with tools such as normalization and scaling ■ Cross-validation and hyperparameter tuning
SciPy	SciPy provides algorithms for optimization, integration, interpolation, eigenvalue problems, algebraic equations, differential equations, and statistics, and is intended for use with scientific data. It is based on NumPy, with tools for array computing. It allows data structures to be designed for this purpose.	■ Solving problems, including linear and nonlinear programming ■ Numeric integration, including quadrature and ordinary differential equations solvers ■ Linear algebra advanced routines for matrix operations, eigenvalue computations, and decompositions ■ Statistical distributions, tests, and random number generation ■ Fourier transforms, filtering, and convolution ■ Image manipulation, including resizing and filtering
seaborn	seaborn, as you already know, is based on Matplotlib and provides visualizations of statistical data. It integrates well with pandas data structures, making it ideal for Python in Excel, which is why it is preloaded.	■ Built-in functions to visualize distributions and relationships within data ■ Predefined themes, including darkgrid, whitegrid, and ticks ■ Creation of complex grids to visualize subsets of data ■ Automatic estimation and aggregation functions ■ Wide range of color palettes for categorical and continuous data
snowballstemmer	snowballstemmer is an algorithm library that is useful for *stemming*, which is the process of reducing a word to its base or root form (stem) for use in search engines and information retrieval.	■ Multilanguage support, including English, German, French, Dutch, Italian, Spanish, Russian, Danish, Norwegian, Portuguese, Swedish, and Finnish ■ Well-defined rules for each language that yield consistent stemming results ■ Speed optimization, making it efficient for handling large datasets

continues

Library	Description	Functionality
squarify	The squarify library is used to generate treemaps, which make it possible to visualize hierarchical data using nested rectangles, where the size of a rectangle corresponds to the value associated with that data point.	■ squarified algorithm, which ensures that rectangles have aspect ratios close to those of a square, improving readability and presentation ■ Customization of colors, labels, and sizes ■ Integration with Matplotlib, which facilitates creating treemaps and adding them to visualization projects
statsmodels	As you have already seen, statsmodels is preloaded into Python in Excel and allows access to statistical computations and models. It complements SciPy, another of the recommended libraries in this table.	■ Extensive support for regression analysis, including ordinary least squares (OLS), weighted least squares (WLS), and generalized least squares (GLS) ■ Autoregressive (AR) models, moving average (MA) models, and ARIMA models, among others, to study temporal data ■ Hypothesis-testing tools, including t-tests, chi-square tests, and goodness-of-fit tests ■ Accommodation of non-normal distributions of data ■ Error estimation techniques ■ Ability to create new models ■ Residual plots and influence diagnostics for regression models
SymPy	SymPy is designed to allow the use of symbolic mathematics with Python. It provides symbolic computations rather than numeric approximations, allowing you to work with exact mathematical results. Symbolic calculations are inherently more computationally intensive than numeric ones, and SymPy can be slower than NumPy or SciPy for large-scale computations.	■ Definition of symbols and manipulation of algebraic expressions ■ Operations such as differentiation, integration, and limits ■ Symbolic solutions to algebraic and differential equations ■ Matrix algebra, eigenvalues, and other related computations ■ Combinatorics and number theory ■ Built-in visualization capabilities for mathematical expressions and graphs ■ Builds on functionality from Matplotlib
tabulate	tabulate is designed to enable you to produce data tables that are well structured and easy to read. It supports many Python data types, including NumPy arrays and pandas DataFrames.	■ Customization of table styles, alignment, and formatting ■ Predefined formats to allow quick generation of tables for specific use cases ■ Integration with pandas and other data analysis libraries
TheFuzz	TheFuzz, as the name suggests, uses fuzzy matching for text matching, deduplication, and fuzzy searching. Be careful when using this library because incorrect configuration can result in false positives, and TheFuzz may perform poorly when text strings lack meaningful or consistent structure.	■ Calculation of the Levenshtein distance between strings (the number of changes to convert one string into another) ■ Ability to search for terms within larger text bodies ■ Token-based similarity matching (in which strings are tokenized, sorted, and then compared) ■ Customized scoring mechanisms ■ Integration with pandas for handling large datasets, enabling efficient processing of column-wise string comparisons
wordcloud	Word clouds are popular text visualization tools in which the sizes of words are based on their frequency of use. The wordcloud library helps you create word clouds easily and customize them to your requirements.	■ Customization of fonts, colors, shapes, and sizes ■ Integration with Matplotlib and pandas, which makes it possible to create word clouds directly from DataFrames ■ Creation of word clouds in specific shapes, such as logos or icons, using image masks

Licensing of recommended Python libraries

Six different licenses apply to the recommended Python libraries (see Table 3-2). They are all free to use, and the restrictions mainly apply to library amendments and redistribution.

TABLE 3-2 Python library licenses

Library license	Description	For more information
Apache License, Version 2.0	NLTK is licensed under the Apache License, Version 2.0, which is a permissive open-source license. Key attributes of this license include the following: ■ It allows free use, modification, and distribution of the software. ■ Users can integrate NLTK into proprietary products without opening their source code. ■ It provides strong protection against patent claims. Use or redistribution of the library requires proper attribution to the original authors.	*https://www.apache.org/licenses/LICENSE-2.0*
2-Clause BSD License	snowballstemmer is licensed under the 2-Clause BSD License. This license allows users to use, modify, and redistribute the software without significant restrictions. You are allowed to use the library for commercial and academic projects. If you redistribute versions of the library, you are required to include the original copyright notice.	*https://opensource.org/license/bsd-2-clause*
3-Clause BSD License	The 3-Clause BSD License applies to the following libraries: ■ Astropy ■ NetworkX ■ NumPy ■ pandas ■ scikit-learn ■ seaborn ■ statsmodels ■ SciPy ■ SymPy The 3-Clause BSD License is the same as the 2-Clause BSD License but with an additional clause: It provides no warranty or liability for the software provided by the developers.	*https://opensource.org/license/bsd-3-clause*

continues

Library license	Description	For more information
MIT License	The MIT License applies to the following libraries: ■ beautifulSoup4 ■ Faker ■ imbalanced-learn ■ mlxtend ■ Pillow ■ plotnine ■ Prince ■ PyTables ■ PyWavelets ■ qrcode ■ squarify ■ tabulate ■ TheFuzz ■ wordcloud This license allows you to freely use, modify, and distribute the library, even in commercial applications. In particular, it allows you to adapt the library and share modified versions, provided that you include the original copyright notice in redistributed versions.	*https://opensource.org/license/mit*
PIL License	Pillow is licensed under the PIL License. The rules are simple: You have permission to use, copy, modify, and distribute the library and its associated documentation for any purpose, provided the following: ■ The copyright notice appears in all copies. ■ Both the copyright notice and the permission notice appear in supporting documentation. The name Secret Labs AB or the name of the author is not used in advertising or publicity pertaining to distribution of the software without specific, written prior permission.	*https://openhub.net/licenses/pil*
Python Software Foundation (PSF) License	■ Matplotlib is licensed under the Python Software Foundation (PSF) License, and the rules are more open: ■ You may freely use, modify, and distribute the library. ■ Matplotlib is suitable for both academic and commercial applications. ■ There are no restrictions on the type of projects or industries where Matplotlib can be employed.	*https://spdx.org/licenses/PSF-2.0.html*

Summary

Like Chapter 2, this chapter provided the building blocks you need to create your own Python code and to interpret code produced by AI. Because of the open-source approach and the enthusiasm of the Python community, you have numerous resources available to you as a Python user. If you are a beginner, it can be hard to know where to start. The goal of this chapter has been to introduce you to the core preloaded libraries and give you an idea of how you can explore additional recommended libraries.

Most examples you worked through in this chapter have multiple lines of Python code, and it becomes difficult to use the formula bar with so much code. The next chapter is all about the Python Editor, which you can use to create, edit, and examine Python code in a larger editing space. You can also use the Python Editor to find and view multiple Python cells using the filters available. The Python Editor allows you to create Python code, go back to the worksheet, work on other Excel formulas, and then return to the Python Editor to commit the code when you're ready.

## CHAPTER 4

Using the Python Editor

In this chapter, you will:

- Discover the history and benefits of the Python Editor
- Learn how to use the Python Editor and customize the information it displays

> **Note** To follow along with the examples in this chapter, you must download the resources that accompany this book. If you don't already have these resources, visit *https://www.sumproduct.com/python-in-excel-book-resources* and download the files to a folder associated with your Python in Excel license. For this chapter, you will begin by accessing the workbook **SP Python in Excel Example Starter File Chapter 4.xlsm**.

As you learned in Chapter 2, "Getting to know Python in Excel," you can use the Python Editor as an alternative to entering formulas in the formula bar. As you will see in this chapter, there are advantages to entering and viewing code in the Python Editor—for example, it is ideal for longer blocks of code. In addition, using the Python Editor will be the preferred method for interacting with Python in the following chapters.

A brief history of the Python Editor

When the preview version of Python in Excel was first released, there was no Python Editor. Users had to enter Python code in the formula bar, and if any errors occurred, the Diagnostics pane would be displayed. The Diagnostics pane could also be accessed from the Formulas tab (see Figure 4-1).

FIGURE 4-1 The preview version of Python in Excel initially had a Diagnostics pane but no Python Editor.

The Diagnostics pane essentially listed the issues in a worksheet. It associated each issue with a cell reference. If a cell containing an issue was refreshed and the same issue occurred again, another entry would be created. Depending on the calculation mode, the list of issue messages could build up quickly, and the only way to get rid of the messages was for the user to clear all messages in the Diagnostics pane by using a trashcan icon. In that preview version of Python in Excel, users could view and edit code only in the formula bar.

Users of the preview version quickly provided feedback that it would be much more user-friendly to allow users to create and edit Python code in a pane, in addition to using the formula bar for each cell. In other platforms, Python is usually created and edited in a notebook format, and users expected to see a similar facility in Excel. When the Python Editor was added to another preview version of Python in Excel, it incorporated the functionality of the Diagnostics pane and provided a space to enter and edit Python code in individual cells and to view the Python code in multiple cells.

Using the Python Editor

The Python Editor is an integrated development environment (IDE). These are some of the features it includes:

- More editing space than in the formula bar, which makes the Python Editor especially helpful for larger code blocks

- A filterable view of all Python cells in a workbook, with the cells shown in execution order

- The ability to edit code in Python cells and run the code when you are ready

- The ability to change the view of the cell results

- IntelliSense to help you efficiently create code

- Use of color to distinguish between code objects

- Hover-over functions for viewing the full syntax

This section provides a tour of the Python Editor's features and also shows you how to use it to view and modify Python code.

Getting to know the Python Editor

To follow along with the examples in this chapter, open the workbook **SP Python in Excel Example Starter File Chapter 4.xlsm**, which contains examples from earlier chapters. Then open the sheet **New Sheet**.

You can open the Python Editor by selecting **Editor** in the **Python** section of the **Formulas** tab. When the Python Editor opens, it shows all the Python cells (see Figure 4-2).

> **Note** When you first open the Python Editor, the default behavior is to show all the Python cells in the workbook in execution order.

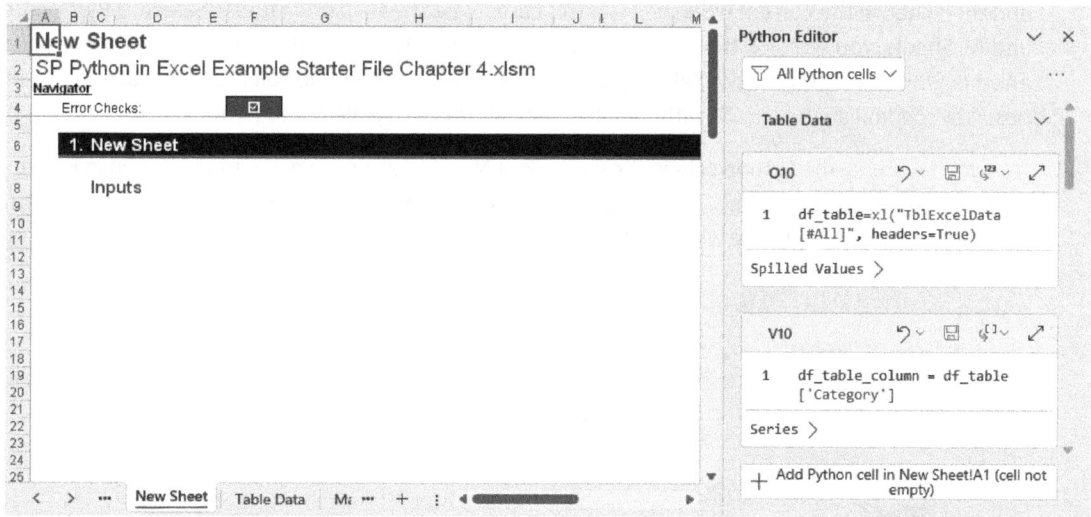

FIGURE 4-2 In a workbook that contains Python cells, when you first open the Python Editor, it defaults to showing all cells unless you change the settings.

The prompt window at the bottom of the Python Editor allows you to add Python code to the currently selected cell (if it doesn't already contain Python code) or the next available cell in the execution order. As you can see in Figure 4-2, if the cell contains something other than Python code, the Python Editor uses the phrase (cell not empty) to indicate this.

You can open the filter dropdown menu at the top of the Python Editor to see the available options, which allow you to control what Python cells are displayed (see Figure 4-3).

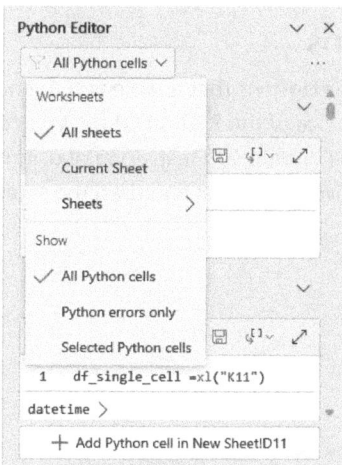

FIGURE 4-3 The filter at the top of the Python Editor allows you to control what Python cells are displayed.

The options in the filter dropdown menu give you many options, some of which overlap. To see all Python cells on the current sheet, you can either select Current Sheet or select the Sheets menu and then choose the current worksheet (in this case, New Sheet). If you choose Selected Python Cells and All Sheets, you see only the Python cells in the range selected on the current sheet. If you specify another worksheet and choose Selected Python Cells, you see the cells selected on that worksheet. The best way to familiarize yourself with the filter behaviors is to try the combinations.

If you view only the Python cells in the worksheet New Sheet, you see the image shown in Figure 4-4 instead of an empty pane. This image is probably included to help new users of Python in Excel who have opened the pane to see what it does.

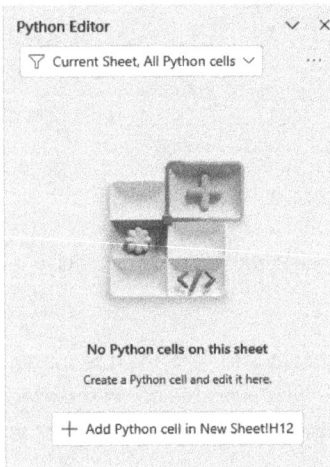

FIGURE 4-4 If no Python cells are selected by the filter, an image representing Python in Excel appears.

Exploring the Python Editor display options

Before we look at Python code in the Python Editor, let's look at the options that enable you to change how the Python Editor is displayed. To change the position and/or size of the Python Editor, you can use the options in the dropdown menu at the top of the pane (see Figure 4-5). Or, instead of using these menu options, you can simply click and drag the pane to move it and click and drag the sides of the pane to resize it.

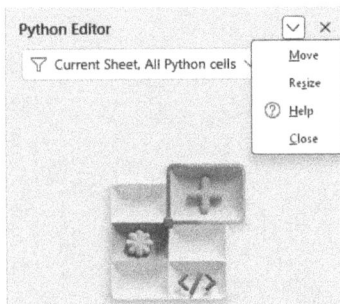

FIGURE 4-5 There are options to move, resize, and close the pane from the dropdown menu at the top of the Python Editor.

The Help option opens the Excel Help pane rather than anything specific to Python in Excel (see Figure 4-6).

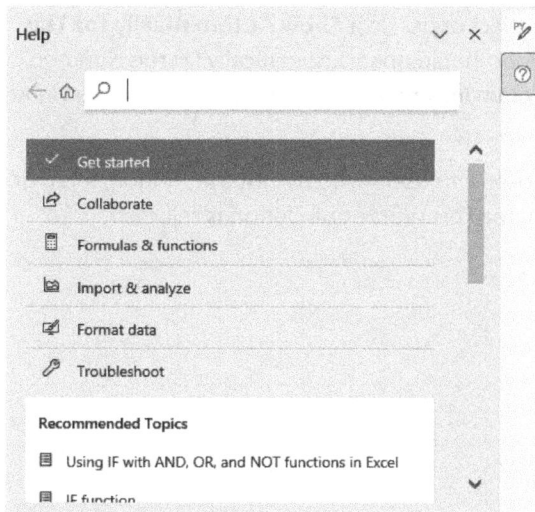

FIGURE 4-6 The Help option in the Python Editor accesses the Excel Help pane.

If you want to access help for Python in Excel from the Help pane, you can search for the word **Python** (see Figure 4-7).

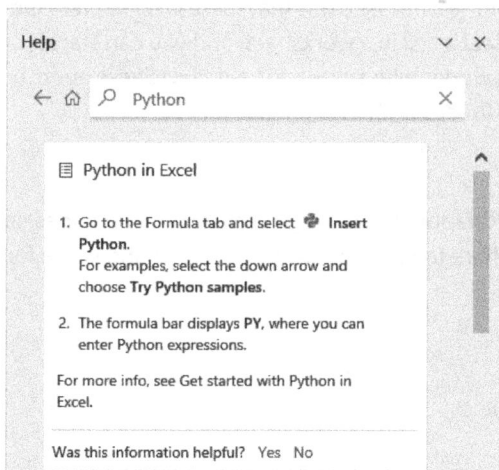

FIGURE 4-7 To get Python in Excel help from the Excel Help pane, search for **Python**.

Recall from Chapter 2 that the Python Editor will open automatically if there are any Python cells in the workbook containing errors or the `print()` function, unless you have changed a particular setting. That setting is called Show Automatically for This Workbook. To find it, click the **...** (More Options) menu at the top of the Python Editor. You can select or deselect **Show Automatically for This Workbook** to indicate whether the Python Editor should open automatically for this workbook when Python cells with errors or using the `print()` command are refreshed in the workbook (see Figure 4-8).

> **Note** When you plan to share the workbook with users who do not use Python, it is a good idea to make sure the Show Automatically for This Workbook option is selected.

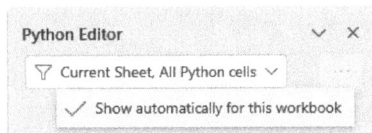

FIGURE 4-8 You can indicate whether the Python Editor should appear automatically when Python cells exist.

Entering code in the Python Editor

Now that you know what settings are available for the Python Editor, you're ready to see how entering Python code here compares to entering it in the formula bar.

One advantage of using the Python Editor over the formula bar is that there is no need to indicate that a cell will be used for Python code. Simply select a cell in a worksheet, and you can start typing Python code in the Python Editor. To see how this works, with the worksheet New Sheet open, enter the following Python code into the Python Editor for cell D10:

```
print("Hello World")
```

Figure 4-9 shows the results. You may recall from Chapter 2 that the `print()` command does not display the text value in the Excel cell. We're using it here to compare using this command in the formula bar and in the Python Editor.

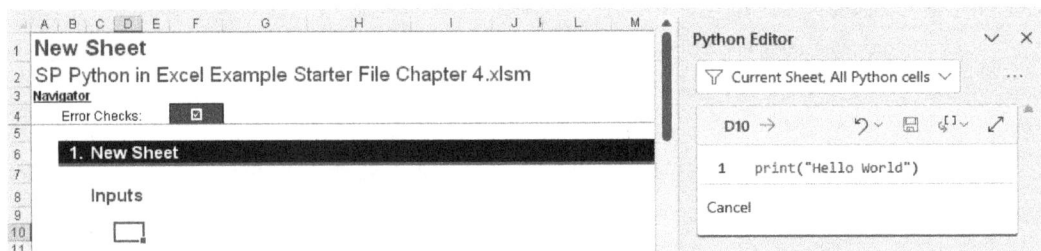

FIGURE 4-9 Entering Python code in the Python Editor

When you enter code for a cell in the Python Editor without committing it, it is retained but does not appear in the formula bar for the cell. You can go to another part of the worksheet, enter Excel cells and Python cells, and then return to the Python Editor, where the code in the D10 box will be retained unless you click the Cancel command at the bottom. To see what happens when you commit the Python code for cell D10, press **Ctrl+Enter** or click the **Save** icon in the cell box, which looks like a floppy disk (see Figure 4-10).

> **Note** When you commit the Python code for one cell, the impact on the other cells depends on the calculation mode. If you have the paid Python in Excel add-on and your calculation mode is set to manual, only the cell you are working on will be updated. This can save valuable processing time.

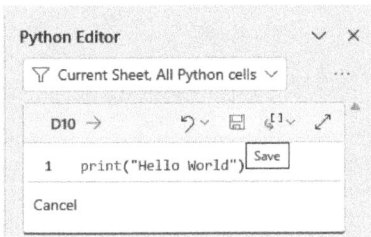

FIGURE 4-10 To commit the Python code, click the **Save** icon, which looks like a floppy disk.

As you can see in Figure 4-10, there are a few other icons at the top of the Python Editor cell box:

- **D10 arrow:** This takes you to cell D10 in the worksheet.

- **Undo dropdown menu:** You can select Undo, Redo, or Discard All Changes from this dropdown menu.

- **Object View toggle:** You can choose Excel or Python Object view. Your selection applies to the cell box in the Python Editor and the cell in the worksheet.

- **Expand arrow:** This diagonal arrow expands the cell box, making it easier to view multiple lines of code.

Creating code with Python Editor features

The Python Editor is designed to help you create Python code. Getting to know the features available will help you learn to recognize how to fix—and avoid—errors. In this section, we'll walk through some examples that show you what's available.

Hover over the `print()` command in the Python code, and you see a description of how to use the function (see Figure 4-11).

FIGURE 4-11 Hovering over the function brings up a full description of how to use it.

In the Python Editor, different objects have distinctive colors. For example, comments are green, text is red, functions are brown, and variables are blue. To see how colors are used in code, commit the `print()` command you entered in cell D10 by entering **Ctrl+Enter** or clicking the **Save** icon. Figure 4-12 shows the results in the Python Editor.

> **Note** Remember that if you are reading a printed copy of this book, you will see only black-and-white text and figures. But if you're following along in the workbook, which we strongly recommend, you will see all the colors we discuss in this chapter.

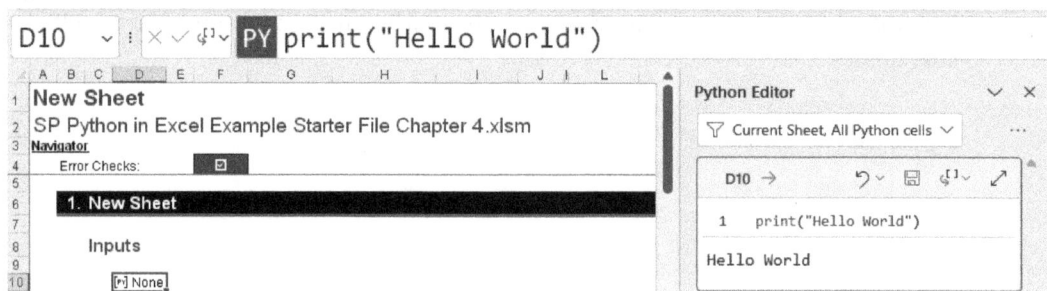

FIGURE 4-12 When you commit the `print()` command in the Python Editor, the text is recognized but not output to the cell.

Now, change to the Excel Value view in the cell box and commit the change. Figure 4-13 shows the results. In the Python Editor, you can see that the code has been accepted, but the final result is 0 in the cell box and None in the cell on the worksheet.

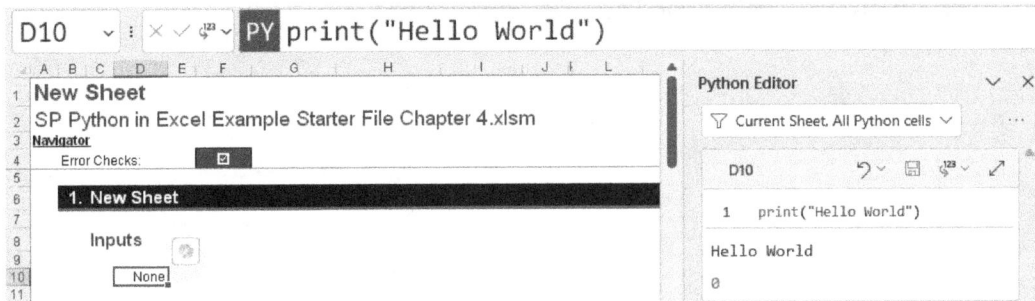

FIGURE 4-13 When you switch to Excel Value view, the text is recognized for the print() command in D10, but the Excel value is 0 in the cell box.

Let's look again at another example from Chapter 2, using the `input()` function. Enter the following code in cell D11:

```
"Enter your name:"
x=input()
"Hello, " + x
```

Before committing the code, hover over the `input()` function. As you can see in Figure 4-14, the Python Editor recognizes the `input()` function.

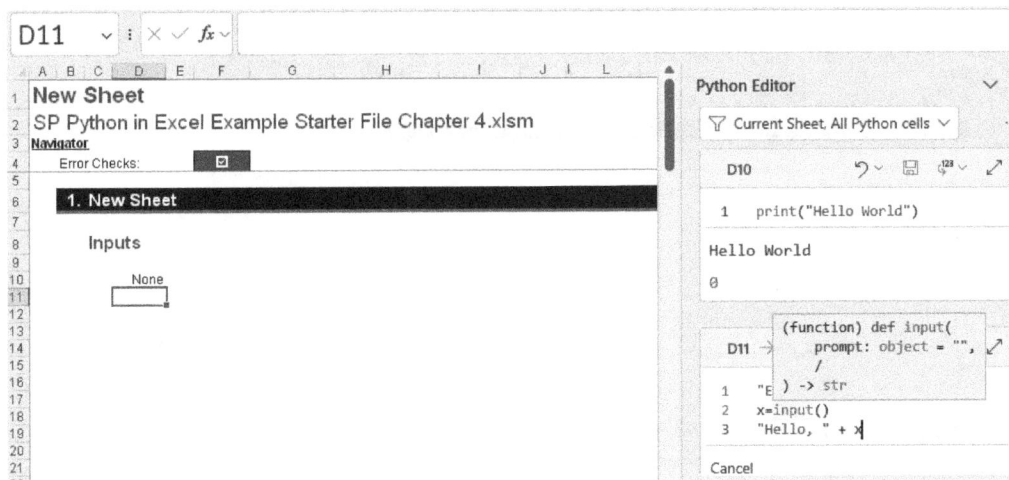

FIGURE 4-14 The `input()` function is recognized in the Python Editor.

Now, commit the Python code in cell D11. Figure 4-15 shows the results: A #PYTHON! error appears in cell D11, and the Python Editor provides an error message.

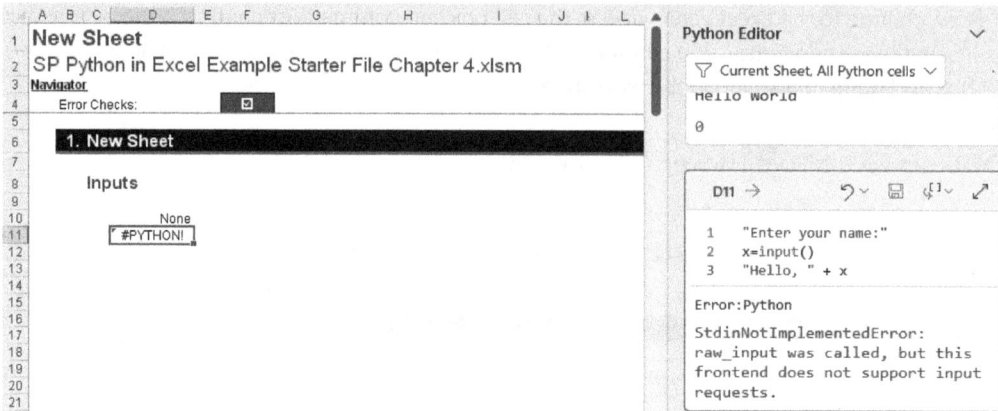

FIGURE 4-15 The `input()` function causes a Python error.

You can view the error in the Python Editor immediately. It was not picked up before execution because the Python syntax was correct until it was run in the Excel frontend.

Although IntelliSense can help you enter the correct syntax, it does not warn you if there will be an error, since errors are not triggered until you commit the code. You also don't get a warning if you enter a function that does not exist. To see this in action, enter the following code in cell D12 and commit it:

```
notafunction("Hello")
```

Figure 4-16 shows that another error results.

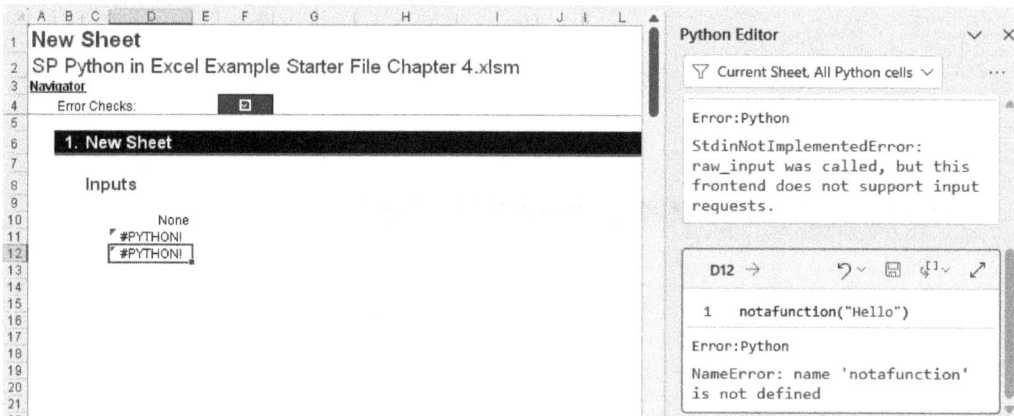

FIGURE 4-16 Invalid Python code is detected when the code is committed.

When entering the code, you may notice that Python tries to display help for `notafunction()` because it recognizes from the parentheses after the name that it should be a function. However, it can't find that function. If no details are supplied and you don't see the function name as a suggestion from IntelliSense as it is entered, check whether the function name is correct and whether you created the function before the current code (in terms of calculation order). The error message triggered when the code is committed provides enough detail to locate the source of the error.

The Python Editor also provides a way to quickly check the values in a cell. To see how it works, open the **Table Data** sheet. Figure 4-17 shows a DataFrame in cell Y10 of this sheet, which is displayed as an Excel value in the worksheet.

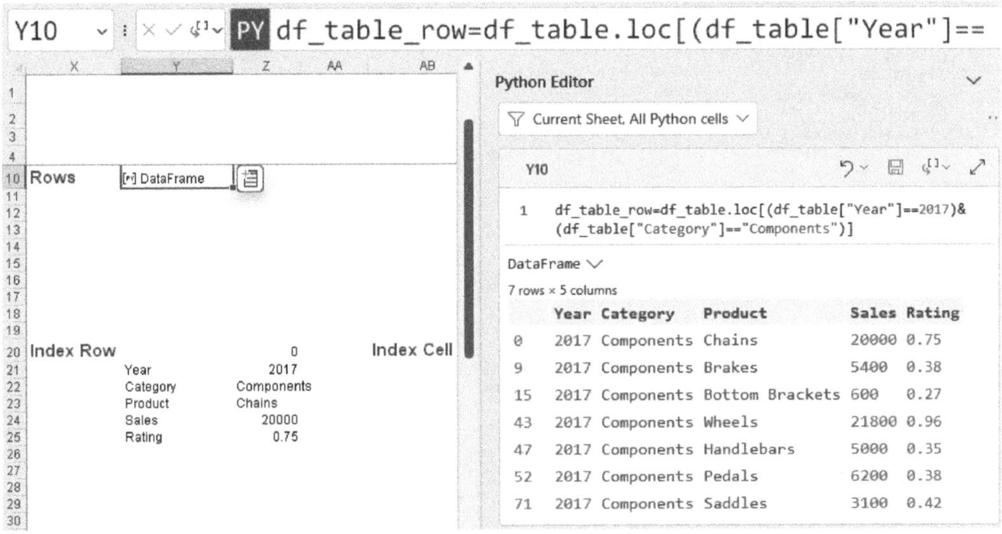

| Y10 | ∨ : × ✓ ↺∨ PY | df_table_row=df_table.loc[(df_table["Year"]== |

Python Editor

▽ Current Sheet, All Python cells ∨

Y10   ↺∨ 🖫 ↺∨ ↗

1   df_table_row=df_table.loc[(df_table["Year"]==2017)&
     (df_table["Category"]=="Components")]

DataFrame ∨
7 rows × 5 columns

	Year	Category	Product	Sales	Rating
0	2017	Components	Chains	20000	0.75
9	2017	Components	Brakes	5400	0.38
15	2017	Components	Bottom Brackets	600	0.27
43	2017	Components	Wheels	21800	0.96
47	2017	Components	Handlebars	5000	0.35
52	2017	Components	Pedals	6200	0.38
71	2017	Components	Saddles	3100	0.42

FIGURE 4-17 You can use the Python Editor to view the data in a DataFrame when the cell is in Python Object view.

You can use the Python Editor to view the values in any Python cells. This is particularly useful when a worksheet has insufficient space to spill the Excel Value view.

Using the Python Editor can also be a quicker way to view images. To try this, open the sheet **Matplotlib**, which shows one of the examples from Chapter 3, "Using Python libraries." In the Python Editor, locate the cell box for cell J36 and ensure that the Excel Value view has been selected for that cell. Figure 4-18 shows the results.

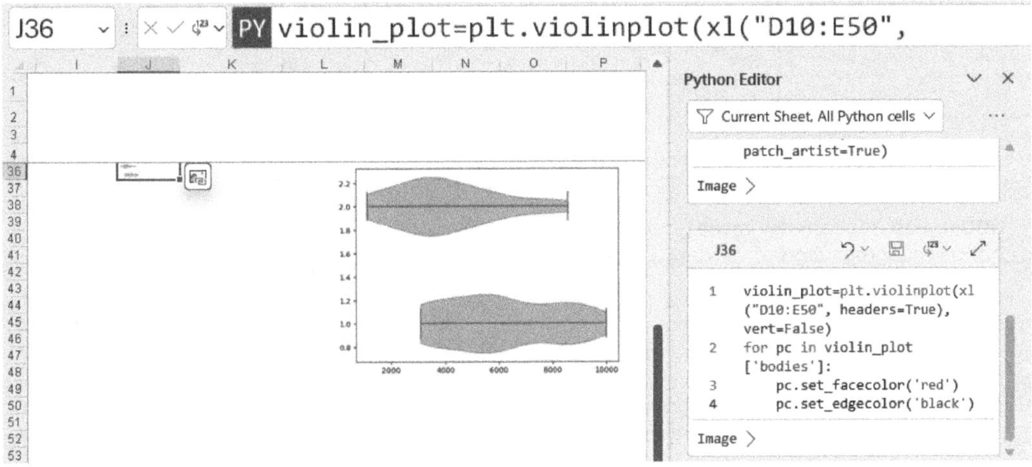

| J36 | ∨ : × ✓ ↺∨ PY | violin_plot=plt.violinplot(xl("D10:E50", |

Python Editor   ∨ ×

▽ Current Sheet, All Python cells ∨

    patch_artist=True)

Image >

J36   ↺∨ 🖫 ↺∨ ↗

1   violin_plot=plt.violinplot(xl
     ("D10:E50", headers=True),
     vert=False)
2   for pc in violin_plot
     ['bodies']:
3   pc.set_facecolor('red')
4   pc.set_edgecolor('black')

Image >

FIGURE 4-18 Viewing the code to create and modify a violin chart

Notice that the result in the cell box is an image. Click the arrow next to it to view the image in the cell box. Figure 4-19 shows the results.

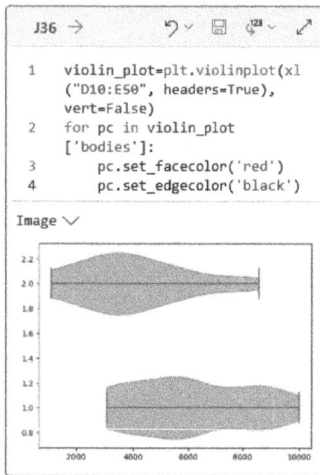

FIGURE 4-19 You can view image results in the Python Editor.

The image is displayed even if the Python Object view is selected (see Figure 4-20).

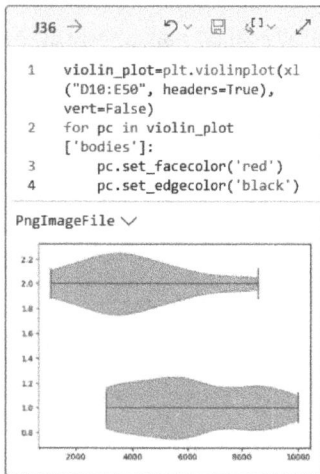

FIGURE 4-20 You can view image results in the Python Editor regardless of the view selected.

You can use the violin chart example to discover the options available in the context menu, which you open by right-clicking a cell box in the Python Editor (see Figure 4-21). These options have been included for more advanced Python coders.

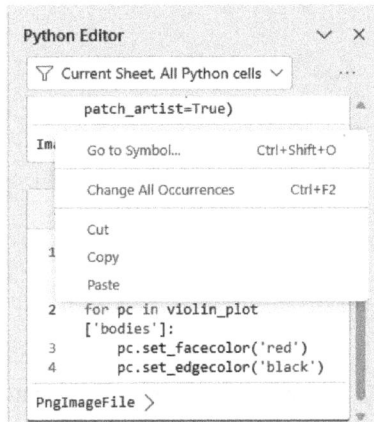

FIGURE 4-21 The context menu in the Python Editor

The top option, Go to Symbol, allows you to search for decorators or defined Python functions to see where they are used in more complex Python code. Select the **Go to Symbol** option for a list of suggested functions (see Figure 4-22).

> **Note** A *decorator* is a function that takes another function as an argument, adds more functionality to it, and returns a new function.

FIGURE 4-22 The option Go to Symbol has located two Python functions in the code.

If you select a symbol and then go back to the context menu and choose Change All Occurrences, the symbol is highlighted each time it occurs. To see this in action, select the suggested option **violin_plot**, return to the context menu, and select **Change All Occurrences**. Figure 4-23 shows the results.

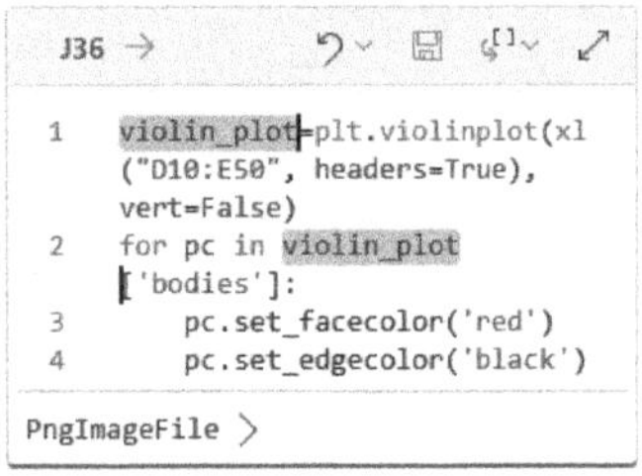

```
J36  →              ↰∨  ⊟  ⊄¹∨  ↗

1   violin_plot=plt.violinplot(xl
    ("D10:E50", headers=True),
    vert=False)
2   for pc in violin_plot
    ['bodies']:
3       pc.set_facecolor('red')
4       pc.set_edgecolor('black')

PngImageFile  ⟩
```

FIGURE 4-23 When you choose **violin_plot** and then return to the context menu and select **Change All Occurrences**, the Python Editor highlights each occurrence of that symbol.

The other options in the context menu allow you to cut, copy, and paste the sections of code associated with the selected symbol.

Summary

The Python Editor is designed to make it easy to enter and view Python code without selecting individual Python cells. It is an IDE that allows you to create Python code and store it until you are ready to commit it. The large editing space lets you view large blocks of code and see the values in the Python objects. You can filter to view all the Python cells in a workbook or focus on the errors in a range.

The Python Editor includes several helpful features. For example, IntelliSense helps you enter correct code in the Python Editor. In addition, you can hover over a function in the Python Editor to see how to use it. The Python Editor also displays errors in a way that helps you identify and fix them, and it shows code in various colors that identify the different parts of the code.

You will use the Python Editor to view and customize the examples in Chapters 6 and 7, but first you need to meet your new assistant, Copilot.

## CHAPTER 5

Introduction to AI and Copilot

In this chapter, you will:

- Discover how artificial intelligence (AI) can help you do your job

- Learn the history of AI

- Understand the different types of AI, including generative AI and chatbots

- Explore and learn to use the Microsoft Copilot interface

- Use Copilot in Excel to complete business tasks.

> **Note** To follow along with the examples in this chapter, you must download the resources that accompany this book. If you don't already have these resources, visit *https://www .sumproduct.com/python-in-excel-book-resources* and download the files to a folder associated with your Python in Excel license. For this chapter, you will begin by accessing the workbook **SP Python in Excel Example Starter File Chapter 5.xlsm**.

Learning how AI can help you

AI is a tool; it is not inherently negative or positive, despite some of the warnings of impending doom that news articles and clickbait use to get your attention. AI will probably not replace you in the workplace, although it may change your role. Although AI can replace formulaic tasks, such as answering frequently asked questions (FAQs) on a shopping site, most workers continued and expanded use of AI in the workplace will involve retraining to work with AI. A coder may begin to use AI to generate code, but we still need a human coder skilled in debugging and auditing that code to make it work.

As organizations continue to use AI, roles will be redefined. For example, if a chatbot takes over as the first point of contact for customers needing help with orders, then the employees who formerly had that role will need to train for new roles. New roles will be created to manage the AI workflows. Many employees will need to adapt to using AI for parts of their jobs. Your organization may already have a strategy for using AI in the workplace that considers the impact of AI on the workforce.

AI can save you time on mundane tasks. You can use it to create a first attempt at a report or presentation, or, more pertinently to this book, code. You can then apply finishing touches and move on to more valuable and interesting areas. At some point, most of us have stared at a blank page and wondered where to start. You can now enter prompts into an AI tool and use it to get started.

> **Note** You can ignore AI or use it to help you with your work. Either way, you can be sure that your competitors will use it.

As with many other tools, you will get the best results from AI if you know how to use it well. With practice, you will learn how to phrase prompts and refine your questions to get the answers you need. The examples in this book focus on Python in Excel and Microsoft's Copilot AI. As you practice using Copilot throughout the rest of the book, you will understand how to use prompts and how to adapt the prompts provided in this book to your own scenarios.

Let's look at a Copilot interaction. Suppose you are wondering how you could use AI to become more productive. You could ask Copilot that question, as shown in Figure 5-1.

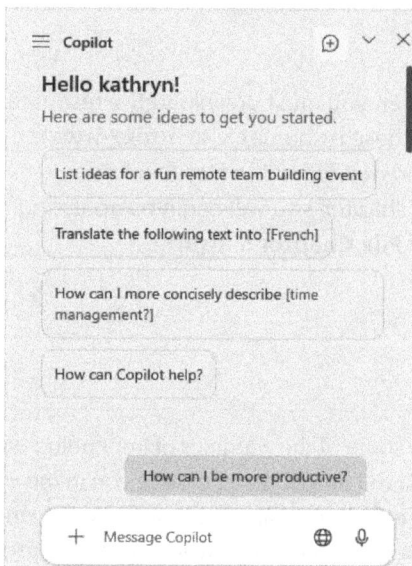

FIGURE 5-1 You can ask open-ended questions in the Copilot interface.

Figure 5-2 shows a sample response to this question, where the top suggestions are related to Microsoft.

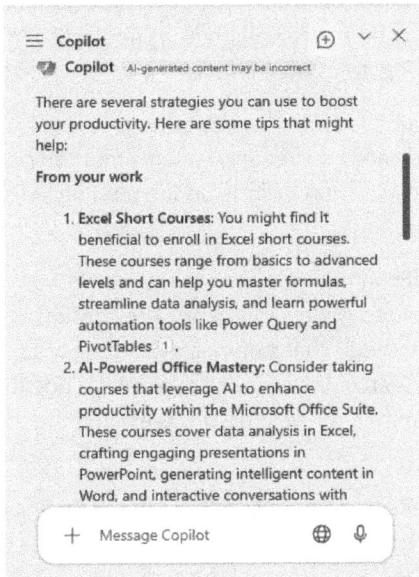

FIGURE 5-2 Copilot's reply to a prompt is likely to include multiple ideas.

If you scroll down to the end of the suggestions, you see that Copilot provides further prompts to continue the conversation (see Figure 5-3). You can ask more questions or click the links provided to find out more.

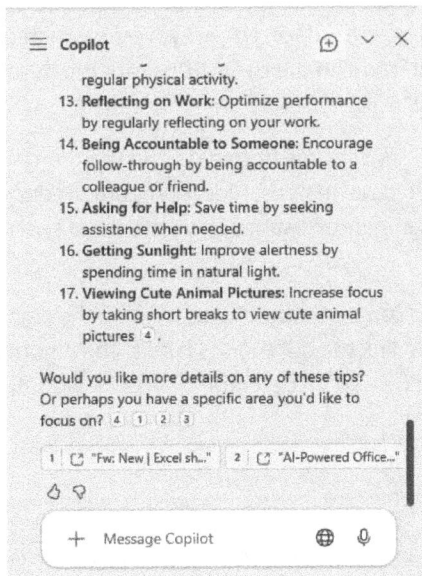

FIGURE 5-3 The reply to a prompt also suggests further questions you can ask and links to some of the ideas.

Exploring the evolution of AI

You may be tempted to skip this section since you are already bombarded with news about AI and how it will change the world. But understanding how AI works is key to using it effectively, so let's step back from all the hype and consider the origins of AI.

Artificial intelligence is a branch of computer science dedicated to creating systems that can perform tasks that traditionally require human intelligence. Specific areas include understanding language, making decisions, and recognizing objects in images.

As with many other technological advancements, it is difficult to pinpoint the first time AI was conceived. Over the years, many institutions have contributed to AI developments. The consensus is that John McCarthy invented the term *artificial intelligence* in 1955. That summer, a group of academics was invited to a workshop at Dartmouth College, a US research university, to explore the possibility of "thinking machines." As a result of the work done that summer, the field of AI was established as a branch of computer science.[1]

The path of AI development has not been smooth. There were some successes in the 1970s, including the creation of ELIZA, which is regarded as the first chatbot. But then came the "AI winter"—a time of dissatisfaction with the progress of AI—which ran from the late 1970s until the early 1990s.

When AI was first conceived, and for the first few decades, the main approach was symbolic, or rule-based, AI. Experts provided the computer with "if-then" rules and created algorithms that followed flowcharts. This meant experts had to think of every possible scenario and provide rules to manage decision-making. This method initially created expert systems used in industries such as manufacturing and finance. The main problems were that experts were required to maintain the algorithms, and the models were difficult to scale. Investment stalled as the initial promise of AI faltered.

Since the late 1990s, AI has developed rapidly, even making it to space. NASA's rovers navigated Mars using AI in addition to remote control. A breakthrough came in the early 2010s with the development of machine learning (ML) and deep neural networks (DNNs).[2]

Machine learning is the process whereby computers discern patterns from data and use them to make decisions. Machine learning is an important concept in data analysis. Algorithms are used to find patterns and connections in data and then provide insights and information. There are three types of machine learning:

- **Supervised learning:** This type of machine learning can be thought of as training the algorithms. The system is given labeled data so that it can link the data to the labels. The algorithms can then be applied to new data. An example would be a spam detector, where the algorithm must detect the characteristics of spam.

---

[1] "The History of AI: A Timeline of Artificial Intelligence," Coursera, accessed June 26, 2025, *https://www.coursera.org/articles/history-of-ai.*

[2] "2010–2019: The Rise of Deep Learning," TNW, accessed June 26, 2025, *https://thenextweb.com/news/2010-2019-the-rise-of-deep-learning.*

- **Unsupervised learning:** With this type of machine learning, data is provided with no labels, and the goal is pattern recognition. An example of unsupervised learning would be fraud detection, where the algorithm must detect unusual data points that don't fit the pattern.

- **Reinforcement learning:** With this type of machine learning, the model receives feedback on the results and then adjusts the algorithms. An example of reinforcement learning would be training a model to play a strategic game, which would prompt a change to the algorithms. You might think that all models should use reinforcement learning, but it has disadvantages: It is complex to set up and requires more computational resources.

A deep neural network is a type of artificial neural network (ANN) that has layers between the data received and the results. This gives the ANN depth. Each layer further refines the result. DNNs use this layering to detect complex patterns in the data. This takes processing power, as well as lots of relevant data, which hadn't been available before this time. Graphics processing units (GPUs), which were originally designed to render graphics and video, can process lots of data simultaneously, and they began to be used for machine learning. The data used for machine learning now comes from the internet, social media, and devices such as smartphones and tablets that consume and create information.

Understanding the types of AI

AI is everywhere today. It helps manage spam filters in email platforms, powers smart replies in messaging apps, and supports virtual customer service agents on many websites. In agriculture, AI is used to detect plant diseases through images. In banking, it detects fraud by identifying unusual patterns in transactions.

Narrow AI

The AI you encounter in many daily tasks is referred to as narrow AI, or *weak AI*, and it is designed to perform specific tasks. When you ask a virtual assistant for the weather forecast or choose your next TV series from the recommendations on a streaming app, you are interacting with narrow AI.

Narrow AI often performs very well at a narrow range of tasks, but it lacks human intelligence characteristics such as common sense and the ability to apply knowledge to different contexts. You will quickly see its limitations when you try to have a conversation with a virtual assistant.

General AI

The term *general AI* is used when the goal is to replicate human intelligence. Although general AI is the inspiration for some excellent (and terrible) movies, it does not truly exist yet. A general AI system would be able to solve problems using available data, and it would also learn from solving problems and adapt to new situations. AI systems currently rely on being trained on vast amounts of data, and they are limited by the quality of the data available. This can sometimes cause problems, especially when the data comes from unreliable sources.

AI is developing rapidly. Although general AI is not available yet, the range of narrow AI applications is increasing. Thanks to improved technology and progress, many AI applications are already helping you manage your home and work lives.

Discriminative, predictive, and generative AI

The AI produced in the early days of AI development is often defined as one of two types: discriminative AI or predictive AI. *Discriminative AI* analyzes data and orders it into classes or categories. With *predictive AI*, data is analyzed, and through the patterns detected, trends are identified to predict future outcomes.

More recently, another type of AI, *generative AI* (GenAI), has evolved. GenAI models are deep learning applications trained using the data available to them to produce new content, which might be text, images, or code. One area of GenAI is conversational AI, where computers can participate in conversations using natural language. Deep learning trains the AI to understand language, interpret the meaning, and respond appropriately, based on the context. We will look more closely at GenAI when we talk about chatbots a little later in this chapter.

Natural language processing

Natural language processing (NLP) is a branch of artificial intelligence that enables computers to create and understand human language. The goal of NLP is to simulate human understanding in an AI system so that it can understand and answer questions and develop conversations with humans.

NLP encompasses two types of analysis: syntactical and semantic. *Syntactical analysis* means ensuring that the syntax of a sentence follows grammatical rules so that prompts are interpreted correctly and responses are understandable for the user. *Semantic analysis*, on the other hand, involves interpreting meaning from context and experience. Both syntax and semantics are important for a sentence to make sense. It is possible, for example, to create a sentence that uses correct syntax but still doesn't make sense—such as "AI writes empty sentences full of red information."

To create prompts that will obtain the desired results, you must consider how those prompts will be interpreted. NLP algorithms are designed to interpret and respond to human language. These are some of the techniques they use:

- **Parsing:** NLP algorithms attempt to split a sentence into related components through a process called *parsing*. AI can parse an unstructured natural language prompt and create a structured representation. It can then use algorithms to process the structured representation and determine the meaning of the prompt.

- **Stemming:** Stemming is the process of reducing a word to its base or root form (or stem) for use in search engines and information retrieval. NLP algorithms use stemming to group words that have the same stem. For example, "work" is the stem of "worked" and "working."

- **Text segmentation:** Rather than splitting a prompt into related components, NLP algorithms can divide text into meaningful segments to extract meaning from the prompt. This process, called *text segmentation*, is part of semantic analysis.

Tips for creating effective prompts for AI

Understanding the techniques that the NLP algorithms use can help you create better prompts. When composing prompts, you can use these techniques to help the AI parse your input and give you helpful results:

- **Use steps:** You don't have to enter a prompt as one long sentence. In fact, asking several related questions in succession to refine the results often works better.

- **Be specific:** Specificity helps AI understand what you're looking for. If you need to know sales trends, for example, asking AI to tell you the sales trends is more likely to get the results you are looking for than just asking it to analyze the data.

- **Give AI context:** It helps to provide relevant background information, such as variable names associated with the data. If you want Microsoft Copilot to change the format of a Python DataFrame, for example, it helps to give the name df_sales_data rather than refer to "sales data." Similarly, you can refer to Excel entities such as cell references and table names.

- **Iterate:** To iterate means to take steps to get closer to the correct answer. Asking the same question another time can yield a different response. Following up a prompt with a more targeted prompt can also get you closer to the answer you expect.

Chatbots

Chatbots are one application of conversational AI that has become available to the public in recent years, and several major companies have invested time and money in developing them. OpenAI is a US company founded in 2015, whose mission is "to ensure that artificial general intelligence benefits all humanity."[3] OpenAI produced GPT-1 in 2018. GPT stands for Generative Pre-trained Transformer, where *Pre-trained* refers to extensive training on language datasets, and *Transformer* is the architecture that made scalable parallel processing possible.[4] GPT-1 was predictive and did not possess the capacity for deep thinking; instead, it relied on training data and pattern recognition.

In 2019, Microsoft invested $1 billion in OpenAI, which led to the release of ChatGPT's predecessor, GPT-3, in 2020.[5] In November 2022, after years of research and investment, OpenAI released ChatGPT. The model was built on a deep learning architecture called a *large language model* (LLM) trained to predict and generate human-like text. ChatGPT brought AI and chatbots into the public eye. By 2024, the

---

[3] "Our Vision for the Future of AGI," OpenAI, accessed June 30, 2025, *https://openai.com/about/*.

[4] "What Are Transformers in Artificial Intelligence," AWS, accessed June 30, 2025, *https://aws.amazon.com/what-is /transformers-in-artificial-intelligence/#:~:text=Transformers%20are%20a%20type%20of,sequence%20into%20an %20output%20sequence*.

[5] "OpenAI Forms Exclusive Computing Partnership with Microsoft to Build New Azure AI Supercomputing Technologies," Microsoft, accessed Jun 30, 2025, *https://news.microsoft.com/source/2019/07/22/openai-forms-exclusive-computing -partnership-with-microsoft-to-build-new-azure-ai-supercomputing-technologies/*.

ChatGPT app was in the top 10 most downloaded apps.[6] In 2023, Microsoft invested more than $10 billion in OpenAI and began using OpenAI's LLM to create tools such as Bing and Copilot in Microsoft Excel.

Microsoft was not the only large corporation to develop chatbot technology, however. Google introduced Bard (now known as Gemini), another AI chatbot, based on its own LLM technology at around the same time that ChatGPT was released. Additional companies have released chatbots in recent years.

Potential problems with chatbot responses

Chatbots' responses to prompts are not always as accurate as you might like them to be. GenAI creates new content based on the training and information available, but it does have some weaknesses, including these:

- **No real understanding:** GenAI doesn't actually understand the text it reads or produces. For example, it has no understanding of sarcasm.

- **Hallucinations:** AI sometimes presents invented facts and quotes as if they are true. This is not the same as being creative. It happens because of poor training data or flaws in the design and training of the system. Vague or contradictory prompts can also trigger hallucinations.

- **Potential for bias:** If the data that an AI system is trained on is biased—for example, if it is sexist or racist data—then the AI will be biased too.

- **Problems with calculations and logic:** Although you might be accustomed to computers as giant calculators, chatbots look for contextual information and can struggle with mathematical concepts.

- **Reliance on old data:** Depending on the version and user plan, AI might give you a snapshot of data that it has found online but that is not the latest information.

ChatGPT features

ChatGPT dynamically responds to natural language prompts. It is trained to use a language similar to the language in the prompt, which may be casual, formal, or technical. If you ask, "Is it raining?" ChatGPT will probably just give you the weather forecast. If you ask, "Dude, do I need my umbrella?" you are more likely to get an answer that includes "dude" and describes whether an umbrella is needed for today's weather. ChatGPT may also interpret your casual tone as a conversation starter and continue the chat by asking about your plans.

ChatGPT's replies are grammatically correct and usually contextually relevant. The context includes information exchanged in the current conversation. This is a particularly powerful feature, as ChatGPT can build on a conversation, provide more relevant information, and respond to any rejected responses with clarification. In some versions, and with enough memory available, ChatGPT can retain preferences and use them consistently in all exchanges.

---

[6] "Most Popular Apps (2025)," Business of Apps, accessed June 30, 2025, *https://www.businessofapps.com/data/most-popular-apps/*.

ChatGPT is particularly useful for summarizing data. It can summarize any text, from a short email to a long, boring book. (Don't even think about it!) It can create a succinct summary if the prompt is to ascertain the key insights, such as from a company report. ChatGPT can also rewrite text using a different style, which can be useful for complicated legal documents or technical specifications. There are limitations to ChatGPT's abilities to summarize and rewrite, though: It will summarize using its training and may not pick out the same key information that a knowledgeable researcher would choose.

With ChatGPT, you are not limited to using English. ChatGPT currently supports more than 50 languages and can translate between them, allowing you to prepare reports for colleagues and clients in their preferred language. It can correctly interpret and translate local idioms, and it preserves the tone and meaning of the original text.

Earlier in this chapter, when Copilot offered ideas about improving productivity (refer to Figure 5-1), you saw that a chatbot can generate new ideas. You could, for example, ask ChatGPT to brainstorm a new article or a new marketing slogan. Since ChatGPT has no personality, it can also take on roles when prompted to do so, such as becoming a teacher or a creative writing partner. It can also respond to voice prompts if you prefer. Using ChatGPT as an assistant to plan your work can save time and help you focus on key ideas. Since ChatGPT can adapt to prompts, if you need to pivot from creating a summary to having a more detailed focus, you can do so while also retaining information about the current exchange.

The aspect of ChatGPT most relevant to this book is its ability to use programming languages to analyze data and create visualizations. ChatGPT can also interpret visualizations to assist with data analysis. To get accurate answers from ChatGPT or any other AI platform, including Microsoft Copilot, you must enter prompts that include enough information about what you need, as you will see in the next section.

Getting to know Microsoft Copilot

Microsoft Copilot uses elements of ChatGPT, but whereas ChatGPT is a general-purpose chatbot, Copilot was designed to assist users of Microsoft 365. As you saw in the example earlier in this chapter, Copilot's first responses to the prompt "How can I be more productive?" suggested Microsoft courses and using AI with Microsoft apps (refer to Figure 5-1).

How you use Copilot depends on the app you use. Copilot consists of a suite of AI assistants embedded into and tailored to work with each app. To access Copilot in all the apps listed next, you will need a Copilot Pro license, which we will discuss later in this chapter. In PowerPoint, you might ask Copilot to design slides and create new pictures, but in Excel, you might need help with Excel formulas or, as you will see later, advanced data analysis performed with Python.

Copilot is available in desktop applications as well as in the following online applications:

- **Copilot for Microsoft 365:** Copilot is integrated into Word, Excel, PowerPoint, Outlook, and Teams.

- **Copilot for Power Platform:** Copilot is available in Power Apps, Power Automate, Power Pages, and Power BI, enabling users to build apps, automate workflows, and analyze data.

- **Copilot for Dynamics 365:** There are two areas where Copilot can be used with Dynamics 365:

  - **Customer relationship management (CRM):** Copilot enables companies to better manage customer and prospect data.

  - **Enterprise resource planning (ERP):** Copilot supports ERP activities with predictive insights, payment tracking, and task automation.

- **GitHub Copilot:** Copilot helps developers create code in Visual Studio Code, Visual Studio, and other IDEs.

- **Copilot in Azure:** Copilot can assist with the design and operation of Azure cloud and edge services.

- **Copilot Security:** Copilot quickly provides intelligent insights and recommendations to optimize performance and secure infrastructure.

- **Copilot Studio:** Through a simple, low-code graphical interface, organizations can build their own customized conversational agents (referred to as *copilots*, lowercased) in Copilot Studio to work with their data, workflows, and business scenarios.

We will not go into detail about how to use Copilot in each of these areas, but we want you to understand that AI is now an integral part of the Microsoft 365 ecosystem. When you use Copilot in an application such as Word, you can access information from the rest of the Microsoft 365 ecosystem. You saw this in the example shown in Figure 5-2, where the first heading is "From Your Work." Copilot uses the Microsoft Graph gateway to access data from all your Microsoft apps and provide information relevant to your prompt. However, since we focus on Copilot in Excel in this book, the primary source of information will be the data in Excel workbooks.

You may recall from the Introduction that the examples in this book require a Microsoft 365 Copilot license and files in a OneDrive or SharePoint folder associated with the license. Users who do not have such a license can access Copilot at *https://copilot.microsoft.com* (see Figure 5-4). However, this free version of Copilot is not integrated into the apps. The free version of Copilot is a natural language chatbot that can accept uploaded files and images and maintain a conversation.

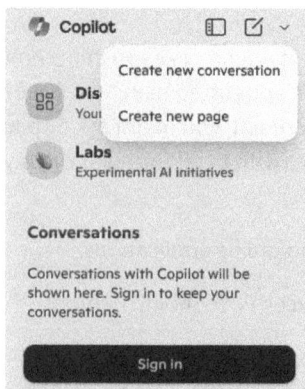

FIGURE 5-4 The free version of Copilot can save previous conversations under your Microsoft login.

The free version of Copilot is available on desktop and mobile devices. Figure 5-5 shows the free version of Copilot being asked, "What versions of Copilot are available?" Copilot responds by providing an answer in table format. It also provides a prompt window with the option to select Quick Response, which takes just 2 to 3 seconds and is "best for everyday conversation," or Think Deeper, which takes more computational time to return with a more detailed or accurate answer, depending on the context. (We will look at Think Deeper mode in more detail when we get to examples of using Copilot advanced analysis with Python in Chapter 6, "Using Copilot with Python in Excel.")

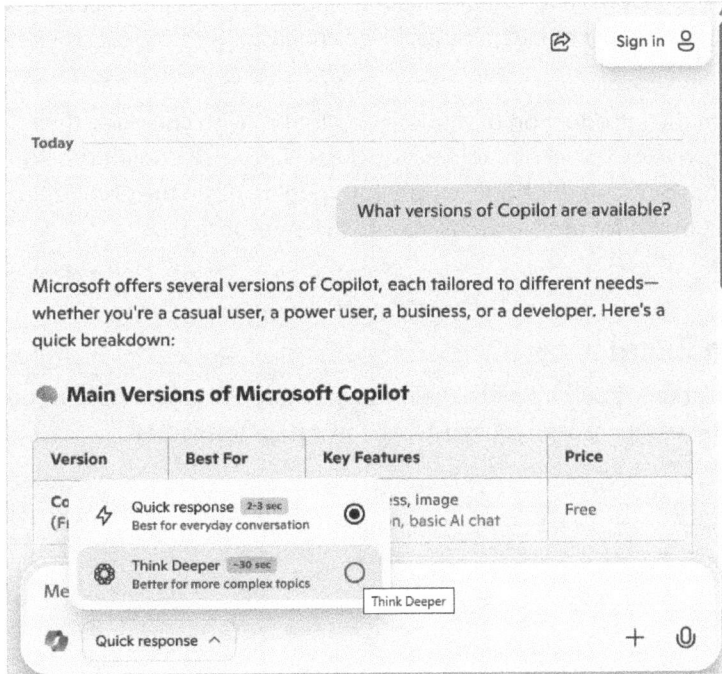

FIGURE 5-5 The free version of Copilot allows you to access Think Deeper mode.

Again, to work through the examples in this book—which we highly recommend—you need more than the free version of Copilot. You need a Microsoft 365 Copilot Pro license. Copilot Pro is available as a paid add-on for Microsoft 365 users or as part of Copilot for Microsoft 365 (Enterprise plan) for larger organizations.

A Copilot Pro license offers several benefits over the free version, including the following:

- **Copilot in Microsoft 365 apps:** Use AI directly in Word, Excel, PowerPoint, Outlook, and OneNote (with a Microsoft 365 Personal or Family subscription).

- **Data analysis in Excel:** Create formulas, analyze trends, and visualize data with natural language prompts.

- **Advanced writing and editing:** Rewrite, summarize, and polish documents and emails with ease.

- **Priority access to GPT-4 Turbo:** Get faster, more reliable responses—even during peak times.

- **Early access to new features:** Be among the first to try experimental tools and updates.

- **Custom GPTs:** Build your own AI assistants tailored to specific tasks or interests.

The paid Copilot Pro add-on for Microsoft 365 works across the web, on mobile platforms, and in Windows and Microsoft Edge. It supports more than 20 languages and currently costs $20 per month, with no annual commitment.

Users on a Microsoft 365 Enterprise plan can purchase the Microsoft 365 Copilot add-on, which gives the same benefits as the Copilot Pro add-on while maintaining enterprise-grade security, privacy, and compliance. It currently costs $30 per month per user, billed annually.

> **Note** You may recall from the introduction that to use Copilot Pro with your files, they must be located in a OneDrive or SharePoint folder associated with your Copilot Pro license. When we use the term Copilot Pro in this book, we are referring to either the Copilot Pro add-on or Microsoft 365 Copilot for users on a Microsoft 365 Enterprise plan.

Enabling Copilot in Excel

Copilot in Excel is an AI assistant specifically trained to help you get more out of your data. If you don't see Copilot on your Home tab (see Figure 5-6), you must take some steps to enable it.

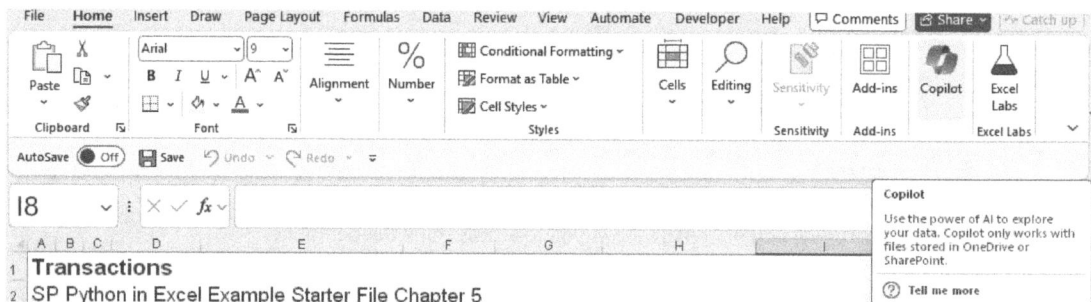

FIGURE 5-6 The Copilot icon appears on the Home tab if Copilot is enabled in Excel.

If the Copilot icon does not appear, the first step is to ensure you have a Copilot Pro license (or Microsoft 365 Copilot license if you are on a Microsoft 365 Enterprise plan). Then, ensure that your license is updated. Depending on your setup, the features enabled by the license update may take time to update automatically. To update your license manually, go to **File** > **Account**. When the screen shown in Figure 5-7 appears, click **Update License**.

> **Note** If you are outside the United States or if the billing address for your Copilot plan is in another region and you are having trouble enabling Copilot on your Home tab, you should check the latest Microsoft public roadmap for Microsoft 365 Copilot, as there could be some differences in your region. If you have issues, contact Microsoft support.

FIGURE 5-7 To access the option to manually update your license, go to the **File** tab, select **Account**, and then click **Update License**.

As mentioned, if you want Copilot to work with a file, that file must be saved to a OneDrive or SharePoint folder associated with your license. If you have a personal OneDrive folder and a business OneDrive folder and your Copilot license is associated with the business folder, you must use the business OneDrive folder. You must also switch on AutoSave. Copilot will let you know if you haven't done that yet (see Figure 5-8).

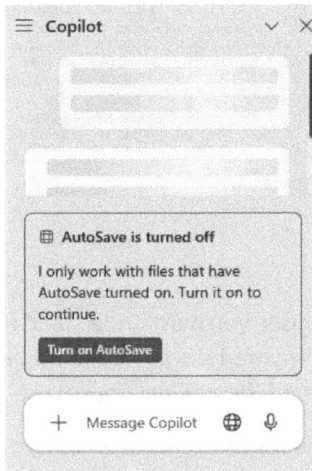

FIGURE 5-8 Copilot requires you to turn on AutoSave before you can use Copilot.

> **Note** When you attempt to use Copilot in a Microsoft app, you will be prompted to enable AutoSave.

Exploring data with the help of Copilot

We're finally getting to the hands-on part of the chapter, where we'll look at how to use Copilot. To follow along with the examples in this chapter, open the workbook **SP Python in Excel Example Starter File Chapter 5.xlsm**. Then, open the sheet Transactions, which contains a sales transactions dataset, as shown in Figure 5-9. The data on the Transactions sheet consists of 11 columns and 1,500 rows.

	Store ID	Store Name	City	Area m2	No. Sellers	Rental/month/m2	Analysis Priority	Transaction Date	Product	Sales
11	Store 1	Liberty's Delightful Bakery & Café	New York	122	9	49.29	3	2 May 22	cookies	
12	Store 2	Northwind Traders	Chicago	223	1	46.37	8	23 Oct 24	ice cream	
13	Store 3	VanArsdel, Ltd.	Los Angeles	207	1	48.44	5	20 Dec 23	cookies	
14	Store 4	Northwind Traders	New Orleans	152	6	59.31	2	19 Jul 24	chocolate cake	
15	Store 5	VanArsdel, Ltd.	Seattle	191	2	46.68	10	23 Jun 22	chocolate cake	
16	Store 6	Liberty's Delightful Bakery & Café	New York	253	10	55.18	2	17 Apr 22	chocolate cake	
17	Store 7	Wide World Importers	New York	249	1	55.38	2	26 Feb 23	spread	
18	Store 8	Wide World Importers	Chicago	208	7	55.91	3	22 Dec 23	spread	
19	Store 9	Proseware, Inc.	Tacoma	242	1	55.28	4	22 Jul 24	cookies	
20	Store 10	VanArsdel, Ltd.	Seattle	147	10	45.73	4	30 Sep 24	spread	
21	Store 11	Proseware, Inc.	Boston	196	10	45.1	7	1 Jan 24	chips	
22	Store 12	VanArsdel, Ltd.	Tacoma	255	5	57.8	9	12 Jul 22	spread	
23	Store 13	Northwind Traders	New York	156	4	49.11	2	27 Jan 23	ice cream	
24	Store 14	Proseware, Inc.	Boston	105	1	52.11	4	21 Jan 22	spread	

FIGURE 5-9 The Transactions sheet contains the data you will use in this chapter.

Understanding Copilot's data requirements

Before you begin using Copilot with this worksheet or any other dataset, you must understand that to get the best out of Copilot, you need to ensure that the data is formatted in a particular way. In this example, the data is in an Excel table called Transactions, which is set up for optimal Copilot use.

If you use any range of data with Copilot, make sure it meets the following requirements, many of which are also properties of an Excel table, as we covered in Chapter 2, "Getting to know Python in Excel":

- Only one header row, with any heading at the top of a column

- No duplicate headings and no blank headings

- Consistently formatted data

- No empty rows or columns

- No subtotals

- No merged cells

The data for this example is already in a suitable format, so you're ready to use it with Copilot.

Getting to know the Copilot pane

The Copilot pane is an AI interface where you can prompt Copilot to help you perform analytical tasks. To get familiar with the Copilot pane and how to use it, open the pane by locating **Home > Copilot**. Due to a recent development in Copilot in Excel, you may need to take an extra step at this point depending on your version of Excel. There may be a dropdown menu that enables you to choose between Chat and App Skills (see Figure 5-10a). If you have this option, you must choose App Skills. If you take the default, or choose Chat, you will not be able to complete the exercises.

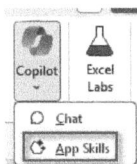

FIGURE 5-10a In some versions of Excel you must select App Skills.

The Copilot pane appears, providing several general prompt buttons to help you get started, as shown in Figure 5-10b.

> **Note** When we refer to the Copilot pane in Excel in the rest of this book, you should always choose App Sklls if the dropdown menu shown in Figure 5-10a is available.

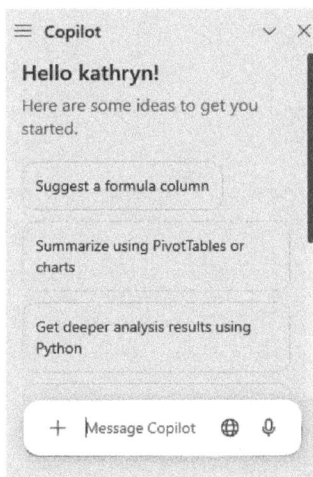

FIGURE 5-10b When the Copilot pane is opened in Excel, Copilot detects any data and suggests prompts.

We will examine the options for using Copilot with Python in the next chapter. For now, click the prompt **Summarize Using PivotTables or Charts**. After you click this button, Copilot starts its analysis. While it is thinking, a green circle around a down arrow rotates to indicate that the results are coming soon (see Figure 5-11).

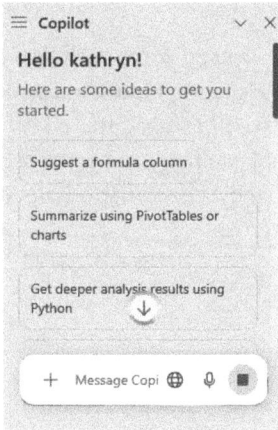

FIGURE 5-11 The green circle around the down arrow rotates as the analysis takes place.

> **Note** Remember that if you are reading a printed copy of this book, you will see only black-and-white text and figures. But if you're following along in the workbook, which we strongly recommend, you will see all the colors mentioned in this chapter.

Figure 5-12 shows sample results, where Copilot has produced a PivotTable of the Sum of Sales Amount for each product.

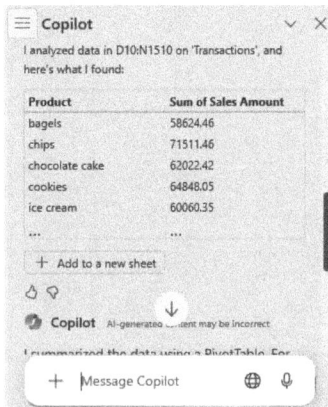

FIGURE 5-12 Copilot presents insights based on its analysis in a table.

> **Note** When you generate the results for this example, don't forget that when you use Copilot or any other AI platform, you must check the data generated by AI to ensure that the results are correct. As we have stressed throughout this book, you cannot assume that responses generated by AI are correct. You must check any code produced.

Note Although you are using the same data we used to generate the results shown here, you may receive different insights. Because you will be reading this in the future, you will be using a better version of Copilot and will get better results and more insights.

Under the PivotTable displayed in the Copilot pane, there is an option to add the PivotTable to a new sheet. In addition to showing the PivotTable, the Copilot pane includes descriptive text below, with an option to copy that text (see Figure 5-13).

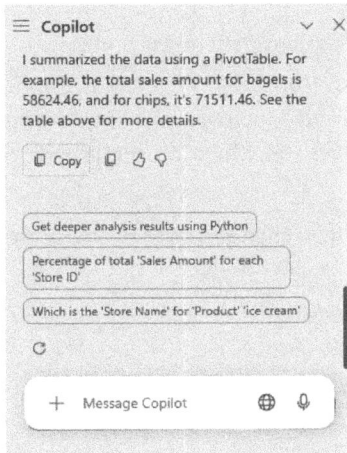

FIGURE 5-13 Copilot describes the analysis and suggests further prompts.

Note As you can see, Copilot uses natural language to describe the results.

If you click the **Add to a New Sheet** button that appears under the PivotTable, a sheet containing the PivotTable is added to the end of the workbook. Figure 5-14 shows the PivotTable added to a new sheet, along with a description pasted onto the sheet from the results Copilot provided.

Product	Sum of Sales Amount
bagels	58624.46
chips	71511.46
chocolate cake	62022.42
cookies	64848.05
ice cream	60060.35
spread	70460.54
Grand Total	387527.28

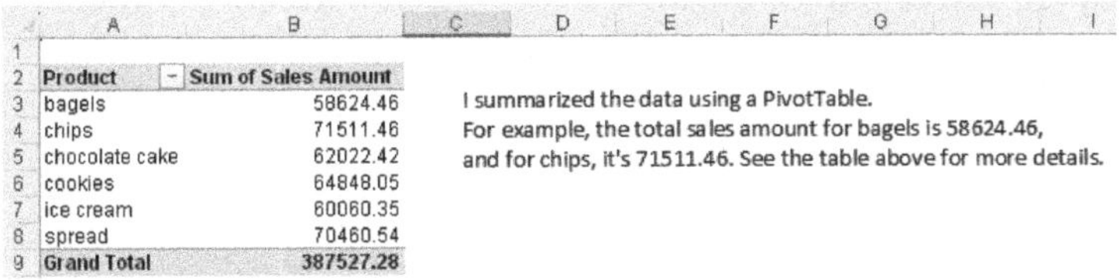

FIGURE 5-14 Copilot inserts the PivotTable into a new sheet, and the description is manually copied and pasted into a textbox for reference.

Rename this sheet **Copilot Pane Prompts** and move it to the right of the Transactions worksheet. Now open the Transactions sheet again, and notice that when you select a cell, you see the Copilot icon (see Figure 5-15a).

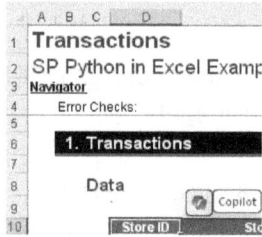

FIGURE 5-15a The Copilot icon is displayed next to the active cell.

Note At the time of writing, Copilot in Excel is in a period of transition. We have written this book ensuring our version of Excel was up to date—or beyond. However, printing deadlines do mean there is a gap between when the book is completed and when it is published.

And Copilot has taken advantage of that! The in-cell icon has now changed its appearance (see Figure 5-15b).

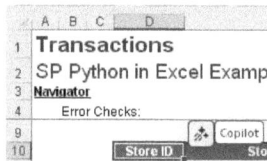

FIGURE 5-15b The Copilot icon may look different in your version of Excel.

If you do not see the icon, check the following setting in File > Options > Copilot. If 'Show Copilot icon only for highly relevant suggestions' is checked, you can uncheck it to see the icon more frequently.

Click the **Copilot** icon, and the menu shown in Figure 5-16 appears.

Note The Copilot menu is contextual, which means it shows different options depending on the data available.

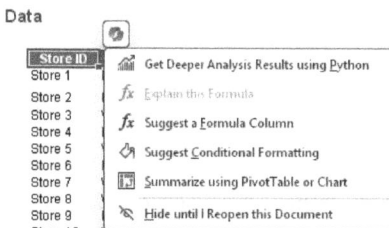

FIGURE 5-16 Clicking the Copilot icon next to the active cell reveals a menu.

In this case, choose **Suggest Conditional Formatting** from the Copilot menu. The Copilot pane appears, showing the results (see Figure 5-17).

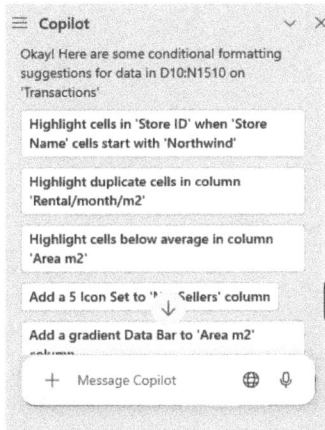

FIGURE 5-17 Choosing a prompt from the Copilot menu opens the Copilot pane, where the results are displayed.

The Copilot pane shows some conditional formatting suggestions for the data in D10:N1510 on the Transactions sheet. There is a button for each suggestion. In this case, click **Highlight Cells Below Average in Column 'Area m2'**. As you can see in Figure 5-18, Copilot suggests applying a conditional formatting rule to highlight the values that are below average. It suggests using a yellow fill color and black text.

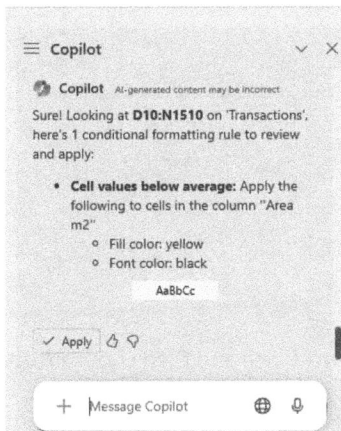

FIGURE 5-18 Copilot suggests a formatting rule and displays an example.

Click the **Apply** button, and Copilot applies the suggested formatting to the existing table in the Transactions worksheet, as shown in Figure 5-19. This is a great example of how Copilot can save you time on simple tasks.

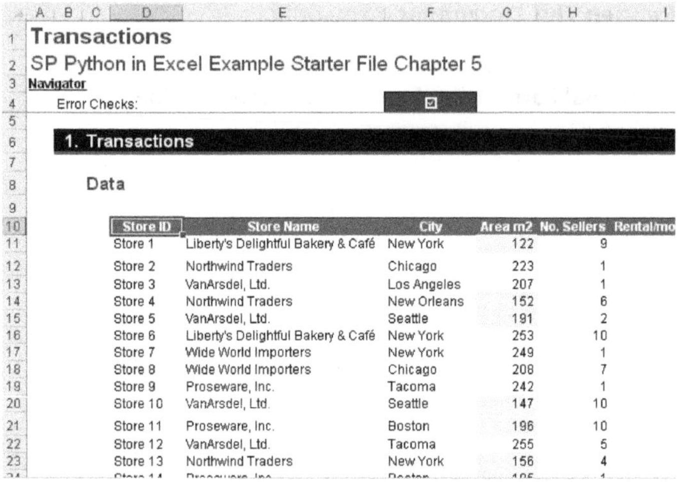

	Store ID	Store Name	City	Area m2	No. Sellers	Rental/mo
	Store 1	Liberty's Delightful Bakery & Café	New York	122	9	
	Store 2	Northwind Traders	Chicago	223	1	
	Store 3	VanArsdel, Ltd.	Los Angeles	207	1	
	Store 4	Northwind Traders	New Orleans	152	6	
	Store 5	VanArsdel, Ltd.	Seattle	191	2	
	Store 6	Liberty's Delightful Bakery & Café	New York	253	10	
	Store 7	Wide World Importers	New York	249	1	
	Store 8	Wide World Importers	Chicago	208	7	
	Store 9	Proseware, Inc.	Tacoma	242	1	
	Store 10	VanArsdel, Ltd.	Seattle	147	10	
	Store 11	Proseware, Inc.	Boston	196	10	
	Store 12	VanArsdel, Ltd.	Tacoma	255	5	
	Store 13	Northwind Traders	New York	156	4	

FIGURE 5-19 Copilot applies the formatting to the existing data.

You can also enter your own prompts into the Copilot pane. To see how this works, enter the general prompt **Show data insights**. Figure 5-20 shows sample results.

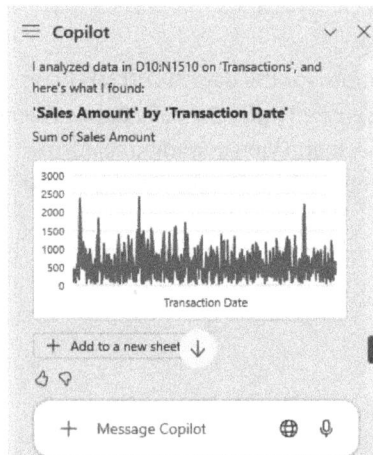

FIGURE 5-20 Copilot creates a chart when asked for insights.

To go a step further, select the prompt **Can I see another insight?** twice and then choose **Add all insights to grid**. Figure 5-21 shows sample results.

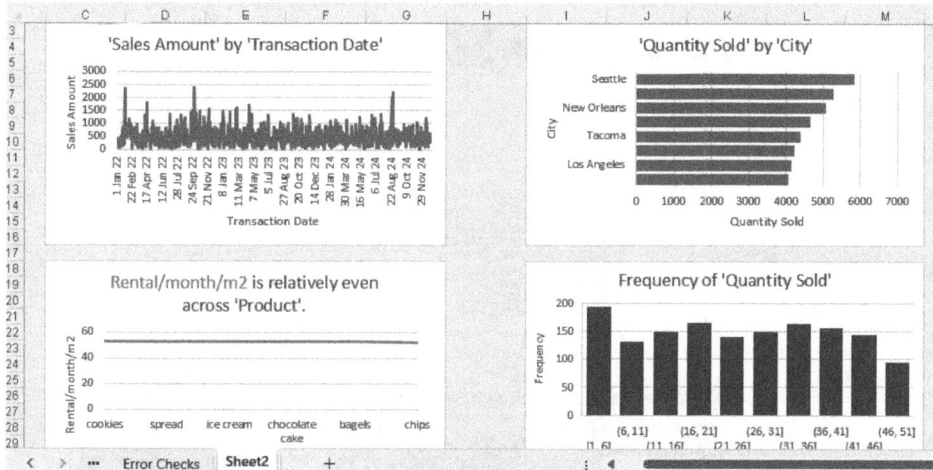

FIGURE 5-21 Copilot can create a new sheet with multiple insights.

The first three visualizations are PivotCharts, which you can customize. To access the settings for one of the PivotCharts, simply click the chart, and the settings should appear in the PivotChart Fields pane, as shown in Figure 5-22.

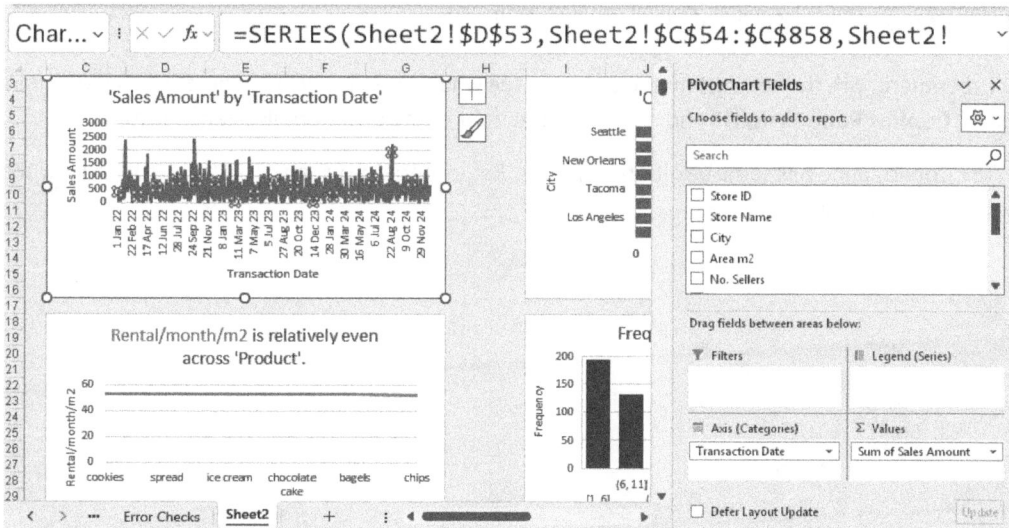

FIGURE 5-22 The PivotCharts created by Copilot can be customized.

Note If the PivotChart Fields pane is not displayed, select the PivotChart and access the **PivotChart Analyze** tab. In the **Show** section, click the **Field List** button.

The fourth chart Copilot has created is simpler—a (rather unusual) column chart that can also be customized (see Figure 5-23).

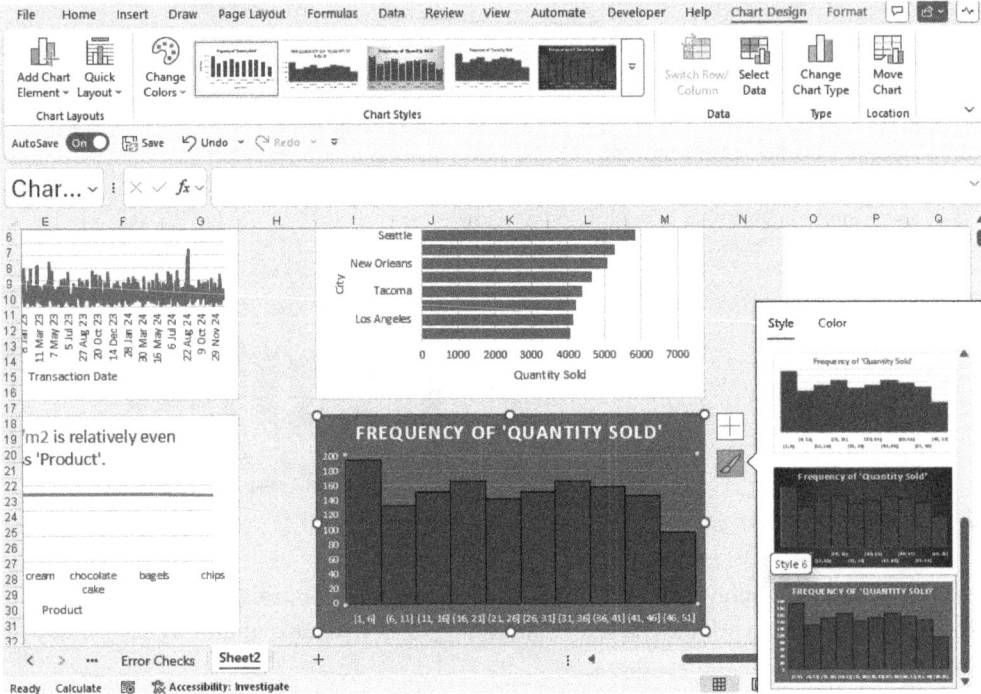

FIGURE 5-23 The charts created by Copilot can be customized.

Experiment with the settings on the charts to see what's possible. When you are finished, rename Sheet2 **Copilot Pane Insights** and move it to the right of the sheet Copilot Pane Prompts.

The Copilot pane has some additional options. For example, you can click the + icon to view the menu shown in Figure 5-24.

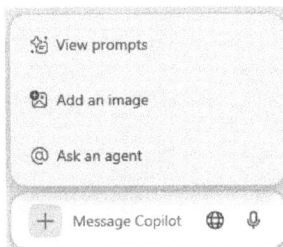

FIGURE 5-24 You can click the + icon to reveal a menu of options.

The Add an Image menu option in the Copilot pane is similar to the Excel From Picture dropdown menu on the Data tab (see Figure 5-25).

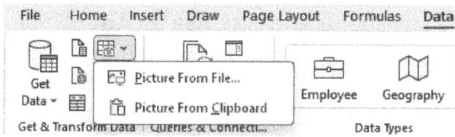

FIGURE 5-25 The From Picture dropdown menu on the Data tab of the Excel ribbon is similar to the Add an Image menu option in the Copilot pane.

When you select Add an Image, you can paste a picture into the prompt box or choose one of the other two options: Upload From This Device or Upload From Phone (see Figure 5-26). The Add an Image option currently supports several file types, including the following:

- .bmp

- .jpg/jpeg

- .gif

- .tiff

- .ico

- .png

- .webp

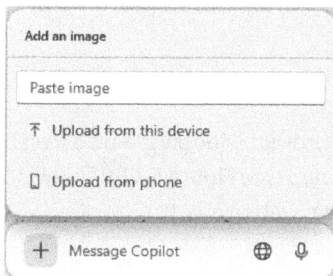

FIGURE 5-26 You can select images from a device or paste them into the Copilot prompt box.

The other option on the Copilot + menu is Ask an Agent. When we looked at the functionality offered by Copilot Pro earlier in this chapter, we saw that Copilot Studio can be used to build customized conversational agents. If you have already created agents in Copilot Studio, you can access them by clicking **Ask an Agent**. If you haven't already added any agents and click **Ask an Agent**, you are taken to the Apps dialog, which shows all the prebuilt agents—and not just those suitable for Excel (see Figure 5-27).

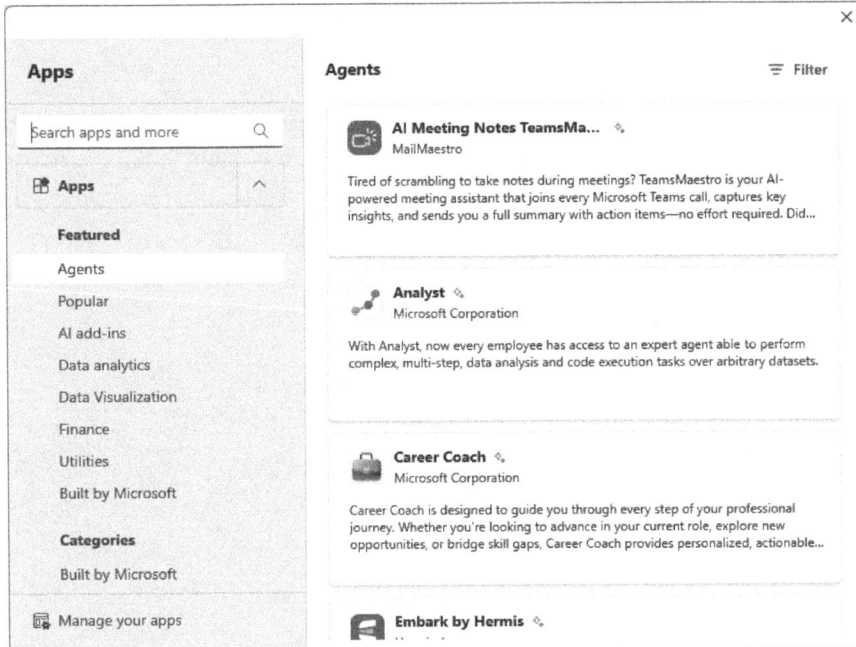

FIGURE 5-27 Agents are available in the Apps dialog.

The Copilot pane includes more options. At the bottom of the prompt window is a web icon (which looks like a globe) that gives you the option to use data from the web (see Figure 5-28). The window warns that some Microsoft 365 data may be shared if you toggle on web content.

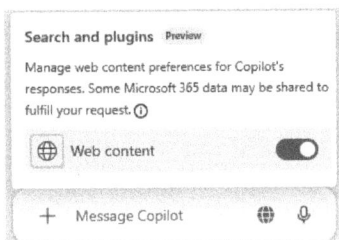

FIGURE 5-28 You can enable or disable web content in Copilot.

At the top of the Copilot pane is the option Switch Copilots. This allows you to switch between Copilot and an agent (see Figure 5-29). If you click **Get Agents**, Copilot takes you back to the Apps dialog.

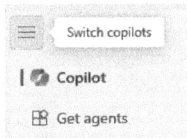

FIGURE 5-29 Switch Copilots allows you to use an agent instead of Copilot.

Crafting targeted prompts

Now that we have walked through the options available in the Copilot pane, let's look at how to enter targeted prompts to extract specific insights. Getting the results you want from Copilot is an art form. If you have ever spent time trying to find obscure information on the web, you know that each time an answer comes back, you need to refine your question to get to the correct information.

As mentioned when we discussed natural language processing earlier in this chapter, the iterative prompting process is often an important part of getting the results you need from chatbots. It also helps you determine what keywords could have helped you get to the answer more directly. By working through the examples in this chapter and the next one, you will learn how to use keywords to guide Copilot toward the answers you need, and you will begin to get a sense of how to craft effective prompts.

Even when using a targeted prompt, you may find that you must ask the same question more than once to get the results you are looking for. Copilot does not calculate the correct answer the way you're used to seeing computers calculate answers; instead, it uses algorithms to access the data it has been trained on and returns a relevant answer. Basically, it finds an answer that it has seen before. Because Copilot has been trained on a huge amount of data, its answers will vary. (It's not all that different from how two humans who independently provide a dashboard for the same scenario will produce dashboards that differ from one another.) So, when you repeat a prompt, the process Copilot uses to find an appropriate answer will vary, and so will the results. You might receive a table or a chart, for example, or the answer might be all text. You can use this idea of repeating the same prompt to have Copilot generate a range of insights to answer your question.

It's time to start experimenting with prompts to see Copilot in action. Open the **Transactions** worksheet. In the Copilot pane, enter the prompt **Show the amount only by year and store name in a table**. Here, you are specifying the data relationship you want to see and the format you want the results to be in. Copilot shows the results—in this case, a PivotTable—in the Copilot pane (see Figure 5-30).

The device you're using and your screen settings determine how much of Copilot's reply you can view at once in the Copilot pane. For this example, you might see only the first two or three columns of the PivotTable in the Copilot pane. You can scroll to see different parts of the response. You can also expand the Copilot pane to view more of the response, but you can't always expand it enough to see all of the response at once.

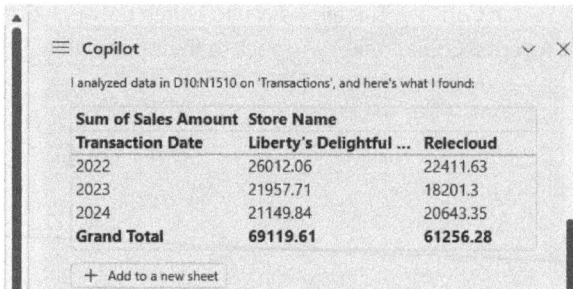

FIGURE 5-30 By entering a specific prompt, you can guide Copilot to give you output tailored to your requirements.

Note Remember that your results will differ from those shown here, even though you are using the same data that the examples in the book are based on. For one thing, the Copilot you are using will be superior to the version we used to create these examples. Also, as we said earlier in this chapter, even with the same version of Copilot using the same data and the same prompt, Copilot usually returns different answers when asked the same question more than once.

Notice that the prompt said *amount* and *year*. Based on this input, Copilot determined that it needed to access data from the Sales Amount and Transaction Date columns.

Putting the PivotTable on a new sheet makes it easy for Copilot to create and position the PivotTable without further interaction. However, if you want to change the location of the PivotTable, you can either copy and paste it to a new location or select the **Move PivotTable** option from the **PivotTable Analyze** tab (see Figure 5-31).

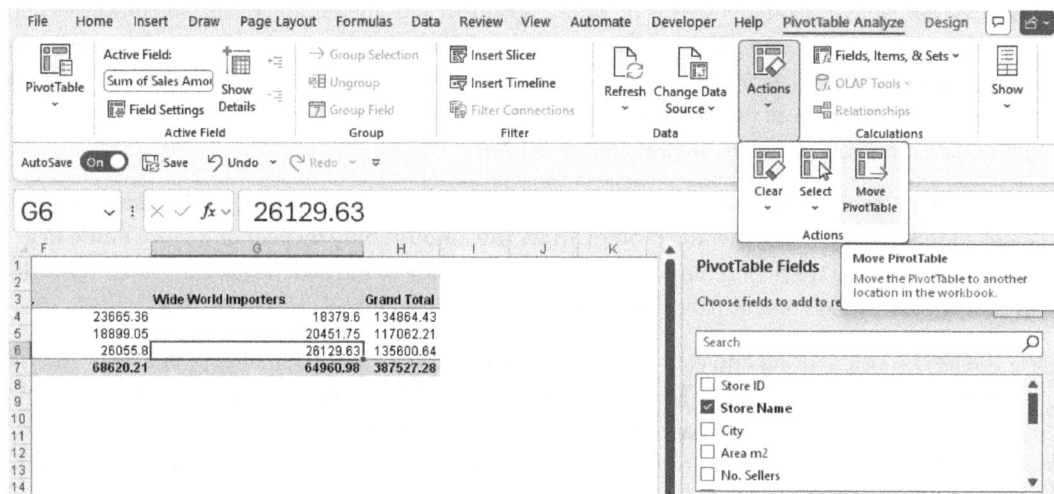

FIGURE 5-31 A PivotTable can be copied and pasted to a new location or moved using the Move PivotTable option on the PivotTable Analyze tab.

To see another example, in the Transactions worksheet, enter this prompt into the Copilot pane: **Show the top 3 products based on amount in a bar chart**. Figure 5-32 shows sample results.

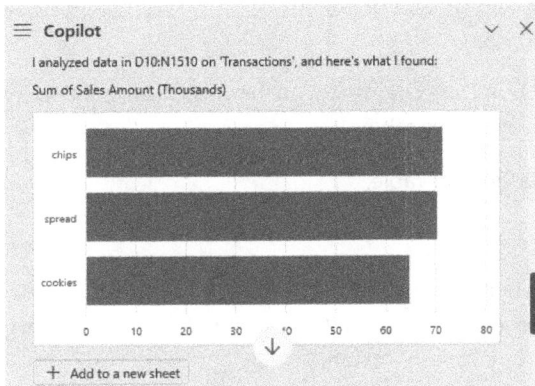

FIGURE 5-32 Copilot has returned a bar chart showing the top three products, based on sales amount.

You can also use Copilot to add other useful columns to the data. To see how it works, enter the following prompt in the Copilot pane on the Transactions sheet: **Add columns for the quarter and year of the date**. Figure 5-33 shows sample results in full-screen mode, so it is possible to view more of the results in the Copilot pane.

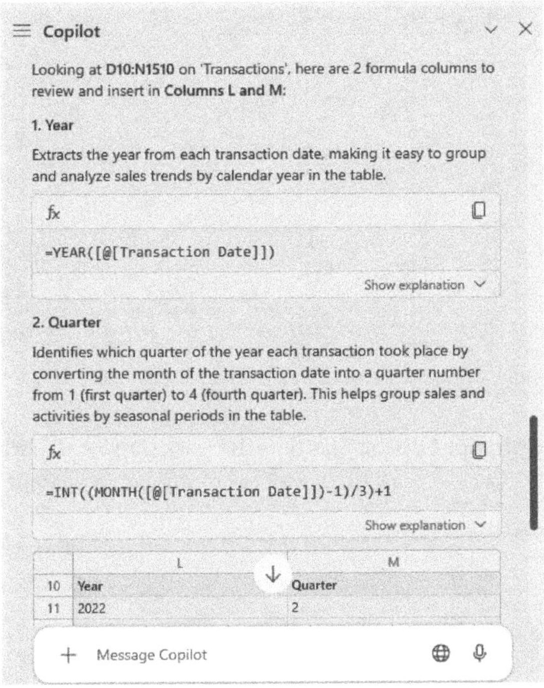

FIGURE 5-33 Copilot has returned formulas for the Year and Quarter columns and a table of values for the two columns.

Copilot generates two Excel formulas to create the columns specified in the prompt, along with a table of the values that would appear in columns L and M in the current sheet if you were to accept Copilot's solution. For the Year column, it creates the following formula:

```
=YEAR([@[Transaction Date]])
```

This formula extracts the year from the Transaction Date column for each transaction, making it easy to group and analyze sales trends by calendar year in the table.

Copilot creates the following formula for the Quarter table:

```
=INT((MONTH([@[Transaction Date]])-1)/3)+1
```

This formula identifies the quarter of the year when each transaction occurred by converting the month from the Transaction Date column into a quarter number, from 1 (first quarter) to 4 (fourth quarter). This helps group sales and activities by seasonal periods in the table.

If the columns Copilot has suggested look right, you can choose the option **Insert Columns**. Figure 5-34 shows sample changes to the Transactions table.

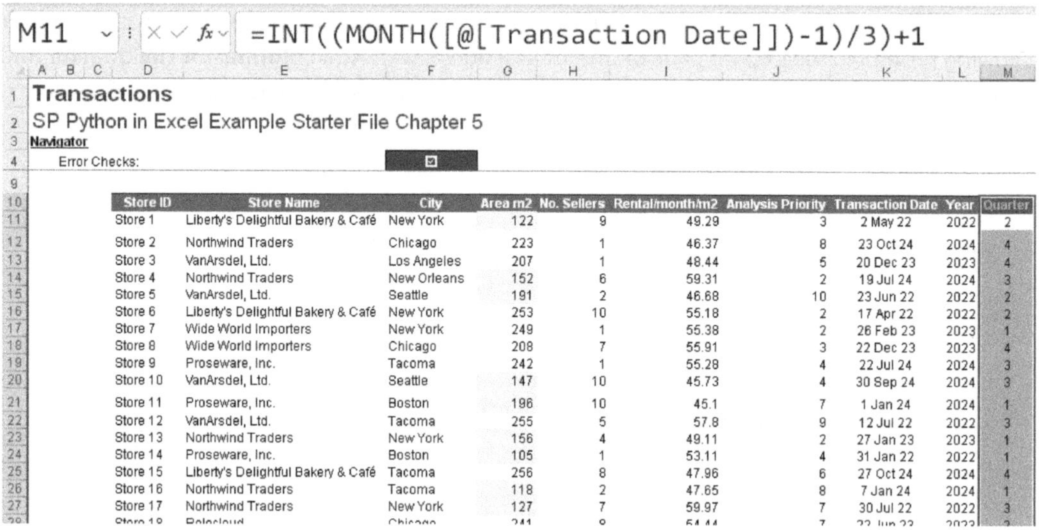

M11 =INT((MONTH([@[Transaction Date]])-1)/3)+1

Transactions

SP Python in Excel Example Starter File Chapter 5

Navigator

Error Checks:

Store ID	Store Name	City	Area m2	No. Sellers	Rental/month/m2	Analysis Priority	Transaction Date	Year	Quarter
Store 1	Liberty's Delightful Bakery & Café	New York	122	9	49.29	3	2 May 22	2022	2
Store 2	Northwind Traders	Chicago	223	1	46.37	8	23 Oct 24	2024	4
Store 3	VanArsdel, Ltd.	Los Angeles	207	1	48.44	5	20 Dec 23	2023	4
Store 4	Northwind Traders	New Orleans	152	6	59.31	2	19 Jul 24	2024	3
Store 5	VanArsdel, Ltd.	Seattle	191	2	46.68	10	23 Jun 22	2022	2
Store 6	Liberty's Delightful Bakery & Café	New York	253	10	55.18	2	17 Apr 22	2022	2
Store 7	Wide World Importers	New York	249	1	55.38	2	26 Feb 23	2023	1
Store 8	Wide World Importers	Chicago	208	7	55.91	3	22 Dec 23	2023	4
Store 9	Proseware, Inc.	Tacoma	242	1	55.28	4	22 Jul 24	2024	3
Store 10	VanArsdel, Ltd.	Seattle	147	10	45.73	4	30 Sep 24	2024	3
Store 11	Proseware, Inc.	Boston	196	10	45.1	7	1 Jan 24	2024	1
Store 12	VanArsdel, Ltd.	Tacoma	255	5	57.8	9	12 Jul 22	2022	3
Store 13	Northwind Traders	New York	156	4	49.11	2	27 Jan 23	2023	1
Store 14	Proseware, Inc.	Boston	105	1	53.11	4	31 Jan 22	2022	1
Store 15	Liberty's Delightful Bakery & Café	Tacoma	256	8	47.96	6	27 Oct 24	2024	4
Store 16	Northwind Traders	Tacoma	118	2	47.65	8	7 Jan 24	2024	1
Store 17	Northwind Traders	New York	127	7	59.97	7	30 Jul 22	2022	3

FIGURE 5-34 Copilot can insert new columns in a table, using the Excel formulas it has calculated.

Let's consider one more example of how to prompt Copilot. This time, let's ask Copilot to find an insight that will help with business planning. In this case, we'll focus on how modifying a prompt can move you closer to the insights required.

On the Transactions sheet, enter the following prompt in the Copilot pane: **What insights can you give me about underperforming stores?** Figure 5-35 shows sample results.

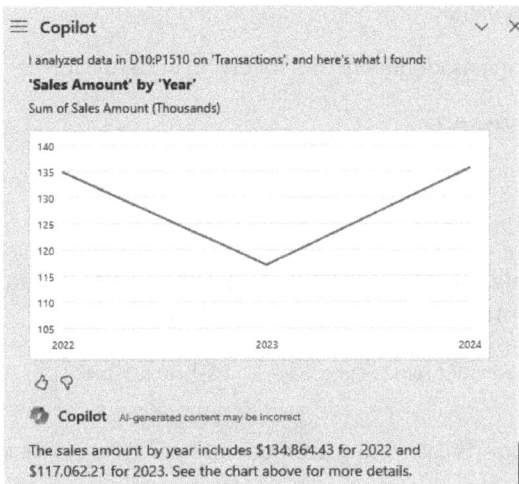

FIGURE 5-35 Copilot returned information about which years the stores underperformed.

We can now see which year all the stores underperformed, but we can't see which particular stores underperformed. We need to give Copilot more information about what we want to see. Enter the following prompt in the Copilot pane: **What insights can you give me about which stores are underperforming?** Copilot returns with a plan like the one shown in Figure 5-36.

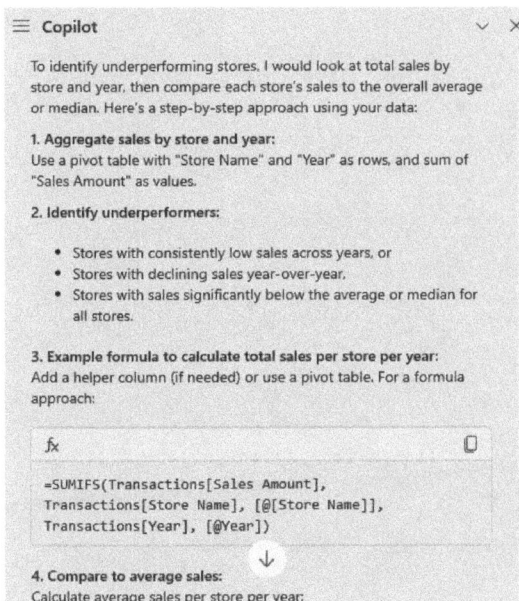

FIGURE 5-36 Copilot returns information about how to get the insights we requested.

This is the full plan:

- **Aggregate sales by store and year:** Copilot proposes using a PivotTable with Store Name and Year as rows and Sum of Sales Amount as values.

- **Identify underperformers:** Copilot suggests identifying the following underperformers:

  - Stores with consistently low sales across years

  - Stores with declining sales year-over-year

  - Stores with sales significantly below the average or median for all stores

- **Example formula to calculate total sales per store per year:** Copilot suggests adding a helper column (if needed) or using a PivotTable. It recommends this formula:

  ```
  =SUMIFS(Transactions[Sales Amount], Transactions[Store Name], [@[Store Name]],
  Transactions[Year], [@Year])
  ```

- **Compare to average sales:** Copilot suggests calculating average sales per store per year by using this formula:

  ```
  =AVERAGEIFS(Transactions[Sales Amount], Transactions[Year], [@Year])
  ```

- **Flag underperformers:** Copilot proposes adding a column that contains the following formula to flag stores that are below average:

  ```
  =IF([@[Total Sales]] < [@[Average Sales]], "Underperforming", "OK")
  ```

Figure 5-37 shows the rest of the Copilot response to the prompt, which provides some insights and ideas on how to proceed with this plan.

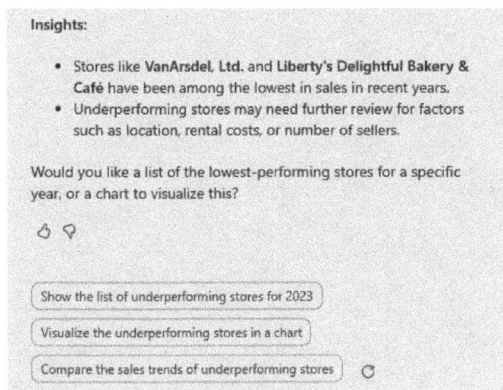

Insights:

- Stores like **VanArsdel, Ltd.** and **Liberty's Delightful Bakery & Café** have been among the lowest in sales in recent years.
- Underperforming stores may need further review for factors such as location, rental costs, or number of sellers.

Would you like a list of the lowest-performing stores for a specific year, or a chart to visualize this?

Show the list of underperforming stores for 2023

Visualize the underperforming stores in a chart

Compare the sales trends of underperforming stores

FIGURE 5-37 Copilot returns some basic insights and further suggestions.

In this case, the next step is to choose **Compare the sales trends of the underperforming stores**. Figure 5-58 shows sample results.

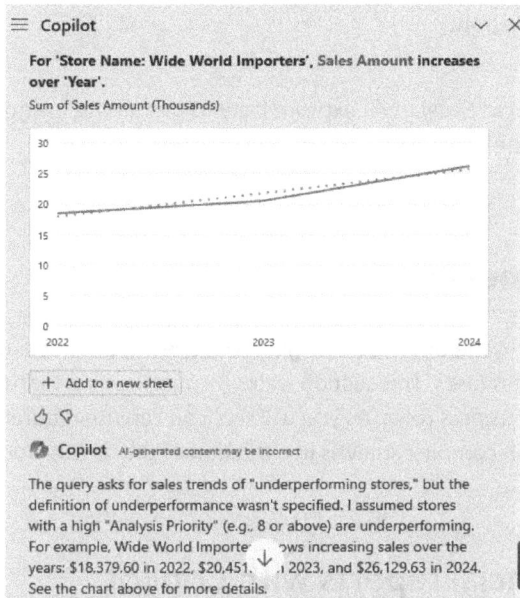

FIGURE 5-38 Copilot returns a chart that indicates how the store Wide World Importers performed.

Since Wide World Importers has been identified as a potential problem and 2023 seems to be the year of poor performance, we can complete the conversation with Copilot by providing a final prompt: **Give me insights on Wide World Importers sales trends in 2023**. Figure 5-39 shows sample results.

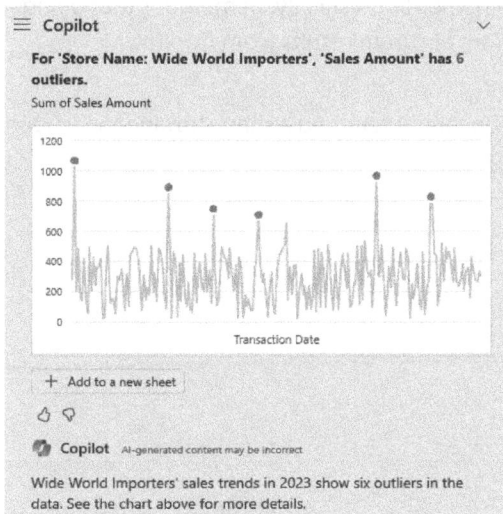

FIGURE 5-39 Copilot returns a chart that shows the outliers for Wide World Importers.

We will stop our interrogation about the fate of Wide World Importers here. As you have seen in this example, you can repeat questions multiple times and ask new questions to see if you get more suitable results. Based on what you have seen in this section, you should now have an idea of how to craft multiple prompts to zero in on the desired information.

> **Note** Chapter 6, "Using Copilot with Python in Excel," will explore how to get all the insights and information gleaned from Copilot on one sheet.

Using Copilot to assist with business tasks

Now that you know how to use Copilot in Excel in general, it's time to get more specific and look at how to use Copilot to assist with particular business tasks. This section walks through scenarios showing tasks that may be carried out by a variety of business roles. As you will see, you can use natural language prompts to get your AI assistant to perform complex analysis in a fraction of the time it would take you to perform the same task on your own.

Creating visualizations for financial reports with Copilot

For this first scenario, let's say that you are a finance manager and need to prepare a monthly performance report based on the **Financial** sheet. Here's one prompt you might use: **Create a line chart displaying monthly totals for Amount (in Finance table) and Expenses (in Finance table) over the past 12 months**.

> **Note** This prompt specifies the table in which the data can be found. If you don't specify the table, Copilot may try to interpret the column names linguistically. Remember that being more specific in your prompt helps you get more accurate results from Copilot.

Figure 5-40 shows sample results. In this case, Copilot has returned a chart showing the amount and expenses data over the past 12 months.

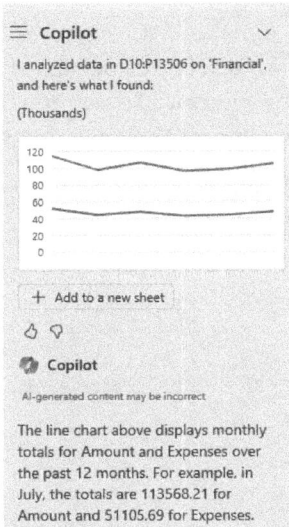

FIGURE 5-40 Copilot returns a chart showing the amount and expenses data over the past 12 months.

However, the chart in the Copilot pane lacks a lot of detail. If you click **Add to a New Sheet**, Copilot adds the information to a new sheet that shows the PivotChart next to the underlying PivotTable (see Figure 5-41). Thanks to Copilot, you now have a key visualization for your report, which you can format using the company template.

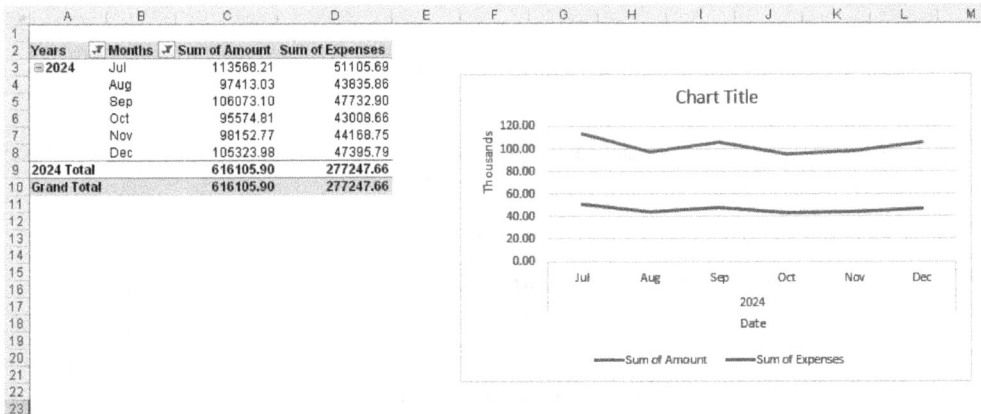

FIGURE 5-41 A PivotChart with lines for Sum of Amount and Sum of Expenses has been created in a new sheet, along with the underlying PivotTable.

If you add the chart Copilot created to a new sheet and then decide you don't want to use it, you can simply delete the new sheet.

Tracking projects using Copilot

Now let's say that you're a project manager. You are managing multiple marketing campaigns and need to get a snapshot of the current situation based on data from the **Project** worksheet. You could use this prompt: **Summarize project status by team, highlighting tasks past their due dates**.

Figure 5-42 shows sample results. In this case, Copilot has returned a bar chart that shows the number of tasks past their due dates for the IT, Sales, and Operations teams.

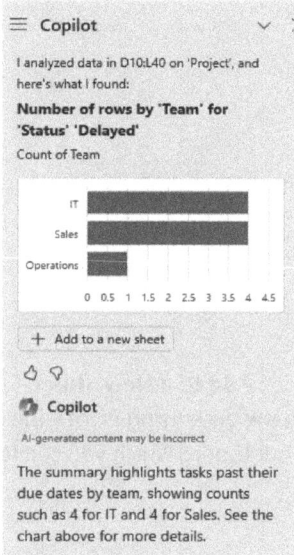

FIGURE 5-42 Copilot returns a bar chart showing the number of tasks past their due dates, by team.

Based on Copilot's results, you might look into why the Operations team is struggling and consider solutions such as reallocating resources.

Using Copilot for decision-making

For this example, suppose you are an analyst who must evaluate product performance across sales regions, using data from the sheet **Financial**. You could use this prompt: **Show the top 5 products by sales in each Store ID for 2023 in a column chart**. Figure 5-43 shows some sample results. In this case, Copilot has provided a column chart that shows clusters of five colored bars for the top five products, by quantity.

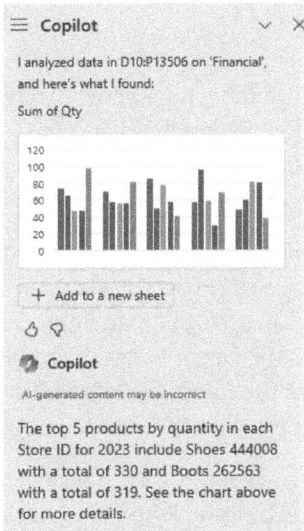

FIGURE 5-43 Copilot returns a chart that shows the top five products by quantity.

Again, the chart in the Copilot pane shows only some of the details. If you click **Add to a New Sheet**, Copilot adds the information to a new sheet that shows the PivotChart below the underlying PivotTable (see Figure 5-44).

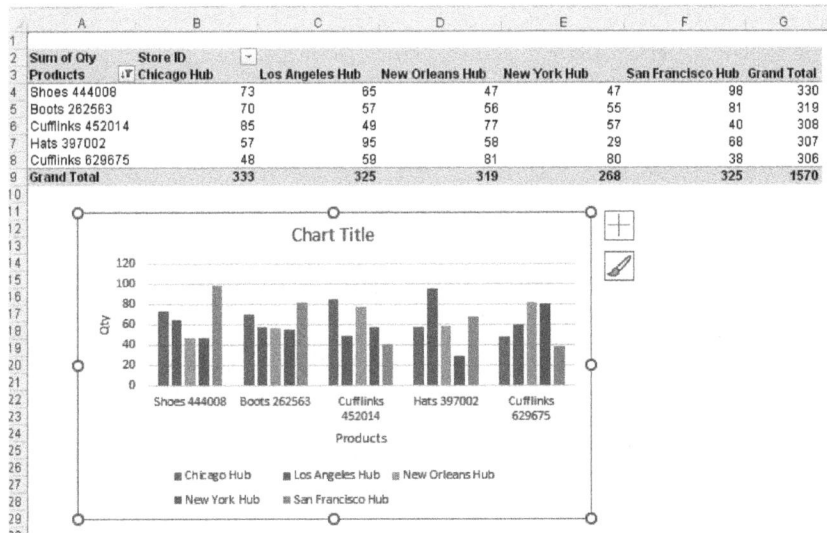

Sum of Qty	Store ID					
Products	Chicago Hub	Los Angeles Hub	New Orleans Hub	New York Hub	San Francisco Hub	Grand Total
Shoes 444008	73	65	47	47	98	330
Boots 262563	70	57	56	55	81	319
Cufflinks 452014	85	49	77	57	40	308
Hats 397002	57	95	58	29	68	307
Cufflinks 629675	48	59	81	80	38	306
Grand Total	333	325	319	268	325	1570

FIGURE 5-44 When the Copilot results are added to a new sheet, more details are displayed.

Summary

This chapter introduced the potential of AI as an intelligent assistant. Understanding how AI has evolved helps you understand the algorithms and training that go into creating the chatbots we use today. Microsoft has committed time and money to furthering the AI capabilities of the Microsoft 365 ecosystem.

Although this book focuses on Excel, Copilot can provide time-saving assistance in all the Microsoft 365 apps, and you should take advantage of that help. In Excel, Copilot is available from the Home tab and from any cell you select (via the Copilot icon). You can use Copilot to help create formulas and provide insights. You may need to prompt Copilot more than once to get the results you need, and as you use it more, you will discover the best phrases to use to get the information you need. You must also check all the results you get because there is no guarantee of accuracy.

In this chapter, you saw several examples where using Excel was enhanced by the assistance of Copilot. The next step is to perform more in-depth data analysis in Excel by using Python in Excel with Copilot. Using natural language prompts with Copilot, you can create complex Python analysis and insightful visuals. You won't need to write the Python code, but you can apply your Python in Excel skills to customize and check the code to ensure the results suit your business requirements. Knowing how to use Python in Excel, how to use AI in general, and Copilot in particular, will allow you to interrogate your Excel data and produce the information your business needs.

## CHAPTER 6

Using Copilot with Python in Excel

In this chapter, you will:

- See how Python in Excel and Copilot have come together

- Explore Copilot advanced analysis

- Use Copilot advanced analysis in a forecasting example

- Create a simple dashboard using Copilot as an assistant

Note To follow along with the examples in this chapter, you must download the resources that accompany this book. If you don't already have these resources, visit *https://www .sumproduct.com/python-in-excel-book-resources* and download the files to a folder associated with your Python in Excel license. For this chapter, you will begin by accessing the workbook **SP Python in Excel Example Starter File Chapter 6.xlsm**.

Bringing together Python in Excel and Copilot

You've already learned a lot about Python in Excel and Microsoft Copilot—two key players that were not available in Excel until recently. Now, however, you can use them together to approach data analysis more easily and powerfully than ever before.

Python is ideal for data analysis because much of the code needed to analyze data has already been written and is available in free libraries. In Chapter 3, "Using Python libraries," you explored some of the capabilities of the preloaded and recommended libraries. Another key feature of Python is its scalability; Python helps you analyze large datasets easily.

Before the release of Python in Excel, analysts were already creating and sharing apps that allowed them to use Python with Excel data. As mentioned in earlier chapters, many companies see Python in Excel (making Python available in Excel natively) as a safer way to access the power of Python. To harness this power, analysts must learn how to use Python in Excel. In Chapter 2, "Getting to know Python in Excel," you started with some basic Python, but accessing detailed data analysis and extensive visualizations requires more advanced Python. Copilot is your ideal assistant to reach this next level.

As you already know, Microsoft Copilot uses elements of the general chatbot ChatGPT but has been specifically designed to assist users of Microsoft 365. The Copilot Pro add-on (or Microsoft 365 Copilot if you are on an Enterprise plan) encompasses a suite of AI assistants embedded into and tailored to work with each Microsoft Office 365 app. For example, in Excel, Copilot can assist you with Excel formulas. In Chapter 5, "Introduction to AI and Copilot," you saw examples of how Copilot in Excel can help in common business scenarios, such as by creating Excel formulas and applying formatting to a workbook in response to simple natural language prompts. As you saw with some more specific data analysis tasks, sometimes this means having a conversation with Copilot rather than just entering one prompt, and it always means checking to ensure that Copilot's results are accurate. Copilot helps you quickly conduct trend analysis and produce insightful visualizations.

While you can ask other AI interfaces for help producing Python code, Copilot is designed to use Python in Excel to solve data analysis challenges. This chapter explores Copilot advanced analysis and illustrates some ways it can help you perform detailed data analysis without having to create Python code. This chapter doesn't demonstrate everything that Copilot can do, but it does provide examples that show the processes involved and the steps you can take to interact with Copilot and Python in Excel to produce useful results.

Performing advanced analysis with Copilot and Python in Excel

When you use Copilot with Excel, its solutions are based on Excel functions and visualizations; in this chapter, we call this "standard Copilot." Copilot has now been integrated with Python in Excel to use Python code to analyze data and provide insights; in this chapter, we call this "Copilot advanced analysis." The same natural language prompts that can help you create an insightful PivotChart can now be used to access the Python libraries preloaded into Python in Excel, as well as any other libraries it has been trained to use. This helpful Excel expert is now a Python specialist too! You can describe the analysis you need to carry out in Python, and Copilot can generate Python code using Copilot advanced analysis to give you insights and explain each step.

To use Copilot advanced analysis, you must have some knowledge of Python. As you learned in Chapter 5, Copilot can make mistakes, and you need to know enough Python basics to spot problems. Equipped with your knowledge of Python, and with Copilot at your side, you will soon learn many more Python functions that can help you perform complex data analysis.

Before we get into new examples, let's try out Copilot advanced analysis, using the workbook **SP Python in Excel Example Starter File Chapter 6.xlsm**, which contains data from Chapter 5. Open the Transactions worksheet and then open the Copilot App Skills pane using the dropdown menu under the Copilot button.

Figure 6-1 shows the Copilot App Skills pane and the transactions data you worked with in Chapter 5. The Copilot App Skills pane shows several prompt suggestion buttons based on the transactions data.

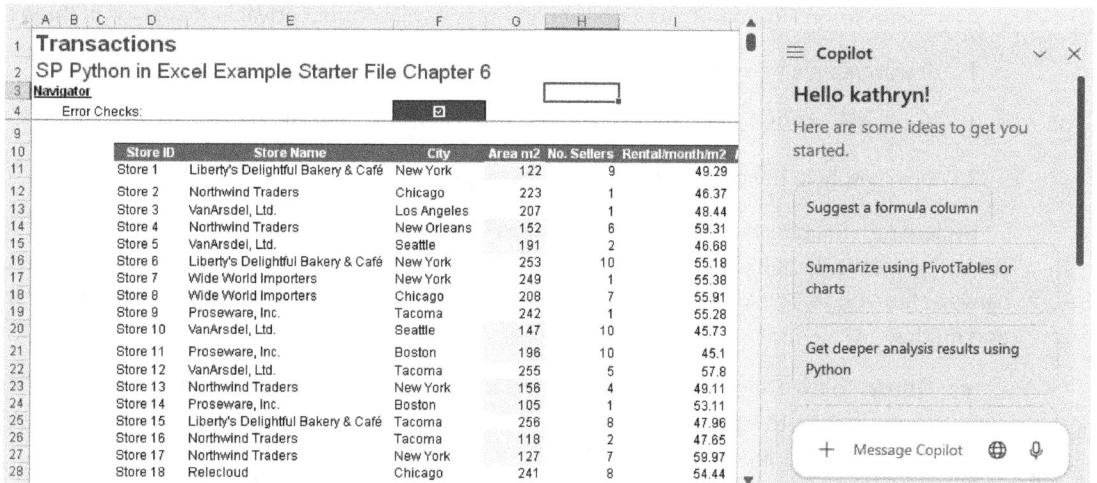

FIGURE 6-1 The transactions data

As you can see in Figure 6-1, one of the prompts Copilot gives you is Get Deeper Analysis Results Using Python. No button explicitly says "Copilot Advanced Analysis," but if you proceed to enter or choose a prompt that contains keywords that Copilot recognizes as being associated with Python functionality (the most obvious being "Python"), Copilot will suggest using advanced analysis to proceed. To see this in action, click the suggested prompt **Get Deeper Analysis Results Using Python**. Copilot responds by offering to use advanced analysis (see Figure 6-2).

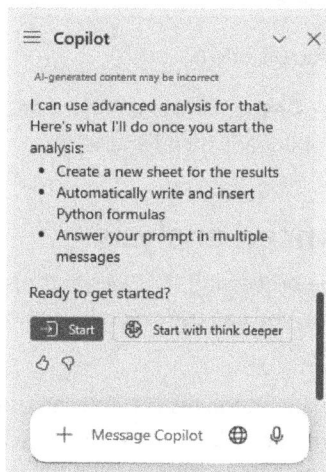

FIGURE 6-2 Copilot offers to use advanced analysis and describes the process.

As you can see in Figure 6-2, the Copilot pane says it will conduct advanced analysis in three steps:

1. It will create a new sheet.

2. It will create Python formulas and insert them in the workbook.

3. It will reply to the prompt in multiple messages.

Underneath the question Ready to Get Started? are two buttons: Start and Start with Think Deeper. Start triggers the default conversation mode, Quick mode. Start with Think Deeper triggers the other conversation mode, Think Deeper. Microsoft has designed Copilot to support three different conversation modes:

- **Quick:** To use Quick mode, click the Start button in the Copilot pane that provides advanced analysis (refer to Figure 6-2). This mode is ideal for quick interactions where the responses you are looking for are straightforward.

- **Think Deeper:** In Think Deeper mode, Copilot takes longer to consider the analysis because it uses advanced reasoning models; it may take up to 30 seconds to respond. This mode is best for complex examples where more thoughtful responses are required. When accessing Copilot at *https://copilot.microsoft.com*, you can also access Think Deeper mode, but your prompts have less processing priority than those created by Copilot Pro users. Think Deeper is available in all supported Copilot regions and languages.

- **Deep Research:** This mode is currently available only with Copilot Pro. The response time is between 3 and 6 minutes because this model is programmed to research the problem and return a detailed response. It is currently available only with US English selected as the language.

Once you select a conversation mode, it remains active unless you disable it.

In a moment, we'll look more closely at how the Quick and Think Deeper conversation modes work, but first let's look at some ideas for getting the best results from Copilot advanced analysis.

Getting the best results from Copilot advanced analysis

In Chapter 5, we discussed the techniques used by natural language processing (NLP) algorithms. As also discussed in Chapter 5, when you compose prompts for Copilot, you can use several techniques to help the AI parse your input and provide helpful results:

- **Use steps:** You will notice that Copilot uses steps when explaining the results. You can use the same method when creating a prompt. You don't have to enter one long sentence. In fact, asking several related questions in succession to refine the results often works better.

- **Be specific:** Copilot can use Python to produce a wide variety of insights and charts. To help it understand which direction you want to go, you must be specific. If you need to focus on departments that are struggling, for example, prompting Copilot to provide sales trends may not produce the results you are looking for. Asking Copilot to focus on the sales performance of departments in 2024 would be a better choice.

- **Give Copilot context:** To guide Copilot, it is important to give it some relevant background information to help it focus on the data you need to analyze. For example, providing table names and column names will ensure that the relevant data is analyzed. You can also use the variable names created when the Python code is generated to focus on the initial results and produce more targeted insights.

- **Iterate:** Just as you saw when using standard Copilot to generate Excel code, you can use the suggested prompts or create your own prompts to drill down into the Python insights that Copilot creates when performing advanced analysis.

- **Use the suggested prompts:** The suggested prompts can help you learn about the kinds of insights that are possible when Copilot uses Python to provide advanced analysis.

Using the Quick mode of Copilot advanced analysis

After you enter a prompt or select a prompt suggestion, Copilot gives you the option of continuing with advanced analysis by selecting Start Advanced Analysis or entering a new message. In this case, click **Start Advanced Analysis**, and Copilot gives you the familiar rotating green circle around a down arrow to indicate that the results are coming soon (see Figure 6-3).

> **Note** Remember that if you are reading a printed copy of this book, you will see only black-and-white text and figures. But if you're following along in the workbook, which we strongly recommend, you will see all the colors we mention in this chapter.

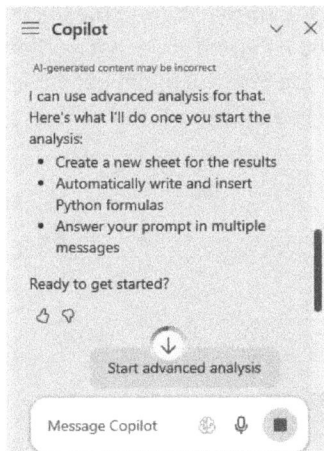

FIGURE 6-3 The advanced analysis process takes a few seconds to complete.

Figure 6-4 shows sample results.

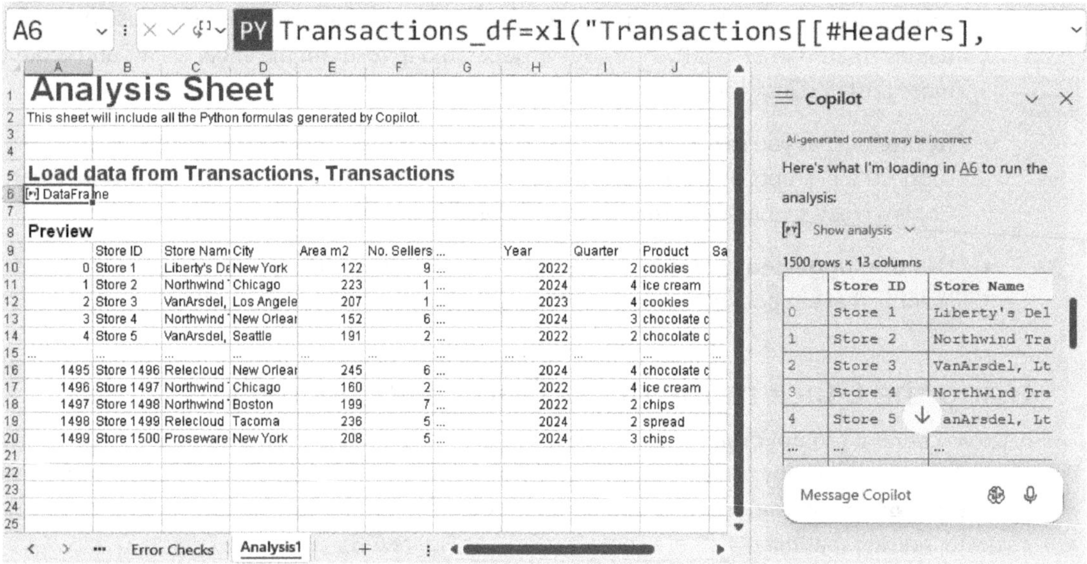

FIGURE 6-4 The advanced analysis process has added a new worksheet that contains a DataFrame.

A few things have happened. A new worksheet, Analysis1, has been added to the end of the workbook. Under the title Analysis Sheet, the first section is titled Load Data from Transactions [the table], Transactions [the worksheet]. Cell A6 is a Python cell that contains the DataFrame `Transactions_df`.

The Copilot pane indicates what is loaded in cell A6. You can click the A6 hyperlink in the Copilot pane to go to A6 in the grid. You can also click Show Analysis to view the Python code that has been created. In this case, click **Show Analysis**. Figure 6-5 shows sample code that you might get in the Copilot pane. The first line of the code is a comment, and the second line creates a DataFrame.

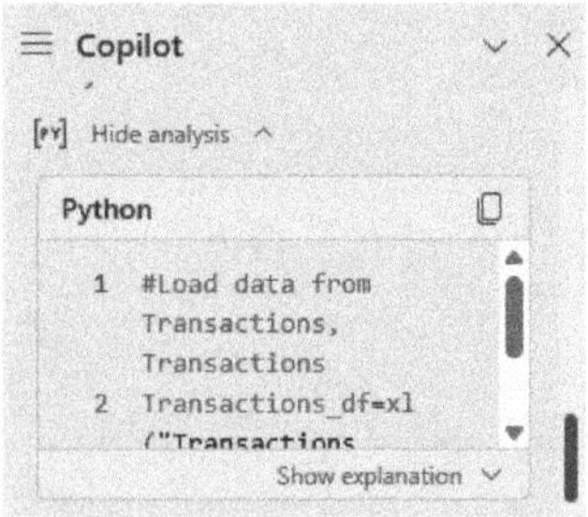

FIGURE 6-5 The Python code that has been generated for cell A6

In the window shown in Figure 6-5, click **Show Explanation** to get Copilot's code description. Figure 6-6 shows sample results. In this figure, the Copilot pane has been expanded to show both the Python code and the description in full.

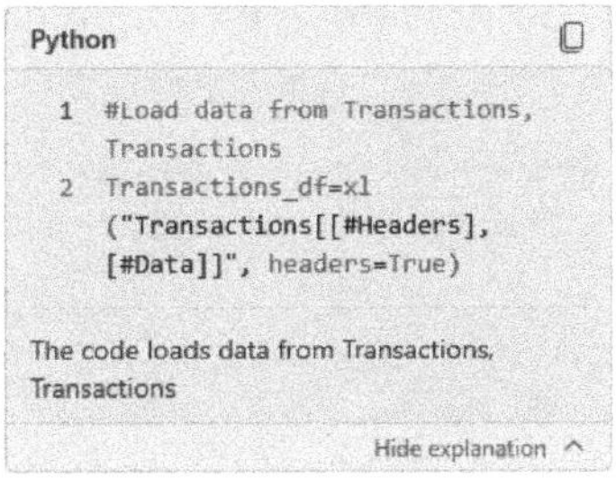

```python
1  #Load data from Transactions,
   Transactions
2  Transactions_df=xl
   ("Transactions[[#Headers],
   [#Data]]", headers=True)
```

The code loads data from Transactions,
Transactions

Hide explanation ∧

FIGURE 6-6 The Copilot pane now explains what
the Python code generated for cell A6 does.

In this simple example, Copilot has extracted the original data to a DataFrame on a new sheet, so if
you make any changes to the data in the DataFrame, the original data is unaffected. Copilot has not yet
performed any actual analysis because more information is needed. Figure 6-7 shows that at the end of
the response, Copilot offers two suggestion buttons for the directions it thinks the analysis could take
next: Show Sales Trends over Time for Each Product and Identify Top-Performing Stores by Total Sales.
It also gives you the option to Stop Advanced Analysis.

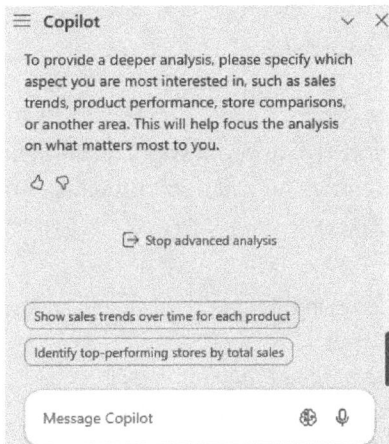

FIGURE 6-7 Copilot asks for more
information to target the analysis.

To get sales trends, click **Show Sales Trends over Time for Each Product**. Figure 6-8 shows sample
results, indicating that Copilot hasn't had any luck with the prompt—even though it suggested that
prompt. In this case, you can try using the same prompt a second time.

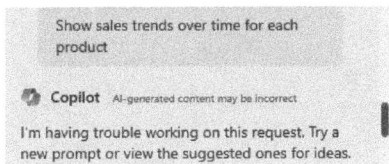

FIGURE 6-8 Copilot sometimes fails to
provide results.

Click **Show Sales Trends over Time for Each Product** again. Figure 6-9 shows that the results for a second attempt with this prompt are more successful.

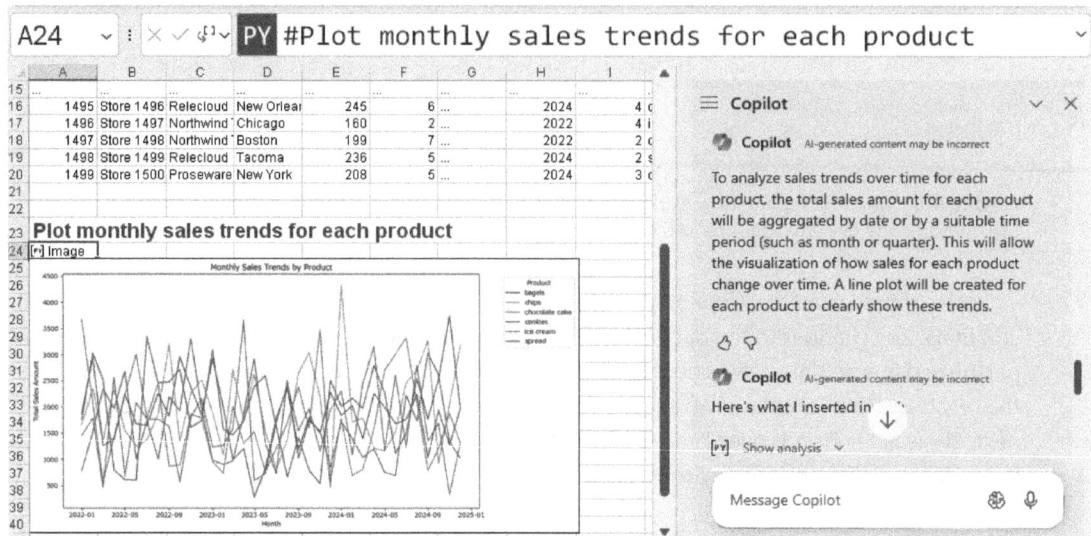

FIGURE 6-9 When you repeat the same prompt, Copilot produces a visualization.

> **Note** Remember that you sometimes must ask a question in a different way, and sometimes you just need to ask the same question again. With generative AI, you don't usually get the same answer twice.

Figure 6-9 shows Copilot's description of the process it is using in this case:

> To analyze sales trends over time for each product, the total sales amount for each product will be aggregated by date or by a suitable time period (such as month or quarter). This will allow the visualization of how sales for each product change over time. A line plot will be created for each product to clearly show these trends.

Copilot creates Python code in cell A24, which you can view by opening the Python Editor (see Figure 6-10).

> **Note** Remember that you can access the Python Editor by clicking Editor in the Python section of the Formulas tab.

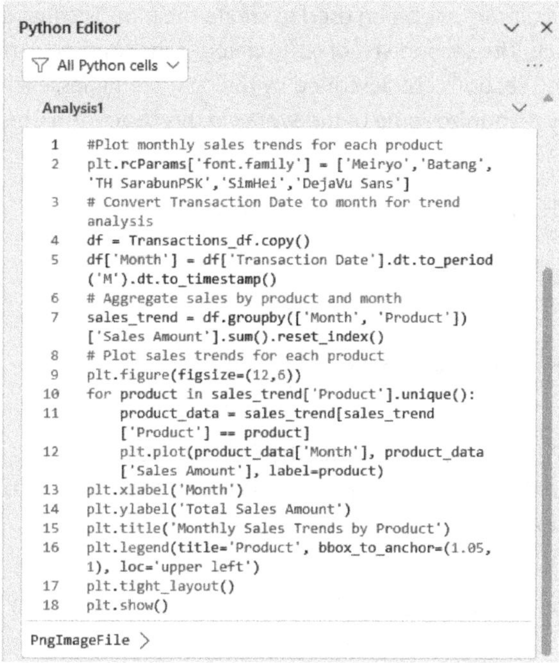

FIGURE 6-10 You can use the Python Editor to view the Python code that Copilot produced.

While it is easier to see the flow of the process in the Copilot pane, the Python Editor is more convenient for viewing large blocks of code, like the one in this case:

```python
#Plot monthly sales trends for each product
plt.rcParams['font.family'] = ['Meiryo','Batang','TH SarabunPSK','SimHei','DejaVu Sans']
# Convert Transaction Date to month for trend analysis
df = Transactions_df.copy()
df['Month'] = df['Transaction Date'].dt.to_period('M').dt.to_timestamp()
# Aggregate sales by product and month
sales_trend = df.groupby(['Month', 'Product'])['Sales Amount'].sum().reset_index()
# Plot sales trends for each product
plt.figure(figsize=(12,6))
for product in sales_trend['Product'].unique():
    product_data = sales_trend[sales_trend['Product'] == product]
    plt.plot(product_data['Month'], product_data['Sales Amount'], label=product)
plt.xlabel('Month')
plt.ylabel('Total Sales Amount')
plt.title('Monthly Sales Trends by Product')
plt.legend(title='Product', bbox_to_anchor=(1.05, 1), loc='upper left')
plt.tight_layout()
plt.show()
```

In this code, functions from the Matplotlib library are being used to create the plot. The first comment serves as a title for the entire code block. The second line of code changes the runtime configuration (rc) to choose the fonts. The remaining sections are described by the comment lines, each of which starts with a hash symbol (#). You may recognize some of the syntax in this code from Chapter 3, where you created your own plots.

It is worthwhile to review the Python code that Copilot generates for three reasons:

- You need to make sure nothing looks incorrect.

- You may want to customize it.

- You can learn from it and expand your Python vocabulary.

Note We do not step through all the Python code generated by Copilot in this chapter, although we do point out interesting features. The main purpose is to see the analysis you can access with Copilot and Python in Excel.

Let's look more closely at the visualization Copilot produced in this example (see Figure 6-11).

FIGURE 6-11 The Python plot showing monthly sales trends for each product

The Copilot pane displays a smaller version of this image as part of Copilot's response (see Figure 6-12).

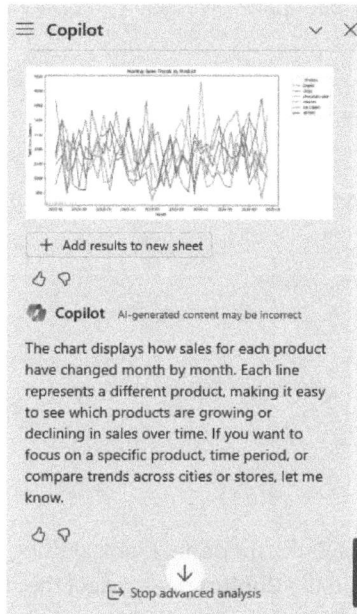

FIGURE 6-12 Copilot displays a small version of the plot in its response.

Copilot outputs the results to the analysis sheet. As shown in Figure 6-12, you can click Add Results to New Sheet to create a new sheet containing the selected insight. You could then copy other insights to the new sheet and quickly create a dashboard from the information produced by Copilot.

> **Note** When copying insights, keep the calculation order in mind. If you copy a chart from the analysis sheet to an existing sheet in the workbook, that chart might depend on one or more DataFrames in the analysis sheet. You must ensure that the analysis sheet is moved so that it is to the left of the sheet that you copy the chart to. You can play around with creating your own dashboards from the examples in this chapter to become familiar with the process.

Using the Think Deeper mode of Copilot advanced analysis

Recall that when you first choose to use advanced analysis, the Copilot pane gives you two options: Start and Start with Think Deeper (see Figure 6-13).

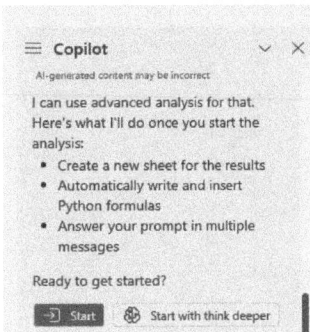

FIGURE 6-13 When your prompt specifies Python, you can use advanced analysis in either Quick mode or Think Deeper mode.

Now that you've seen what happens when you click Start to use Quick mode, let's look at using Think Deeper mode. With the **Transactions** worksheet open, go to the **Copilot** pane. Select the suggested prompt **Get Deeper Analysis Results Using Python**, and when Copilot offers to use advanced analysis, click **Start with Think Deeper**.

As you already know, your results will probably differ from those discussed here. In our results, Copilot provided a seven-step plan and showed the results in a new sheet called Analysis2 that contains 16 Python cells. You can view the sample results in the workbook SP Python in Excel Example Completed File Chapter 6.xlsm on the sheet Transactions Deep Analysis. The plan that Copilot uses to create the Python code is summarized at the beginning of the response:

1. **Data Quality & Preprocessing:**

   - Verify completeness of the dataset by checking for missing or inconsistent values.

   - Convert the Transaction Date to datetime format if needed and create additional time-based columns (e.g., Month, Week).

   - Validate data types for numerical and categorical features.

2. **Exploratory Data Analysis (EDA):**

   - Summary statistics: Calculate means, medians, and quartiles for numerical columns like Sales Amount, Quantity Sold, Area m2, and Rental/month/m2.

   - Distribution analysis: Plot histograms or density plots for key numerical variables.

   - Category counts: Obtain counts for categorical variables such as Product, City, and Store Name.

3. Time Series Analysis:

   - Reproduce and extend the monthly sales trends by product and aggregate overall sales trends.

   - Identify seasonal patterns via grouping by Year/Quarter/Month.

   - Perform moving average smoothing to highlight trends over time.

4. Comparative Analysis:

   - Group data by City and Product to compare performance across regions.

   - Analyze the impact of store characteristics (Area m2, No. Sellers, and Rental/month/m2) on Sales Amount using aggregations.

5. Correlation & Regression Analysis:

   - Compute correlation matrices to inspect relationships between numerical variables.

   - Consider running a simple regression or multiple regressions to understand the influence of store features on Sales Amount.

6. Advanced Insights:

   - Outlier detection: Identify unusual transactions or stores with significantly different performance metrics.

   - Segmentation: Perform clustering on stores based on sales performance and store attributes to identify segments.

   - Trend decomposition: If time series modeling is needed, decompose the sales series to inspect seasonal, trend, and residual components.

7. Reporting & Visualization:

   - Summarize the findings in plots and tables to highlight key insights from the deeper analysis.

   - Ensure that the entire dataset (all 1500 rows) is used in the computations to avoid biases from data preview.

Copilot concludes by saying, "Once these steps are implemented in Python, they will provide comprehensive insights into both temporal performance trends and the influence of store characteristics on sales performance."

This is an impressive plan. If you were looking at a dataset for the first time, using a plan like this from Think Deeper mode would be a great way to get an overview of the data and spot any issues.

However, if you were looking for a few key visualizations to add to a dashboard, you would probably choose to use Quick conversation mode instead.

We won't go through all 16 Python cells in this example, but let's consider the first one, cell A6. In the description associated with cell A6, Copilot describes the step to create the Python code in cell A6 as follows: "The first step is to assess data quality and perform preprocessing. This includes checking for missing or inconsistent values, validating data types, and ensuring the Transaction Date is in the correct format."

Figure 6-14 shows the Python code for cell A6 in the Python Editor.

Python Editor

A6 →

```
1   #Check for missing values, data types, and unique
    counts in key columns
2   # Step 1: Data Quality & Preprocessing
3   # Check for missing values and data types
4   missing_values = Transactions_df.isnull().sum()
5   data_types = Transactions_df.dtypes
6   # Check for unique values in categorical columns
7   unique_products = Transactions_df['Product'].nunique()
8   unique_cities = Transactions_df['City'].nunique()
9   unique_stores = Transactions_df['Store Name'].nunique
    ()
10  # Ensure Transaction Date is datetime
11  Transactions_df['Transaction Date'] = pd.to_datetime
    (Transactions_df['Transaction Date'], errors='coerce')
12  # Output summary
13  pd.DataFrame({
14      'Missing Values': missing_values,
15      'Data Type': data_types
16  })
```

FIGURE 6-14 Copilot advanced analysis in Think Deeper mode has begun by analyzing the data available to check its quality.

This is the complete Python code block that appears in the Copilot pane for cell A6:

```
#Check for missing values, data types, and unique counts in key columns
# Step 1: Data Quality & Preprocessing
# Check for missing values and data types
missing_values = Transactions_df.isnull().sum()
data_types = Transactions_df.dtypes
# Check for unique values in categorical columns
unique_products = Transactions_df['Product'].nunique()
unique_cities = Transactions_df['City'].nunique()
unique_stores = Transactions_df['Store Name'].nunique()
# Ensure Transaction Date is datetime
Transactions_df['Transaction Date'] = pd.to_datetime(Transactions_df['Transaction Date'],
errors='coerce')
# Output summary
pd.DataFrame({
    'Missing Values': missing_values,
    'Data Type': data_types
})
```

> **Note** Throughout this chapter, we have included the full code blocks for each example for your reference. Sometimes, we point out features to help you become more familiar with how the Python code is constructed. Depending on the format of the book you are reading, you may be able to copy and paste the full code block to a cell in your workbook. In any case, the code can be found in the workbook SP Python in Excel Example Completed File Chapter 6.xlsm. We recommend that you try the code and experiment by changing parameters.

The comments in the code in cell A6 mirror the description of step 1 of the full plan in Copilot's response. The first line of Python code in cell A6 informs you about the quality of the data. If you were unfamiliar with the dataset, this would be very helpful. In addition, you can learn a little about Python code from this code block. For example, you can see that it is possible to use `nunique()` to check the values in the categorical columns to ensure that there are no unexpected duplicates.

The results of this quality check are displayed in a DataFrame preview. Figure 6-15 shows the results of the code in cell A6 spilling from cell F9 in order to show the results in the Excel Value view and include all the rows. If you had a larger dataset, you could put the results of this step on a new sheet instead.

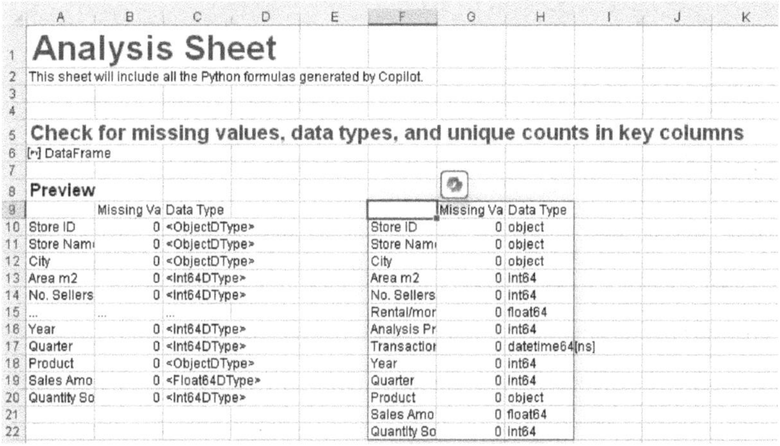

FIGURE 6-15 Copilot advanced analysis Think Deeper mode has begun by analyzing the available data to check its quality.

> **Note** If you use automatic calculation mode in Excel, adding cells will cause the other Python cells to recalculate, which will take a short time. The extra time is often worth it, though, because adding cells to the sheet can help you interpret the results and decide how to proceed.

You may find that some of Copilot's insights are not particularly useful for your data. For example, in the sample results shown in Figure 6-16, there is an Outlier Detection in Sales Amount section that hasn't found any outliers. While this provides information, it would be better expressed as a statement than an empty table.

FIGURE 6-16 Copilot advanced analysis Think Deeper mode sometimes returns DataFrames with no rows.

Think Deeper mode suggests visualizations that would be valuable additions to a dashboard. For example, in the results shown on the Analysis2 worksheet in Figure 6-17, in cell A74, Copilot has generated the Python code to create a plot that shows an overall monthly sales trend with a moving average. As shown in the figure, Copilot displays the floating image under cell A74.

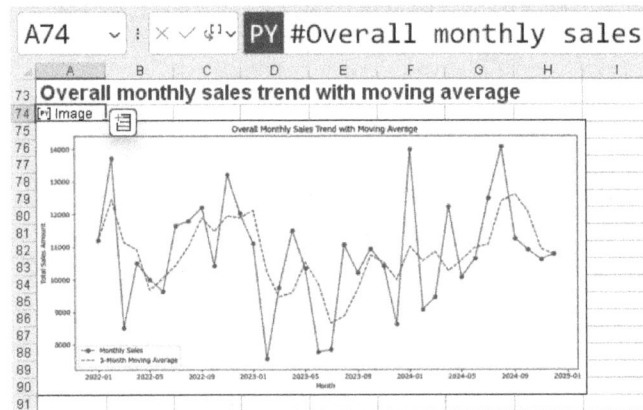

FIGURE 6-17 Copilot advanced analysis Think Deeper mode can generate useful plots.

We looked at creating a moving average using pandas in Chapter 3, and the Python code in this example uses similar functionality. We can use the Python Editor to examine the Python code in cell A74 (see Figure 6-18). A quick way to find this cell is to select the filter Selected Python Cells at the top of the Python Editor to see only the cell or cells you currently have selected in the sheet or workbook. This trick is especially helpful in a workbook or worksheet that contains lots of Python cells.

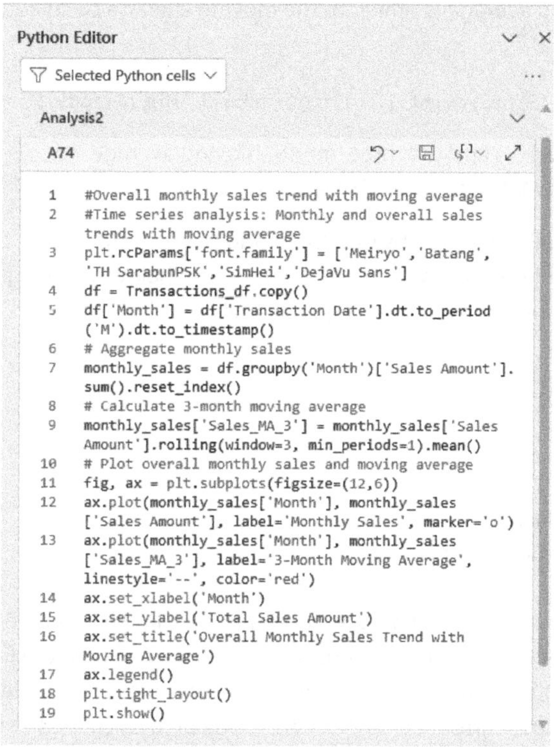

FIGURE 6-18 In advanced analysis Think Deeper mode, Copilot creates this Python code to create a moving average plot.

This is the Python code block that appears in the Python Editor for cell A74:

```python
#Overall monthly sales trend with moving average
#Time series analysis: Monthly and overall sales trends with moving average
plt.rcParams['font.family'] = ['Meiryo','Batang','TH SarabunPSK','SimHei','DejaVu Sans']
df = Transactions_df.copy()
df['Month'] = df['Transaction Date'].dt.to_period('M').dt.to_timestamp()
# Aggregate monthly sales
monthly_sales = df.groupby('Month')['Sales Amount'].sum().reset_index()
# Calculate 3-month moving average
monthly_sales['Sales_MA_3'] = monthly_sales['Sales Amount'].rolling(window=3, min_periods=1).mean()
# Plot overall monthly sales and moving average
fig, ax = plt.subplots(figsize=(12,6))
ax.plot(monthly_sales['Month'], monthly_sales['Sales Amount'], label='Monthly Sales', marker='o')
ax.plot(monthly_sales['Month'], monthly_sales['Sales_MA_3'], label='3-Month Moving Average',
linestyle='--', color='red')
ax.set_xlabel('Month')
ax.set_ylabel('Total Sales Amount')
ax.set_title('Overall Monthly Sales Trend with Moving Average')
ax.legend()
plt.tight_layout()
plt.show()
```

The calculation for the three-month moving average is similar to the moving average calculation you performed in Chapter 3. It looks like this:

```
monthly_sales['Sales_MA_3'] = monthly_sales['Sales Amount'].rolling(window=3, min_periods=1).mean()
```

Copilot plots the monthly sales (`'Sales Amount'`) and the three-month moving average (`'Sales_MA_3'`) in a single chart by using the Matplotlib `subplots` functionality.

Sometimes you need to amend a Python cell generated by Copilot or add new cells to display the results. For example, Figure 6-19 shows that cell A94 contains a Python tuple, and below it, in the pre-view, there are two DataFrames, although the results cannot be displayed fully.

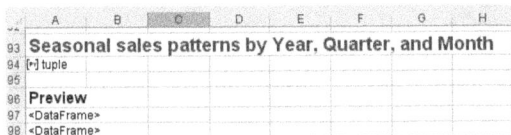

FIGURE 6-19 Copilot advanced analysis Think Deeper mode sometimes returns results that cannot be displayed fully.

As you may recall from Chapter 2, a *tuple* is a static list that cannot be changed. In this example, cell A94 contains a Python tuple that is a list of DataFrames. The problem is that we can't see the Excel values of two DataFrames in one cell. To view the results, we could add more Python cells to display each DataFrame, or we could create a copy of the current cell, amend the original to calculate the first DataFrame, and amend the copy to show the second DataFrame. How you approach this issue depends on how you intend to use the results. In this example, we will take the second approach. Let's look at the code for cell A94 in the Python Editor (see Figure 6-20).

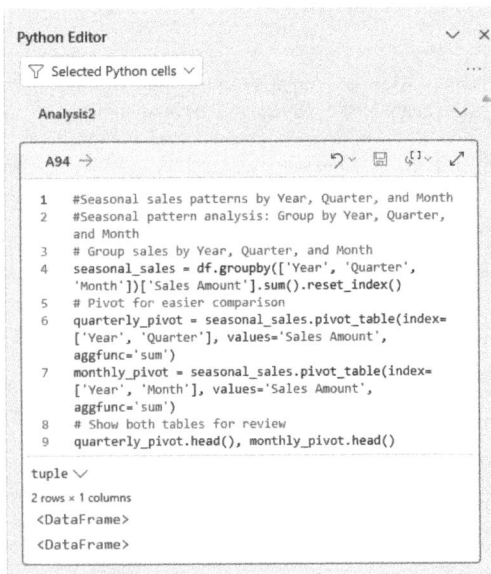

FIGURE 6-20 The result in this example is a tuple and cannot be displayed fully.

This is the Python code block that appears in the Python Editor for cell A94:

```
#Seasonal sales patterns by Year, Quarter, and Month
#Seasonal pattern analysis: Group by Year, Quarter, and Month
# Group sales by Year, Quarter, and Month
seasonal_sales = df.groupby(['Year', 'Quarter', 'Month'])['Sales Amount'].sum().reset_index()
# Pivot for easier comparison
quarterly_pivot = seasonal_sales.pivot_table(index=['Year', 'Quarter'], values='Sales Amount',
aggfunc='sum')
monthly_pivot = seasonal_sales.pivot_table(index=['Year', 'Month'], values='Sales Amount',
aggfunc='sum')
# Show both tables for review
quarterly_pivot.head(), monthly_pivot.head()
```

This Python code begins by grouping sales amounts by year, quarter, and month. It then creates two pivoted tables, one showing grouping by year and quarter and the other showing grouping by year and month. The final line tries to show both pivoted tables in one cell. This would work in a different Python platform, but Excel cannot show two tables in one cell. To see both tables, we will use two cells. Because there is not enough room to spill the Excel value from cell A94, we need to copy A94 twice. Let's copy it once to cell G94 and once to cell K94. In cell G94, we can change the Python code to remove references to the monthly calculation and show only `quarterly_pivot.head()`. It ends up looking like this:

```
#Seasonal sales patterns by Year and Quarter
#Seasonal pattern analysis: Group by Year and Quarter
# Group sales by Year and Quarter
seasonal_sales = df.groupby(['Year', 'Quarter'])['Sales Amount'].sum().reset_index()
# Pivot for easier comparison
quarterly_pivot = seasonal_sales.pivot_table(index=['Year', 'Quarter'], values='Sales Amount',
aggfunc='sum')
# Show table for review
quarterly_pivot.head()
```

In cell K94, we can change the Python code to remove references to the quarterly calculations and display only `monthly_pivot.head()`. It ends up looking like this:

```
#Seasonal sales patterns by Year and Month
#Seasonal pattern analysis: Group by Year and Month
# Group sales by Year and Month
seasonal_sales = df.groupby(['Year', 'Month'])['Sales Amount'].sum().reset_index()
# Pivot for easier comparison
monthly_pivot = seasonal_sales.pivot_table(index=['Year', 'Month'], values='Sales Amount',
aggfunc='sum')
# Show table for review
monthly_pivot.head()
```

Figure 6-21 shows the Excel values for these cells.

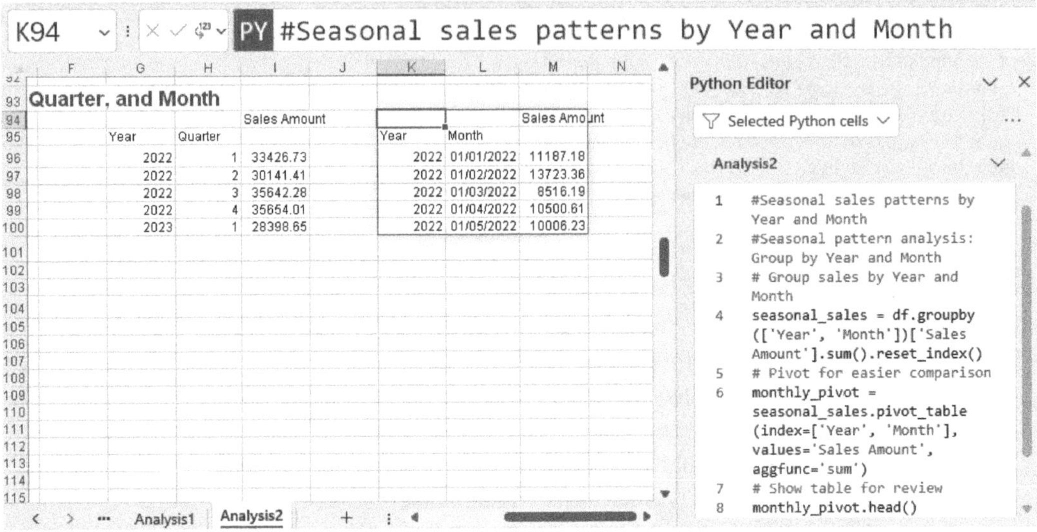

FIGURE 6-21 You can amend the Python code produced by Copilot in advanced analysis Think Deeper mode to view the results in Excel.

> **Note** As you have seen in this example, some knowledge of Python is helpful for interpreting the results returned by Copilot and amending them for inclusion in an Excel report.

In addition to the Python cells created in the Analysis2 worksheet, Copilot summarizes the results of the analysis by dividing the findings into six areas:

A comprehensive analysis of your transaction data was performed:

1. **Data Quality:** No missing values were found, and all columns have appropriate data types.

2. **Exploratory Data Analysis:** Summary statistics and histograms revealed the central tendency and spread of sales amount, quantity sold, area, number of sellers, and rental rates. Category counts showed the diversity of products, cities, and stores in the dataset.

3. **Time Series Analysis:** Monthly and quarterly sales trends were visualized, with a 3-month moving average highlighting overall sales patterns and seasonality.

4. **Comparative Analysis:** Sales were compared across cities and products, and average store characteristics were summarized. This revealed how different regions and store features relate to sales performance.

5. **Correlation & Regression:** Correlation analysis showed weak relationships between store features and sales. Regression analysis confirmed that area, number of sellers, and rental rates do not have a statistically significant impact on sales amount in this dataset.

6. **Advanced Insights:** No outliers were detected in sales amount. Clustering segmented stores into three groups based on their attributes and sales, which can help identify similar-performing stores for targeted strategies.

These results provide a thorough understanding of your sales data, highlighting trends, regional differences, and the limited influence of store features on sales. If you need further breakdowns or visualizations, please specify your focus area.

Copilot then provides more suggested prompts (see Figure 6-22).

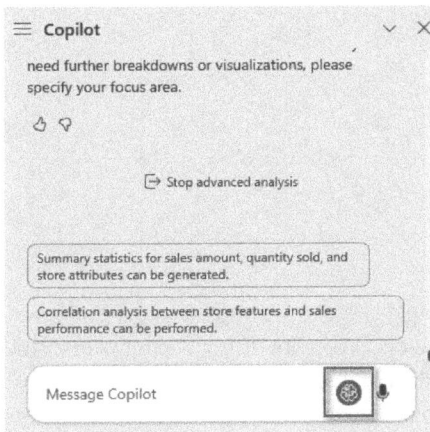

FIGURE 6-22 Copilot advanced analysis Think Deeper mode suggests further prompts.

Before moving on to the next section, rename the Analysis1 sheet **Transactions Quick Analysis** and rename the Analysis2 sheet **Transactions Deep Analysis**. Then move these sheets to the right of the Transactions sheet. End Think Deeper conversation mode by clicking the green button on the right side of the prompt box, highlighted in Figure 6-22, to return to Quick conversation mode.

Now that we have worked with both the Quick and Think Deeper conversation modes of Copilot advanced analysis, let's look at some more involved examples of how to use Copilot advanced analysis. The following two sections walk through examples of using Quick mode to help you learn more about crafting targeted prompts to get key insights from data.

Calculating a forecast based on planned and actual sales

In this section, we'll follow a forecasting example that uses a targeted prompt with Copilot advanced analysis to provide specific insights. To walk through this example yourself, open the **Forecasting** sheet in the current workbook (SP Python in Excel Example Starter File Chapter 6.xlsm). This worksheet, shown in Figure 6-23, contains the data you will use for this example.

	A	B	C	D	E	F
1	**Forecasting**					
2	SP Python in Excel Example Starter File Chapter 6					
3	Navigator					
4	Error Checks:				☑	
5						
6		1. Forecasting				
7						
8		Data				
9		Month	Planned Sales		Actual Sales	
10		January	$ 159,467.95	$	287,042.31	
11		February	$ 196,216.22	$	353,189.20	
12		March	$ 112,762.59	$	202,972.67	
13		April	$ 143,578.70	$	258,441.66	
14		May	$ 178,463.04	$	321,233.47	
15		June	$ 170,645.49	$	307,161.89	
16						
17						
18		Month	Planned Sales	Forecast Sales		
19		July	$ 169,189.00			
20						

FIGURE 6-23 In this example, you must calculate a forecast based on planned and actual sales.

The tasks for this example are to plot planned sales against actual sales and calculate predicted sales for July. If you are already using advanced analysis (that is, if you are using Copilot with Python in Excel), then ensure that you are in Quick conversation mode and not Think Deeper mode. Don't worry, though, if you have come out of advanced analysis and are now using standard Copilot. Either way, you can enter the following prompt. If you are using standard Copilot, you will just have an extra step to get back into advanced analysis. Enter this prompt: **Use the data in the range C9:E15 to Plot Planned Sales and Actual Sales, then fit a linear model and show the prediction for Planned Sales of $169,189.00 for July.**

If you have come out of advanced analysis and are now using standard Copilot to enter the prompt, you should see a response similar to the one shown in Figure 6-24. If you get suggestions for achieving this in Excel instead of using Python in Excel, add the words "using Python" to the prompt.

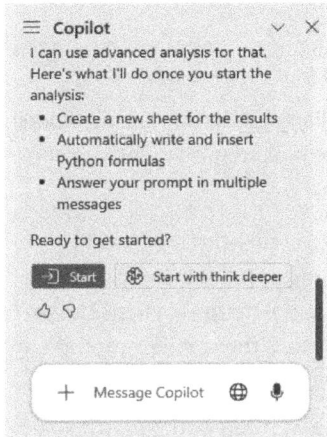

FIGURE 6-24 Copilot offers to use advanced analysis and describes the process.

Click the **Start** button. Figure 6-25 shows sample results. (Remember that your results will probably not look the same as those shown here.)

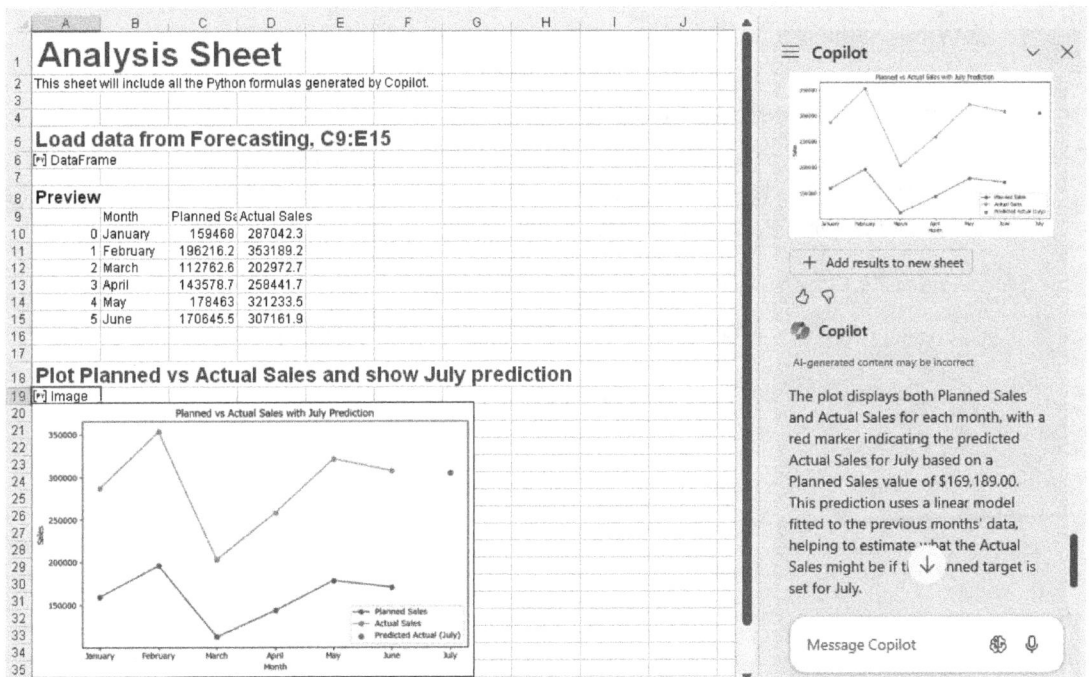

FIGURE 6-25 Copilot has used advanced analysis to create a plot that includes the predicted sales for July.

Copilot has generated Python code in cell A6 to load the data specified into a DataFrame, and it displays a preview of the data in the DataFrame in cell A9. Python code to create a line plot has been generated in cell A19, and the floating image for this chart shows two lines—one for Planned Sales and one for Actual Sales—and a prediction for July sales.

Moving Copilot-generated Python insights

Sometimes you will want to move the insights created in advanced analysis to an existing worksheet. In the example we've been working with, you might want to move the plot created in the previous section to the Forecasting sheet. To do so, you can take several approaches:

- **Move the sheet and the floating image:** Move the Analysis2 sheet to the left of the Forecasting sheet and move the floating image to the Forecasting sheet. This preserves the calculation order, but when you use this method, you cannot delete the Analysis2 sheet because the floating image is using the Python code on that sheet. This is the simplest method and requires no further explanation.

- **Copy Python cells to another sheet:** Copy Python cells A6 and A19 to the Forecasting sheet and ensure that the copy of A19 comes after the copy of A6 to preserve the calculation order. When copying Python cells, it is important to pay attention to the cell referencing in the new location. (We will look closely at this in a moment.)

- **Copy the Python code into a new cell:** Copy cell A6 to the Forecasting sheet and then use the Python Editor to copy the Python code from cell A19 into the new cell.

Let's look at the second and third methods in more detail.

Copying Python cells to another sheet

When copying Python cells, you must check any Excel references. If you don't, you may end up with errors caused by Python code accessing the wrong cells. For example, cell A6 in the Analysis2 sheet contains the following Python code that Copilot created:

```
Forecasting_C9_E15_df=xl("Forecasting!C9:E15", headers=True)
```

If you copy this cell to cell F9 on the Forecasting sheet, the formula changes to the following:

```
Forecasting_C9_E15_df=xl("Forecasting!H12:J18", headers=True)
```

The original formula created by Copilot uses relative referencing, so if the formula is moved, it changes to reference different cells. You can check and adjust the formula accordingly, but a better approach is to anchor the referencing—using absolute referencing instead of relative referencing—before you copy the cell. To do this, change the Python code in cell A6 to:

```
Forecasting_C9_E15_df=xl("Forecasting!$C$9:$E$15", headers=True)
```

The Excel cell references in the formula will now be preserved if you copy the Python cell to a new location.

> **Note** To explain relative and absolute referencing, let's use the formula =SUM(A1,A2) as an example. If you move this formula one cell to the right, the formula becomes =SUM(B1,B2). This is relative referencing, and it is useful if you are copying a formula across a range of data. On the other hand, if you change the original formula to =SUM($A1, $A2), the dollar sign ($) acts as an anchor so that if you move the formula one cell to the right, it will still be =SUM($A1, $A2). This is absolute referencing, and it is useful when you always want the formula to use the same cells.

Copying the Python code into a new cell

Now let's look at the third method of moving the plot to the Forecasting sheet, which involves copying the Python code from the Python Editor for cell A19 on the Analysis2 worksheet to cell G9 on the Forecasting sheet. Figure 6-26 shows all the Python code copied to one cell, G9, on the Forecasting sheet and the floating image displayed with it.

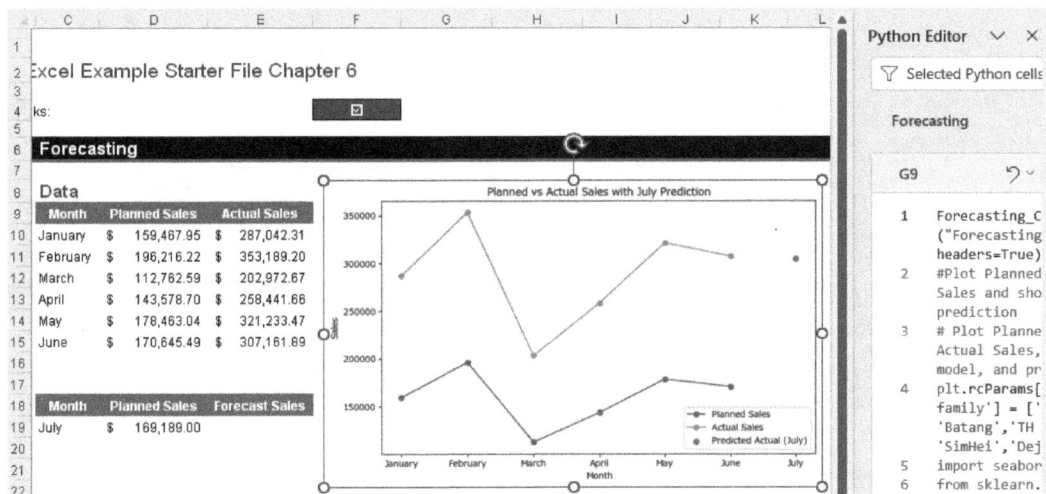

FIGURE 6-26 The Python code from the Analysis2 worksheet has been copied to cell G9 on the Forecasting sheet.

Remember from Chapter 3 that you can display a floating image for a Python image cell. To do so, click the **Insert Data** icon and choose **Display Plot over Cells** (see Figure 6-27).

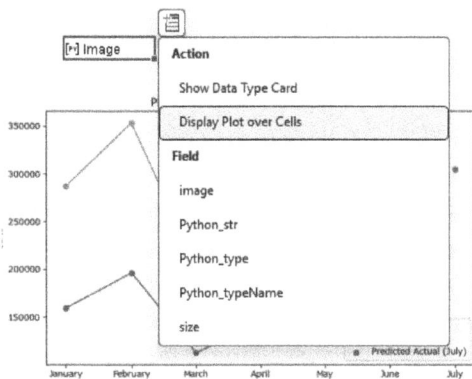

FIGURE 6-27 To display a floating image, you can choose **Display Plot over Cells**.

Copilot is not restricted to using the preloaded Python libraries. If you look at the Python code generated for cell G9 in this example, you can see that Copilot has imported appropriate Python libraries as part of the process. Figure 6-28 shows the first section of Python code in cell G9.

```
G9 →

1   Forecasting_C9_E15_df=xl("Forecasting!$C9:$E15",
    headers=True)
2   #Plot Planned vs Actual Sales and show July prediction
3   # Plot Planned Sales and Actual Sales, fit linear
    model, and predict for July
4   plt.rcParams['font.family'] = ['Meiryo','Batang','TH
    SarabunPSK','SimHei','DejaVu Sans']
5   import seaborn as sns
6   from sklearn.linear_model import LinearRegression
7   # Prepare data
8   X = Forecasting_C9_E15_df['Planned Sales'].values.
    reshape(-1, 1)
9   y = Forecasting_C9_E15_df['Actual Sales'].values
10  # Fit linear regression
11  model = LinearRegression()
12  model.fit(X, y)
```

FIGURE 6-28 The Python code for cell G9 imports the LinearRegression module from the sklearn (aka scikit-learn) library.

Figure 6-28 shows the following lines of Python code:

```
Forecasting_C9_E15_df=xl("Forecasting!$C9:$E15", headers=True)
#Plot Planned vs Actual Sales and show July prediction
# Plot Planned Sales and Actual Sales, fit linear model, and predict for July
plt.rcParams['font.family'] = ['Meiryo','Batang','TH SarabunPSK','SimHei','DejaVu Sans']
import seaborn as sns
from sklearn.linear_model import LinearRegression
# Prepare data
X = Forecasting_C9_E15_df['Planned Sales'].values.reshape(-1, 1)
y = Forecasting_C9_E15_df['Actual Sales'].values
# Fit linear regression
model = LinearRegression()
model.fit(X, y)
```

The first line imports the data from C9:E15 into a DataFrame. There are comments after this line, and then the seaborn library is imported. This import is unnecessary for Python in Excel because the seaborn library is preloaded. However, seaborn was one of the later additions to the preloaded libraries, and Python in Excel has not yet been updated to omit the import. Your version of Python in Excel may have been updated so that no import statement for seaborn is generated. The next import accesses the LinearRegression submodule of the sklearn.linear_model module. The following line of code from this example produces a 2D array for the X parameter:

```
X = Forecasting_C9_E15_df['Planned Sales'].values.reshape(-1, 1)
```

> **Note** sklearn is an alternative name for scikit-learn, which is one of the Microsoft-recommended libraries listed in Chapter 3.

You can use single brackets ([]) with `reshape()` to explicitly convert a series to a 2D array. (Later in this chapter, in the car sales example, you will see a different line of code used to achieve a similar result.) For this example, this code would also work:

```
X = Forecasting_C9_E15_df[['Planned Sales']].values
```

In this case, Copilot uses double brackets to select a DataFrame and preserve the 2D structure. This is a stylistic choice and indicates that Copilot has been trained using different samples of Python code.

> **Note** Recall from Chapter 5 that Copilot uses algorithms to access the data it has been trained on and returns a relevant answer (not necessarily the "right" answer). There is often more than one way to code Python to get the same result, and because Copilot is trained using code examples, if you repeat the prompt, Copilot may use different Python code to generate the results.

The `LinearRegression()` function is assigned to the variable model, and then the relevant sections of data are added to the model.

Although the Analysis2 worksheet displays the DataFrame and plot, it does not display a numeric value that forecasts sales for July. It is possible to extract this numeric value from the code in the Python Editor. The remaining lines of the code block are as follows (see Figure 6-29):

```
# Predict for July
planned_july = 169189.00
predicted_july = model.predict([[planned_july]])[0]
# Plot
fig, ax = plt.subplots(figsize=(8,5))
months = Forecasting_C9_E15_df['Month']
ax.plot(months, Forecasting_C9_E15_df['Planned Sales'], marker='o', label='Planned Sales')
ax.plot(months, Forecasting_C9_E15_df['Actual Sales'], marker='o', label='Actual Sales')
ax.scatter('July', predicted_july, color='red', label='Predicted Actual (July)', zorder=5)
ax.set_xlabel('Month')
ax.set_ylabel('Sales')
ax.set_title('Planned vs Actual Sales with July Prediction')
ax.legend()
plt.tight_layout()
plt.show()
```

FIGURE 6-29 The Python code for cell G9 calculates the prediction for July so that it can be added to the chart.

Let's look at how the Python code generates the chart. The line `predicted_july = model.predict([[planned_july]])[0]` calculates the sales forecast, although the value of `predicted_july` is not explicitly returned because this is not a necessary step to create the chart. To create the chart, having the value in the variable is sufficient. However, the goal of this part of the exercise is to get more information from the Python code, so we might want to know the value. One way to find the forecast value is to copy this line of code to another cell that follows cell G9 in the calculation order.

Figure 6-30 shows the result that appears if we create a new Python cell H9 and paste in this line of code: 304540.2. This gives us the value of the forecast sales figure for July. (Note that we could have entered only the variable `predicted_july` here because it is already calculated in the Python code in cell G9, but we wanted to highlight the Python code used to calculate the value.)

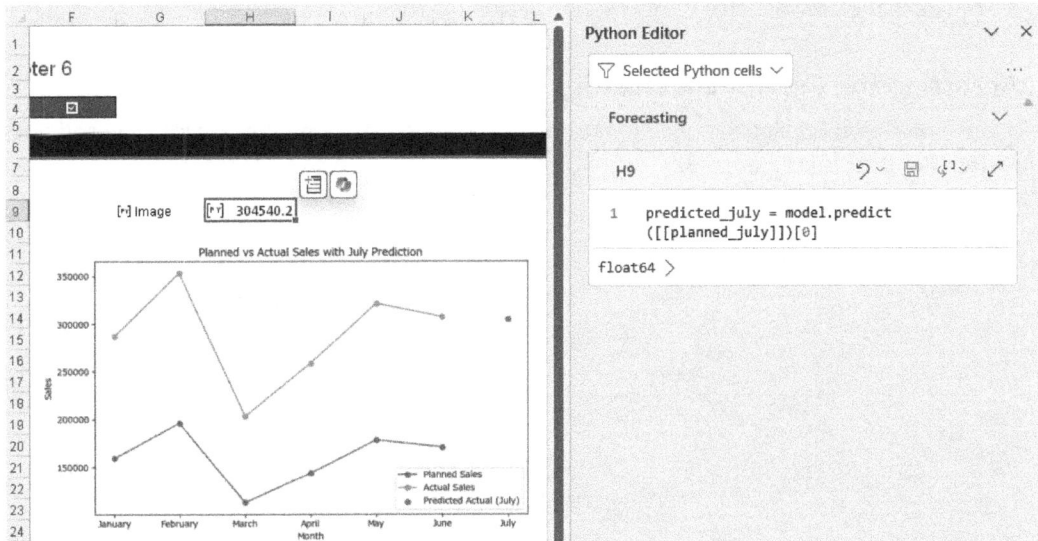

FIGURE 6-30 The Python code in cell H9 returns a forecast sales value for July.

This example uses cell H9 to make it easier to display the Python code next to the result. Let's also show the result in cell E19, with the rest of the data, by referencing the `predicted_july` variable. Let's also assume that new information has come in for the first six months, and the actual sales values for January and June must be modified to $300,050.36 and $400,266.67, respectively. Figure 6-31 shows that, with automatic calculation mode turned on, the results and the plot change when we change these values.

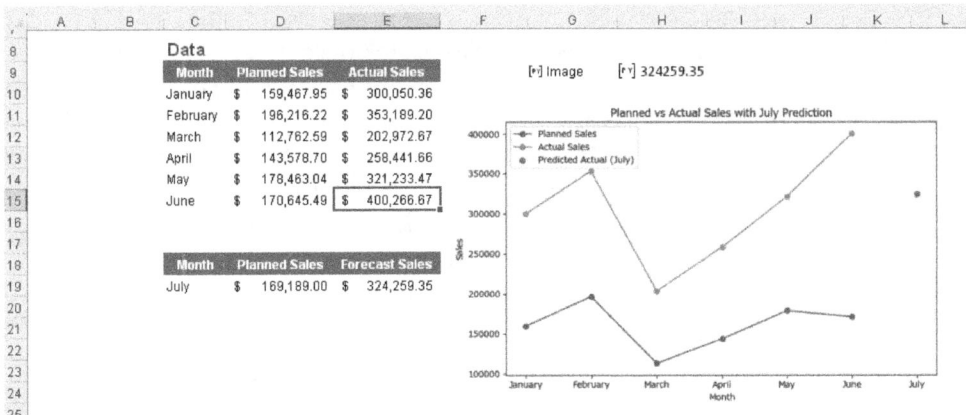

FIGURE 6-31 When the actual sales value for the first six months changes, the forecast sales value for July is dynamically updated.

Using Copilot to modify the results

So far in this example, we have used our knowledge of Python code to change the displayed results, but we can also get Copilot to change the results in the Analysis2 sheet. Since we have already copied the cells we need to the Forecasting sheet, let's change the forecasting model used. In sheet Analysis2, we can open the previous chat or refer to the data in the sheet.

Accessing the Copilot chat history

If you have closed Copilot and need to return to a previous chat, open the Copilot pane and select **Switch Copilots** (see Figure 6-32).

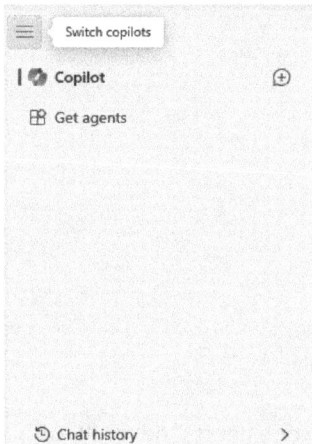

FIGURE 6-32 The Switch Copilots menu

Note If your version of Excel features a dropdown menu under the Copilot button, you must ensure you select App Skills and not Chat.

You can click the plus (+) sign in the speech bubble next to Copilot to start a new Copilot chat. In this case, though, you're looking for the chat history, so choose the **Chat History** option at the bottom of the pane (refer to Figure 6-32). Figure 6-33 shows sample results, where you can view the chat history, select a chat, delete a chat, or delete all Copilot history. To determine how long Copilot conversations in Excel are retained, consult your organization's Microsoft Purview retention policies. You can find more about this at *https://learn.microsoft.com/en-us/purview/retention-policies-copilot*.

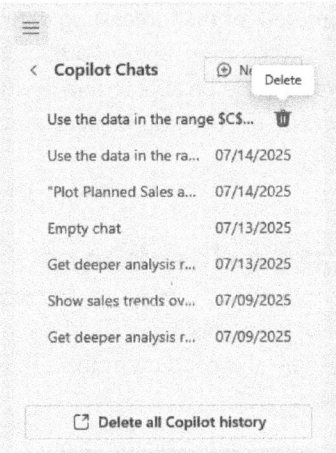

FIGURE 6-33 You can view your Copilot chat history, select a chat, delete a chat, or delete all your Copilot history.

Continuing to analyze the data in the forecasting example

To continue with the forecasting example, select the chat that begins with the prompt **Use the data in the range C9:E15 to plot planned sales and actual sales, then fit a linear model and show the prediction for planned sales of $169,189.00 for July**. If you don't have access to the Excel conversations in Copilot chat history because of your company settings, you will need to start a new conversation by entering the following prompt: **Change the Python code in this sheet to use the polynomial regression method**.

No matter which of these prompts you choose, Copilot returns a plot that looks similar to the one it created earlier, using linear regression. Figure 6-34 shows the Analysis2 sheet with the Python Editor open to show that the code in cell A23 uses polynomial regression. (In Figure 6-34, we have moved the floating images to allow you to compare the plots.)

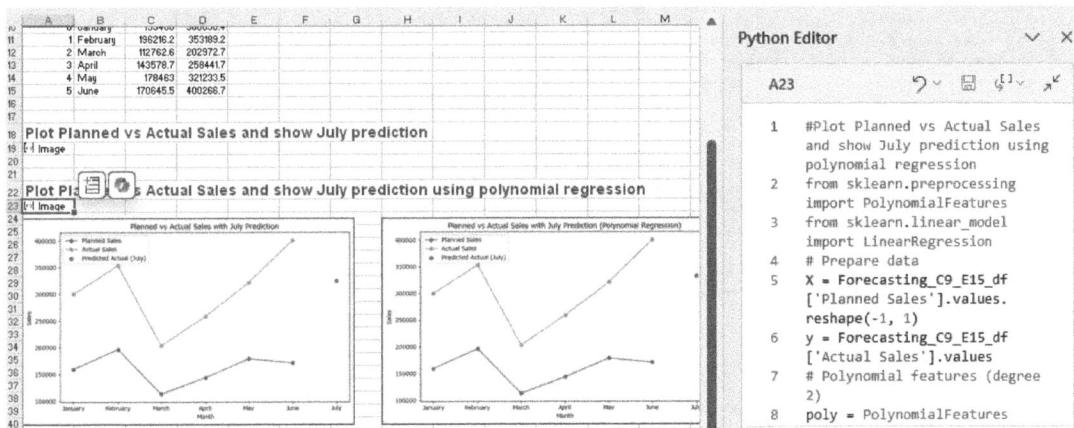

FIGURE 6-34 Using polynomial regression on the same data as before produces a similar plot to the one created using linear regression.

To finish this example, rename the Analysis2 sheet that Copilot created for the forecasting data to **Forecasting Quick Analysis** and move it to the right of the Forecasting sheet. In the workbook SP Python in Excel Example Completed File Chapter 6.xlsm, which you should be able to find in your downloaded files, we have saved the sheet before polynomial regression as Forecasting Quick Analysis1 and after polynomial regression as Forecasting Quick Analysis2.

Using car sales data to get insights and create a dashboard

Now you are ready for a more comprehensive example where you will learn about investigating data. In this example, you will work with Copilot to analyze and refine the data and produce insights that you will use to create a simple dashboard.

The data for this example, which comes from the Kaggle website, *https://www.kaggle.com /datasets/suraj520/car-sales-data*, is available in the workbook SP Python in Excel Example Starter File Chapter 6.xlsm, on the sheet Car_Sales_Data in the Excel table Car_Sales. This dataset includes more than 240,000 rows of car sales transactions, including all the key information you would expect (see Figure 6-35).

> **Note** As you can see in Figure 6-35, the Date column on the Car_Sales_Data sheet uses the general format, which means it is displayed as a serial number. This will be important later in the chapter!

Date	Salesperson	Customer Name	Car Make	Car Model	Car Year	Sale Price	Commission Rate	Commission Earned
44728	Eric Lopez	Vanessa Jones	Honda	Silverado	2022	20256	0.113489793	2298.85
44806	Scott Parker	Stephanie Smith	Ford	Corolla	2021	27337	0.099503651	2720.13
44997	Harold Nelson	Isaac Patton	Honda	Silverado	2021	41259	0.09254116	3818.16
44955	Richard Richardson	Justin Gray	Toyota	Silverado	2022	48224	0.090592146	4368.72
45022	Carrie Howard	Rodney Black	Chevrolet	Altima	2021	10313	0.103874895	1071.26
44760	Matthew White	Nancy Martinez	Chevrolet	Altima	2020	30184	0.136991193	4134.94
44809	Stephanie Trujillo	April Morales	Ford	Silverado	2022	43188	0.099220141	4285.12
44744	Jacob Bishop	Marc Caldwell	Nissan	Corolla	2021	21224	0.093014227	1974.13
44790	Kristen Martinez	Colleen Fischer	Chevrolet	Altima	2021	17832	0.051852876	924.64
45029	Valerie Sanchez	Carlos Fields	Nissan	Altima	2022	13508	0.146756353	1982.38
44919	Kevin Mitchell	Christie Odonnell	Chevrolet	F-150	2022	13280	0.122885977	1631.93
44841	Monique Green	Audrey Perry	Toyota	Corolla	2022	26862	0.09513501	2555.52
44958	Walter Robinson	Jeffrey Gillespie	Honda	Civic	2020	19526	0.128314718	2505.47
44929	Kathy Evans	Claudia Ali	Toyota	Altima	2022	43019	0.146540852	6304.04
44881	Katherine Harris	Lori Byrd	Ford	Altima	2022	33493	0.146898115	4920.06
44695	Tyler Freeman	Shannon Sutton	Honda	Altima	2021	27067	0.104673188	2833.19
44850	Matthew Ortiz	Mr. Kyle Patrick MD	Honda	Civic	2022	31238	0.098555281	3078.67
44812	Ashley English	Adrian Miller	Chevrolet	Corolla	2022	45561	0.116254342	5296.66
44735	Christopher Oneill	Phillip Cox	Toyota	Altima	2022	18209	0.0972776	1771.33

FIGURE 6-35 The Car_Sales_Data sheet

Asking Copilot for an overview of the data

When encountering a dataset for the first time, it is often useful to get an overview of the data, which is something Copilot can help you with. To get an overview of the data for this example, go to the Car_Sales_Data sheet and open the Copilot pane. Then select the prompt **Get Deeper Analysis Results Using Python**. When Copilot suggests using advanced analysis, click **Start** to use Quick conversation mode.

As you have learned in this chapter, when using advanced analysis, Copilot first extracts the data from the source sheet to a new analysis sheet, Analysis1 (see Figure 6-36).

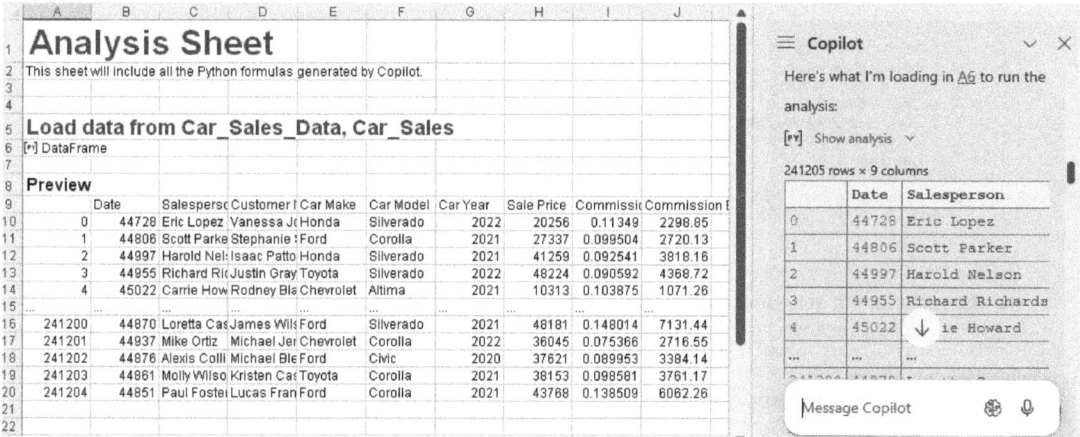

FIGURE 6-36 Copilot begins by extracting the source data into a DataFrame on a new sheet.

From this point, your results will probably differ from what we show. These are the steps Copilot planned for the example shown here:

> *A deeper analysis of the car sales data can be approached from several angles, such as identifying top-performing salespeople, analyzing sales trends over time, examining the most popular car makes and models, and evaluating commission patterns. To provide a comprehensive overview, the following steps will be taken: 1) summarize total sales and commissions by salesperson, 2) analyze monthly sales trends, 3) identify the most sold car makes and models, and 4) examine the distribution of commission rates and earned commissions. Each of these analyses will be performed using the full dataset.*

To achieve these results, Copilot generates Python code in cell A24, as shown in Figure 6-37.

```
1    #Comprehensive car sales analysis   summary
2    # 1. Total sales and commissions by salesperson
3    salesperson_summary = Car_Sales_df.groupby
     ('Salesperson').agg(
4        Total_Sales=('Sale Price', 'sum'),
5        Total_Commission=('Commission Earned', 'sum'),
6        Num_Cars_Sold=('Sale Price', 'count')
7    ).sort_values('Total_Sales', ascending=False)
8    # 2. Monthly sales trends
9    Car_Sales_df['Date'] = pd.to_datetime(Car_Sales_df
     ['Date'], unit='d', origin='1899-12-30')
10   Car_Sales_df['YearMonth'] = Car_Sales_df['Date'].dt.
     to_period('M')
11   monthly_sales = Car_Sales_df.groupby('YearMonth').
     agg(
12       Total_Sales=('Sale Price', 'sum'),
13       Num_Cars_Sold=('Sale Price', 'count')
14   )
15   # 3. Most sold car makes and models
16   make_model_counts = Car_Sales_df.groupby(['Car
     Make', 'Car Model']).size().reset_index
     (name='Num_Sold')
17   make_model_counts = make_model_counts.sort_values
     ('Num_Sold', ascending=False)
18   # 4. Distribution of commission rates and earned
     commissions
19   commission_stats = Car_Sales_df[['Commission Rate',
     'Commission Earned']].describe()
20   # Output all summaries as a dictionary for review
21   analysis_results = {
```

FIGURE 6-37 Copilot generates Python code in cell A24
to provide a comprehensive car sales analysis summary.

This is the code that appears in cell A24:

```python
#Comprehensive car sales analysis summary
# 1. Total sales and commissions by salesperson
salesperson_summary = Car_Sales_df.groupby('Salesperson').agg(
    Total_Sales=('Sale Price', 'sum'),
    Total_Commission=('Commission Earned', 'sum'),
    Num_Cars_Sold=('Sale Price', 'count')
).sort_values('Total_Sales', ascending=False)
# 2. Monthly sales trends
Car_Sales_df['Date'] = pd.to_datetime(Car_Sales_df['Date'], unit='d', origin='1899-12-30')
Car_Sales_df['YearMonth'] = Car_Sales_df['Date'].dt.to_period('M')
monthly_sales = Car_Sales_df.groupby('YearMonth').agg(
    Total_Sales=('Sale Price', 'sum'),
    Num_Cars_Sold=('Sale Price', 'count')
)
# 3. Most sold car makes and models
make_model_counts = Car_Sales_df.groupby(['Car Make', 'Car Model']).size().reset_
index(name='Num_Sold')
make_model_counts = make_model_counts.sort_values('Num_Sold', ascending=False)
# 4. Distribution of commission rates and earned commissions
commission_stats = Car_Sales_df[['Commission Rate', 'Commission Earned']].describe()
# Output all summaries as a dictionary for review
analysis_results = {
    'salesperson_summary': salesperson_summary,
    'monthly_sales': monthly_sales,
    'make_model_counts': make_model_counts,
    'commission_stats': commission_stats
}
analysis_results
```

A problem surfaces when Copilot runs the code. Copilot encounters an error when dealing with the format of the Date column in the Car_Data table: "A #PYTHON error occurred while I tried to execute the code in A24. I'm generating new code to continue with the analysis." We have included the Date column part of the process to demonstrate how Copilot can recover from this type of problem and continue with the analysis. Your version of Copilot may be more proactive and check the data before running the code. For our data, Copilot spotted the problem:

> *The error occurred because the 'Date' column, which is in Excel serial date format, was not converted correctly to a datetime object. The correct unit for Excel serial dates is 'D' (uppercase), not 'd'. The conversion step will be fixed, and the analysis will be rerun to provide the comprehensive summary.*

Copilot then reruns the code with the amended conversion step 2, as shown in Figure 6-38.

```
10    # 2. Monthly sales trends
11    Car_Sales_df['Date'] = pd.to_datetime(Car_Sales_df
      ['Date'], unit='D', origin='1899-12-30')
12    Car_Sales_df['YearMonth'] = Car_Sales_df['Date'].dt.
      to_period('M')
13    monthly_sales = Car_Sales_df.groupby('YearMonth').
      agg(
14        Total_Sales=('Sale Price', 'sum'),
15        Num_Cars_Sold=('Sale Price', 'count')
16    )
17
```

FIGURE 6-38 Copilot generates amended Python code in cell A24 to convert the date format and prevent an error from occurring.

This is the Python code step 2 that now appears in cell A24:

```
# 2. Monthly sales trends
Car_Sales_df['Date'] = pd.to_datetime(Car_Sales_df['Date'], unit='D', origin='1899-12-30')
Car_Sales_df['YearMonth'] = Car_Sales_df['Date'].dt.to_period('M')
monthly_sales = Car_Sales_df.groupby('YearMonth').agg(
    Total_Sales=('Sale Price', 'sum'),
    Num_Cars_Sold=('Sale Price', 'count')
)
```

Copilot then summarizes the results:

> *A comprehensive analysis of the car sales data has been completed. The results include summaries of total sales and commissions by salesperson, monthly sales trends, the most sold car makes and models, and statistics on commission rates and earnings. Let me know if you would like to see any specific details or visualizations from these results.*

The results are output as a Python `dict` object. We can see from the Copilot pane shown in Figure 6-39 that the `dict` object is constructed of four pairs of labels and DataFrames. In Figure 6-39, we have formatted cell A27 to wrap the text. The preview is a stream of data.

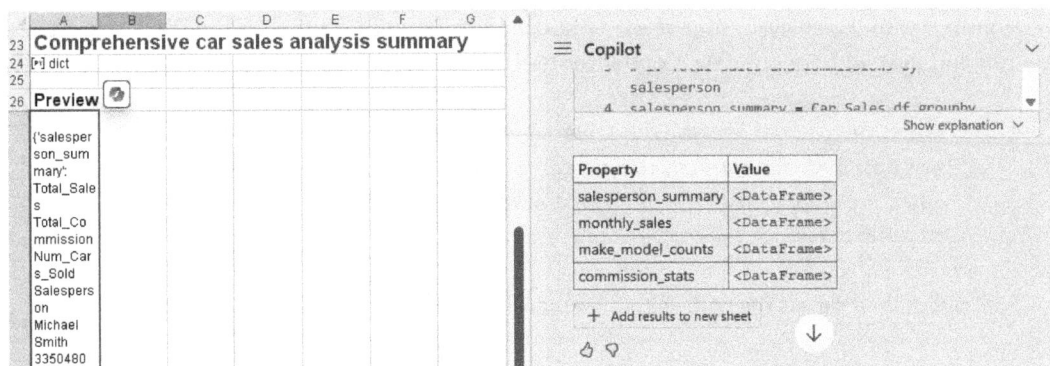

FIGURE 6-39 The preview of the `dict` object shows one cell that contains all the data.

We can delete this preview because it doesn't allow us to see the data. We could create Python cells to display each DataFrame ourselves, but we have an expert on hand to do that for us. Enter this prompt in the Copilot pane: **display the DataFrames in the Python object in cell A24.**

Copilot previews the individual DataFrames in separate sections of the worksheet. Figure 6-40 shows the first DataFrame.

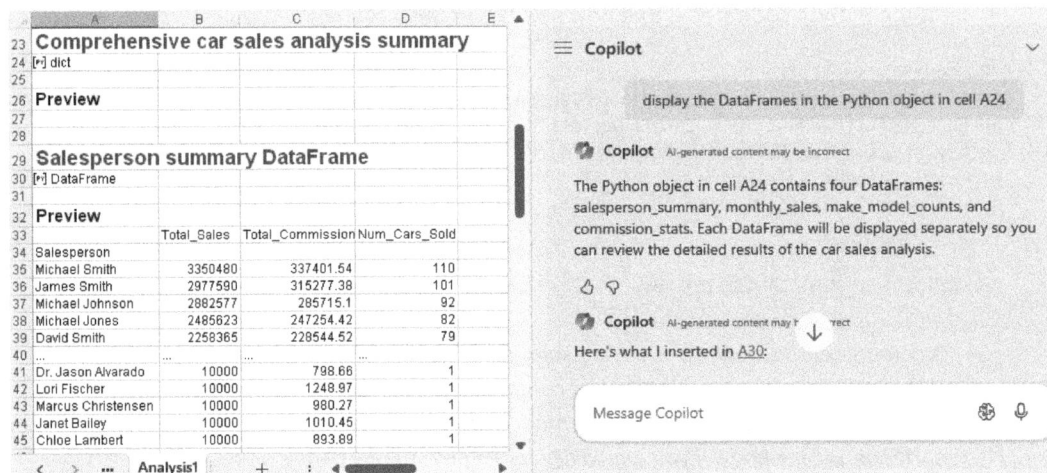

FIGURE 6-40 Copilot extracts and provides a preview of the first DataFrame from the `dict` object.

As you have seen in this section, if Copilot returns data in a way that is not user-friendly, you can solve the problem by prompting Copilot to show the information in a different way.

Formatting column names

Let's assume for now that a manager has reviewed our analysis, and their feedback doesn't mention any insights Copilot has provided. However, the manager complains about the underscores in column names in the generated DataFrames.

To change the offending column name formatting, we can enter the following prompt: **Replace underscores with spaces in column names in salesperson_summary, monthly_sales, and make_model_counts and convert column names to sentence case**.

Copilot creates the Python code to update each of the DataFrames and provides a preview of each (see Figure 6-41).

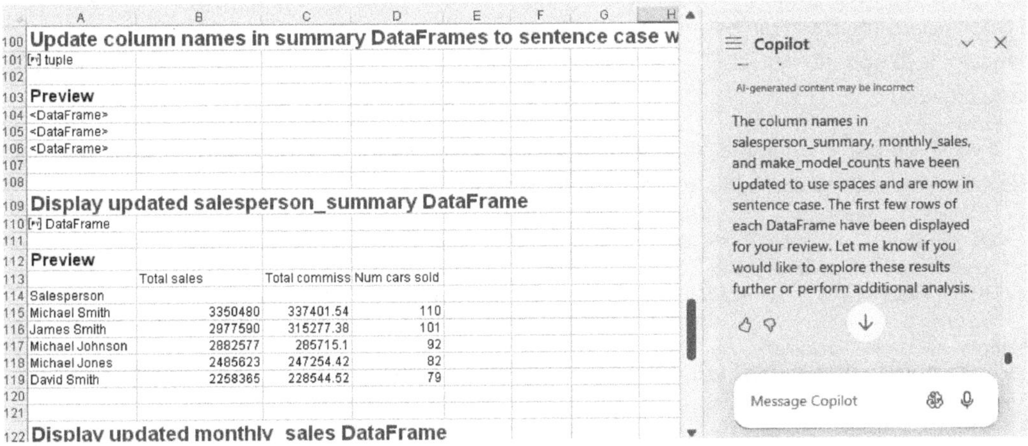

FIGURE 6-41 Copilot reformats the column names to meet the requirements of the prompt.

Figure 6-42 shows the Python code that Copilot generated to create the tuple in cell A101.

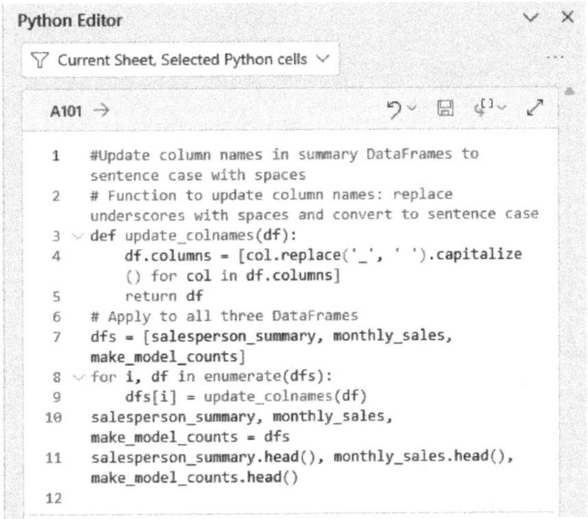

FIGURE 6-42 Copilot generates Python code to reformat the column names to meet the requirements of the prompt.

This is the Python code that appears in cell A101:

```
#Update column names in summary DataFrames to sentence case with spaces
# Function to update column names: replace underscores with spaces and convert to sentence case
def update_colnames(df):
    df.columns = [col.replace('_', ' ').capitalize() for col in df.columns]
    return df
# Apply to all three DataFrames
dfs = [salesperson_summary, monthly_sales, make_model_counts]
for i, df in enumerate(dfs):
    dfs[i] = update_colnames(df)
salesperson_summary, monthly_sales, make_model_counts = dfs
salesperson_summary.head(), monthly_sales.head(), make_model_counts.head()
```

This code defines the function `update_colnames(df)`, which receives and returns a DataFrame. It then groups the DataFrames and uses a `for` loop to update each one. Note that Copilot's default behavior is to update the DataFrames and not change the original Python code where the DataFrames were created.

If we wanted to change the column names in the code block where they were created, we could add the following code to cell A24 after the original step 4 code (shown in Figure 6-37):

```
# 5. Function to update column names: replace underscores with spaces and convert to sentence case
def update_colnames(df):
    df.columns = [col.replace('_', ' ').capitalize() for col in df.columns]
    return df
# Apply to three DataFrames
dfs = [salesperson_summary, monthly_sales, make_model_counts]
for i, df in enumerate(dfs):
    dfs[i] = update_colnames(df)
salesperson_summary, monthly_sales, make_model_counts = dfs
```

After we commit this Python code, the column names in the summary DataFrames are formatted correctly (see Figure 6-43).

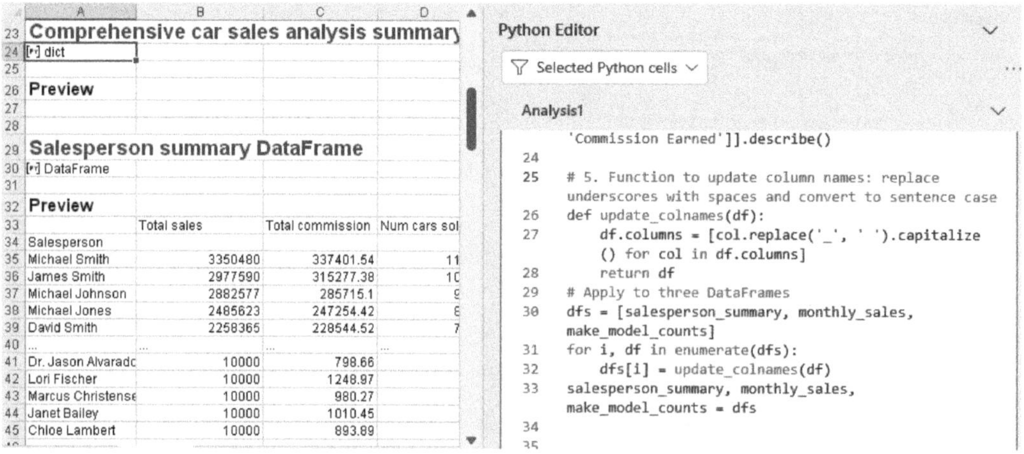

FIGURE 6-43 The Python code that Copilot originally generated has been modified to show column names formatted correctly.

Now that we have inserted the code to reformat the headings earlier in the analysis sheet, as step 5, we can remove the section to change the column names that Copilot generated in rows 100 to 142.

Investigating data relationships

Now that we've fixed the formatting of the table heads, the report looks better, but some of the figures do not look great. Some salespeople are struggling to sell cars. One reason for this could be that they are not reducing the prices to get sales because doing so would also reduce their commissions. We can check the correlation between the sales price and the commission earned by entering the following prompt: **Show the correlation between sale price and commission earned**.

Because there are so many data points, the scatter plot that Copilot returns looks like a solid area. The correlation coefficient 0.78 shows a strong correlation (see Figure 6-44).

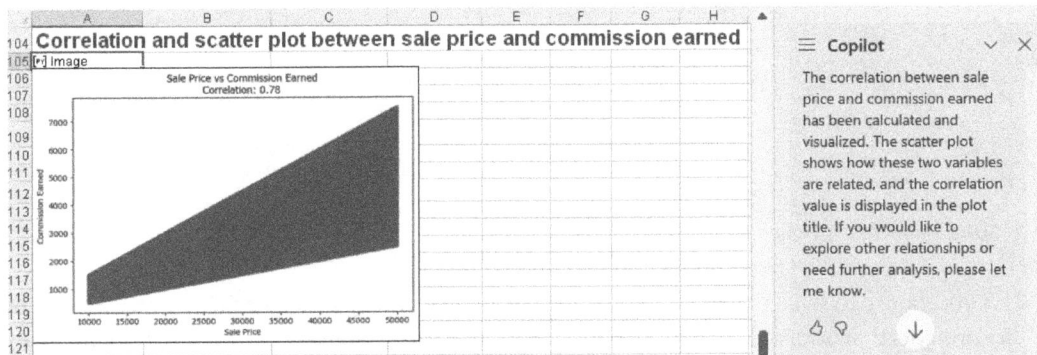

FIGURE 6-44 The correlation between sale price and commission earned is returned with a scatter plot.

We can look at the commission a different way: Do some types of cars generate more commission, and is this related to the sale price? To find out, enter the following prompt in the Copilot pane: **Group data by car make and calculate the average sale price and total commission**.

Copilot returns the data in a DataFrame and offers to create a chart (see Figure 6-45).

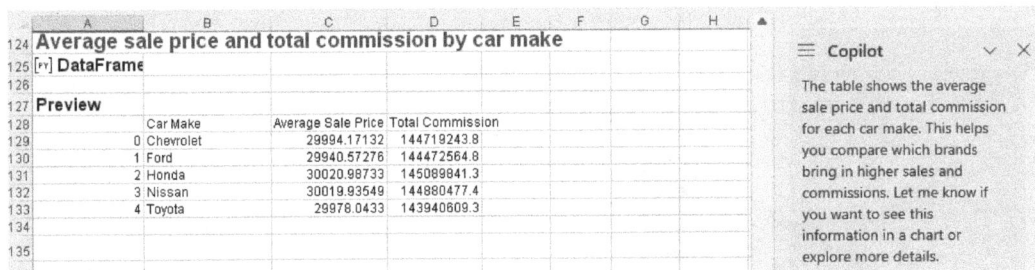

FIGURE 6-45 The data for each car make doesn't reveal any new information about the commission.

Since the data is fairly similar for each car make, there is no point in creating a visualization. Instead, let's create a predictive model for commission earned by entering the following prompt: **Train a linear regression model to predict commission earned from sale price**. The goal is to use linear regression to mathematically model the unknown commission and known sales price as a linear equation. (We used a similar method earlier in this chapter, in the forecasting example.)

Copilot initially returns the data required for the model and offers to create a visualization (see Figure 6-46).

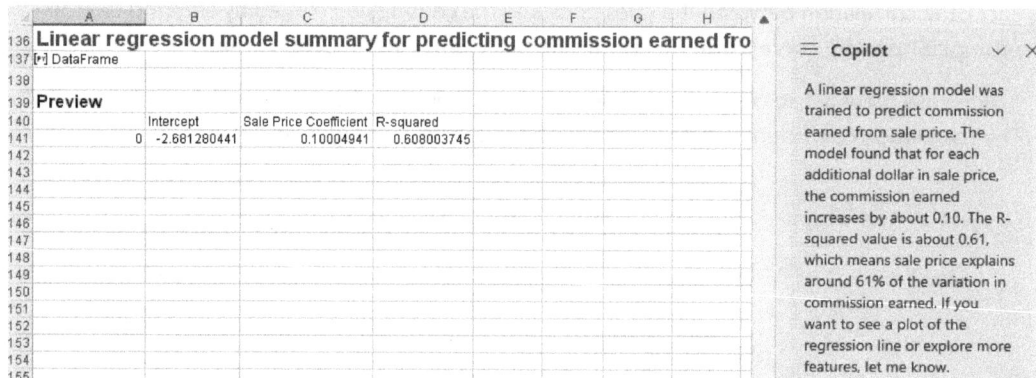

FIGURE 6-46 Creating a linear regression model with Copilot

Let's choose to see a plot of the regression line to help visualize this model. We can use one of the prompts that Copilot suggests: **Show a scatter plot with the regression line for sale price vs commission earned**.

Copilot shows the scatter plot we saw earlier but now with a regression line drawn on it (see Figure 6-47).

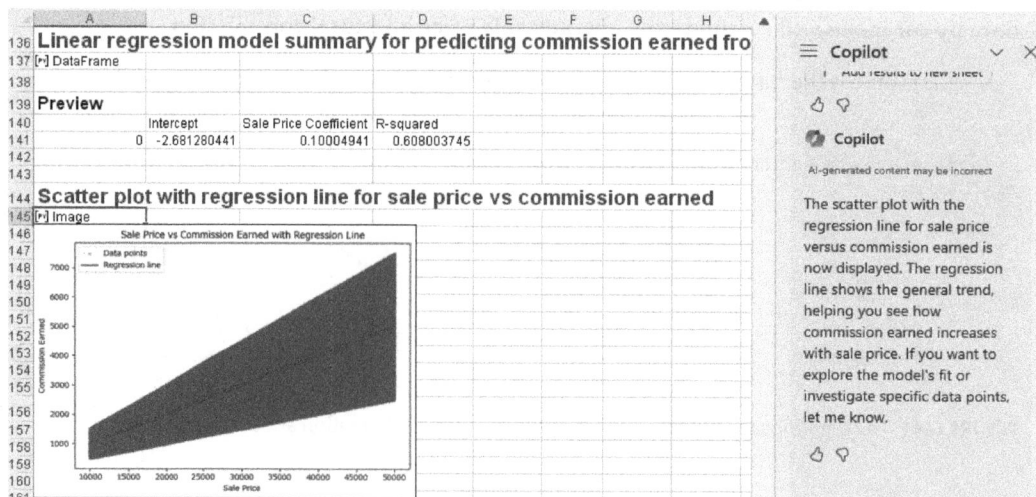

FIGURE 6-47 Creating a visualization of the linear regression model with Copilot

Copilot generates Python code in cell A137 to create a linear regression model summary, as shown in Figure 6-48.

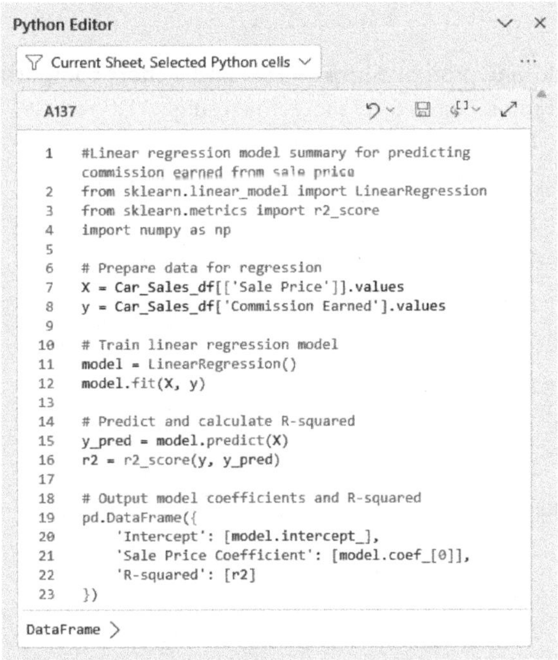

FIGURE 6-48 Copilot generates Python code to create a linear regression model summary.

The Python code in cell A137 is reproduced here:

```
#Linear regression model summary for predicting commission earned from sale price
from sklearn.linear_model import LinearRegression
from sklearn.metrics import r2_score
import numpy as np
# Prepare data for regression
X = Car_Sales_df[['Sale Price']].values
y = Car_Sales_df['Commission Earned'].values
# Train linear regression model
model = LinearRegression()
model.fit(X, y)
# Predict and calculate R-squared
y_pred = model.predict(X)
r2 = r2_score(y, y_pred)
# Output model coefficients and R-squared
pd.DataFrame({
    'Intercept': [model.intercept_],
    'Sale Price Coefficient': [model.coef_[0]],
    'R-squared': [r2]
})
```

> **Note** In this code, notice the alternative method to define the X parameter that we mentioned in the forecasting example.

To check the model, we can input the following prompt: **Show a table and a chart comparing actual and predicted commissions for all sales**. Figure 6-49 shows the results.

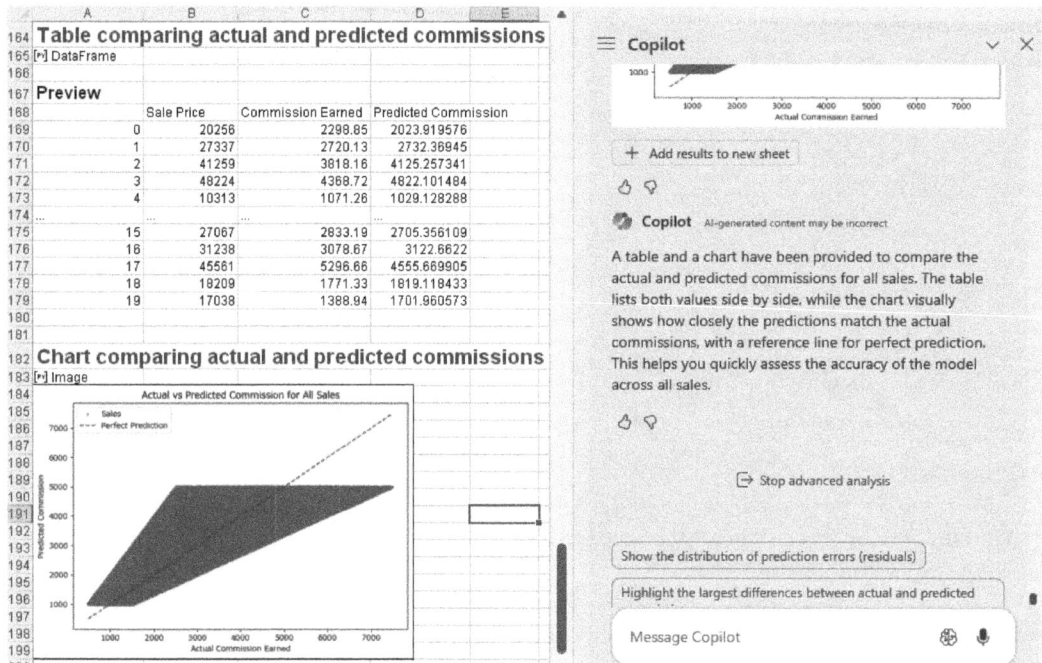

FIGURE 6-49 Checking the accuracy of the linear regression model with Copilot

The model looks good, and management is happy to use it. But now they would like you to create an Excel dashboard for them.

Creating a simple dashboard

You are now tasked with creating a dashboard showing top-performing salespeople and revenue trends. To get this started, enter the following prompt: **Create a dashboard layout to show top-performing salespeople and revenue trends**.

Copilot generates a table and a plot (see Figure 6-50).

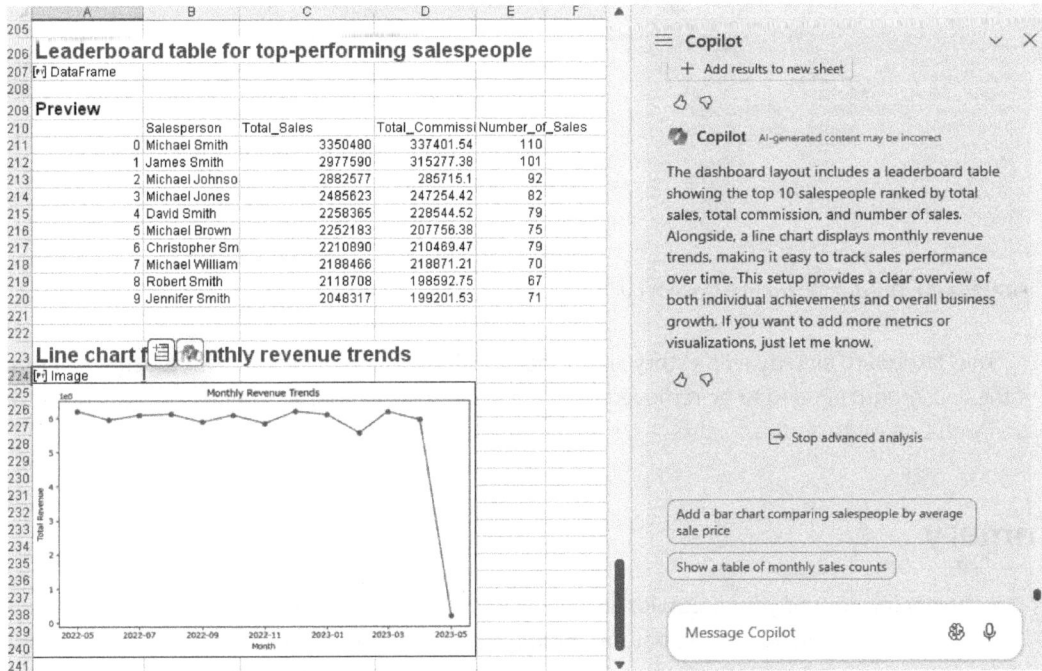

FIGURE 6-50 Copilot can create DataFrames and plots for a dashboard of your choice.

The dashboard isn't currently arranged in an acceptable way. Of course, Copilot can help design a suitable dashboard. We can ask it to do so by entering this prompt: **How can I organize a dashboard to show top-performing salespeople and revenue trends clearly**.

Copilot responds as follows:

> To make your dashboard clear and effective, place a leaderboard table of top-performing salespeople on one side, ranking them by total sales, commissions, and number of sales. Next to it, include a line chart that shows revenue trends over time, such as by month. This arrangement lets you quickly see who your best salespeople are and how your revenue is changing. You can also add summary cards at the top for quick stats like total revenue or the top salesperson.

Figure 6-51 shows what it looks like if we add the DataFrames and plots that Copilot creates to a new sheet and follow Copilot's advice.

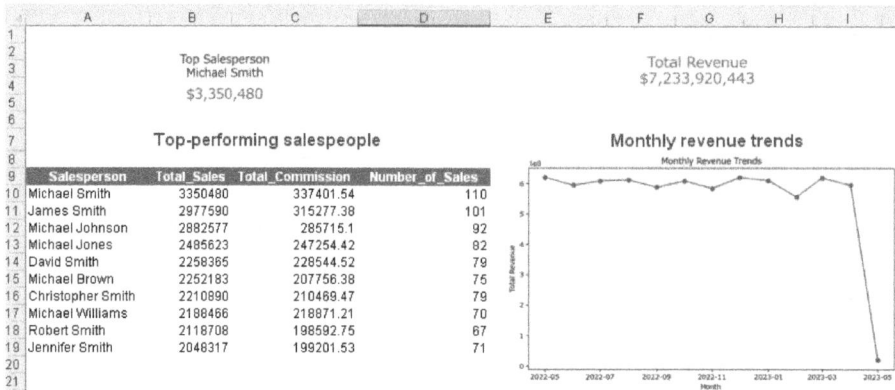

	Salesperson	Total_Sales	Total_Commission	Number_of_Sales
10	Michael Smith	3350480	337401.54	110
11	James Smith	2977590	315277.38	101
12	Michael Johnson	2882577	285715.1	92
13	Michael Jones	2485623	247254.42	82
14	David Smith	2258365	228544.52	79
15	Michael Brown	2252183	207756.38	75
16	Christopher Smith	2210890	210469.47	79
17	Michael Williams	2188466	218871.21	70
18	Robert Smith	2118708	198592.75	67
19	Jennifer Smith	2048317	199201.53	71

FIGURE 6-51 The dashboard that Copilot built

This dashboard already tells a story about the data, but we could add our own touches. For example, if the final month needed to be removed from the trends calculation, we could continue the conversation with Copilot to do this.

Summary

This chapter introduced you to Copilot advanced analysis, which means Copilot working with Python in Excel. You have seen how to use natural language prompts to get Copilot to create extensive Python code blocks, using functionality from Python libraries, to reveal patterns and extract insights from data. You have seen that you can have conversations using multiple prompts in Quick conversation mode or use Think Deeper mode to prompt Copilot to investigate the data and return detailed observations.

We encourage you to create your own prompts and use Copilot's advanced analysis to explore the data. Nothing you do using advanced analysis will change the source data, and by exploring the data yourself, you will become familiar with how to work with Copilot. In addition, this exploration will allow you to see how much better your version of Copilot is than the one we used as we wrote this book!

This chapter, which combined everything you have learned so far in this book, showed how to use Copilot with Python in Excel. You have seen how you can use Copilot advanced analysis to create Python code that you can modify and use to create dynamic reports and dashboards. The final step is to create a link between external data and Copilot with Python in Excel, using Power Query. So, in the next chapter, you will add Power Query to the tools you use to perform data analysis.

## CHAPTER 7

Using Copilot and Power Query with Python in Excel

In this chapter, you will:

- See through examples why Python in Excel cannot import external data

- Become familiar with Power Query

- Learn the basics of extracting external data using Power Query

- Explore the Power Query functionality to check and fix data quality

- Use Copilot, Power Query, and Python in Excel together to transform and analyze external data

> **Note** To follow along with the examples in this chapter, you must download the resources that accompany this book. If you don't already have these resources, visit *https://www .sumproduct.com/python-in-excel-book-resources* and download the files to a folder associated with your Python in Excel license. For this chapter, you will begin by accessing the workbook **SP Python in Excel Example Starter File Chapter 7.xlsm.**

Trying to use external data with Python in Excel

The sample data you have been working with up to this point has been in the same Excel workbook you use to access Python in Excel and Copilot. In Chapter 2, "Getting to know Python in Excel," you learned how Python in Excel can extract and manipulate Excel data, and in Chapter 5, "Introduction to AI and Copilot," you discovered how Copilot can help you perform data analysis in Excel. In Chapter 6, "Using Copilot with Python in Excel," you learned how to use natural language prompts with Copilot advanced analysis to create Python code that provides information and insights.

In this book, you have seen how to use natural language prompts to generate Python code to clean data, perform statistical analysis, build predictive models, and create dashboards. You have seen that Copilot can help you visualize insights by using Python libraries such as pandas, Matplotlib, and scikit-learn (also known as sklearn). The examples in Chapter 6, which show how to forecast sales and analyze customer behavior, demonstrate how Copilot works with Excel to provide a smart, AI-assisted analytics tool.

As you discovered in Chapter 2, not all Python code is compatible with Python in Excel. For example, Python in Excel recognizes the `input()` function but does not allow its use. As you can see in Figure 7-1, Python in Excel throws the following Python error when it encounters `input()`:

```
StdinNotImplementedError: raw_input was called, but this frontend does not support input requests.
```

FIGURE 7-1 The Python Editor shows an error when it encounters `input()`.

This error doesn't present a problem in our data analysis because we are using Excel data as the input, and there is no need to prompt the user for input. If the user enters a value in an Excel cell that is then imported into a Python cell, the value will be uploaded to that Python cell when it is refreshed. If the calculation mode is automatic, then changing the Excel cell prompts the Python cell to recalculate.

However, in some cases, you may need to bring data from other sources into Python in Excel. Because Python in Excel uses the data in the workbook, if you try to import external data directly into Python cells, you will encounter errors. To see how this works, let's look again at the car sales data example from Chapter 6. Open the workbook for this chapter: **SP Python in Excel Example Starter File Chapter 7.xlsm**. The data for this example, which comes from the Kaggle website, *https://www.kaggle.com/datasets/suraj520/car-sales-data*, is available for download in the file car_sales_data.csv. This file is also available as a download for this chapter. For this example, you need to make sure the file is downloaded and move it into the same folder on your computer as the workbook for this chapter. (Moving it to the same folder as the workbook will make the results of this exercise clear.)

In the SP Python in Excel Example Starter File Chapter 7.xlsm workbook, open the **Car_Sales_Data** sheet. You'll see that it is currently empty. Open the Python Editor and enter the following Python code in cell C10:

```
csv_file_path = 'car_sales_data.csv'
df_car_sales_data = pd.read_csv(csv_file_path)
```

This code uses the pandas library function `read.csv()` to access the .csv file, which is how Python accesses CSV files on platforms other than Python in Excel. Commit the code, and you get the following error (see Figure 7-2):

```
FileNotFoundError: [Errno 2] No such file or directory: 'car_sales_data.csv'
```

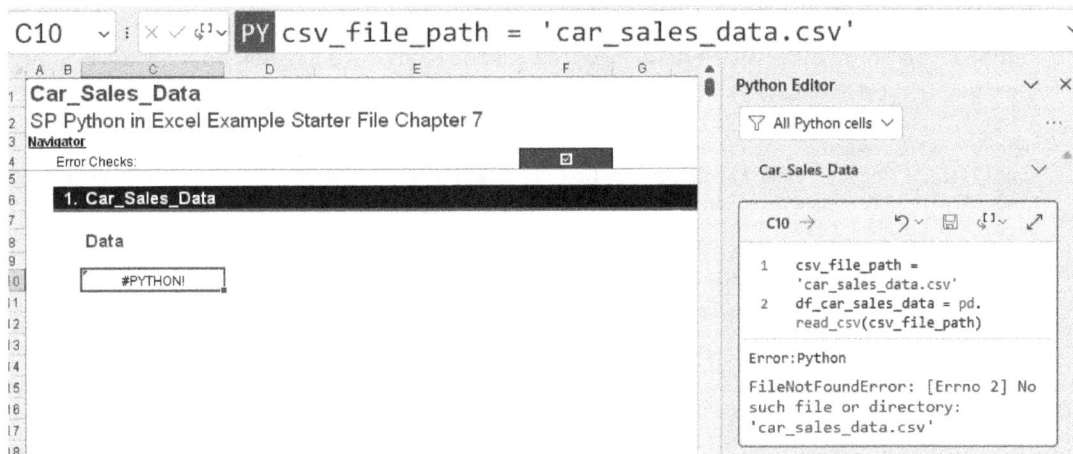

FIGURE 7-2 The Python Editor encounters an error when it tries to read a .csv file in the same location as the workbook.

Now you can see why we had you put the downloaded data file in the same directory as the workbook: You know for sure that you entered the correct file path. The file is there, but as you can see, it can't be imported this way. Figure 7-3 shows that we get similar results if we try to use advanced analysis to import the .csv file from this folder.

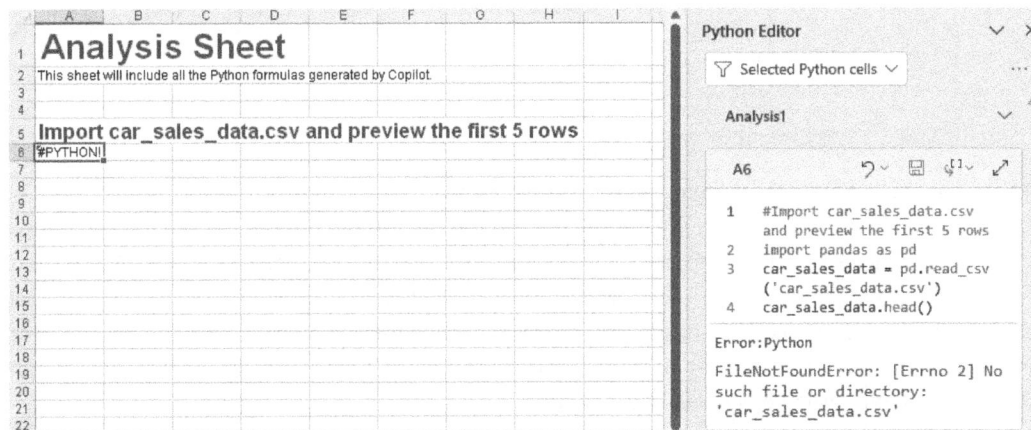

FIGURE 7-3 When you try to use Copilot advanced analysis to extract a .csv file in the same directory as the workbook, the Python Editor encounters an error.

What happens if you try to get the file directly from the Kaggle website? The easiest way to do this in Python on platforms other than Python in Excel would be to import a function from the urllib library. To see if this method works in Python in Excel, replace the Python code in cell C10 with the following code:

```
import urllib.request
kagglesite = "https://www.kaggle.com/datasets/suraj520/car-sales-data?resource=download"
readurl = urllib.request.urlopen(kagglesite)
getdata = readurl.read()
```

As you probably expect by now, when you commit the code, you get an error again. This time, though, the error is a little different (see Figure 7-4):

```
URLError: <urlopen error Tunnel connection failed: 400 Bad Request>
```

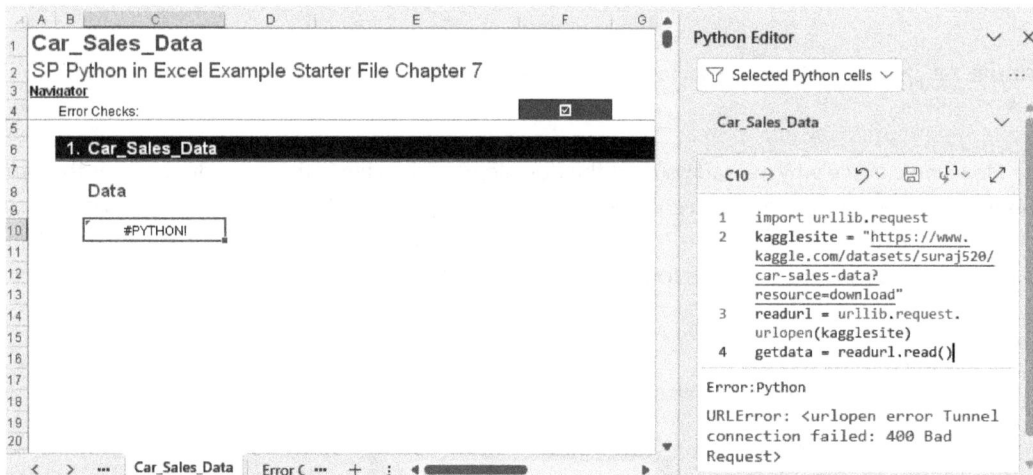

FIGURE 7-4 The Python Editor encounters an error when Python in Excel tries to read a URL.

Figure 7-5 shows an attempt to get Copilot advanced analysis to perform the same task. As you can see, Copilot gives a more human-readable error message: "The URL provided is a Kaggle download page, which cannot be accessed directly for data import. Please upload the CSV file or provide a direct link to the raw data file for further analysis." This is better than the response to the previous prompt, but we're still not getting anywhere with the data.

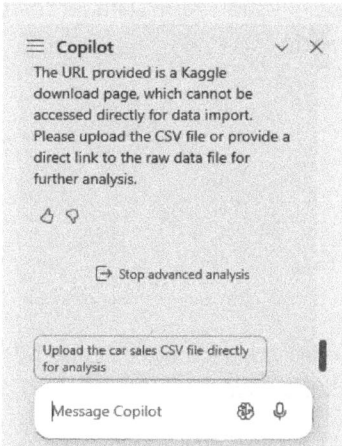

FIGURE 7-5 Copilot responds to the prompt to access data from the Kaggle website.

As you have seen, Python in Excel does not currently support the functionality to import external data. The only way to import data into Python in Excel is to load a connection in Excel first. That is why you need Power Query. If you are not familiar with Power Query, the next section provides some background.

> **Note** The version of Copilot used in this example has not been trained to recognize that uploading of external data is not achievable with Python in Excel. We asked the question again several times to be sure. Still, although some responses we received mentioned using Power Query as an alternative import method, Copilot also suggested using Python code to import the .csv file.

Before moving on to the next section, delete cell C10 from the Car_Sales_Data sheet, as well as any analysis sheets that Copilot has generated.

Getting to know Power Query

Power Query is the engine behind data importing, cleaning, and transformation in the Microsoft 365 ecosystem. Power Query is an extract, transform, and load (ETL) tool, which means that when you use it, the external data is not changed; rather, the extracted data is changed. This section aims to familiarize you with the features of Power Query that you need to use to extract and check data from an external source. You will also see in some examples later in the chapter how to use Power Query and Python to transform data, and you will learn about the functions needed as you encounter them in the examples.

> **Note** This section focuses on Power Query in the desktop version of Excel, but similar functionality is available in other familiar Microsoft applications, such as Power Apps and Power BI.

The Power Query functionality is located on the Data tab, in the Get & Transform Data section (see Figure 7-6). For this reason, Power Query is also known as Get & Transform.

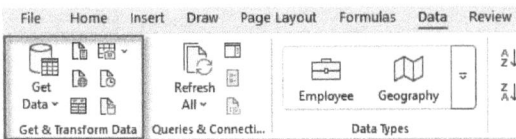

FIGURE 7-6 Power Query functionality can be accessed on the Data tab, in the Get & Transform Data section.

The Get Data dropdown menu provides access to external data via a connector (see Figure 7-7). A *connector* is a tool that can be configured to access an external data source.

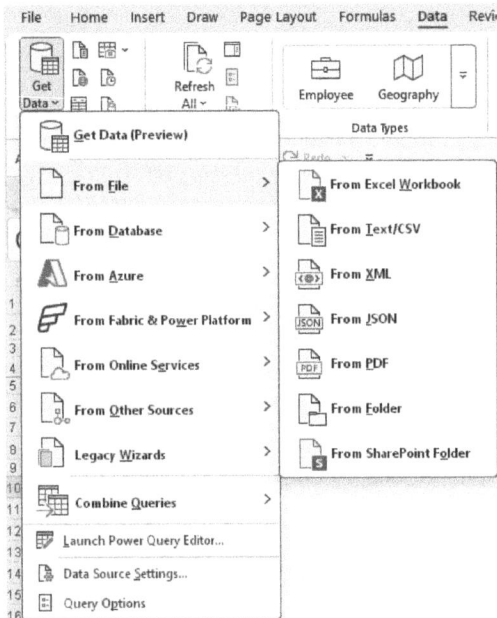

FIGURE 7-7 The Get Data dropdown menu provides access to lots of data sources.

At the top of the Get Data dropdown menu is the Get Data (Preview) option. When you click this option, you see the Get Data (Power Query) dialog, where you can search for any data source (see Figure 7-8).

> **Note** At the time of writing, we are viewing a preview of the Get Data option, and we assume that it will be generally available for you, since this is similar to how the connectors are accessed in other Microsoft apps, such as Power BI. So while we see the Get Data (Preview) option in the Get Data dropdown menu, you will likely see just Get Data.

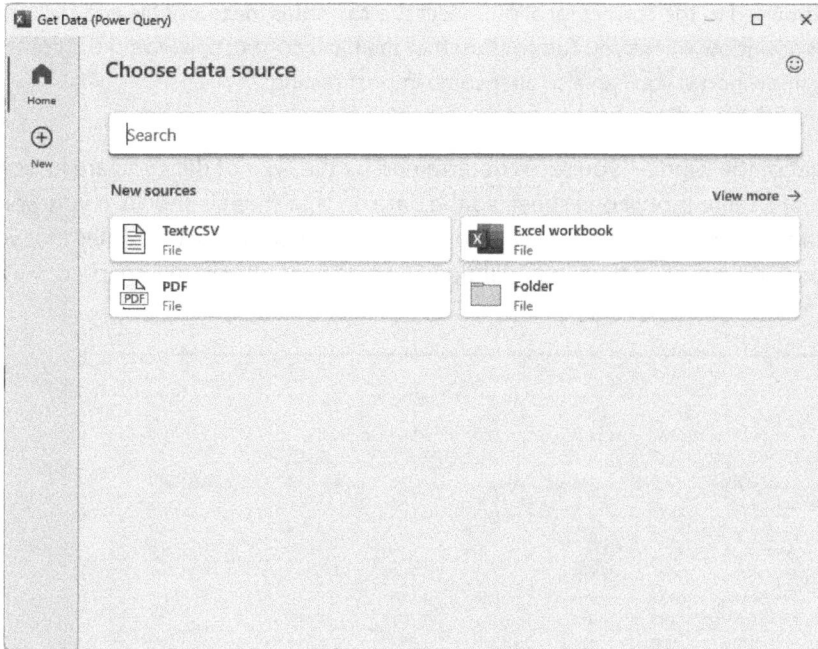

FIGURE 7-8 The Get Data dialog allows you to search for and access lots of data connectors.

For this example, let's use the car_sales_data.csv file as the source to explore some Power Query functionality. In the Get Data dialog, click the **Text/CSV** option. When the Import Data dialog appears, browse to the location where you saved the file car_sales_data.csv (see Figure 7-9).

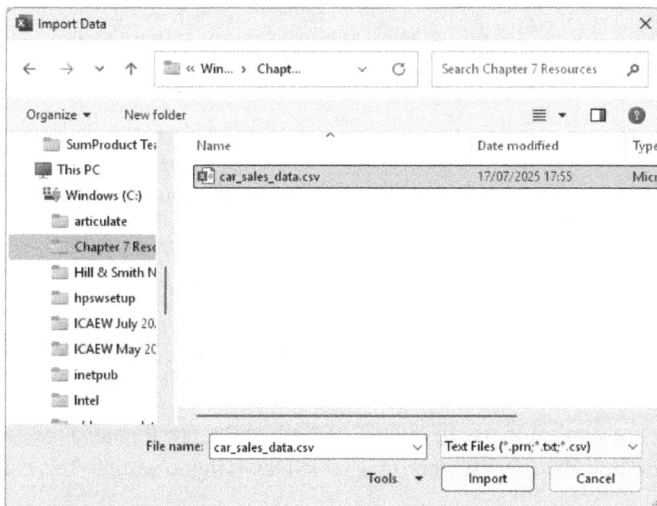

FIGURE 7-9 When you choose the Text/CSV connector, you are prompted to browse to the correct file.

Once you have browsed to the correct location, select the **car_sales_data.csv** file and click **Import**. Power Query opens a window where you can confirm that the file is correct by viewing the contents (see Figure 7-10). In this window, you can also alter some import settings.

> **Note** The format of the window you see is determined by the type of data you are importing. In this example, there is only one sheet, so the data on that sheet is shown. If you were accessing a database, you would see a Navigator window displaying a list of tables that you could select. You will notice the Navigator window in some examples in this chapter.

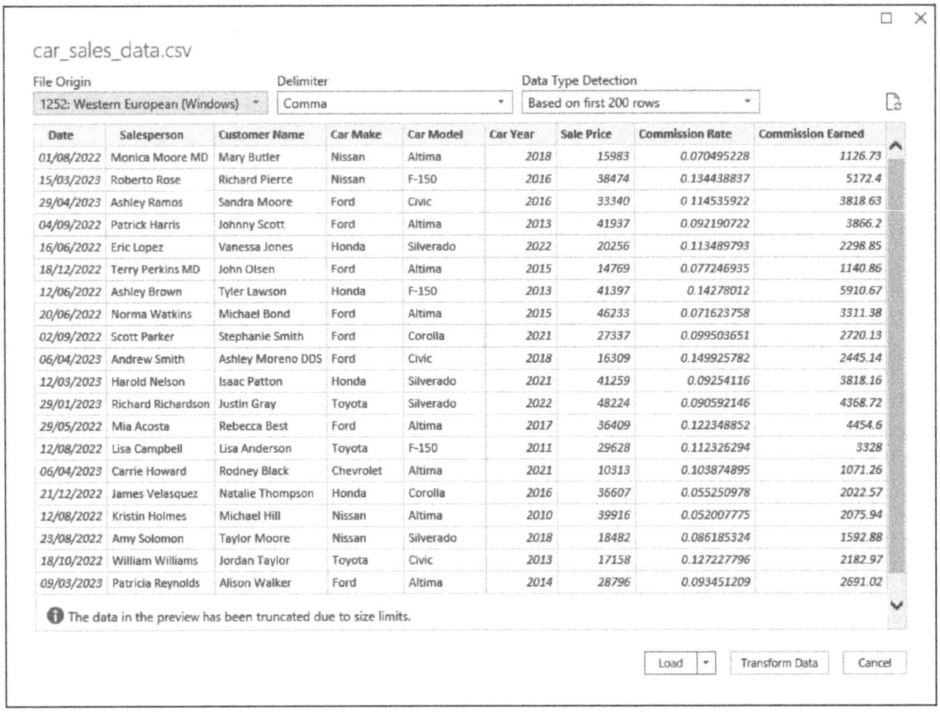

car_sales_data.csv

File Origin		Delimiter			Data Type Detection			
1252: Western European (Windows) ▾		Comma ▾			Based on first 200 rows ▾			

Date	Salesperson	Customer Name	Car Make	Car Model	Car Year	Sale Price	Commission Rate	Commission Earned
01/08/2022	Monica Moore MD	Mary Butler	Nissan	Altima	2018	15983	0.070495228	1126.73
15/03/2023	Roberto Rose	Richard Pierce	Nissan	F-150	2016	38474	0.134438837	5172.4
29/04/2023	Ashley Ramos	Sandra Moore	Ford	Civic	2016	33340	0.114535922	3818.63
04/09/2022	Patrick Harris	Johnny Scott	Ford	Altima	2013	41937	0.092190722	3866.2
16/06/2022	Eric Lopez	Vanessa Jones	Honda	Silverado	2022	20256	0.113489793	2298.85
18/12/2022	Terry Perkins MD	John Olsen	Ford	Altima	2015	14769	0.077246935	1140.86
12/06/2022	Ashley Brown	Tyler Lawson	Honda	F-150	2013	41397	0.14278012	5910.67
20/06/2022	Norma Watkins	Michael Bond	Ford	Altima	2015	46233	0.071623758	3311.38
02/09/2022	Scott Parker	Stephanie Smith	Ford	Corolla	2021	27337	0.099503651	2720.13
06/04/2023	Andrew Smith	Ashley Moreno DDS	Ford	Civic	2018	16309	0.149925782	2445.14
12/03/2023	Harold Nelson	Isaac Patton	Honda	Silverado	2021	41259	0.09254116	3818.16
29/01/2023	Richard Richardson	Justin Gray	Toyota	Silverado	2022	48224	0.090592146	4368.72
29/05/2022	Mia Acosta	Rebecca Best	Ford	Altima	2017	36409	0.122348852	4454.6
12/08/2022	Lisa Campbell	Lisa Anderson	Toyota	F-150	2011	29628	0.112326294	3328
06/04/2023	Carrie Howard	Rodney Black	Chevrolet	Altima	2021	10313	0.103874895	1071.26
21/12/2022	James Velasquez	Natalie Thompson	Honda	Corolla	2016	36607	0.055250978	2022.57
12/08/2022	Kristin Holmes	Michael Hill	Nissan	Altima	2010	39916	0.052007775	2075.94
23/08/2022	Amy Solomon	Taylor Moore	Nissan	Silverado	2018	18482	0.086185324	1592.88
18/10/2022	William Williams	Jordan Taylor	Toyota	Civic	2013	17158	0.127227796	2182.97
09/03/2023	Patricia Reynolds	Alison Walker	Ford	Altima	2014	28796	0.093451209	2691.02

ⓘ The data in the preview has been truncated due to size limits.

[Load ▾] [Transform Data] [Cancel]

FIGURE 7-10 Power Query shows a window previewing the selected data source, where you can check your data and change some import settings.

This window includes the following options:

- **File Origin:** This option allows you to select the character set used to generate the file. The default in this case is 1252: West European (Windows), and you can leave it as is.

- **Delimiter:** You can choose the symbol to use to divide the data in the file. Because this is a comma-delimited file, the default delimiter is a comma, which is what you want in this case.

- **Data Type Detection:** Power Query can run algorithms on the imported data to determine the data type of each column. This option allows you to stop checking, check the first 200 rows (the default), or check the whole dataset. The best option is usually the default. Even if you plan to change the data type of your columns, checking the first 200 rows will help you spot any issues (more on this later). Checking the whole dataset will take longer for large datasets like car_sales_data.csv, and you can check the data quality once you are in the Power Query Editor instead.

- **Load:** This dropdown menu allows you to load the data straight into the Excel workbook, bypassing the Power Query Editor. The options are Load and Load To. If you plan to use Python in Excel to clean up the data and do not need to view the data in the Power Query Editor, you can use Load To. (We will look more closely at this option a little later in the chapter.) Unless you need a copy of the data in the workbook in addition to the DataFrame that Python in Excel will use, you should not use the Load option from this dropdown menu.

- **Transform Data:** This option takes you to the Power Query Editor, where you can use the user interface (UI) to check the quality of your data and perform transformations. You will usually use this option instead of Load or Load To.

- **Cancel:** You can click this option to cancel the import and return to the Excel workbook.

You can accept the defaults for the options at the top of the window and click **Transform Data** at the bottom. The Power Query Editor screen appears, as shown in Figure 7-11. In the following sections, we will focus on various parts of the screen as we explore the functionality available.

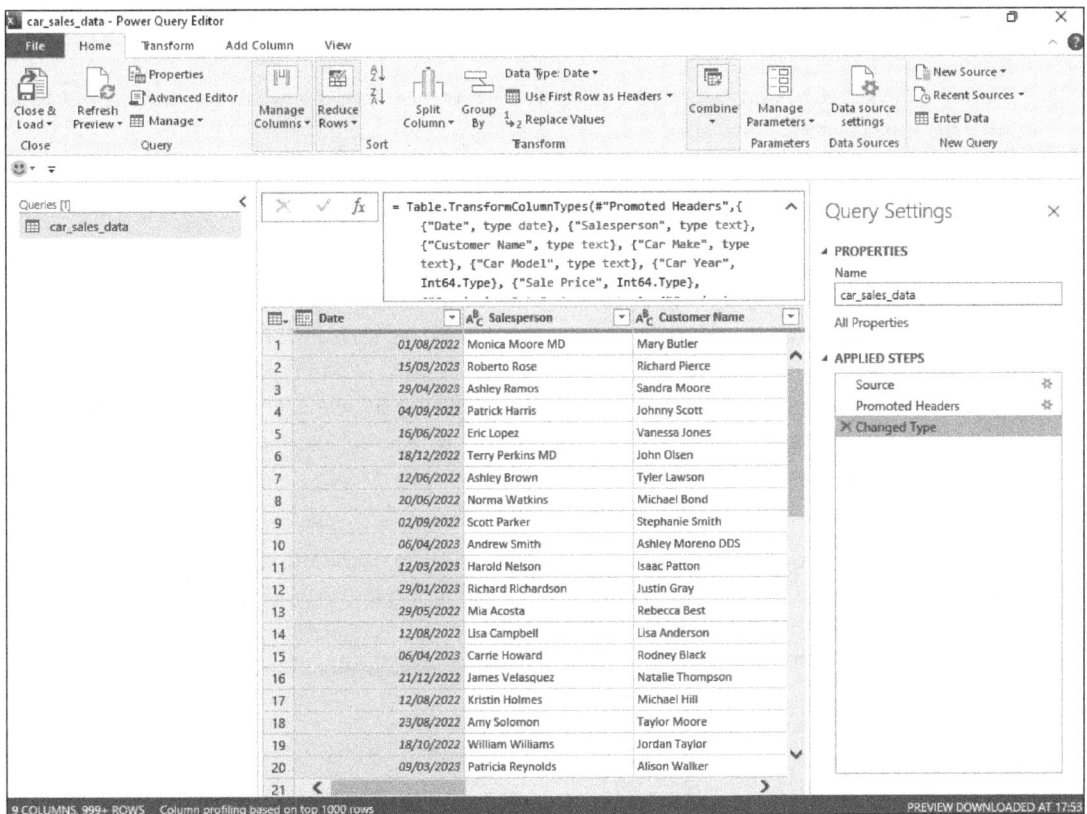

FIGURE 7-11 The Power Query Editor

Allowing Power Query to perform transformations for you

Power Query can perform some data transformations automatically. In Figure 7-11, you can see that the first row of the data has been promoted to be column headings, and the data types have been detected for the columns. The data type is indicated by the symbol to the left of the column name in each heading. The ABC symbol indicates that the column data type is text.

The Query Settings pane, shown on the right side of Figure 7-11, includes a list titled Applied Steps. Power Query works with tables, and you can always access the first table by clicking the Source step in the Applied Steps list. To view the table created in that step, click **Source**, and you will see a table like the one shown in Figure 7-12.

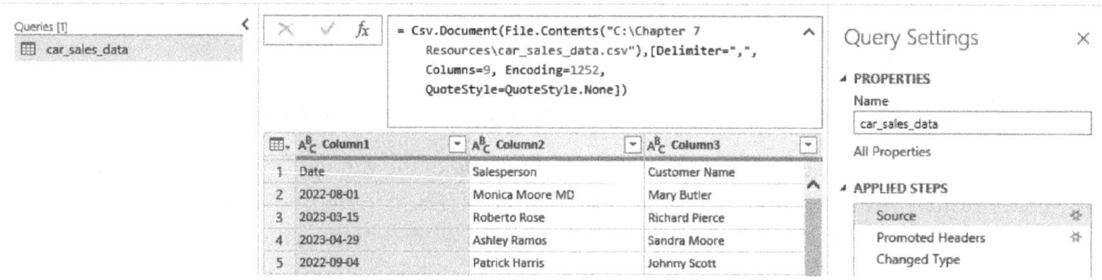

FIGURE 7-12 Viewing the Source step

Power Query uses M (Mashup) code. In Figure 7-12, you can see the following M code for the Source step in the formula bar:

```
= Csv.Document(File.Contents("C:\Chapter 7 Resources\car_sales_data.csv"),
[Delimiter=",", Columns=9, Encoding=1252, QuoteStyle=QuoteStyle.None])
```

The examples in this book do not require you to write any M code. The Power Query UI has been designed to allow you to perform many useful transformations without needing to create or understand M code. All you need to know at this point is that each step transforms the existing table and returns a new table. When you hover over a step, you see an X next to the step name. If you accidentally create a wrong step, you can click the X next to that step to delete it. To see what happens when you delete a step, delete the Changed Type step shown in Figure 7-13. This step determines the column types by analyzing the top 200 rows of data.

> **Note** Remember that if you are reading a printed copy of the book, you will see only black-and-white text and figures. But if you're following along in the workbook, which we strongly recommend, you will see all the colors we mention in this chapter.

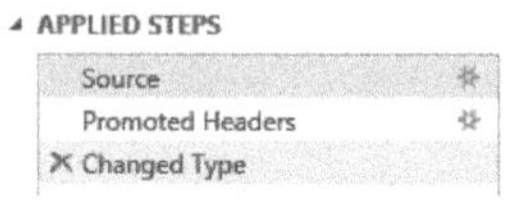

FIGURE 7-13 To delete a step, click the red X that appears to the left of the step name.

> **Note** Before you delete a step from the Applied Steps list, keep in mind that you cannot use Ctrl+Z to undo that action. If you delete a step by accident, you will need to re-create it from the UI.

In Figure 7-14, you can see that the Changed Type step has been deleted.

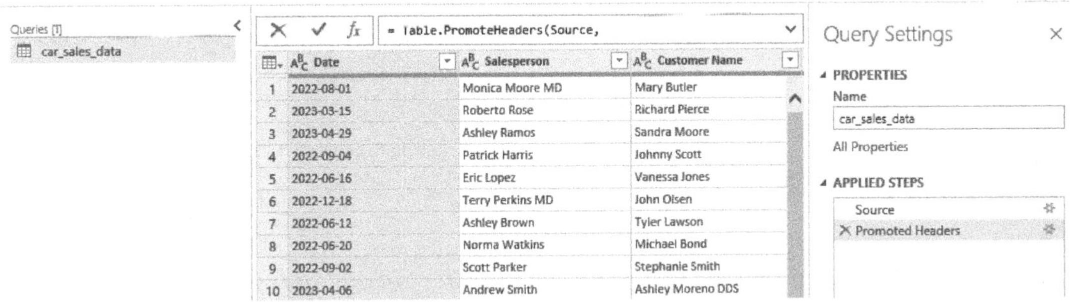

FIGURE 7-14 The Changed Type step has been deleted.

To re-create the Changed Type step, you could click the ABC icon for a column and choose the data type you want from the dropdown menu, as shown in Figure 7-15.

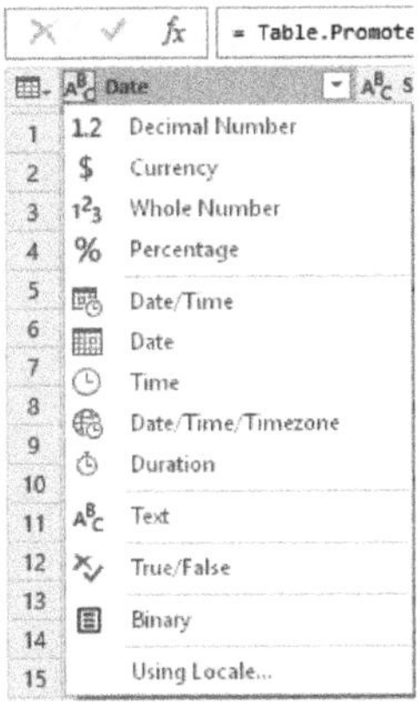

FIGURE 7-15 The icon to the left of each column title reveals a dropdown menu that allows you to select the data type for that column.

Select **Date** from the dropdown menu as the data type for the Date column, and Power Query creates a Changed Type step that only changes the data type for the Date column (see Figure 7-16).

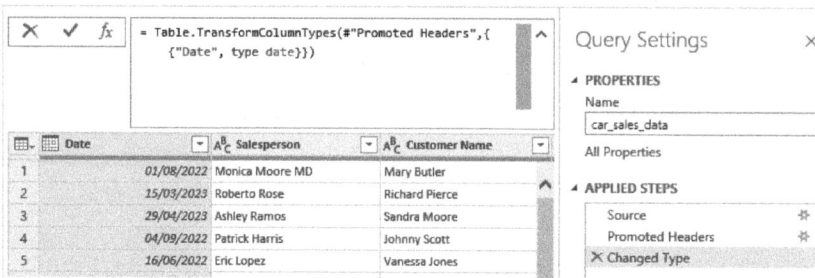

FIGURE 7-16 By changing the Date column's data type, you manually create a Changed Type step that only changes the Date column's data type.

> **Note** The date in Figure 7-16 is displayed in the format dd/mm/yyyy because our locale is set to the United Kingdom.

You can change the data type of multiple columns at one time. When you do so, you must make them all the same data type, although they can start as different data types. To see how it works, hold down the **Ctrl** key and select the **Sale Price**, **Commission Rate**, and **Commission Earned** column headings and then, on the **Transform** tab, click the **Data Type** dropdown menu and select **Decimal Number** (see Figure 7-17).

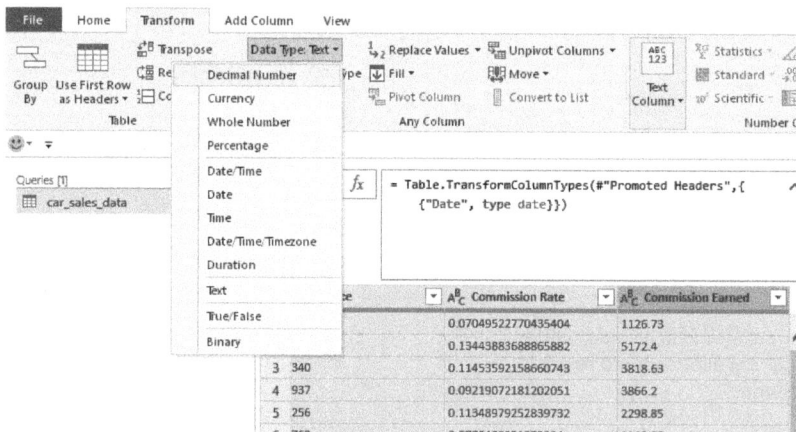

FIGURE 7-17 You can change the data types of columns by using the Data Type dropdown menu on the Transform tab.

The column heads now show the decimal number icon, and the Changed Type step is updated to include this change (see Figure 7-18).

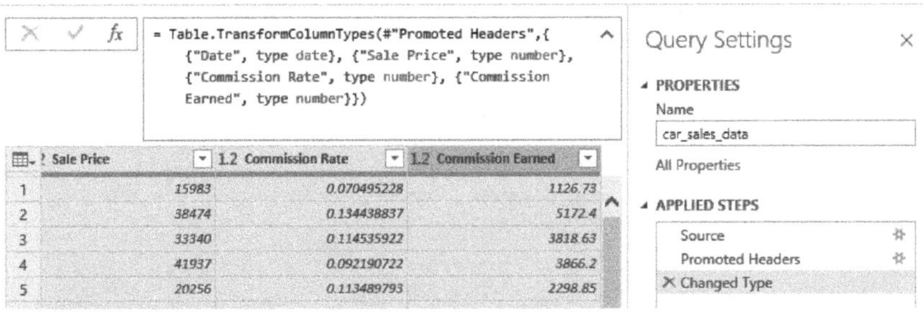

FIGURE 7-18 The data type change has been included in the Changed Type step.

You could build your own Changed Type step this way, but using the Power Query algorithms is usually easier. To see how this works, delete the **Changed Type** step and select all the columns by selecting any column heading and then pressing **Ctrl+A**. Then go to the **Transform** tab and select **Detect Data Type**. Power Query runs the algorithms on the columns selected. Figure 7-19 shows the results: the same Changed Type step you started with.

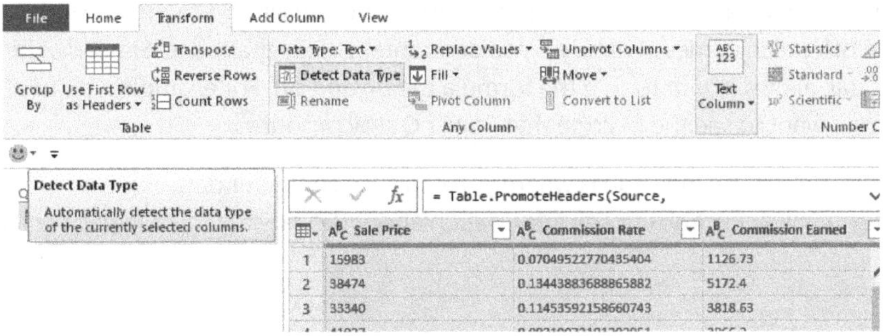

FIGURE 7-19 Detect Data Type can be used on all the columns.

> **Note** As mentioned earlier, this chapter will not cover all the possible transformations, but we will highlight any necessary transformations in the examples.

Checking the quality of your data with the View tab

Even if you choose not to use Power Query to transform your data, you should know about the useful functions that you can access from the View tab to check the quality of the data (see Figure 7-20).

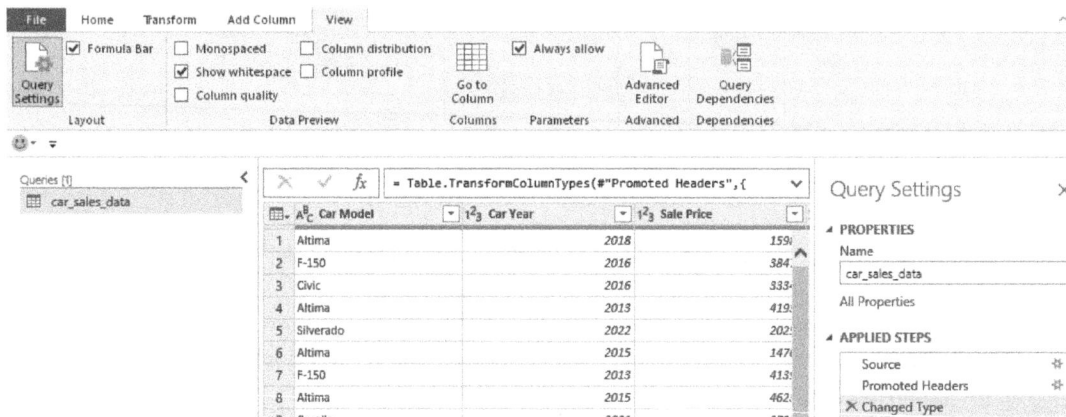

FIGURE 7-20 The View tab

The first option on the View tab, Query Settings, is a button you can click to toggle the Query Settings pane on and off, which comes in handy if you accidentally close that pane. Similarly, the second option, Formula Bar, allows you to toggle the formula bar on and off. For example, you might want to turn it off if you don't want to see the M code that Power Query produces.

The Data Preview section of the View tab is where you can check out your data. For example, you can select the Column Quality checkbox to see information about the car sales data in each column (see Figure 7-21).

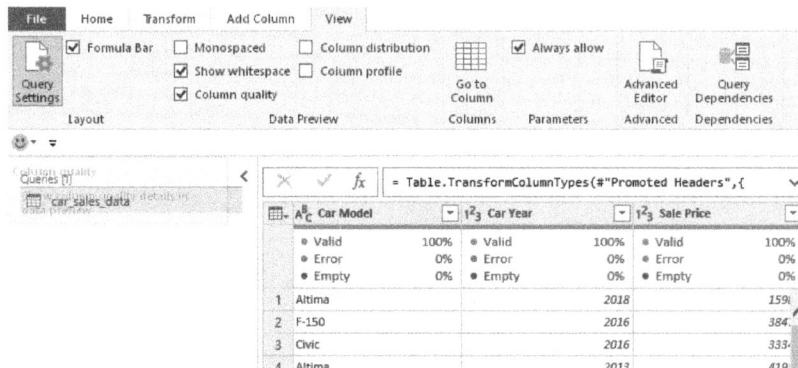

FIGURE 7-21 The Column Quality checkbox allows you to see data quality indicators under the column headings.

The line under each heading also indicates the quality of the data in the column. If all the data in a column is valid, the column heading has a green line under it; if there are empty cells, then part of the line under the column heading will be gray to show the distribution. If the data contains errors, you may also see green dashes under the column heading for unknown or red dashes for unexpected errors. Unknown means that there are errors in the column, and the quality of the remaining data can't be determined. Determining the quality of data in a column is called *column profiling*.

You may recall that when you first viewed the Power Query Editor, a message about the number of rows used to determine column quality was displayed at the bottom of the pane. Figure 7-22 zooms in on this message regarding column profiling settings.

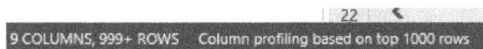

FIGURE 7-22 The settings for column profiling are displayed at the bottom of the Power Query Editor.

If you want to use the whole dataset for column profiling, click this message and select the other setting: **Column Profiling Based On Entire Data Set** (see Figure 7-23). Depending on the number of rows in the dataset you are analyzing, this process may take a while because it causes Power Query to check for null values and errors in the whole dataset. For the examples in this book, you should leave the setting at Column Profiling Based on Top 1000 Rows.

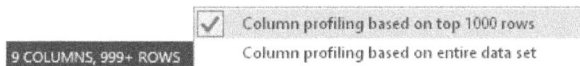

FIGURE 7-23 The setting for column profiling can be changed from the bar at the bottom of the Power Query Editor.

If you hover over the column quality data for a particular column, a pop-up box will appear that shows the numeric distribution of the quality of values in the profiled dataset (see Figure 7-24).

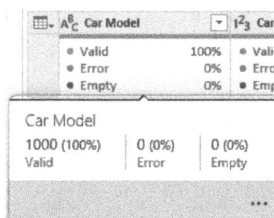

FIGURE 7-24 By hovering over the column quality data for a column, you can get more information.

You can click the ellipsis (…) menu at the bottom of the column quality pop-up box to view options for cleaning the data (see Figure 7-25). When completing a task in Power Query, there is often more than one possible route. The ellipsis menu provides another way to quickly resolve data issues as you find them.

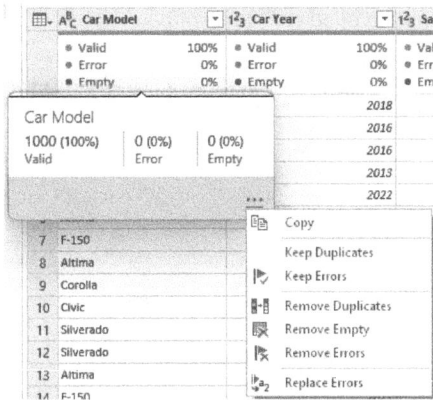

FIGURE 7-25 Hovering over the ellipsis (…) menu at the bottom of the column quality pop-up box allows you to access some data cleansing options.

The next checkbox on the View tab is Column Distribution, which you can select to see visualizations (see Figure 7-26).

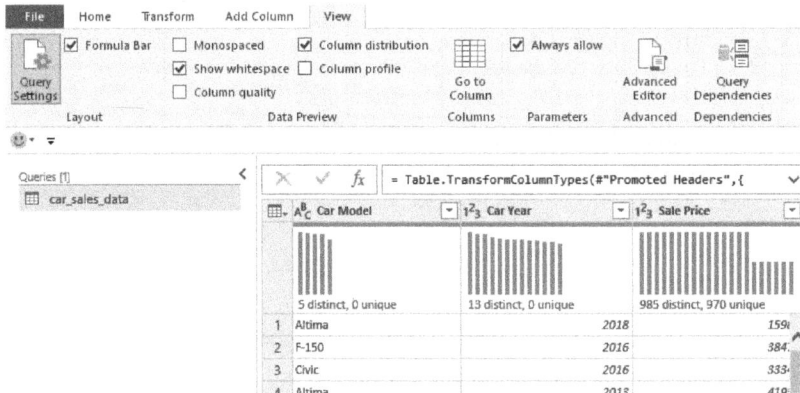

FIGURE 7-26 The Column Distribution option provides a visual representation of unique and distinct values.

The column charts give you an idea of how often values are repeated in each column. You can hover over a visualization to see more details (see Figure 7-27).

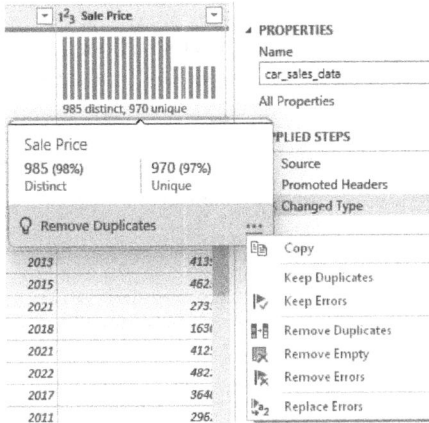

FIGURE 7-27 Hovering over the visual representation of a column distribution reveals more information and an ellipsis menu with options to manipulate the data based on the values in that column.

You can see in this example that the number of distinct values represents 98% of the data, which means the same sales prices are not repeated very often in the data being analyzed (which is 1,000 rows). The 970 unique sales prices make up 970 of the 1,000 rows analyzed, which is 97% of the data analyzed.

The final checkbox in the Data Preview section of the View tab is the Column Profile checkbox. When you select it, Power Query gives you Column Statistics and Value Distribution sections that provide more information (see Figure 7-28).

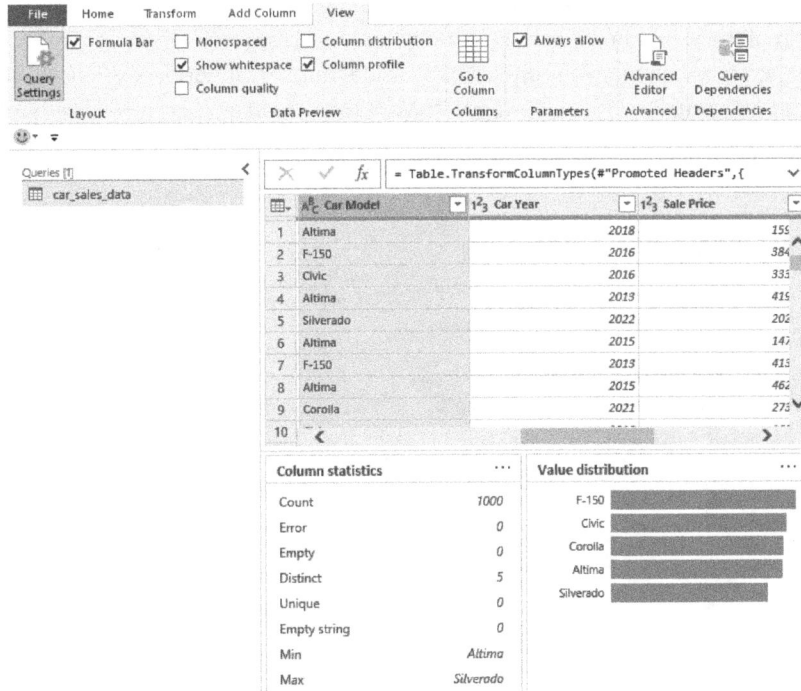

FIGURE 7-28 The Column Statistics box displays contextual statistics for the column selected.

The statistical data is not static; you can interact with it. For example, you can right-click one of the bars in the chart to see transformations available for that value (see Figure 7-29).

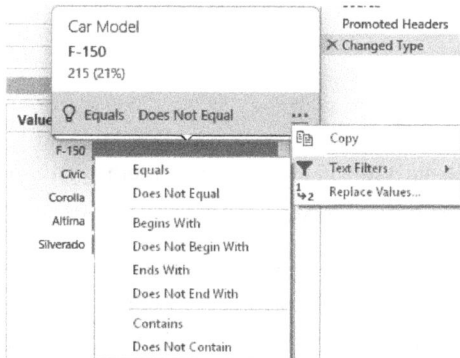

FIGURE 7-29 Hovering over a bar of the value distribution bar chart allows you to view more data, and right-clicking the bar reveals a menu of transformations based on that value.

You may have noticed the ellipsis menu available from the value distribution chart. It allows you to change the grouping of the values in the column. The options available in this menu depend on the data type. For the Car Make column, you can group by value (the default) or by text length (see Figure 7-30). Changing the Group By option allows you to view the data in a different way without changing the data in the query.

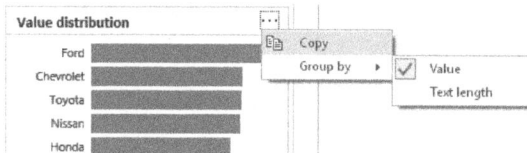

FIGURE 7-30 The ellipsis menu on the value distribution bar chart allows you to copy the data or group by value or by text length.

Detecting and fixing errors

Now that we have looked at various ways of checking the quality of data, let's introduce an error that can be detected and fixed. Change the data type of the Sale Price column to text by clicking the **123** icon next to the column name and choosing **Text**. You will probably see the message shown in Figure 7-31.

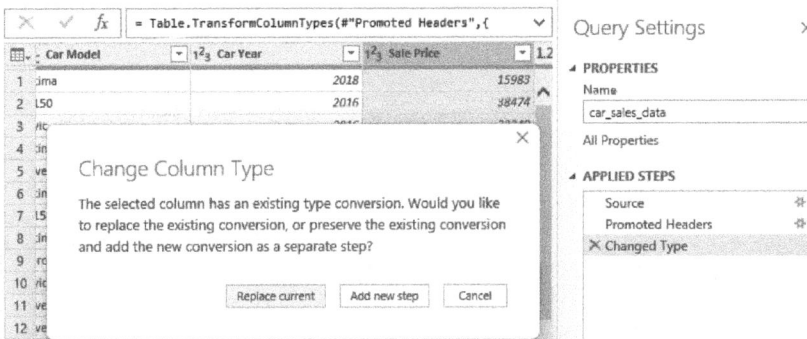

FIGURE 7-31 Changing the data type of the Sale Price column to text results in a prompt to add it to the current step or a new step.

Click **Replace Current** and right-click row 6 of the Sale Price column. The menu shown in Figure 7-32 appears.

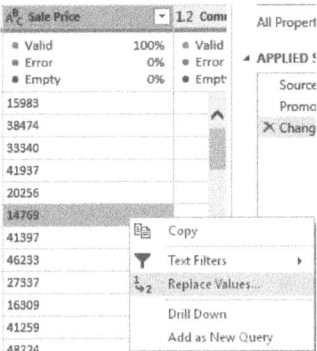

FIGURE 7-32 The context menu for a cell allows you to replace values.

Select **Replace Values** to open the Replace Values dialog. Change the Replace With value to **I am not a number** (see Figure 7-33). (This is where you are introducing the error we mentioned earlier.)

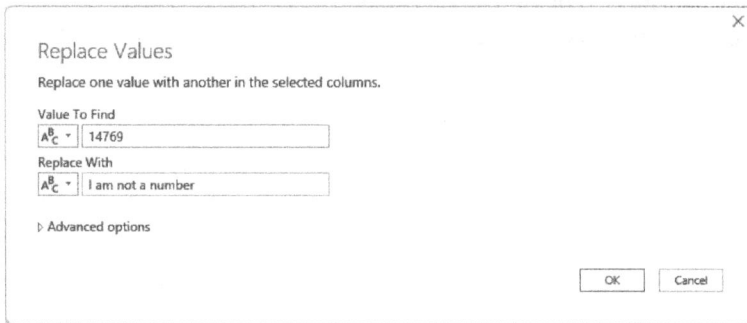

FIGURE 7-33 Entering text in the Sale Price column to generate an error

Click **OK** and view the results, which are shown in Figure 7-34. As you can see, the value on row 6 is I Am Not a Number, and the Applied Steps box now includes a Replaced Value step.

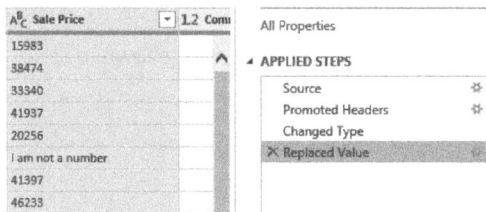

FIGURE 7-34 Row 6 now contains text.

Next, change the data type of the Sale Price column to decimal number. As shown in Figure 7-35, row 6 now contains an error, and the Applied Steps box now includes a Changed Type1 step.

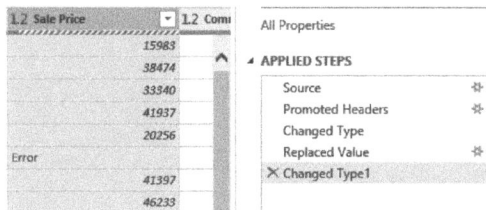

FIGURE 7-35 Row 6 now contains an error.

The bar under the column heading is normally green but is now red with a green dashed line, indicating that the quality of the data cannot be determined because an error occurred. To find the error, go to the **View** menu and select the checkboxes **Column Quality**, **Column Distribution**, and **Column Profile**. Figure 7-36 shows the results.

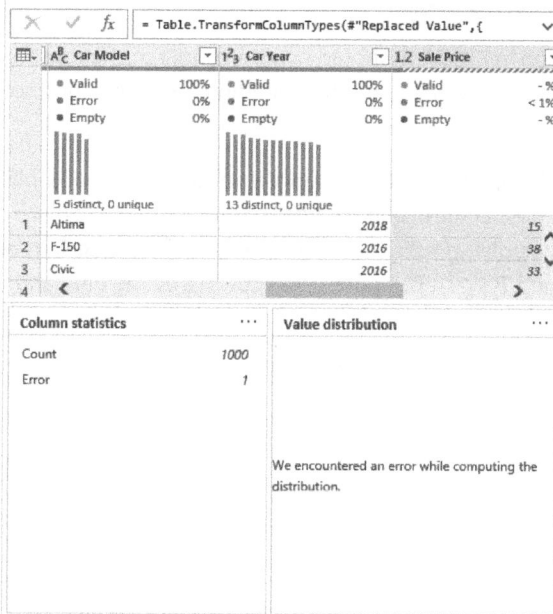

FIGURE 7-36 Because there is an error, the distribution cannot be shown.

By right-clicking the column quality information in the Sale Price column, you open the column quality pop-up box, where you can see that there is one error (see Figure 7-37). You could click the ellipsis menu and then select the Replace Errors option to change the text that is causing the error to a numeric value.

Caution Be careful when using Remove Errors; if you choose to delete an error, you will also delete the rest of the row that contains the error.

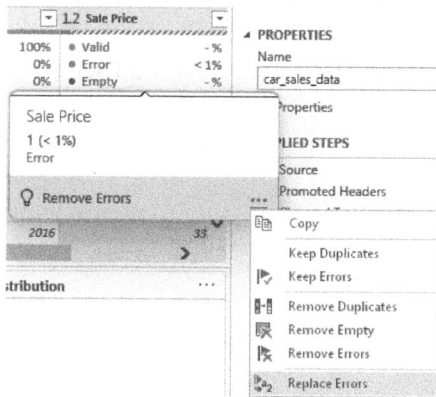

FIGURE 7-37 The value causing the error can be replaced.

Preparing the data for Python in Excel

Before we load the data in the query into Python in Excel, we should make a couple of changes to prepare it. Let's start by restoring the data to its original state and then loading the connection so that Python in Excel can read it.

First, we need to delete the **Changed Type1** step and the **Replaced Value** step from the Applied Steps list. Then, click the ABC icon for the Sale Price column and change its data type to decimal number. When you see the Change Column Type dialog (refer to Figure 7-31), click **Replace Current** to replace the conversion in the current Changed Type step. Figure 7-38 shows what the data and the steps look like after these changes are made.

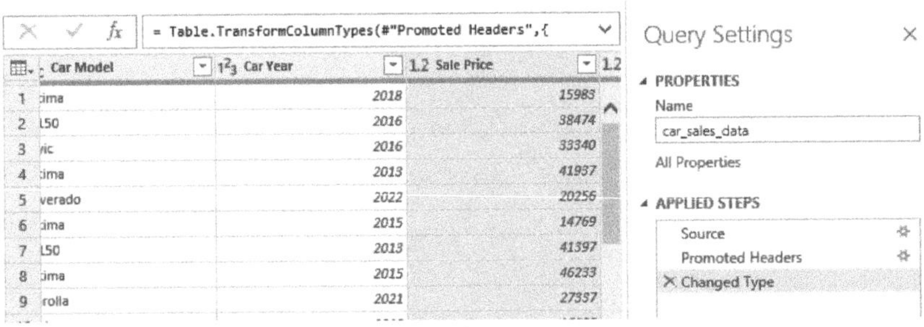

FIGURE 7-38 The car_sales_data query, with no errors and only three steps

> **Note** You might wonder why we would clean the data in Power Query instead of in the Excel workbook. Cleaning large datasets in Excel can take a lot of time and processing power, and the dataset we're working with here is very large. We can also repeat the cleaning process if the external data changes by refreshing the Power Query query.

Counting rows of data with Group By

As we just said, the dataset we're working with in this example is very large. In fact, you will probably be surprised at how many rows it contains. To use the UI to determine just how many rows there are, select the Date column by clicking the column heading, go to the Home tab, and click **Group By**. As shown in Figure 7-39, the Group By dialog appears.

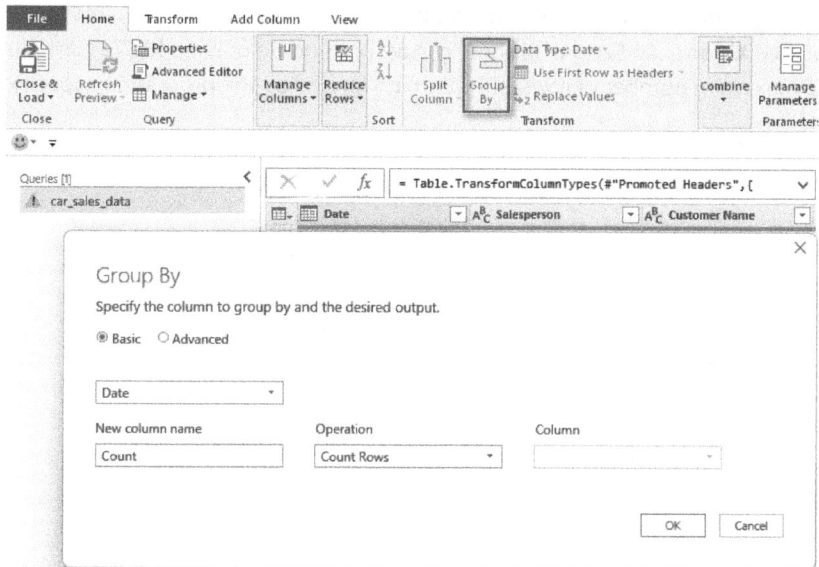

FIGURE 7-39 The Group By dialog

We can use the Group By dialog to get Power Query to count the rows in the dataset. One of the operations available is Count Rows (see Figure 7-39). If we can use this operation for the whole query, we can count all the rows. When the Group By dialog first appears, the Basic format is selected. If you select the **Advanced** radio button instead, the dialog changes to include an ellipsis menu next to the Date selection (see Figure 7-40). You can click the ellipsis and select **Delete** to delete the grouping and have Power Query count all the rows.

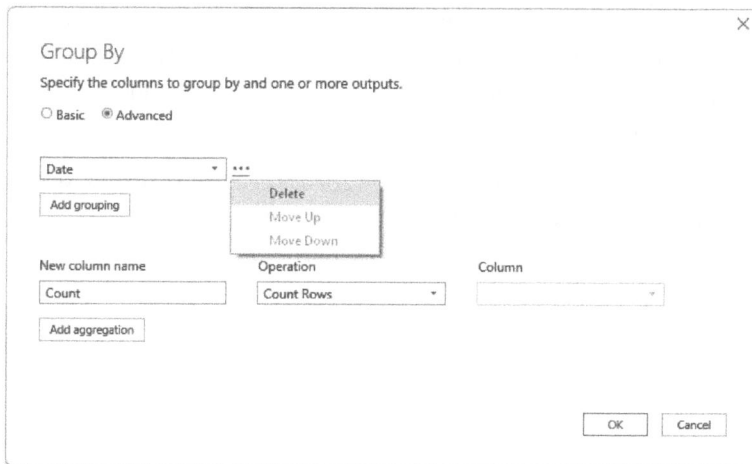

FIGURE 7-40 When the Group By dialog has the Advanced option selected, you can delete the Date grouping.

Click **OK**, and Power Query takes a short time to count the number of rows. Figure 7-41 shows the results: There are 2,500,000 rows. An Excel worksheet can accommodate only 1,048,576 rows, but Power Query has no maximum number of rows, although it is limited by the processing capacity available on the computer.

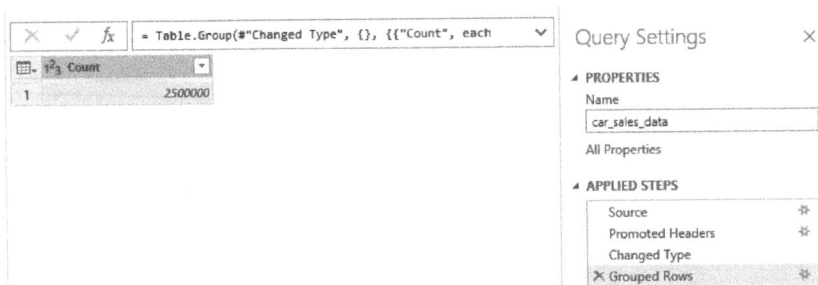

FIGURE 7-41 Power Query has counted the number of rows in the query and found 2,500,000.

Reducing the dataset by using filters

Now that you have seen the number of rows in the query, you can delete the **Grouped Rows** step. We said earlier that the number of rows you can process in Power Query depends on the processing capacity of your computer—and you may have experienced some longer-than-desired waits for some steps to process the data. We do not need all these rows to explore Python in Excel, so let's introduce a filter to trim down the number of rows to a fraction of the 2,500,000 rows we currently have. This will reduce processing time while we work through the example.

Reducing a dataset by removing unnecessary columns and rows should be done as close to the data source as possible to ensure efficiency. By "as close to the data source as possible," we mean as early on in the transformation process as feasible. If you don't reduce a dataset, you will spend computing resources on processing data that will ultimately be deleted. In this case, we will reduce the data before Excel can access it and before Python in Excel can load it into a DataFrame.

We will sample this dataset by selecting cars made between 2020 and 2022. To do this, select the filter arrow next to the Car Year column heading and select the checkboxes next to 2020, 2021, and 2022, as shown in Figure 7-42.

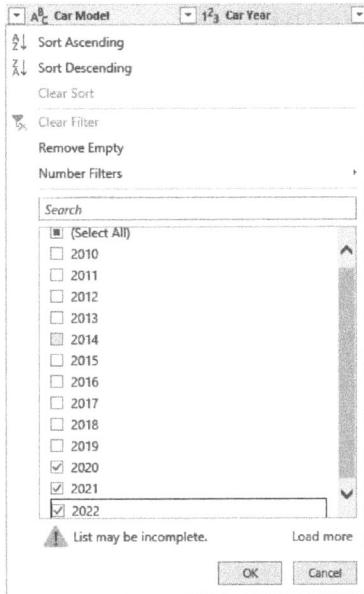

FIGURE 7-42 Filtering on the Car Year column

Click **OK**, and a new step called Filtered Rows is created, as shown in Figure 7-43. This step selects cars made in the years you selected. Now the sample dataset contains more than 500,000 rows. This is still a large dataset, but it's only about one-fifth the size of the original dataset.

> **Note** You can check the number of rows in the dataset by following the process described in the section "Counting rows of data with Group By," earlier in this chapter. If you do that, be sure to delete the Grouped Rows step before continuing.

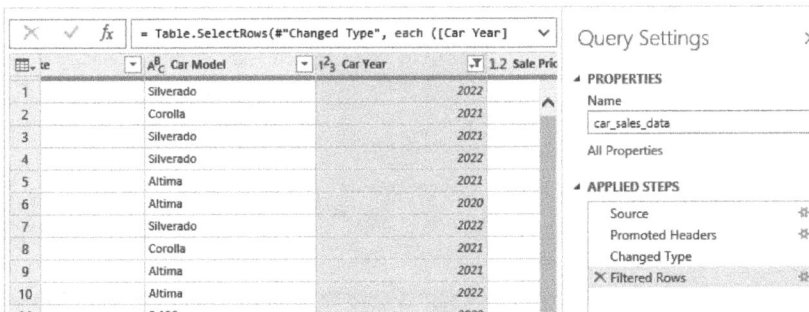

FIGURE 7-43 The car_sales_data query is ready to load.

Creating a connection between the query and Excel

We now have a query that contains a subset of the car sales data so that we can work through the examples without waiting for Python to process the data. To make the query available to Python in Excel, go to the **Home** tab, click the **Close & Load** dropdown menu, and then select **Close & Load To** (see Figure 7-44).

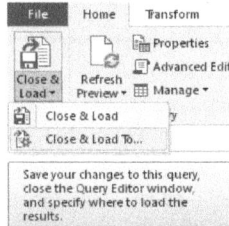

FIGURE 7-44 The Close & Load To option on the Home tab

When you load a query, if you choose Close & Load from the Close & Load dropdown menu on the Home tab instead of Close & Load To, the default Power Query behavior is to create a new Excel worksheet for each new query and load the query to an Excel table on that worksheet. If you delete the worksheets for new queries and ignore any warnings, each query will be converted into a connection-only query. A connection-only query is a query that can be accessed by other queries and Python in Excel, but the data is not loaded in the workbook. In Figure 7-45, Categories is a connection-only query that has been accidentally loaded to the workbook. Deleting the sheet will fix that.

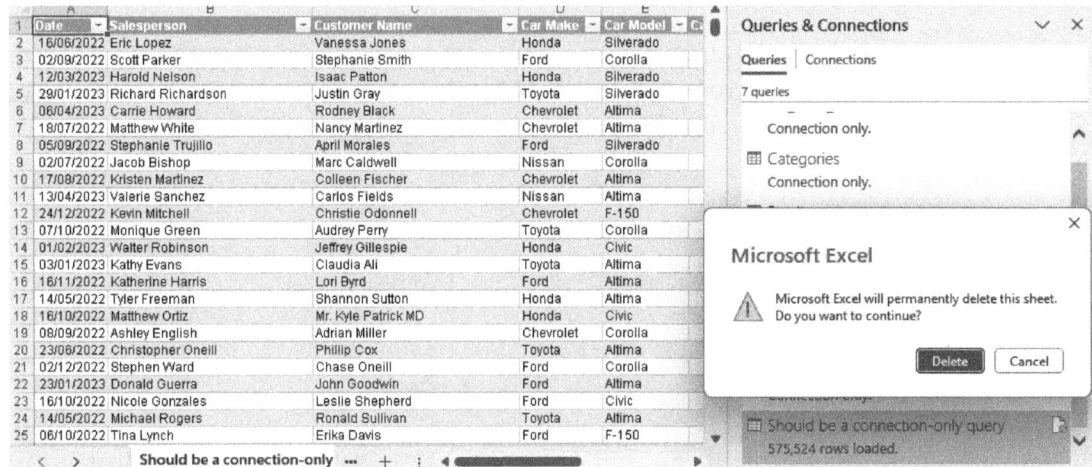

FIGURE 7-45 If you accidentally use Close & Load instead of Close & Load To, you can delete the new sheet created, and the query will be converted to a connection-only query.

As shown in Figure 7-46, the Queries & Connections pane appears in the Excel workbook, and so does the Import Data dialog. This dialog allows you to choose how the query will be loaded.

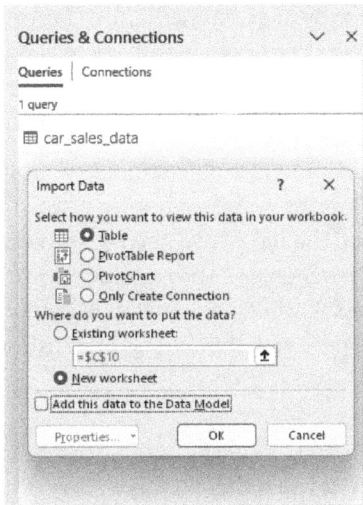

FIGURE 7-46 The Queries & Connections pane has opened in the Excel workbook, and so has the Import Data dialog.

The Import Data dialog has options to load the data into the workbook as a table, PivotTable, or PivotChart. Because you are using the data for Python in Excel, there is no need to load it into the workbook; in fact, loading the data into the workbook unnecessarily would make the workbook less efficient. Therefore, choose the option **Only Create Connection** and click **OK**.

The Queries & Connections pane shows that the car_sales_data query is now ready for Python in Excel (see Figure 7-47).

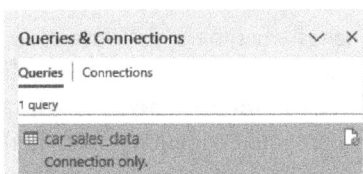

FIGURE 7-47 The Queries & Connections pane shows the car_sales_data query and the message "Connection only."

Figure 7-47 shows a refresh symbol to the right of the car_sales_data query in the Queries & Connections pane. This query is linked to the car_sales_data.csv file. The underlying data is not changed by any transformations in the query, but if the underlying data changes, you can update the query by clicking the refresh symbol.

Note If you have any issues refreshing a connection-only query from the workbook, double-click the query in the Queries & Connections pane to access the Power Query Editor. You can then refresh the data from the Power Query Editor by clicking the Refresh Preview option on the Home tab. When you select the Close & Load dropdown menu, you will not have the option Close & Load To. This is not a problem because you already indicated that it is a connection-only query. When you use Close & Load, the updated data will be available from the connection-only query in the workbook.

In this introductory section on Power Query, you have learned the basics you need to start exploring the use of external data with Copilot, Python in Excel, and Power Query. Throughout the rest of the chapter, we will look at examples that demonstrate how to access Power Query queries in Python in Excel and compare the process of transforming data in Power Query with the process of transforming data in Python in Excel.

Extracting the car sales data into Python in Excel

At the beginning of this chapter, you saw that importing external data into Python in Excel is not currently possible. The only way to import data into Python in Excel is to load a connection in Excel first. You have seen how to use Power Query for that and to spot issues before loading the data into Python in Excel. We have already created a query, called car_sales_data, to link to the data in the car_sales_data.csv file. Now, to show how to link the Power Query query and Python in Excel, let's continue with the car sales data.

Asking Copilot to connect Python in Excel with a Power Query query

We'll begin by using Copilot with Power Query and Python in Excel. Remember if you have access to the dropdown menu under the Copilot button, you must choose App Skills for these exercises. Open Copilot and use this prompt to access the query we've created: **Use Python to analyze the data in the Power Query query car_sales_data**. Figure 7-48 shows a potential Copilot response to this prompt. As you can see, Copilot says it was unable to access the query, and it walks you through the basic steps involved in loading the data into an Excel worksheet and then using the PY function to run the Python code on the data.

Note The Python in Excel functionality you have available is likely more advanced than the functionality shown here.

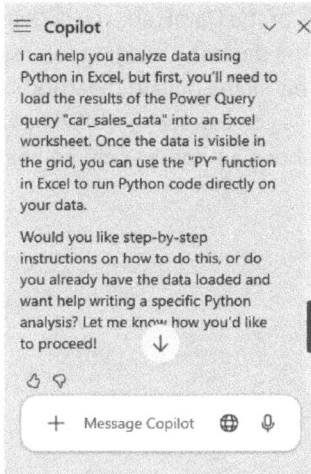

FIGURE 7-48 Copilot could not access the car_sales_data query.

Ideally, we would like Copilot to create a DataFrame from the query for a complete solution, but it didn't do that. In addition, its response is inaccurate: You don't need to load data into the Excel workbook for Python to read it. Python in Excel can read the data directly from a Power Query query.

Creating a DataFrame to access a Power Query query

You can manually create a DataFrame in a new Python cell, cell C10, as shown in Figure 7-49, by entering the following code that you learned in Chapter 2:

```
df_car_sales_query=xl("car_sales_data")
```

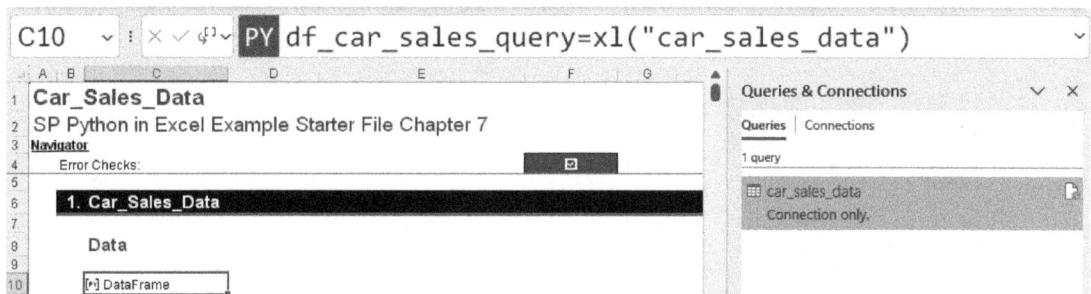

FIGURE 7-49 The car_sales_data query can be extracted into a DataFrame in a Python cell.

As discussed extensively in Chapter 2, you can check the contents of the DataFrame by clicking the PY icon in Excel cell C10 to show the data type card. Since this is a large dataset, changing to the Excel Value view is not necessary—or convenient—unless you need to show all the data in the workbook. Figure 7-50 shows the data type card for the DataFrame in cell C10. As you can see, it is a 575524X9 DataFrame, and the first five rows and the last five rows of data are shown under the column headings.

	Date	Salesperson	Customer Name	Car Make	Car Model
0	16/06/2022	Eric Lopez	Vanessa Jones	Honda	Silverado
1	02/09/2022	Scott Parker	Stephanie Smith	Ford	Corolla
2	12/03/2023	Harold Nelson	Isaac Patton	Honda	Silverado
3	29/01/2023	Richard Richardson	Justin Gray	Toyota	Silverado
4	06/04/2023	Carrie Howard	Rodney Black	Chevrolet	Altima
...	...	...	...	...	...
575519	12/04/2023	Shawn Park	Anna Callahan	Honda	Altima
575520	07/05/2022	Alexandra Charles	Rebecca Mata	Nissan	Silverado
575521	04/07/2022	Matthew Townsend	Nicole Clay	Chevrolet	Civic
575522	26/05/2022	Isabella Moore	Shirley Lee	Chevrolet	Silverado
575523	03/10/2022	Kimberly Snow	Tara Rodgers	Ford	F-150

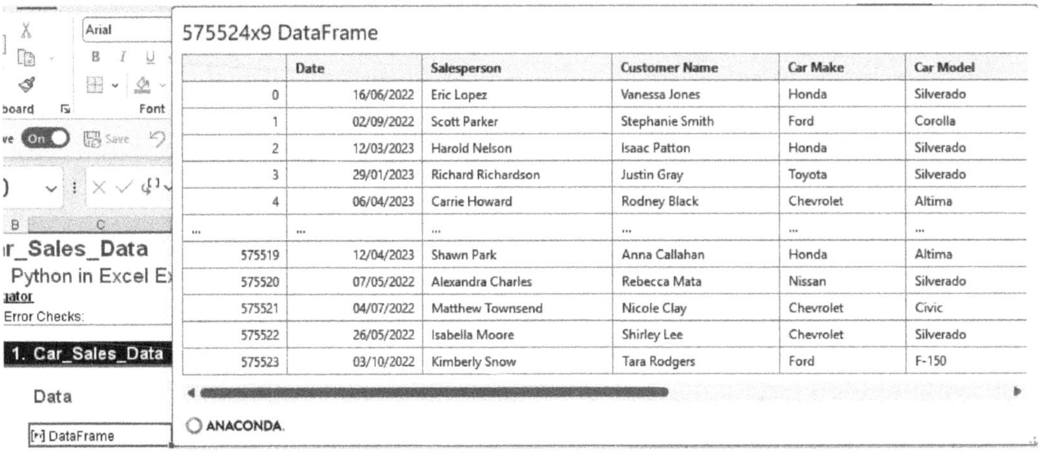

FIGURE 7-50 The data type card for DataFrame df_car_sales_query

Asking Copilot to analyze the car sales data

Now that you have a DataFrame that contains the data from the car_sales_data query, try the following Copilot prompt: **Use Python to analyze the data in df_car_sales_query**.

Copilot should be able to locate the data and offer to use advanced analysis. When you click **Start** to use Quick conversation mode, Copilot begins by outlining the reasonable-sounding plan shown in Figure 7-51.

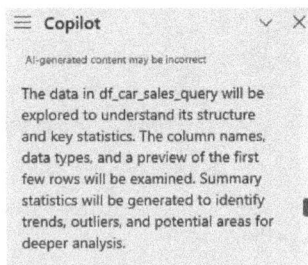

FIGURE 7-51 The plan to analyze the data in DataFrame df_car_sales_query sounds reasonable.

Figure 7-52 shows that Copilot has also created four Python cells, starting with cell A6. As you will see, there is repetition in the data.

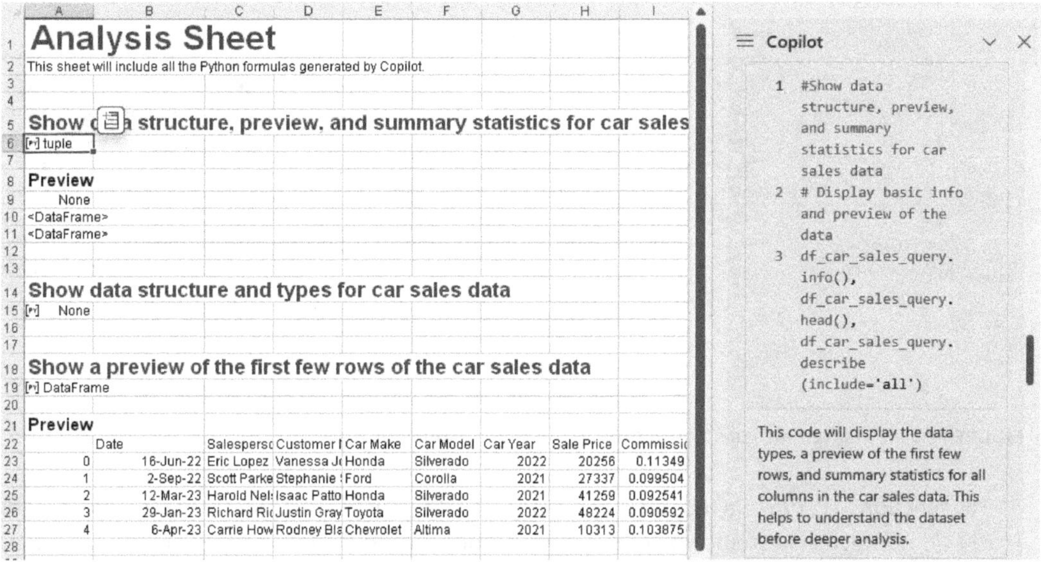

FIGURE 7-52 Cell A6 contains Python code to describe the data structure, preview, and summary statistics.

> **Note** Recall from the Python syntax you learned in Chapter 2 and the examples in Chapter 6 that tuples cannot be displayed as Excel values. This is why the preview for cell A6 doesn't give any more information. And there is another problem: Although the function `df_car_sales_query.info()` would work in a different platform, it does not output a value here because normally it would just print the results to the platform. This is why the result is None in the Excel workbook.

To see more information about the data, you can create your own DataFrame of information by entering the following Python code in cell C6:

```
info = df_car_sales_query.dtypes.to_frame('dtypes')
info['non_null'] = df_car_sales_query.count()
info['unique_values'] = df_car_sales_query.apply(lambda srs: len(srs.unique()))
info['first_row'] = df_car_sales_query.iloc[0]
info['last_row'] = df_car_sales_query.iloc[-1]
info['memory_usage'] = df_car_sales_query.memory_usage().sum()
info
```

Figure 7-53 shows the results, with the data type card showing more information.

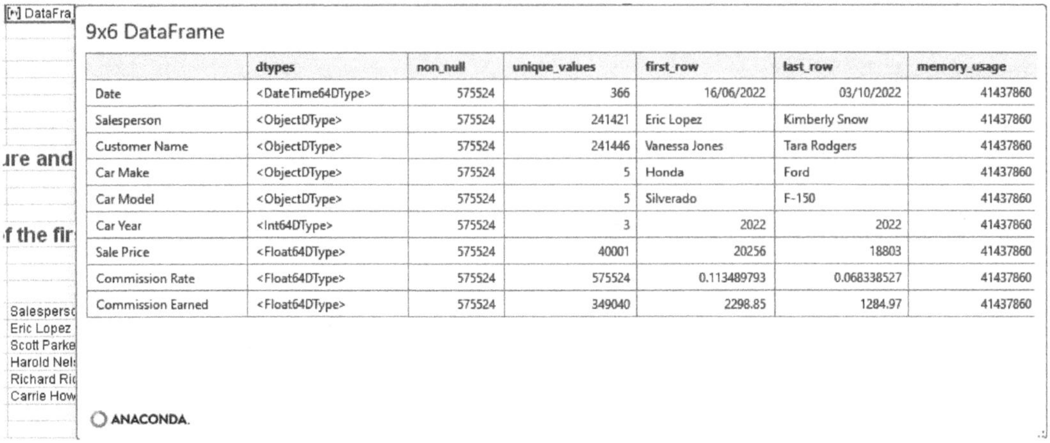

9x6 DataFrame

	dtypes	non_null	unique_values	first_row	last_row	memory_usage
Date	<DateTime64DType>	575524	366	16/06/2022	03/10/2022	41437860
Salesperson	<ObjectDType>	575524	241421	Eric Lopez	Kimberly Snow	41437860
Customer Name	<ObjectDType>	575524	241446	Vanessa Jones	Tara Rodgers	41437860
Car Make	<ObjectDType>	575524	5	Honda	Ford	41437860
Car Model	<ObjectDType>	575524	5	Silverado	F-150	41437860
Car Year	<Int64DType>	575524	3	2022	2022	41437860
Sale Price	<Float64DType>	575524	40001	20256	18803	41437860
Commission Rate	<Float64DType>	575524	575524	0.113489793	0.068338527	41437860
Commission Earned	<Float64DType>	575524	349040	2298.85	1284.97	41437860

ANACONDA.

FIGURE 7-53 You can create your own version of the `info()` function.

The functions `df_car_sales_query.head()` and `df_car_sales_query.describe(include='all')` returned values, and you can copy these functions to the Python cells E6 and G6, respectively. You can also view the data type card to check the values in the DataFrames you have created (see Figure 7-54).

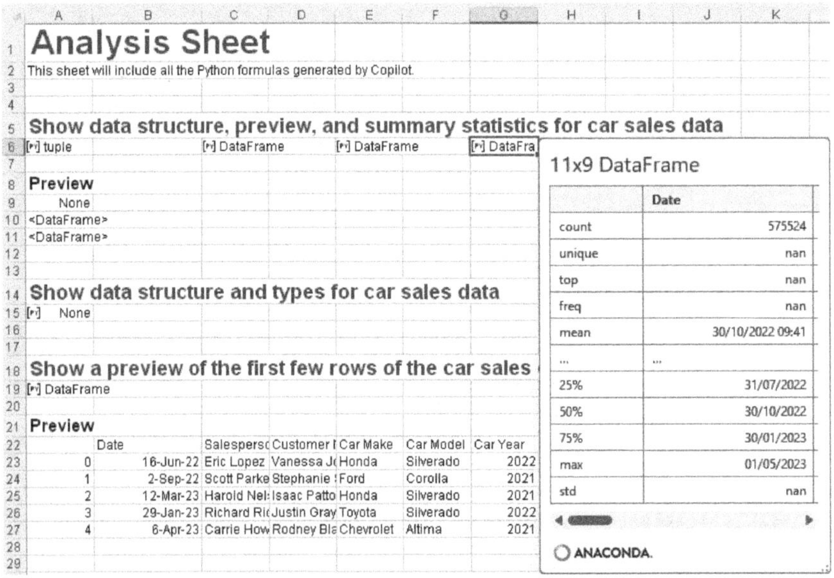

FIGURE 7-54 You can extract the other results from cell A6 to cells E6 and G6 to view the remaining information.

The next Python cell that Copilot created is cell A15. It displays None, so we should check what Copilot entered in this cell (see Figure 7-55). You already know that the `info()` function doesn't work with Python in Excel because nothing is returned as a value. We have already created our own Python code in cell C6 to show this information, so the Show Data Structure and Types for Car Sales Data section of the worksheet is redundant.

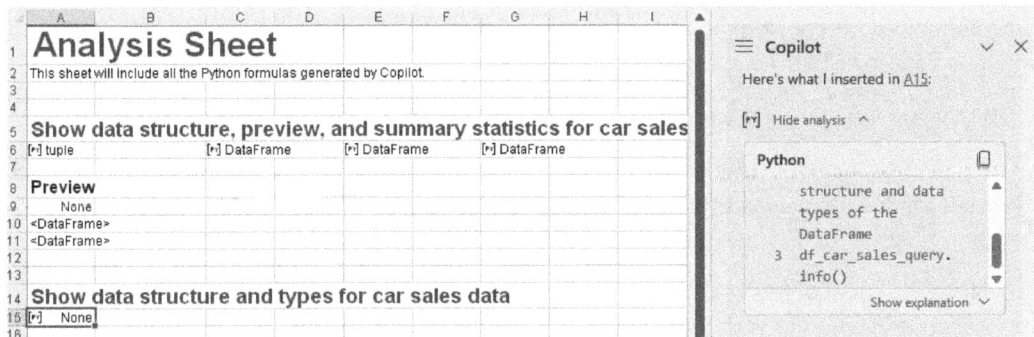

FIGURE 7-55 The Python code for cell A16 uses the `info()` function again.

Now let's look at the next cell that Copilot created, cell A19. This also looks familiar because it is the second DataFrame you copied to cell E6 from the tuple in A6 (see Figure 7-56). The Copilot pane shows that the Python code uses the `head()` function, which was part of the code in cell A6.

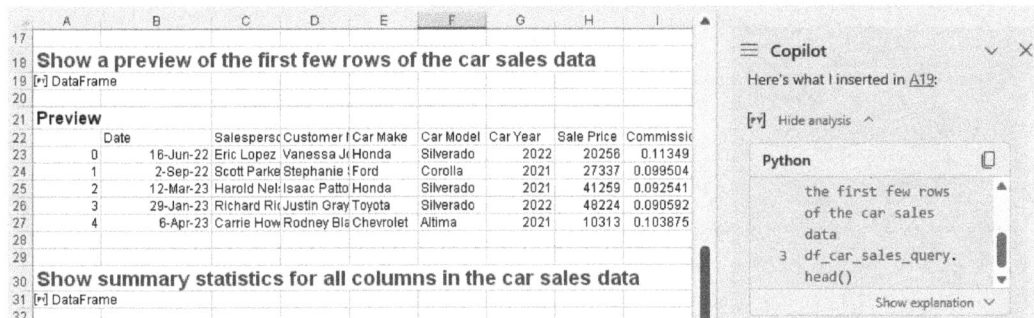

FIGURE 7-56 The Python code in cell A19 uses part of the Python code from cell A6.

The final Python cell, A31, also uses code from cell A6. The Copilot pane shows that this Python code uses the `describe(include='all')` function, which was part of the code in cell A6 (see Figure 7-57).

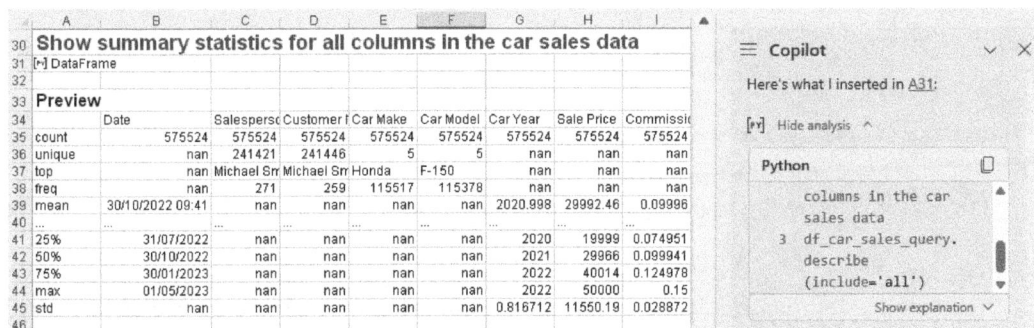

FIGURE 7-57 The Python code in cell A31 uses part of the Python code from cell A6.

You can see that Python has repeated code in multiple cells. This repetition makes it hard to get a good picture of the data. To better see what's going on, we could move the Python code we created in cell C6 to cell A15 and remove cells E6 and G6. We can create a Preview section for cell A15 by creating enough space, copying the code from cell A32 into cell A18, and adjusting the cell reference. The Python code in cell A18 is:

```
=IFERROR(A15.arrayPreview,A15.Python_str)
```

Figure 7-58 shows the results. As you can see, cell A15 now contains a Python DataFrame, and a Preview section has been added under cell A15 to show the data in that DataFrame.

> **Note** The goal of this code is to show `arrayPreview` for the Python cell A15; if an error occurs, `Python_str` is shown instead. The Excel function `IFERROR()` does not currently trap for the error `#SPILL!` because it is an error concerning the output of the result rather than an error concerning the **calculation** of the result. Therefore, if you have not added enough space for `arrayPreview` to spill, you will get a `#SPILL!` error in this cell.

Analysis Sheet

This sheet will include all the Python formulas generated by Copilot.

Show data structure, preview, and summary statistics for car sales data

[·] tuple   [·] DataFrame

Preview

None

<DataFrame>

<DataFrame>

Show data structure and types for car sales data

[·] DataFrame

Preview

	dtypes	non_null	unique_val	first_row	last_row	memory_usage
Date	<DateTime64DTyp	575524	366	16/06/2022	03/10/2022	41437860
Salesperso	<ObjectDType>	575524	241421	Eric Lopez	Kimberly Snow	41437860
Customer I	<ObjectDType>	575524	241446	Vanessa Jon	Tara Rodgers	41437860
Car Make	<ObjectDType>	575524	5	Honda	Ford	41437860
Car Model	<ObjectDType>	575524	5	Silverado	F-150	41437860
Car Year	<Int64DType>	575524	3	2022	2022	41437860
Sale Price	<Float64DType>	575524	40001	20256	18803	41437860
Commissi	<Float64DType>	575524	575524	0.11348979	0.068338527	41437860
Commissi	<Float64DType>	575524	349040	2298.85	1284.97	41437860

Show a preview of the first few rows of the car sales data

[·] DataFrame

Preview

	Date	Salespers	Customer I	Car Make	Car Model	Car Year	Sale Price	Commissi	Commission Earned
0	16-Jun-22	Eric Lopez	Vanessa J	Honda	Silverado	2022	20256	0.11349	2298.85
1	2-Sep-22	Scott Parke	Stephanie	Ford	Corolla	2021	27337	0.099504	2720.13
2	12-Mar-23	Harold Nel	Isaac Patto	Honda	Silverado	2021	41259	0.092541	3818.16
3	29-Jan-23	Richard Ric	Justin Gray	Toyota	Silverado	2022	48224	0.090592	4368.72

FIGURE 7-58 Cell A15 uses the Python code created to replace the `info()` function.

Copilot summarizes the analysis performed so far as follows:

> The car sales data includes information such as date, salesperson, customer name, car make and model, year, sale price, commission rate, and commission earned. There are 575,524 records

with a variety of car makes and models, and the data covers multiple years. If you would like to explore specific trends or insights, please let me know what you are interested in.

Next, we'll move on to a new example using external data from an OData feed. Before you go any further, though, rename the Analysis sheet **Car Sales Data Quick Analysis** and move it to the right of the Car_Sales_Data sheet. Close the Copilot pane. (You will start a new conversation with Copilot once the data in the following example has been extracted using Power Query.)

Using the OData service to access Northwind data

As promised, we will now step through an example of using external data from an OData feed. OData refers to the Open Data Protocol, and OData services allow you to access live data, enabling up-to-date reporting. We'll look at using Power Query to extract data from the Northwind OData service, which is publicly available at *https://services.odata.org/northwind/northwind.svc/*.

In the SP Python in Excel Example Starter File Chapter 7.xlsm workbook, open the **Northwind** sheet. Then go to the **Data** tab, select the **Get Data** dropdown menu in the **Get & Transform** section, and click the **Get Data (Preview)** option (which may be called Get Data in your version). The Get Data dialog appears (see Figure 7-59). In this example, we will use the OData connector, so we need to search for that in the search bar of the Get Data dialog. When we type the letter **O** in the search bar, Excel suggests the new sources, such as OData, Odbc, Oracle Database, and Folder.

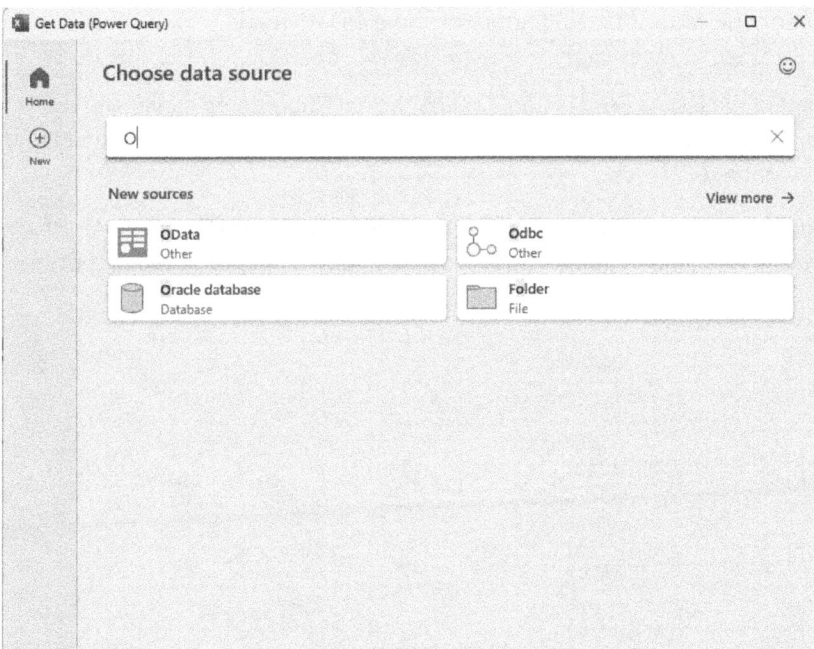

FIGURE 7-59 The OData connector can be found by using the Get Data (Power Query) dialog.

Select the **OData** connector. The OData Feed dialog appears. Enter the URL *https://services.odata.org/northwind/northwind.svc/,* as shown in Figure 7-60.

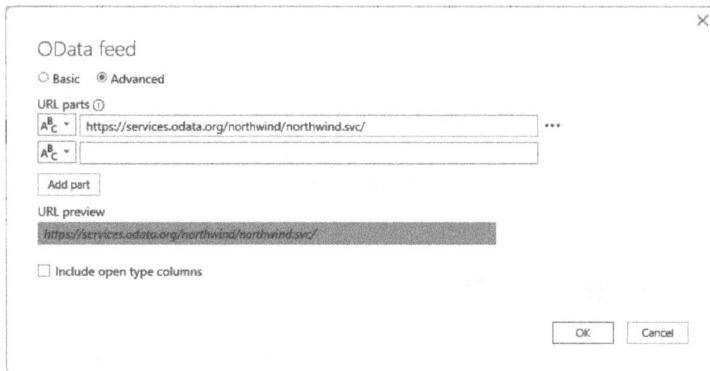

FIGURE 7-60 The OData Feed dialog, with the Advanced option selected

> **Note** Figure 7-60 shows the Advanced option selected in the OData Feed dialog. You don't need the advanced features for this example, but knowing what is available is useful. When Advanced is selected, you get several extra options. For example, you can enter URL parts to make up a full URL. You might want to enter the URL in parts, for example, when part of the URL is held in a Power Query parameter. You can see a dropdown menu for the data type of each URL part, which may be text or a parameter. With Advanced selected, you can also choose to include open-type columns. An open type is a structured type with dynamic properties, and open type columns are a feature of some OData feeds.

The URL Preview part of the OData Feed dialog displays the full URL entered earlier and shows a warning triangle if the URL is invalid. There is no warning in this case, so you can assume that the URL is correct and click **OK** to continue.

Another OData Feed dialog appears (see Figure 7-61). Its title includes the URL for the Northwind database. Because you are accessing that website for the first time, you are prompted to specify how to access it.

FIGURE 7-61 If this is the first time you are connecting to a site, you must specify how to access it.

The details you need to enter here depend on the data you are accessing. The data in this example allows public access, so you should use anonymous access and apply this setting at the top level of the website. (For secure data, you would need to consult with your network administrator to access login details.) For this example, you can use the default settings and click **Connect**. The Navigator dialog appears (see Figure 7-62).

You use the Navigator dialog for connections when you could extract from more than one possible data source. (You will also see it when you access Excel workbooks or databases.)

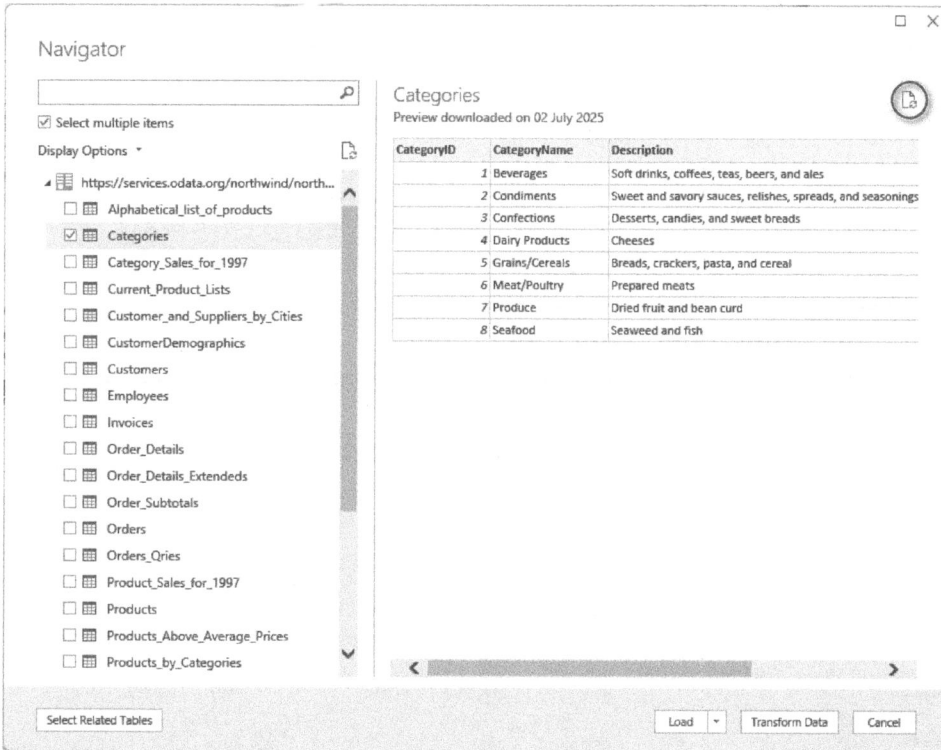

FIGURE 7-62 The Navigator dialog allows you to select more than one data source and create multiple queries.

As shown in Figure 7-62, you can select the checkbox Select Multiple Items to see a list of tables available in the dataset. You can select multiple tables by checking them. Selecting each one provides a preview of that table on the right side of the dialog. If the date shown with the preview is old or if you know the data has changed recently, you can click the Refresh icon (highlighted in the top right) to refresh the connection and extract the data again.

> **Note** If you were connecting to a relational database, you could select one or more tables and then click the Select Related Tables button to automatically select any other tables with direct relationships to the tables you manually selected.

To continue with our example, select the **Categories** table and then click **Transform Data**. As shown in Figure 7-63, the Power Query Editor screen appears, and it contains the Categories query, which has two steps in the Applied Steps list: Source and Navigation. The car_sales_data query from our earlier example also appears in the Queries pane.

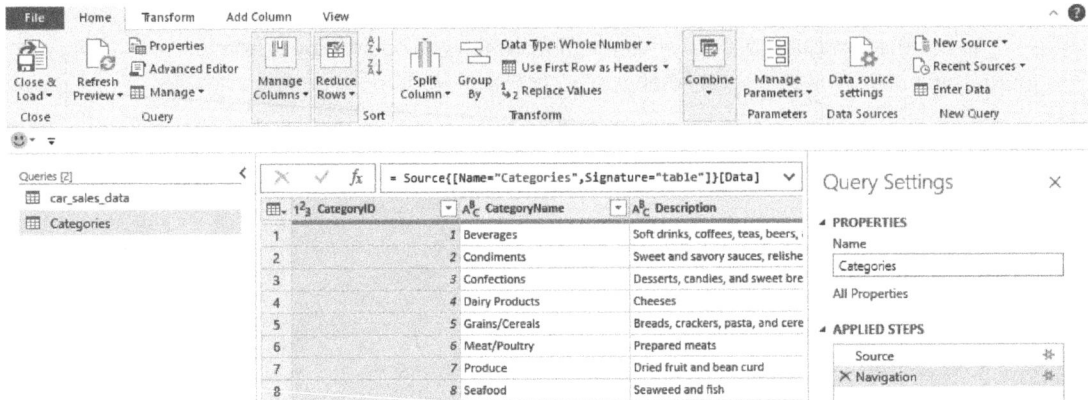

FIGURE 7-63 The Categories query has been created from the OData feed.

If you click the **Source** step for the Categories query, you can see the M code to access the OData feed, as shown in Figure 7-64.

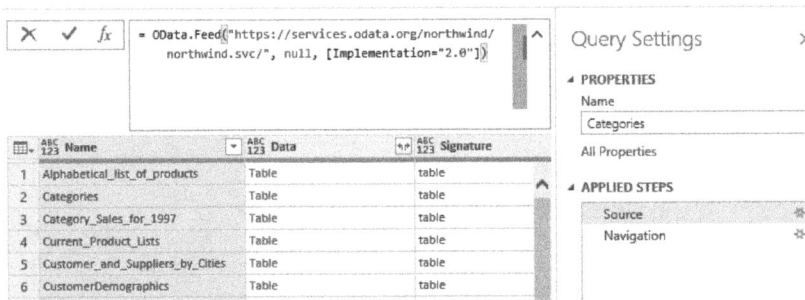

FIGURE 7-64 The Categories query Source step accesses the OData feed.

The Source step always shows the data or connection from which the data was extracted. In this case, the Source step allows you to access any tables in the Navigator dialog. The Navigation step drills down into one of the tables—in this case, the Categories table.

Note Any connection that uses the Navigator dialog will have a Source step and a Navigator step.

You can now load this data into the Queries & Connections pane. Go to the **Home** tab, click the **Close & Load** dropdown menu, and choose **Close & Load To** (as you did for the car_sales_data query). When the Import Data dialog appears, you can choose how to load the data. The choice you make here will apply only to queries that have not had their load status defined, so in this case, the car_sales_data query's load status will be unaffected by this selection. For this example, the query will only be accessed by Python, so choose **Only Create Connection** in the Import Data dialog, as shown in Figure 7-65, and then click **OK**.

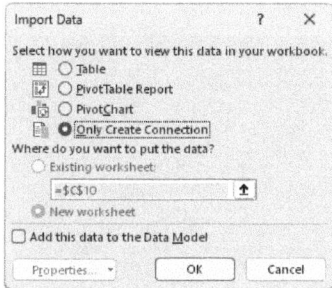

FIGURE 7-65 In the Import Data dialog, choose **Only Create Connection** for queries that are only accessed by Python.

Excel creates the connection-only query Categories, which can be extracted to a Python DataFrame in cell C10, as shown in Figure 7-66. (In this figure, we have also chosen to display the data type card.)

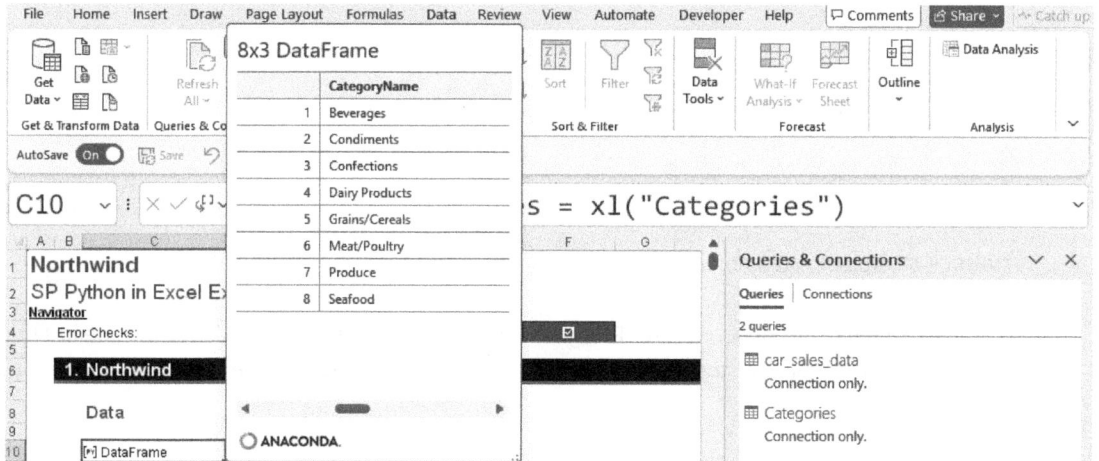

FIGURE 7-66 An 8x3 DataFrame contains the data from the Categories query.

We will use Copilot and Python in Excel with this data soon, so let's prepare by creating a new DataFrame in C10 using the following Python code:

```
df_nw_categories = xl("Categories")
```

Creating another connection-only query from the same OData feed

In this section, let's get another table from the same OData feed we've been working with. To do so, you could go through the same process you used with the Categories table, but there is another way: You can use a recent source. You can access recent sources from the Power Query Editor, or you can access them from the Get & Transform Data section of the Data tab on the Excel ribbon (see Figure 7-67).

FIGURE 7-67 Accessing external data using recent sources

To see how accessing recent sources works, go to the **Get & Transform Data** section of the **Data** tab of the Excel ribbon and click the **Recent Sources** icon (which looks like a clock in front of a sheet of paper). The Recent Sources dialog appears (see Figure 7-68). Select the Northwind database URL from the options listed in the dialog. (You should also see the car_sales_data connection from the previous example. The example here also shows a connection for another source.)

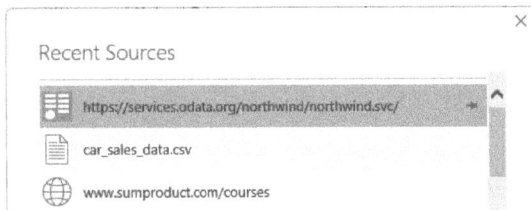

FIGURE 7-68 Accessing recent sources

Click **Connect** to connect to the URL again. You are taken straight to the Navigator dialog because the connection details are stored from the previous connection (see Figure 7-69).

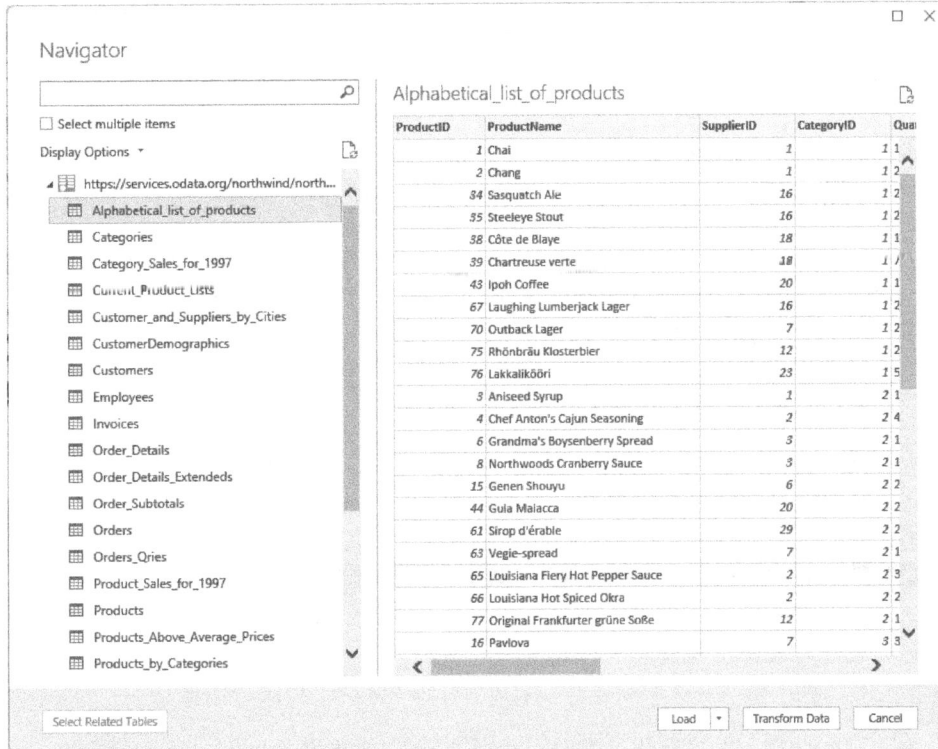

FIGURE 7-69 You are taken from the Recent Sources dialog to the Navigator dialog.

Select **Alphabetical_list_of_products**. Instead of clicking Transform Data, select the **Load** drop-down menu and then select **Load To**. You now see the same Import Data dialog that you saw for car_sales_data and Categories. In the Import Data dialog, select **Only Create Connection** and click **OK** to create a new query. As you can see in Figure 7-70, the Queries & Connections pane now lists Alphabetical_list_of_products along with the car_sales_data and Categories queries.

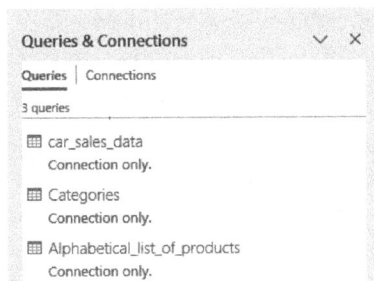

FIGURE 7-70 A third query, Alphabetical_list_of_products, has been created.

Let's set up the DataFrame for Alphabetical_list_of_products. Enter the following Python code in cell C12:

```
df_nw_products = xl("Alphabetical_list_of_products ")
```

Alphabetical_list_of_products is not a friendly name for the query. It would be better to call it Products. You might think this would cause an error in the Python code in cell C12 since the xl() function is using the name Alphabetical_list_of_products, but Python in Excel will retain the link to the query even though the name changes. To see this in action, right-click the query **Alphabetical_list_of_products** in the Queries & Connections **pane**, choose **Rename**, and enter the new name **Products**. As you can see in Figure 7-71, the Python code to create the DataFrame in cell C12 also updates to the new name.

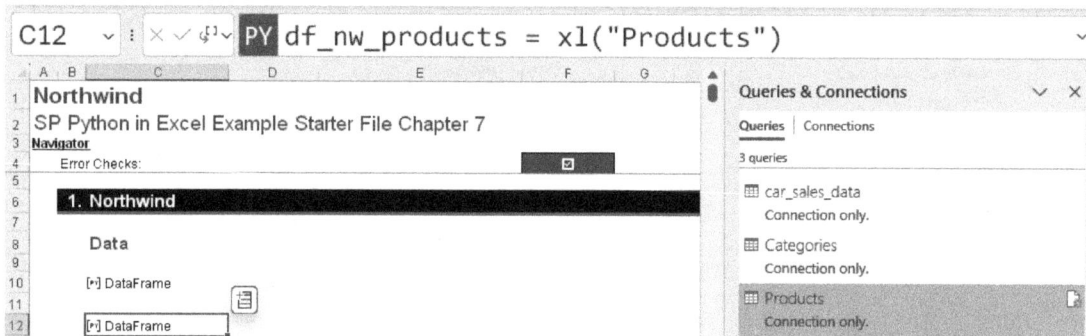

FIGURE 7-71 When the query is renamed to Products, the DataFrame reference is automatically updated.

You could now combine or merge the queries you have extracted from the Northwind database to get information on products and categories in the same DataFrame. You would then be able to produce insights and visualizations using the combined data.

Performing transformations in Power Query vs. Python in Excel

Now that you are using Power Query to extract data from external sources, you have more options for performing transformations. You could merge the data in Power Query or with Python in Excel. Whichever method you use, though, you should check the quality of the data when you extract data from an external data source.

Earlier in this chapter, you used Power Query to detect the data types of columns based on algorithms, and you also manually changed column data types. Given the algorithms available and the column quality features you explored earlier, it makes sense to perform these checks in Power Query. If you intend to reduce a dataset before analysis, it also makes sense to do that in Power Query before you load the data. As we said earlier in this chapter, reducing a dataset by removing unnecessary columns and rows should be done as close to the data source as possible.

Where you take care of other transformations—such as formatting names in order to merge first and last names or extracting day, year, and month from a date column—depends on several factors, including the following:

- If you use Power Query regularly and have existing code and functions that will speed up this process, it makes sense to use them.

- If you use the same query for multiple purposes—such as creating an Excel report or a PivotTable—it makes sense to make the changes once in the query.

- If you need to use the same connection but in different ways—such as if you will use the query to display extra columns for an Excel report, but you only need targeted information for the Python data analysis—then you would want to reduce the data by using Python.

We could go on, but you get the idea.

If you ever find that you should have made more changes at the Power Query stage, you can return to the query and make the changes. With experience, you will learn where to perform transformations. Don't forget that Copilot can also provide you with the M code for Power Query; if you need some help wrangling your data, you only need to ask Copilot the right questions.

For the Northwind example we've been working with, we will show both ways of merging the data.

Using Power Query to merge the Northwind data

To merge the Products and Categories queries in Power Query, right-click **Products** in the Queries & Connections pane and select **Merge** from the context menu (see Figure 7-72).

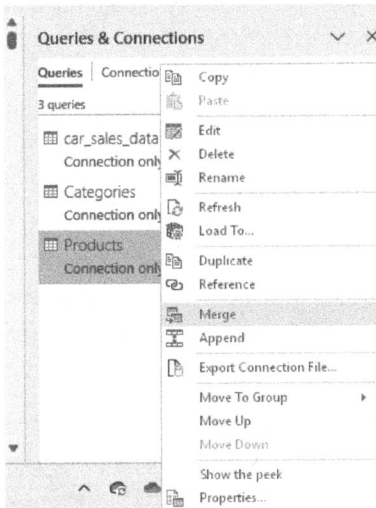

FIGURE 7-72 You can access the Merge option by right-clicking a query in the Queries & Connections pane.

The Merge dialog appears. As you can see in Figure 7-73, the query has defaulted to Products, and the columns of the Products table are shown.

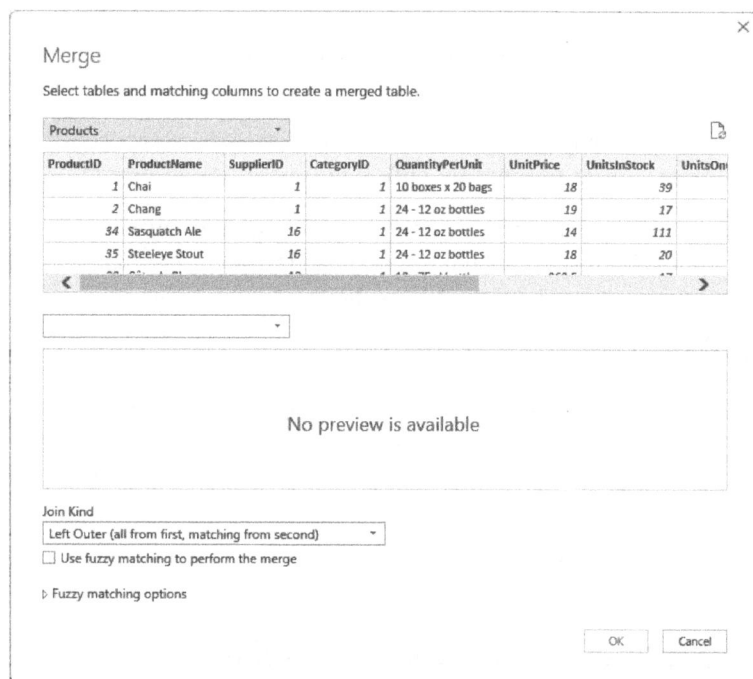

FIGURE 7-73 The Merge dialog allows two queries to be merged.

Merging involves joining two queries that contain related data—the CategoryID column in the case of the Products and Categories queries—by specifying the join type. There are several join types, and we'll discuss them all in a moment. In this case, you will accept the default Join Kind setting, Left Outer, which takes all the values in the column specified in the first (top) table and looks for any matching values in the column selected in the second (bottom) table. It's important to select the same number of columns in each table, and the columns should be the same data type to allow the values to be compared. Select the CategoryID column for Products and Categories, as shown in Figure 7-74.

> **Note** You can use fuzzy matching to use similar values as the join link—for example, the join algorithms could use fuzzy matching to treat "Apple" and "apple" as the same value.

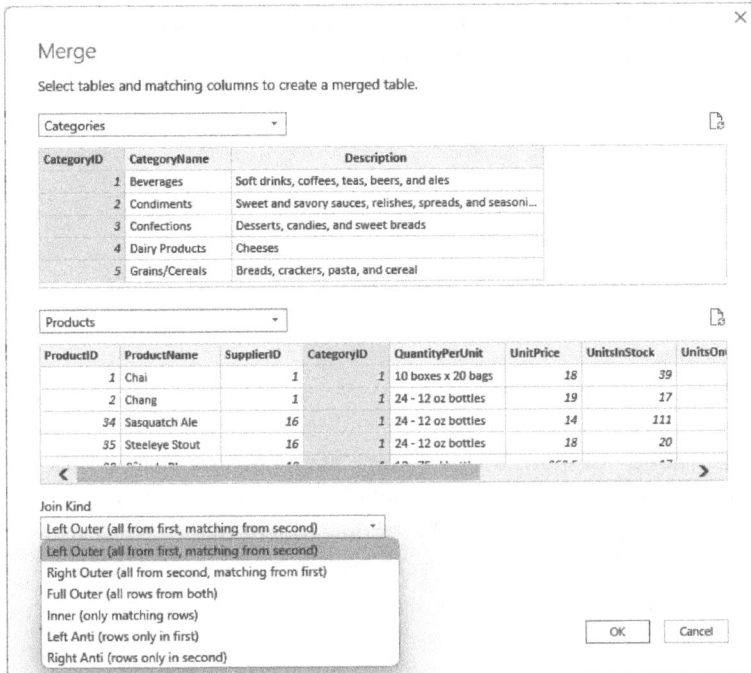

FIGURE 7-74 Six kinds of join are available for merging data.

As you can see in Figure 7-74, there are six join types. Figure 7-75 shows Venn diagrams and descriptions to help you better understand the join types. In this example, we are using a left outer join because it will give us the category data and the products for each category.

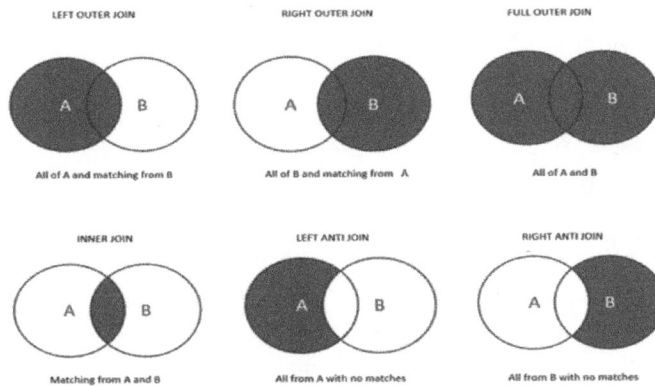

FIGURE 7-75 The join kinds explained

When you are done making selections in the Merge dialog, click **OK**. Power Query creates a merged query, which you can rename **ProductsInCategories** (see Figure 7-76).

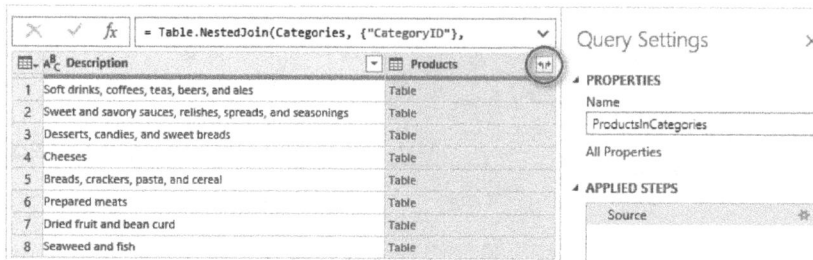

FIGURE 7-76 The Power Query Editor shows the merged query.

In Figure 7-76, the Power Query Editor shows the data from Categories and a column called Products. The Products column contains tables. The highlighted icon to the right of the Products column heading is the expand icon. To see the data from the Products query, click this icon. As shown in Figure 7-77, a dialog containing a list of columns in Products appears.

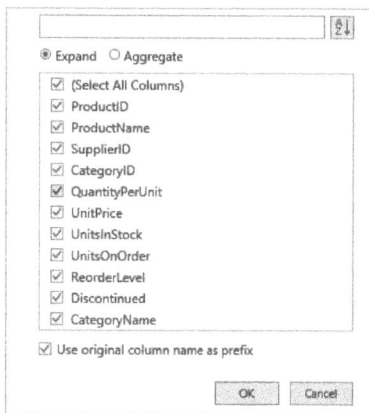

FIGURE 7-77 Selecting the data from the merged query

At the bottom of the dialog is a checkbox labeled Use Original Column Name as Prefix. You need to select this option only if the new column names are the same as existing column names, and you want to associate the new columns with the table the data comes from. In this case, you can deselect the Use Original Column Name as Prefix checkbox and CategoryID, since that column already exists in the Categories query, and click **OK**. ProductsInCategories is now expanded to 69 rows (see Figure 7-78).

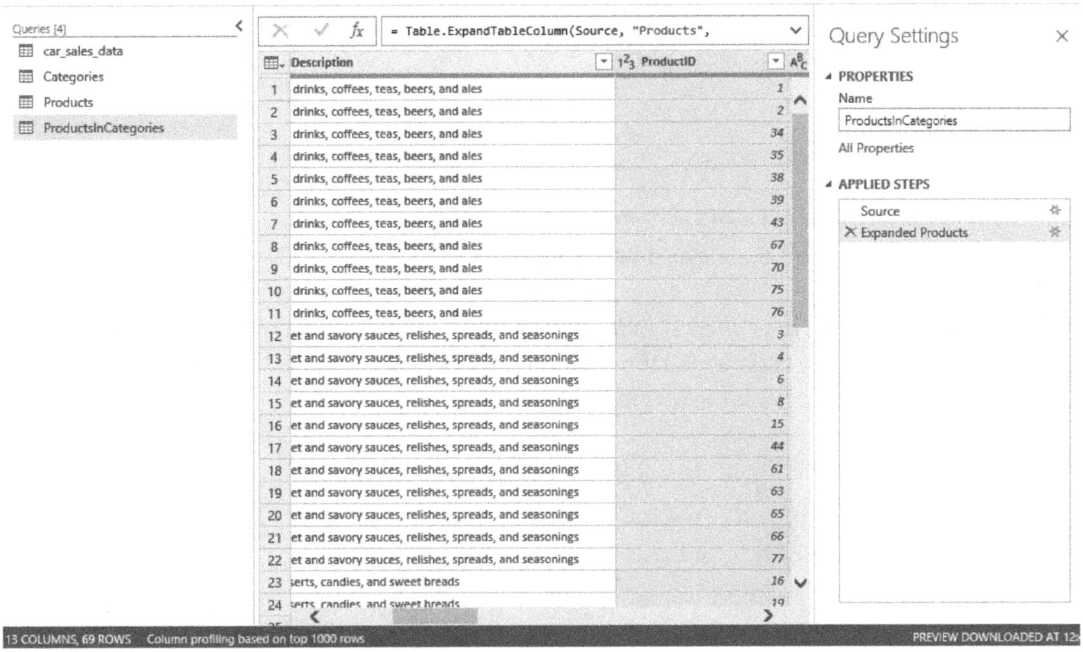

FIGURE 7-78 The query now consists of 13 columns and 69 rows.

You can now create a connection-only query to save your work. If you wanted to, you could create a Python DataFrame now. Next, we'll look at how to merge the data in Python—with Copilot's help, of course!

Using Python in Excel to merge the Northwind data

You have seen how to merge data by using Power Query, and now you're ready to learn about merging data by using Python in Excel. In the Northwind worksheet, open the Copilot pane (by clicking **Copilot** on the **Home** tab) and enter the following prompt: **Merge the data in df_nw_categories with the data in df_nw_products**.

> **Note** If there is a dropdown menu available under the Copilot button in your version of Excel, you must select the App Skills option and not the Chat option, which is the default.

When Copilot offers to use advanced analysis, click **Start** to use Quick conversation mode.

Note that the prompt used in this example is vague; it doesn't specify what column to merge on or what join type to use. Copilot can figure it out for you. It begins by analyzing the data to determine how to join it and gives you a response like the one in Figure 7-79.

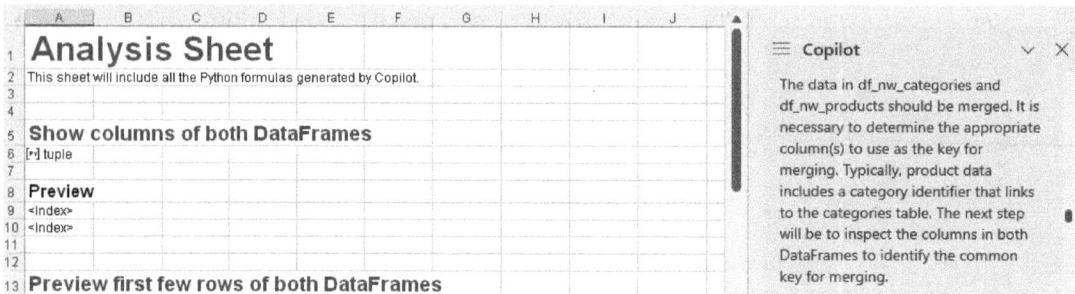

FIGURE 7-79 Copilot starts by locating the key to merge on.

Figure 7-80 shows rows 45 to 57 of the same Analysis sheet. You can see that Copilot has determined the correct key and merged the data. The Copilot pane in Figure 7-80 summarizes what has been achieved and prompts the user for the next request.

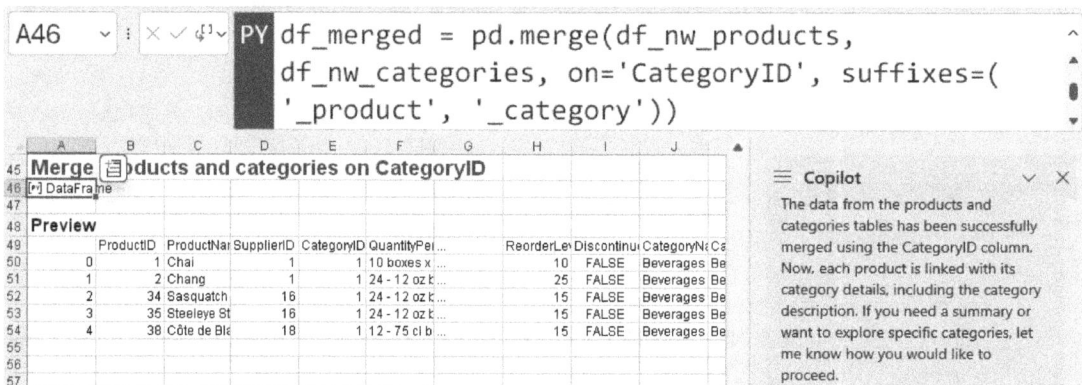

FIGURE 7-80 Copilot has created the Python code to merge Products and Categories.

If you view the data type card for the DataFrame in cell A46, you can see that it currently shows only five rows. This is because the final line of Python code is about showing the heading:

```
#Merge products and categories on CategoryID
# Merge df_nw_products with df_nw_categories on 'CategoryID'
df_merged = pd.merge(df_nw_products, df_nw_categories, on='CategoryID', suffixes=('_product',
'_category'))
df_merged.head()
```

If you remove the final line of this code and commit the remaining code, you can see that the merged DataFrame has the same 69 rows as the merged query from earlier (refer to Figure 7-78). Figure 7-81 shows the DataFrame that was merged in Python in Excel.

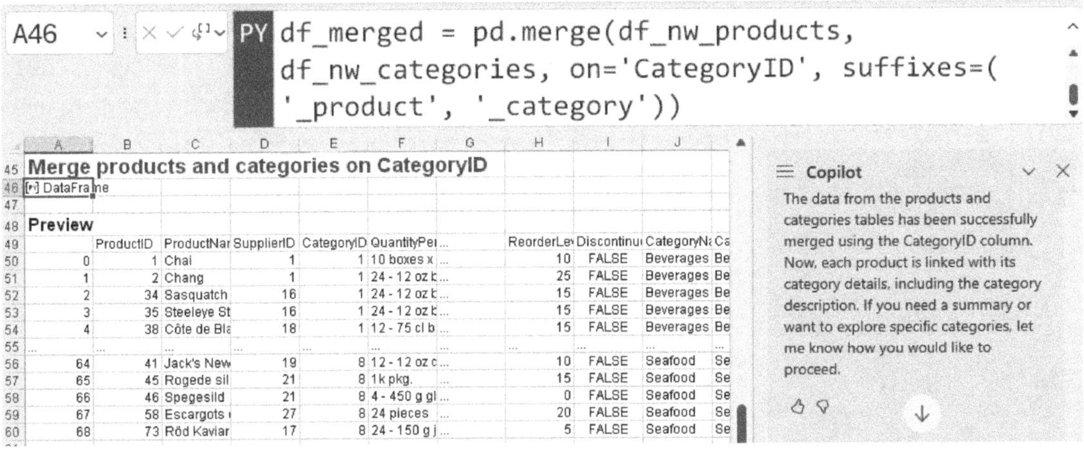

FIGURE 7-81 We have amended the Python code to show the merged Products and Categories DataFrame in full.

Now that you have the code to merge Categories and Products, copy it to cell C14 on the Northwind sheet. From this sheet, prompt Copilot to create a table that shows the number of products in each category. You can use the following prompt: **Summarize the number of products by category**. Copilot returns a new DataFrame on the Analysis sheet in cell A64 as well as a preview (see Figure 7-82). The formula bar for cell A64 shows the Python code to group the data into the new DataFrame.

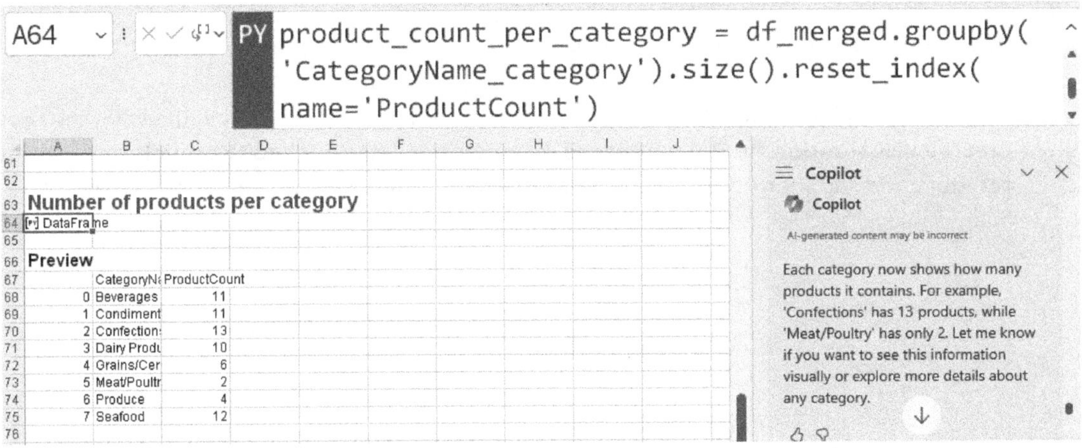

FIGURE 7-82 Copilot has created the Python code to group the data.

To repeat this process to include the supplier, you can use the following prompt: **Summarize the number of products by category and supplier**. Copilot produces another grouped table in cell A79, as shown in Figure 7-83.

```
A79          ×  ✓  ⨍  PY  #Number of products by category and supplier
                          # Count the number of products by category and supplier
                          product_count_by_category_supplier = df_merged.groupby(
```

	A	B	C	D	E	F	G	H	I	J	K	L	M	N	O
61															
62															
63	**Number of products per category**														
64	[+] DataFrame														
65															
66	**Preview**														
67		CategoryName	ProductCount												
68	0	Beverages	11												
69	1	Condiment	11												
70	2	Confections	13												
71	3	Dairy Produ	10												
72	4	Grains/Cere	6												
73	5	Meat/Poultr	2												
74	6	Produce	4												
75	7	Seafood	12												
76															
77															
78	**Number of products by category and supplier**														
79	[+] DataFrame														
80															
81	**Preview**														
82		CategoryName	SupplierID	ProductCount											
83	0	Beverages	1	2											
84	1	Beverages	7	1											
85	2	Beverages	12	1											
86	3	Beverages	16	3											
87	4	Beverages	18	2											
88	...	...	...	...											
89	37	Seafood	13	1											
90	38	Seafood	17	3											
91	39	Seafood	19	2											
92	40	Seafood	21	2											
93	41	Seafood	27	1											
94															

FIGURE 7-83 Copilot has created the Python code to group the data by supplier too.

Next, ask Copilot to provide a visualization for each DataFrame by entering the following prompt: **Create a visualization for the number of products per category and the number of products by category and supplier**. Copilot produces a single Python image object and shows the results in one floating image (see Figure 7-84).

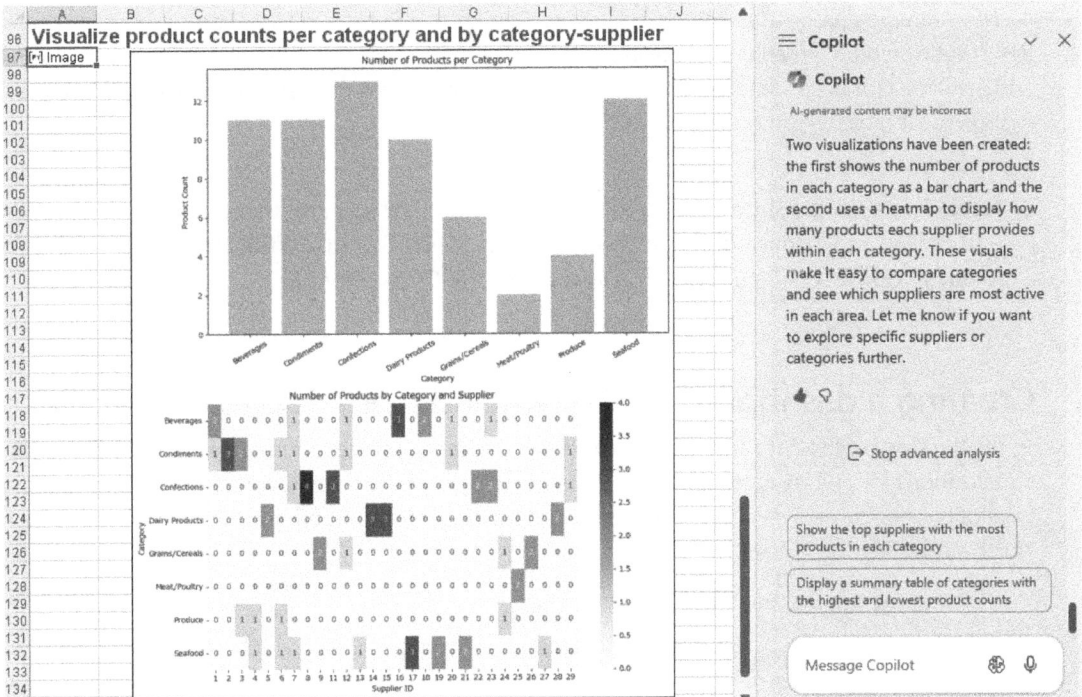

FIGURE 7-84 Copilot has created a floating image that contains two visualizations.

Copilot has created the following Python code in cell A97:

```
#Visualize product counts per category and by category-supplier
plt.rcParams['font.family'] = ['Meiryo','Batang','TH SarabunPSK','SimHei','DejaVu Sans']
fig, axes = plt.subplots(2, 1, figsize=(10, 12))
# Bar chart for products per category
axes[0].bar(product_count_per_category['CategoryName_category'], product_count_per_
category['ProductCount'], color='skyblue')
axes[0].set_title('Number of Products per Category')
axes[0].set_xlabel('Category')
axes[0].set_ylabel('Product Count')
axes[0].tick_params(axis='x', rotation=30)
# Pivot for heatmap
pivot_table = product_count_by_category_supplier.pivot(index='CategoryName_category',
columns='SupplierID', values='ProductCount').fillna(0)
# Heatmap for products by category and supplier
sns.heatmap(pivot_table, annot=True, fmt='.0f', cmap='YlGnBu', ax=axes[1])
axes[1].set_title('Number of Products by Category and Supplier')
axes[1].set_xlabel('Supplier ID')
axes[1].set_ylabel('Category')
plt.tight_layout()
plt.show()
```

This example demonstrates that you can use Copilot and Python in Excel to easily create visualizations that would be difficult to create in Excel (for example, creating a heatmap in Excel is awkward and involves a lot of conditional formatting). This example also demonstrates how easy it is to create a Python pivot table by using the `pivot()` function.

> **Note** This example shows the two charts—the column chart and the heatmap—created in a Python cell and displayed as one floating image. If you would like the charts in two separate images, you can divide up the code yourself or ask Copilot for help.

Creating a dashboard for Northwind from Copilot's analysis

To tell the story of the data and facilitate business decisions, presentations often include dashboards of visualizations for quickly identifying trends and issues. To create a dashboard showcasing the analysis Copilot has performed, let's copy some of the interesting information from the Analysis1 sheet to the Northwind sheet:

- Copy Analysis1!A64 to Northwind!C16.
- Copy Analysis1!A79 to Northwind!C18.
- Copy Analysis1!A97 to Northwind!C20.

To create an impressive summary of the Northwind data you have extracted, click the **Insert Data** icon for cell C20 on the Northwind sheet and choose **Display Plot over Cells**. Move the floating image so that the visualizations appear over Python cells C16, C18, and C20. The image hides the Python DataFrames (which not all recipients of the workbook will understand) below the visualizations that workbook recipients will be interested in. Figure 7-85 shows the results: a column chart that shows the number of products per category and a heatmap that shows the number of products by category and supplier.

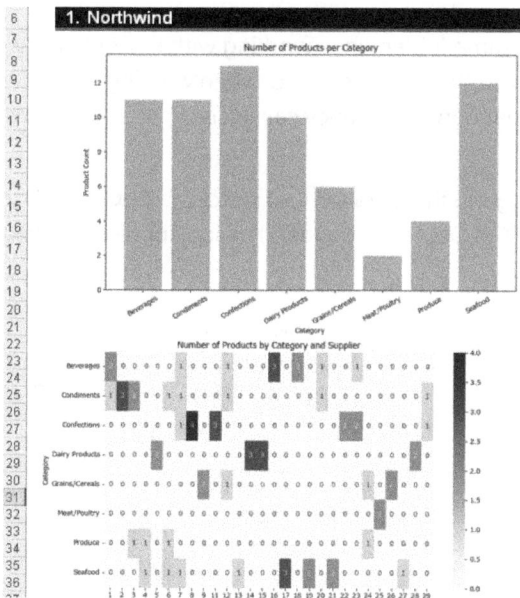

FIGURE 7-85 The visualizations on the Northwind sheet tell the story of the Northwind data.

> **Note** In this example, you have learned about using Power Query and Python in Excel with the help of Copilot to extract and merge data. In this case, the data came from the same source, but you can merge any queries or DataFrames as long as you specify a key to join the data.

Now that you have completed this example, rename the Analysis sheet **Northwind Quick Analysis** and move it to the right of the Northwind sheet.

Cleaning the Kaggle Adventure Works data with Copilot, Python in Excel, and Power Query

When analyzing data to produce insights that will help guide your business, the results will not be reliable if the data you use contains errors or inconsistencies. We have already looked at how to check and fix data quality in Power Query. In this example, we will use Copilot and Python in Excel to clean data that has been extracted using Power Query.

In the downloadable resources for this book, find the Excel workbook **KaggleAdventureWorks.xlsx**, which you will use as a source for this example. Make sure this file is in the same folder as the Chapter 7 workbook.

Open the **Adventure Works** worksheet. Then go to the **Data** tab and select the **Get Data** drop-down menu in the **Get & Transform** section. The Get Data (Power Query) dialog appears, offering several options for the data source (see Figure 7-86).

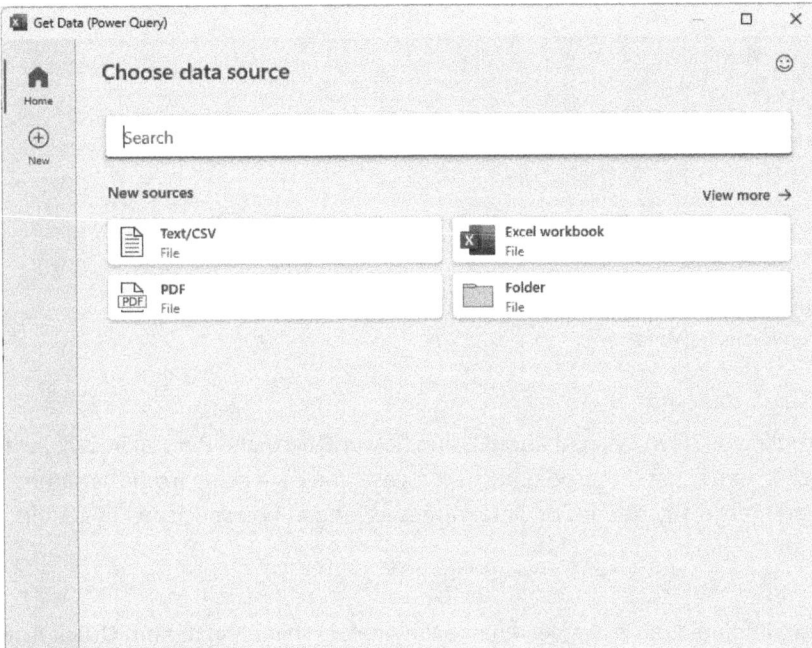

FIGURE 7-86 The Excel Workbook data source connector is available in the Get Data (Power Query) dialog.

In the Get Data (Power Query) dialog, select **Excel Workbook**, locate and select the **KaggleAdventureWorks** file in the browser, and click **Import**.

The Navigator dialog appears, showing the four sheets available in KaggleAdventureWorks.xlsx. Select the Select Multiple Items box and select the Region and Sales sheets (see Figure 7-87).

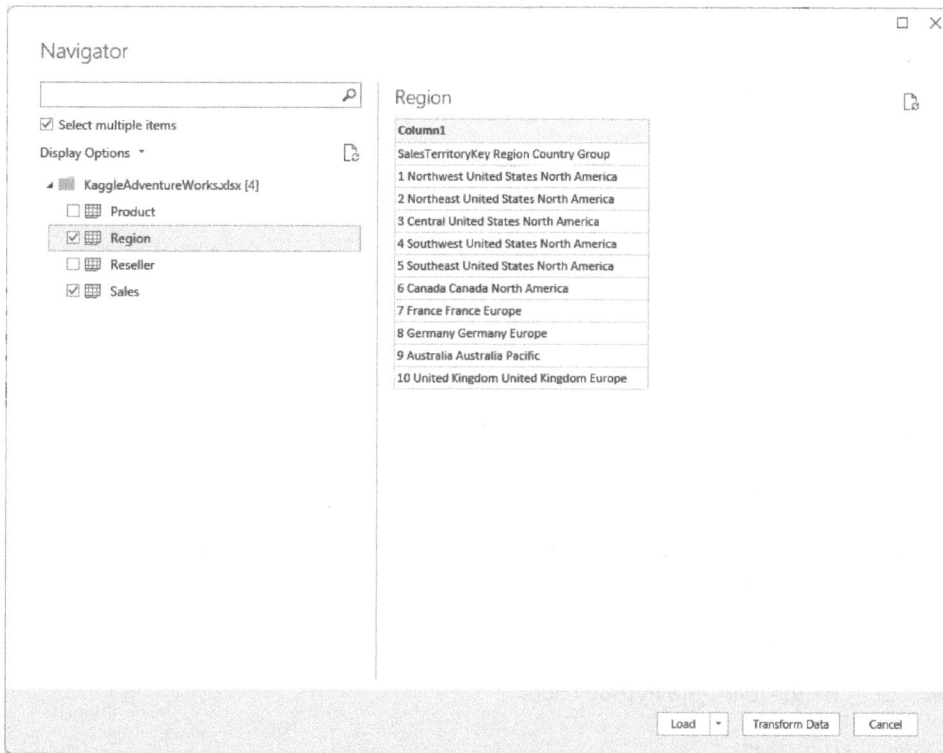

FIGURE 7-87 The Navigator dialog shows the contents of the source workbook.

As you learned in Chapter 2, when preparing data for Python, it is best to use defined ranges or tables. The data for this example is currently entered on the sheets, but it is not organized. Power Query will transform the data into tables. Remember that each step in Power Query results in a new table.

One purpose of this example is to show how Copilot with Python in Excel can handle improperly formatted data. Let's start by creating the queries. In the Navigator dialog (refer to Figure 7-87), click the **Load** dropdown menu and then click **Close & Load To**. In the Import dialog that appears, select **Only Create Connection** and click **OK**. The Queries & Connections pane now shows that you have two new queries, for a total of six queries (see Figure 7-88).

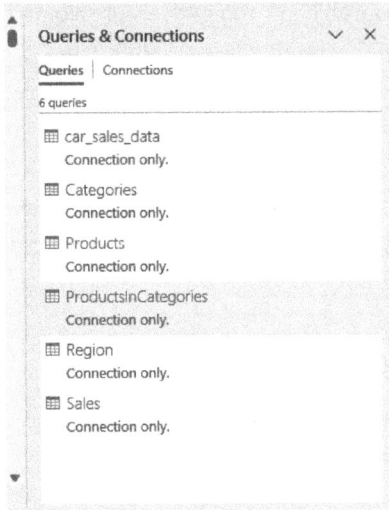

FIGURE 7-88 There are now six queries, including Products and Sales.

You need to create two Python cells to allow Python in Excel to access the data in the new Region and Sales queries. In C10, enter the following Python code:

```
df_aw_region = xl("Region")
```

In cell C12, enter the following Python code:

```
df_aw_sales = xl("Sales")
```

If you look at the data for Region in the data type card, you will find that it doesn't look well organized (see Figure 7-89). The df_aw_region DataFrame has only one column that contains all the data. This is not the correct format. You can use Power Query to sort it out, or you can ask Copilot to help you.

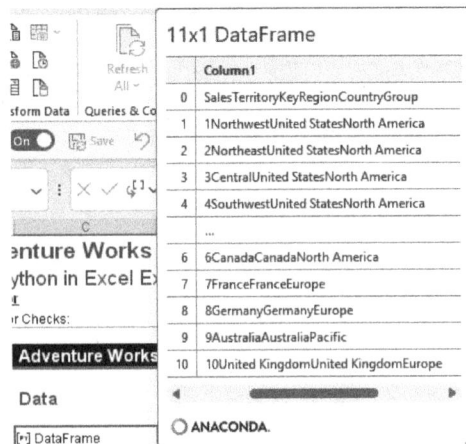

FIGURE 7-89 The df_aw_region DataFrame has only one column that contains all the data.

To use Copilot to sort out the data format, enter the following prompt: **Use Python to clean the data in df_aw_region**. When Copilot offers to use advanced analysis, click **Start** to use Quick conversation mode. Copilot then produces a plan, as shown in Figure 7-90.

FIGURE 7-90 Copilot recognizes what "clean the data" means.

Copilot generates the following Python code, which cleanses the data, for cell A6:

```
#Clean and standardize df_aw_region
# Standardize column names
cleaned_df = df_aw_region.copy()
cleaned_df.columns = cleaned_df.columns.str.strip().str.lower().str.replace(' ', '_')
# Remove duplicate rows
cleaned_df = cleaned_df.drop_duplicates()
# Check and handle missing values (simple fill or drop, depending on context)
missing_summary = cleaned_df.isnull().sum()
# For columns with all missing values, drop them
cols_all_missing = missing_summary[missing_summary == len(cleaned_df)].index
cleaned_df = cleaned_df.drop(columns=cols_all_missing)
# For columns with some missing values, fill with appropriate value (mean for numeric, mode for
categorical)
for col in cleaned_df.columns:
    if cleaned_df[col].isnull().any():
        if cleaned_df[col].dtype in [np.float64, np.int64]:
            cleaned_df[col] = cleaned_df[col].fillna(cleaned_df[col].mean())
        else:
            cleaned_df[col] = cleaned_df[col].fillna(cleaned_df[col].mode()[0])
cleaned_df.head()
```

This code performs a thorough data cleanse. With it, Copilot has tidied up column names, removed duplicates, checked for missing values, and so on. When Copilot finishes cleansing the data, the next part of the Python code for cell A6 transforms the data into a consistent tabular format that makes it easier to create visualizations. Figure 7-91 shows what the data looks like now.

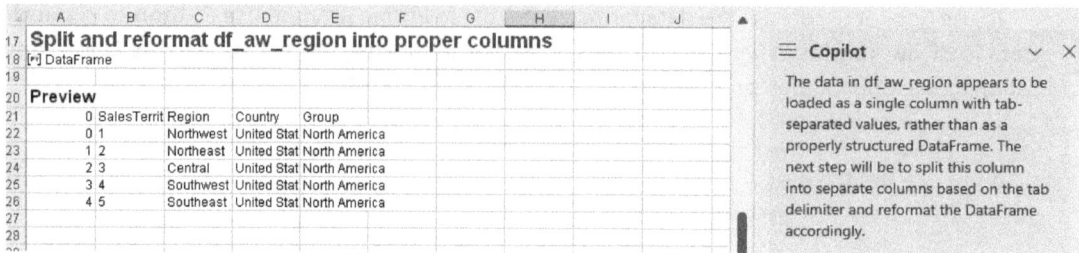

FIGURE 7-91 Copilot transforms the data into usable columns.

Copilot generates the following Python code, which splits the data into columns, for cell A18:

```
#Split and reformat df_aw_region into proper columns
# Split the single column into separate columns using tab as the delimiter
split_df = cleaned_df['column1'].str.split('\t', expand=True)
# Use the first row as header, then drop it from the data
split_df.columns = split_df.iloc[0]
split_df = split_df.drop(0).reset_index(drop=True)
# Show the cleaned and properly structured DataFrame
split_df.head()
```

By combining the Python code that Copilot has created on the Analysis sheet for cells A6 and A18, you can create a new cleaned and split DataFrame for the Product query in cell E10 on the Adventure Works sheet. This is the combined code:

```
#Clean and standardize df_aw_region
# Standardize column names
cleaned_df = df_aw_region.copy()
cleaned_df.columns = cleaned_df.columns.str.strip().str.lower().str.replace(' ', '_')
# Remove duplicate rows
cleaned_df = cleaned_df.drop_duplicates()
# Check and handle missing values (simple fill or drop, depending on context)
missing_summary = cleaned_df.isnull().sum()
# For columns with all missing values, drop them
cols_all_missing = missing_summary[missing_summary == len(cleaned_df)].index
cleaned_df = cleaned_df.drop(columns=cols_all_missing)
# For columns with some missing values, fill with appropriate value (mean for numeric, mode for
categorical)
for col in cleaned_df.columns:
    if cleaned_df[col].isnull().any():
        if cleaned_df[col].dtype in [np.float64, np.int64]:
            cleaned_df[col] = cleaned_df[col].fillna(cleaned_df[col].mean())
        else:
            cleaned_df[col] = cleaned_df[col].fillna(cleaned_df[col].mode()[0])
#Split and reformat df_aw_region into proper columns
# Split the single column into separate columns using tab as the delimiter
split_df = cleaned_df['column1'].str.split('\t', expand=True)
# Use the first row as header, then drop it from the data
split_df.columns = split_df.iloc[0]
df_clean_aw_region = split_df.drop(0).reset_index(drop=True)
```

As you can see in Figure 7-92, the df_aw_sales DataFrame is now organized into columns, and the data looks consistent.

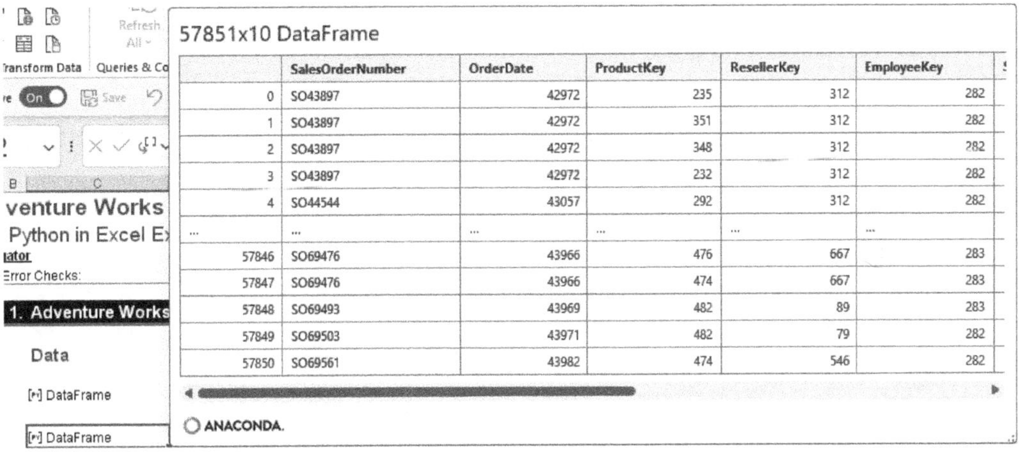

FIGURE 7-92 The df_aw_sales DataFrame is organized into columns.

Now that you have finished this data wrangling, let's see what Copilot can do with your DataFrames. Let's start by asking Copilot to answer a question about the sales data. Enter the following prompt: **Using df_aw_sales forecast future sales trends**. The Copilot response shown in Figure 7-93 indicates a Python error in cell A30 and a possible problem with the data.

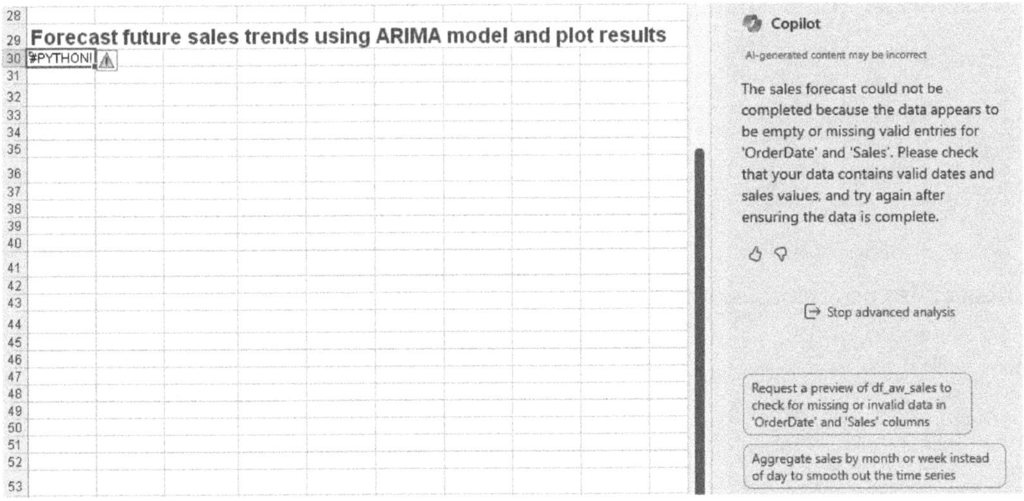

FIGURE 7-93 Copilot has encountered an issue.

Copilot has suggested the following prompt: Request a Preview of df_aw_sales to Check for Missing or Invalid Data in 'OrderDate' and 'Sales' Columns. If you select this option, Copilot checks the data and returns a possible solution, as shown in Figure 7-94.

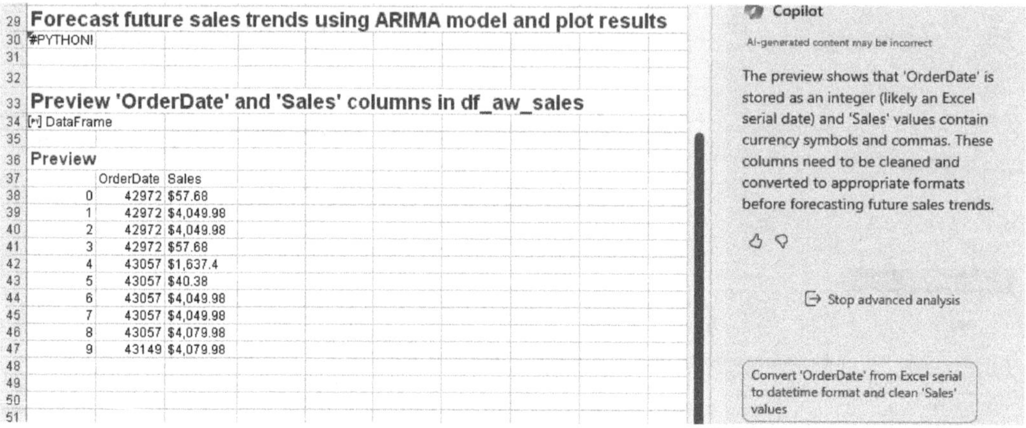

FIGURE 7-94 Copilot suggests a solution.

Copilot has kindly offered to fix the data format in the prompt Convert 'OrderDate' from Excel Serial to Datetime Format and Clean 'Sales' Values. If you select this option, Copilot converts the data and creates a new DataFrame, as shown in Figure 7-95.

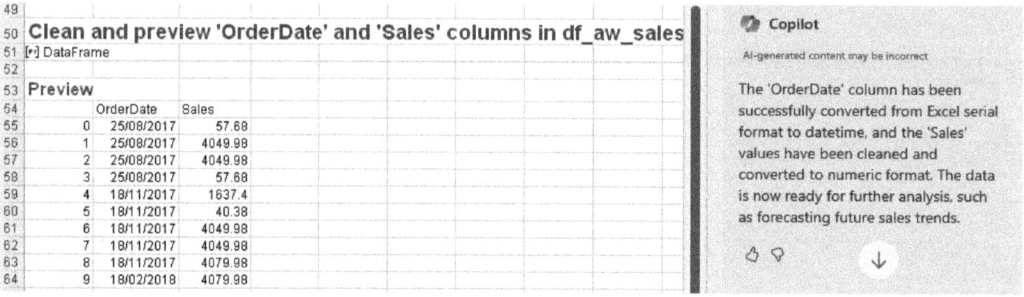

FIGURE 7-95 Copilot has successfully cleaned the data.

Copilot has generated the following data-cleaning Python code for cell A51:

```
#Clean and preview 'OrderDate' and 'Sales' columns in df_aw_sales
# Convert 'OrderDate' from Excel serial to datetime
sales_clean = df_aw_sales.copy()
sales_clean['OrderDate'] = pd.to_datetime('1899-12-30') + pd.to_timedelta(sales_clean
['OrderDate'], unit='D')
# Clean 'Sales' values: remove $ and commas, convert to float
sales_clean['Sales'] = sales_clean['Sales'].replace('[\$,]', '', regex=True).astype(float)
# Preview cleaned columns
display_cols = sales_clean[['OrderDate', 'Sales']].head(10)
display_cols
```

To ensure the correct formats are used, you can modify the original prompt to now use the following wording: **Using display_cols forecast future sales trends**. Now the data is in the correct format, and Copilot produces a visualization (see Figure 7-96).

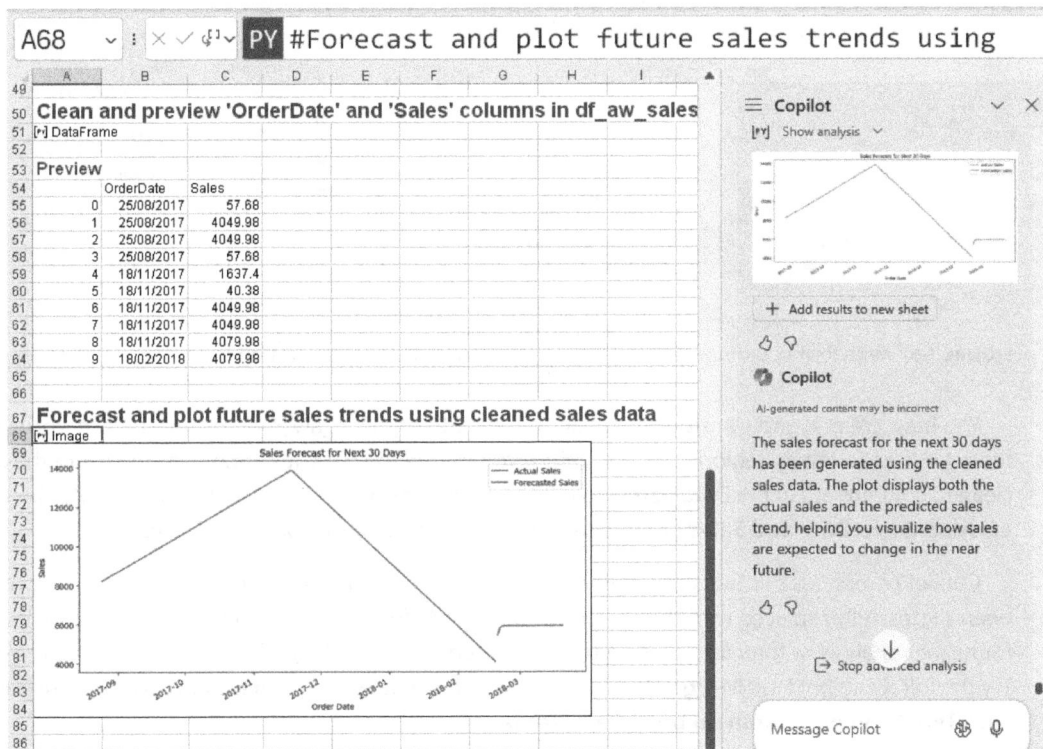

FIGURE 7-96 Copilot can now produce a visualization.

To look at trends, you can use the following prompt: **Forecast future sales trends using the sales column**. Copilot creates another visualization for an alternative presentation (see Figure 7-97).

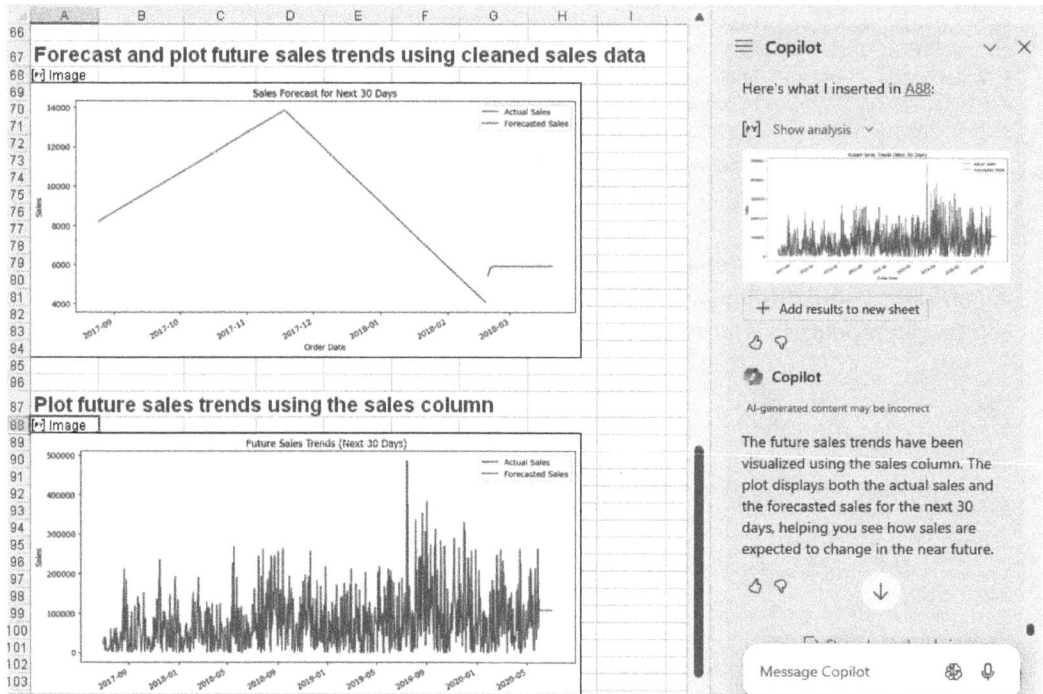

FIGURE 7-97 With further prompting, Copilot produces an alternative visualization.

You have created and transformed df_aw_region into df_clean_aw_region. Now let's merge it with the sales data to obtain regional results. Before you merge the data, it's important to ensure the newly cleaned columns are in the DataFrame you're using for sales. You might use this prompt: **Replace the existing OrderDate and Sales columns in df_aw_sales with the converted columns**.

Copilot completes this task and replies: "The 'OrderDate' and 'Sales' columns in df_aw_sales have been successfully replaced with the cleaned and properly formatted versions. The data is now ready for further analysis or forecasting using these updated columns." This means you can merge the data. Try the following prompt: **Merge the DataFrames df_clean_aw_region and df_aw_sales using the SalesTerritoryKey column on both DataFrames**.

Copilot successfully merges the data, as shown in Figure 7-98.

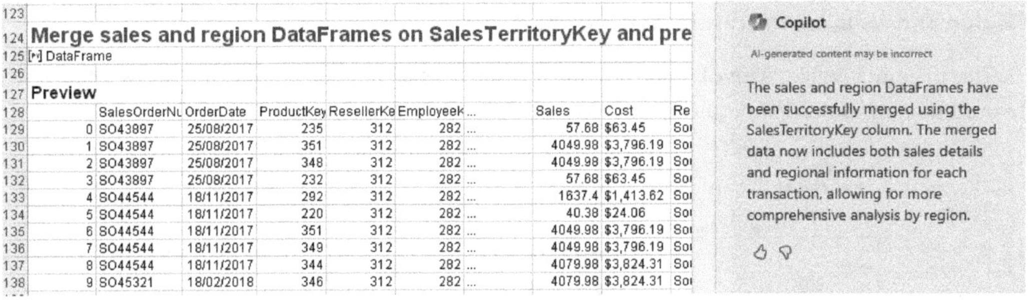

FIGURE 7-98 Copilot successfully merges the two DataFrames.

Copilot has created the following Python code, which merges the two DataFrames, for cell A125:

```
#Merge sales and region DataFrames on SalesTerritoryKey and preview result
# Ensure 'SalesTerritoryKey' is the same type in both DataFrames
region_df = split_df.copy()
region_df['SalesTerritoryKey'] = region_df['SalesTerritoryKey'].astype(int)
df_aw_sales['SalesTerritoryKey'] = df_aw_sales['SalesTerritoryKey'].astype(int)
# Merge on 'SalesTerritoryKey'
merged_df = pd.merge(df_aw_sales, region_df, on='SalesTerritoryKey', how='inner')
# Preview the merged DataFrame
merged_df.head(10)
```

You can use this more detailed prompt to use merged_df to get regional insights: **Calculate descriptive statistics (mean, median, min, max, standard deviation) for the columns Sales, Cost, and Unit Price in merged_df. Group the statistics by Region**.

Copilot produces a new DataFrame with the requested data (see Figure 7-99).

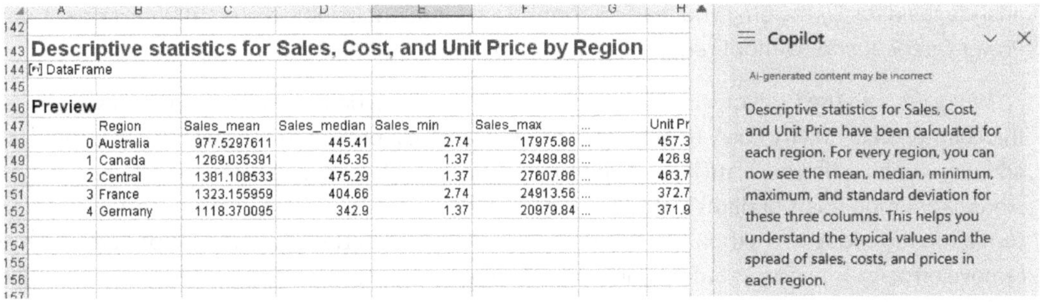

FIGURE 7-99 Copilot has generated regional statistics.

Let's finish the example with a visualization. Enter the following prompt: **Calculate Profit as Sales minus Cost using merged_df. Then compute the average profit and profit margin for each Region and visualize the results as a bar chart**.

This prompt involves a lot of work, and performing this analysis without Copilot's assistance would take some time. But Copilot quickly returns the results shown in Figure 7-100.

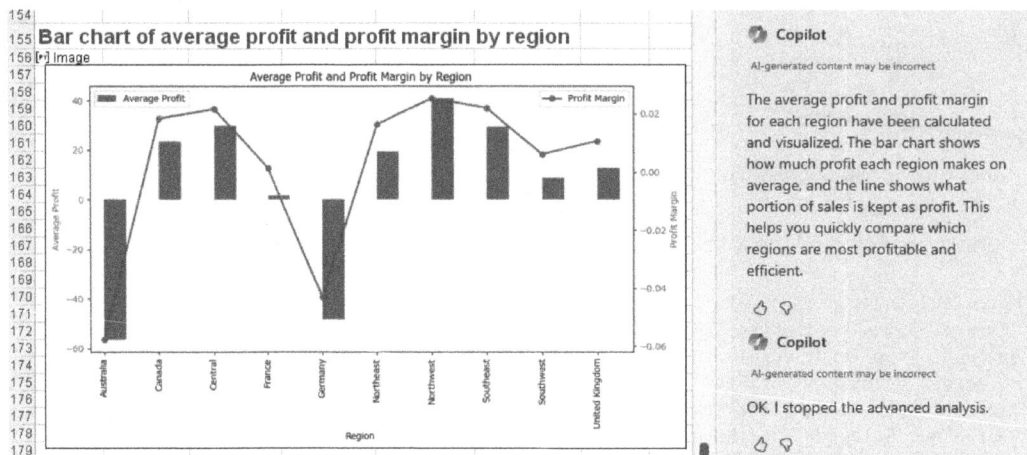

FIGURE 7-100 The requested visualization is created, and Copilot offers suggestions for interpretation.

Summary

In this chapter, you learned the basics of using Power Query to extract external data into Python in Excel. You also learned how to create DataFrames from queries and then use Copilot in Excel to help analyze the data. By the time you read this book, Copilot might be able to create DataFrames from Power Query queries without requiring you to load them into DataFrames first.

While you can use Copilot with Python in Excel to transform data, as you saw in the last example in this chapter, data quality is key to getting impressive and reliable results. You will be better able to spot and remove issues in your data if you learn to recognize problems such as amount columns that are not stored as Python floats or dates stored as Excel serial numbers. By learning data cleansing and transformation techniques in Python and Power Query, you will be better equipped to spot problems and remove error-causing issues before you load data as queries. (For more information about how Excel and Python store numbers and dates, refer to Chapter 2.)

This chapter showed Copilot used in Quick conversation mode, but don't forget that you can use Think Deeper mode to get an overview of external data or to investigate a particular issue.

Epilogue

While this book has covered a lot of code, prompts, and explanations, there is much more to learn about Python in Excel, Copilot, and Power Query. As you should now appreciate, this toolkit enables you to generate complex analyses and impressive insights.

The knowledge you've acquired by working through the examples in this book isn't just about technical proficiency. This introductory text gives you the information you need to explore the functionality available when you use Copilot and Power Query to access Python in Excel. The capabilities of Python in Excel are evolving rapidly. Anaconda and Microsoft continue to enhance Python's capabilities within Excel, including improved performance, richer visualizations, and more intuitive, collaborative features. Keeping an eye on updates and new features will ensure that you stay at the cutting edge.

Now that you know how to analyze data with greater speed and sophistication, you should consider exploring the following:

- **Advanced data visualization:** Go beyond Excel's traditional charting tools using Python libraries such as Matplotlib and seaborn to better interpret and present your information.

- **Machine learning, advanced predictive analytics, and data science:** Move beyond the basic extract, transform, and load (ETL) tools to wrestle your data into submission. With practice, you can create sophisticated statistical analyses, build predictive models, and even build machine-learning pipelines, using libraries such as scikit-learn (aka sklearn), pandas, and NumPy, and AI open-source software such as Google's TensorFlow directly in your workbooks.

- **Developing Python-powered dashboards:** You have already created some simple dashboards in the examples in this book, but you have only scratched the surface of the dashboards that are possible with Python in Excel using refreshable Power Query connectors to source many types of external datasets.

- **Experimenting with Copilot's evolving capabilities:** Copilot can generate Excel formulas, M code, and Python code and provide intelligent suggestions tailored to your organizational requirements. You should remain aware of Copilot's continual development and evolving capabilities.

- **Automation and productivity:** You can develop your own scripts and custom functions using Python code and Excel's formula engine to streamline repetitive tasks. With further reading, you can integrate other Microsoft 365 apps to schedule workflows, trigger events, and design robust, multistep processes that save hours of manual effort.

- **Collaboration and sharing:** By implementing best practices for sharing Python-enhanced workbooks, you can ensure that your solutions are accessible and sufficiently flexible for colleagues and stakeholders.

In a world so wary of the potential of AI, the skills you have developed in this book will put you in a great position to add value, tackle complex challenges, and identify potential opportunities when using Python in Excel with Copilot and Power Query.

If the pace of recent innovations in spreadsheet technology has told us anything, it's that this is not the last chapter. Instead, it is the introduction to a new book—or even a new era. We can only make educated guesses, but trends suggest that the future will create all the following possibilities:

- **More immersive AI integration:** We can expect further, more integrated connections between Excel, Python, and AI, making it increasingly possible to deploy advanced models, automate reasoning over data, and receive intelligent suggestions natively inside your workbooks. AI needs a calculation engine, and Python might just deliver it.

- **Think even deeper:** Think Deeper mode will only improve with time to provide better overviews, greater insights, and more reliable outputs than the current software.

- **Enhanced collaboration:** As cloud platforms evolve, sharing and collaborating on Python-powered Excel workbooks should become more seamless, simplifying teamwork across geographies, skillsets, and organizations.

- **Expanded library support:** As described in Chapter 3, Python in Excel currently touches only the tip of the iceberg when it comes to the vast array of Python libraries available today. Microsoft, Anaconda, and the open-source community are rapidly expanding the set of Python libraries that run securely and efficiently within Excel, opening new doors for analysis, visualization, and connectivity.

- **No-code and low-code enhancements:** Python and AI in Excel will only become more intuitive. Users with no coding ability should soon be able to access the full power and flexibility you've learned in this book.

You're at the forefront. But you must stay there. Use everything you've learned in this book and don't be afraid to make mistakes. You can always try again, just as Copilot does when you ask the same question repeatedly!

Index

P

Plug into learning at

MicrosoftPressStore.com

The Microsoft Press Store by Pearson offers:

- Free U.S. shipping

- Buy an eBook, get multiple formats – PDF and EPUB – to use on your computer, tablet, and mobile devices

- Print & eBook Best Value Packs

- eBook Deal of the Week – Save up to 60% on featured title

- Newsletter – Be the first to hear about new releases, announcements, special offers, and more

- Register your book – Find companion files, errata, and product updates, plus receive a special coupon* to save on your next purchase

P Pearson